About the Au

Educated at Preston Catholic College, Paul played amateur football before qualifying as a Class One referee and being appointed to the Northern Premier League.

Married to Margaret with two daughters and two granddaughters, he is a season ticket holder at Deepdale, home of Preston North End, the subject of his two previous books.

Also by J. Paul Harrison:
Tom Finney's Forgotten Season
ISBN 9780956480309
LizLin Publishing
Published 2010

A Tenth of a Goal from Glory
ISBN 9780956480316
LizLin Publishing
Published 2011

For Ella and Eleanor.

J. Paul Harrison

MANCHESTER UNITED IN TEARS

AUSTIN MACAULEY PUBLISHERS™

LONDON • CAMBRIDGE • NEW YORK • SHARJAH

A CIP catalogue record for this title is available from the British Library.

ISBN 9781786939432 (Paperback)
ISBN 9781786939449 (E-Book)
www.austinmacauley.com

First Published (2017)
Austin Macauley Publishers Ltd.
25 Canada Square
Canary Wharf
London
E14 5LQ

Acknowledgements

The first person to thank is my wife, Margaret, for patiently helping me with the research and painstakingly typing the story. Without her help I could never have completed the project.

The photographs, programme pages, illustrations etc. have been taken from scrapbooks, albums, magazines, programmes and collectors of soccer memorabilia from 60 years ago. The author is grateful to the clubs, newspapers and organisations listed below who have given permission for their reproduction in this book:

Blackpool, Burnley, Chelsea, Leeds United, Leicester City, Manchester City, Manchester United, Newcastle United, Portsmouth, Preston North End, Shamrock Rovers, Sheffield Wednesday, Wolverhampton Wanderers and Workington.

Daily Express, Lancashire Evening Post, Manchester Evening News, Birmingham Central Library, Harris Library in Preston and Manchester Central Library along with the EFL (English Football League Ltd.) and Football Association.

CONTENTS

INTRODUCTION

In January 1958, as a seven year old living no more than 800 yards from Deepdale, my life revolved around football. Watching the North End players train during school holidays, collecting autographs and playing football on nearby Moor Park.

Also playing 'Side Coaster Tippet' across the narrow road outside my house in Curwen Street, with a tennis ball and chalked goal-lines with the backdrop of terraced houses.

I was still too young to attend games on my own and my dad was not a big football fan, but every Saturday, when the first team were at home, I would listen out for a loud roar to signify a Preston goal. As the spectators dashed home after the game I would ask them the final score as you never knew how many goals the opposition had scored. It was also important to ask if they had stayed until the final whistle.

In early February 1958, after attending St Joseph's Primary School, a group of older children breathlessly discussed a plane crash. They said that many Manchester United players had been killed. When my dad returned from working on Preston Docks he related the story to my mum and me as to how the plane, carrying United, had crashed on take-off in Germany. I went to the local shop to buy my dad a copy of the late edition of the Lancashire Evening Post for more details of the incident. For many days afterwards this was the only subject of conversation in the school playground and prayers were said at morning assembly for the dead and injured and their families.

Moving forward 55 years I began researching material for this book telling the story of Manchester United during the 1957/58 season. It was only then that I became aware of the full facts of the disaster which denied a generation of talented players the opportunity to show their skills to the footballing public.

After writing two earlier football books – *Tom Finney's Forgotten Season* (2010) and *A Tenth of A Goal From Glory* (2012) I hope that this third book will once again take the reader back to that black and white era, and the days of the maximum wage when football was still fun.

MANCHESTER UNITED
AFTER 'THE WAR'

Matt Busby was appointed as manager of United in 1945 prior to the reintroduction of League football following the Second World War. In August 1946 United resumed their place in the First Division with Jimmy Murphy, the former West Bromwich Albion and Wales wing-half, working alongside Busby as his assistant.

Home games were played at Maine Road because Old Trafford had suffered severe bomb damage during the hostilities and money was very tight at the Club. During the season over 900,000 spectators flocked to Maine Road to watch United who, despite playing some wonderful football, could only finish runners-up to Liverpool. A 1-0 defeat at Anfield, four games from the end of the season, effectively costing them the title.

Arsenal won the Championship the following season and the game between the clubs at Maine Road in January 1948 attracted a crowd of over 81,000 to witness a 1-1 draw. After finishing second in the League United had the satisfaction of winning the FA Cup defeating Blackpool 4-2 at Wembley despite going behind twice in the game. Many journalists and football 'experts' considered this game to be the best Final ever seen at Wembley.

The 1948/49 season ended with United again runners-up for the third consecutive year and Johnny Carey was named Footballer of the Year.

On the 24th August 1949 they returned to Old Trafford and won their opening game 3-0 against Bolton Wanderers, ending the season in 4th place with Portsmouth as Champions.

Spurs won the title in 1950/51 finishing four points ahead of 'The Red Devils'.

The next three seasons saw United always in the mix with the best teams in England finishing 2nd, 4th and 2nd again and reaching the Quarterfinals of the FA Cup on two occasions and the semi-final once.

On the opening day of the 1951/52 season United fielded the following side away to West Bromwich Albion – *Allen, Carey, Redman, Cockburn, Chilton, McGlen, McShane, Pearson, Rowley, Downie* and *Bond.* The team had an average age of almost 29 with six players aged 30 or over. A Rowley hat trick (he finished the season with 30 goals) earned United a point in a 3-3 draw and they went on to lose only once in their first nine games. This consistency was maintained throughout the season as the experienced players helped the Club to clinch the First Division title 4 points clear of Tottenham Hotspur.

The 1952/53 season proved to be a transitional period in their history as the team finished in 8th position and many of the 'old-timers' found their places in the team challenged by young players being brought on in the reserves and youth teams by Busby and Murphy. Tommy Taylor had been signed from Barnsley for £29,999 in March 1953 and made a sensational start scoring twice on his début against Preston, and went on to score 7 goals in 11 games.

The season heralded the first ever Football Association Youth Cup competition for players under 18 and United easily won the Cup beating Wolves 9-3 on aggregate over the two legs. The first game at Old Trafford on 4th May 1953 saw United win 7-1 with goals from McFarlane (2), Lewis (2), Pegg, Scanlon and Whelan in front of 20,934 spectators. Duncan Edwards, aged just 16, who had made his first team début four weeks earlier, had a storming game with his long range passes continually putting the Wolves defence under pressure.

The following two seasons saw United consolidate their position in English football, finishing 4th then 5th as Busby introduced his youngsters to First Division football. The 'old guard' were gradually replaced and the strength of 'The Babes' could be seen by the fact that United won the FA Youth Cup in each of these seasons.

At the start of the 1955/56 season United had Duncan Edwards aged 18, Eddie Colman (18), David Pegg (19), Albert Scanlon (19), Billy Whelan (20), Eddie Lewis (20), John Doherty (20) and Dennis Viollet (21) amongst the playing squad. The majority of these players came through the Youth system and once again United won the Youth Cup. But 'The Babes' were soon to set football alight by winning the Championship with 60 points, a massive 11 points ahead of Blackpool and Wolves. This was despite a poor start to the season which saw them win 3, lose 3 and draw 2 of their opening 8 games.

Every club had its own 'star players' – Bert Trautmann (Manchester City), Billy Wright (Wolves), Nat Lofthouse (Bolton Wanderers), Stanley Matthews (Blackpool), Tom Finney (Preston North End), Danny Blanchflower (Spurs)-the list went on.

In August 1956 Manchester United were once again clear favourites to win the title and despite objections from the Football League Management Committee, the club decided to enter the 1956 European Cup competition. For the third year running the maximum wage had remained at £15 per week.

The season was tremendously exciting for Manchester United fans with the team scoring 103 goals and losing only 6 games to clinch the title for the second year running. They finished 8 points clear of Spurs and Preston. United also reached the FA Cup Final losing 2-1 to Aston Villa in a game marred by an early injury to United goalkeeper Ray Wood. A victory would have made them the first team to achieve a League and Cup double since Aston Villa in 1897. They also reached the semi-final of the European Cup but were beaten by eventual winners Real Madrid.

The Youth team won the FA Youth Cup final for the 5th consecutive season beating West Ham United 8-2 on aggregate with goals from Dawson (3), Pearson (2), Lawton, Morgans and Hunter. As the opening day of the new season approached the players finally received a pay rise of £2 per week.

Fixture List 1957-58

1957

Aug.	24 Leicester City	a
	28 EVERTON	h
	31 MANCHESTER CITY	h
Sept.	4 Everton	a
	7 LEEDS UNITED	h
	9 Blackpool	a
	14 Bolton Wanderers	a
	18 BLACKPOOL	h
	21 ARSENAL	h
	25 Shamrock Rov. Euro Cup	a
	28 Wolverhampton Wanderers	a
Oct.	2 SHAMROCK R. Euro Cup	h
	8 ASTON VILLA	h
	12 Nottingham Forest	a
	19 PORTSMOUTH	h
	22 ASTON V. Charity Shield	h
	26 West Bromwich Albion	a
Nov.	2 BURNLEY	h
	9 Preston North End	a
	16 SHEFFIELD WED.	h
	23 Newcastle United	a
	30 TOTTENHAM HOTSPUR	h
Dec.	7 Birmingham City	a
	14 CHELSEA	h
	21 LEICESTER CITY	h
	25 LUTON TOWN	h
	26 Luton Town	a
	28 Manchester City	a

1958

Jan.	4 FA CUP 3RD ROUND	
	11 Leeds United	a
	18 BOLTON WANDERERS	h
	25 FA CUP 4TH ROUND	
Feb.	1 Arsenal	a
	8 WOLVERHAMPTON W.	h
	15 Aston Villa	a
	22 NOTTINGHAM FOREST	h
Mar.	1 Portsmouth	a
	8 WEST BROM. ALBION	h
	15 Burnley	a.
	22 NEWCASTLE UNITED	h
	29 Sheffield Wednesday	a
April	4 SUNDERLAND	h
	5 PRESTON NORTH END	h
	7 Sunderland	a
	12 Tottenham Hotspur	a
	19 BIRMINGHAM CITY	h
	26 Chelsea	a
May	3 FA CUP FINAL	

Professional Playing Staff

Details of all the players who have appeared for United in a First Team game prior to the start of the 1957/58 season and are registered by the Club as professionals for the new season.

All records correct as at 23rd August 1957.

Raymond Ernest Wood – Goalkeeper

Born Hebburn, County Durham 11th June 1931
Début 3rd December 1949 v Newcastle United (home) 1-1

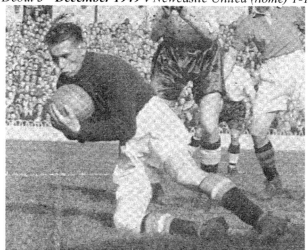

Included with kind permission of the Manchester Evening News

Ray Wood made 12 appearances for Darlington during the 1949/50 season before moving to United for a fee reported to be between £5000 and £6000. He was immediately thrust into the first team due to injury problems and acquitted himself well with a competent performance against Newcastle.

He then learned his trade in the second team before making a total of 15 League and Cup appearances in 1952/53. His agility and speed off the line singled him out and the following season he made 28 appearances against Crompton's 15.

Now the No.1 'keeper for his club, Wood gained the first of three England caps in October 1954 at Windsor Park as England beat Northern Ireland 2-0. Bill Foulkes also made his England début at right-back with Roger Byrne playing at left-back.

He won Championship medals in 1956 and 1957 as the 'Busby Babes' took football by storm. He had the misfortune to suffer a fractured cheekbone in the 1957 FA Cup Final when, after only six minutes, Villa's Peter McParland shoulder charged him after he had caught the ball. Jackie Blanchflower took over in goal and although Wood returned to the field he remained a passenger on the wing for the second half as United lost the match 2-1 missing the opportunity to complete 'the double'. He also suffered the disappointment of bowing out of the European Cup at the semi-final stage when United lost 5-3 on aggregate to eventual winners Real Madrid.

Appearances

Football League	157
FA Cup	15
European Cup	8

****

Jeff Whitefoot – Wing-Half

Born Cheadle, Cheshire 31st December 1933
Début 15th April 1950 v Portsmouth (home) 0-2

There have been many young players over the years who have made their début for United at an early age but none as young as Jeff Whitefoot. He was selected to play at right-half against Portsmouth when still under 16½ years of age.

Over the next three seasons he played a further 15 games before making the right-half spot his own in the 1953/54 season.

Comfortable on the ball and with an eye for a good pass, Whitefoot was unfortunate to lose his place in the team to Eddie Colman in November 1955 and did not make a single appearance the following season. Has made one appearance for the England Under 23 side.

Appearances

Football League	93
FA Cup	2

Mark Jones – Centre-Half

Born Wombwell near Barnsley 15th June 1933
*Debut **7th October 1950** v Sheffield Wednesday (home) 3-1*

After excelling in schoolboy football, Mark Jones signed for United as an amateur in the summer of 1948. Although only aged 17 he made his début against Sheffield Wednesday replacing his injured boyhood hero Allenby Chilton at centre-half. He went on to make a further 3 appearances during the season and was on the winning side each time.

Over the next 3 seasons he played just 5 first team games but was learning his craft and had developed into a strong six-footer whilst undertaking his National Service duties.

At the start of the 1954/55 season Chilton was still the first choice centre-half but in February 1955, following a heavy 5-0 defeat at home against bitter rivals City and then a 4-2 home defeat against Wolves, Jones replaced him in the team for the last 13 games. He was a typical old-fashioned centre-half, strong in the tackle, powerful in the air and fearless.

Nicknamed 'Dan Archer' by his team-mates because of his pipe smoking habit, Jones was easily recognised in his trilby hat and long overcoat. He played every League and Cup game in United's 1955/56 title winning season and was strongly tipped for England honours. He remained first choice No 5 until suffering a knee injury at Bournemouth in March 1957 after which Jackie Blanchflower took his place and kept it for the rest of the season including the FA Cup Final defeat against Aston Villa.

Jones did return to the side for the final League game at Old Trafford, a 1-1 draw against West Bromwich Albion on the day United were presented with the trophy.

	Appearances	Goals
Football League	93	1
FA Cup	5	
European Cup	6	

****

Johnny Berry – Outside-Right

Born Aldershot 1ˢᵗ June 1926
*Debut for Man. U. **1ˢᵗ September 1951** v Bolton W. (away) 0-1*

After making 4 appearances for Birmingham City in the 2ⁿᵈ Division at the start of the 1951/52 season Johnny Berry was transferred to Manchester United for a fee of £25,000. He had made 104 appearances for the 'Blues' scoring 6 goals since joining the club in December 1944.

It was reported that Matt Busby had tracked the player for two seasons before finally obtaining his signature. Although under 5'6" tall his strength, bravery, speed and dribbling skills soon made him a firm favourite with the fans at Old Trafford and he has retained the right-wing spot ever since. Berry has won 3 Football League Championship medals and an FA Cup loser's medal during his 6 seasons at the Club.

His international appearances for England have been limited due to the competition for the outside-right position, mainly from Finney and Matthews, but he has still been selected on 4 occasions for the National team. His last game was in May 1956, a goalless draw against Sweden.

Manchester United	Appearances	Goals
Football League	227	33
FA Cup	15	4
European Cup	8	2

****

Roger William Byrne – Full-Back

Born Manchester 8th February 1929

Debut 24th November 1951 v Liverpool (away) 0-0

Manchester Evening News

Roger Byrne joined United as a teenager and spent his early years playing at wing-half in the reserves side. In November 1951 the team suffered an injury crisis in the left-back position and Byrne was drafted in giving a creditable performance against Liverpool. He occupied the position for the next 18 League and Cup games before being switched to outside-left scoring against Burnley at Turf Moor in a 1-1 draw. He went on to score 6 goals from the left wing in the last 5 games of the Championship winning season.

 He started the following season at outside-left but after only 3 games was switched to the left-back spot, which has been his position ever since.

On 3rd April 1954 he made his international début for England at left-back in Glasgow in a 4-2 victory against Scotland and has played every international since, having now made 30 appearances at the start of the 1957/58 season.

His ability to read a game, sound positional play and attacking runs down the wing to support his forwards have made him popular with supporters. He has captained United for a number of seasons and has 3 Championship medals and an FA Cup loser's medal in his trophy cabinet.

	Appearances	Goals
Football League	219	17
FA Cup	16	2
European Cup	8	

Jackie Blanchflower-
Wing-half/Inside-forward/Centre-half

Born Belfast, Northern Ireland 7th March 1933
Debut 24th November 1951 v Liverpool (away) 0-0

Jackie Blanchflower joined United in March 1949 aged 16 after playing for Northern Ireland Schoolboys turning professional a year later.

With the team suffering a number of injury problems he made his début in November 1951 playing at right-half alongside Roger Byrne who was also making his League début. The following season he made one appearance at left-half before finally breaking into the team in October 1953 when he made the inside-right position his own, playing 28 successive games and scoring 14 League and Cup goals as United finished fourth.

His ability to play the ball with either foot, strength in the air and calmness under pressure earned him his first Irish cap in March 1954 in a 2-1 win against Wales at Wrexham. Playing at inside-right with his brother Danny (then at Aston Villa) playing at right-half, he gave a sound performance and now has 9 caps at the start of the 1957/58 season. He scored his first goal for his country in October 1955 as Ireland beat Scotland 2-1.

The following season he only missed two League games from August 1954 to February 1955 whilst scoring 8 goals at inside-right. The last of these games was a 5-0 home defeat against bitter rivals Manchester City and he lost his place in the regular line-up as Viollet, Taylor and Whelan were all tried in that position. He regained his place for the last three games of the season scoring twice in a 3-2 defeat at Highbury.

With the 'Young Babes' bursting into the team, Blanchflower found himself under a lot of pressure as the 1955/56 season got under way. However he showed his versatility by playing at inside-right, centre-forward and inside-left whilst making 16 appearances in the first 17 games scoring 3 goals.

The outstanding form of first John Doherty and then Liam Whelan resulted in Blanchflower being unable to retain his place in the side and he only made two more appearances that season.

Matt Busby had great faith in his protégé having worked with the player for six years and on the Scandinavian tour, prior to the start of the 1956/57 season, he identified that Blanchflower could make a great centre-half. As the season opened Mark Jones held that position and his strong performances made it impossible for Blanchflower to break back into the team.

However, in March 1957, Jones suffered a knee injury in an FA Cup tie and Blanchflower took his chance. Playing centre-half he appeared in every game but two from that date until the end of the season in the League, FA Cup and Europe.

In the 1957 FA Cup Final Blanchflower had to play in goal for most of the game following an early injury to Ray Wood but in no way disgraced himself whilst conceding two goals in the defeat to Aston Villa.

	Appearances	Goals
Football League	87	26
FA Cup	6	1
European Cup	3	

****

John Doherty – Inside-Right

Born Manchester 12th March 1935
Début 6th December 1952 v Middlesbrough (home) 3-2

John Doherty joined United as a professional aged 17 but missed the opportunity of playing in the 1953 FA Youth Cup Final against Wolves after suffering a knee injury in the semi-final against Brentford at Old Trafford. He had already made his first team début in December 1952 and in only his third game scored twice against Chelsea in a 3-2 win at Stamford Bridge going on to make five appearances that season.

For a young player he has a great understanding of the game and his touch and shooting power have singled him out as a future star.

However he did not make an appearance during the following two seasons whilst undertaking his National Service and surprisingly was discharged from the RAF as he was classified 'medically unfit' due to continued problems with his knees.

He still trained with United prior to the start of the 1955/56 season and was fit enough to replace Blanchflower for a home game against Wolves scoring in a 4-3 victory. In that title winning season he eventually played 17 League and Cup games scoring 4 goals.

With fierce competition for every place in the team, Doherty was only selected on three occasions last season.

	Appearances	Goals
Football League	24	6
FA Cup	1	

****

David Pegg – Outside-Left

Born Doncaster 20th September 1935
Début 6th December 1952 v Middlesbrough (home) 3-2

David Pegg was yet another outstanding youngster who joined the 'Busby Babes' at Old Trafford making his début aged 17 in a victory against Middlesbrough. A tricky, powerful winger with a fierce shot, he retained his place in the team for a further 20 League and Cup games scoring 4 goals.

During the following two seasons he faced stiff competition for the No. 11 slot from Rowley, McShane and then Scanlon and had to be satisfied with just 15 first team appearances.

He also helped United win the FA Youth Cup for the first two years 1953 and 1954 whilst scoring 4 goals in the two-legged finals against Wolves.

At the start of the 1955/56 season he was in the reserve team but after six games replaced Scanlon and has made the position his own ever since whilst winning two Championship medals and an FA Cup loser's medal.

After representing England Schoolboys and England 'B' Team he finally won his first cap in May 1957 in a 1-1 draw against the Republic of Ireland in Dublin. The England side also included his United colleagues Byrne, Edwards and Taylor with Whelan playing for the Irish. Many pundits have tipped him to take over the left-wing position in the future from Tom Finney.

	Appearances	Goals
Football League	106	20
FA Cup	9	
European Cup	8	1

****

William Foulkes – Right-Back

Born St Helens 5th January 1932

Début 13th December 1952 v Liverpool (away) 2-1

Manchester Evening News

Bill Foulkes worked down the mines at Lea Green Colliery at the time he signed for United in March 1950. Although he became a professional the following year, he continued with his job at the pit because of the good wages.

He made his League début at right-back at Anfield in December 1952 and played one further first team game that season.

The 1953/54 season began with Aston and McNulty sharing the right-back position but by mid-September Foulkes had forced his way into the team only missing one game for the rest of the season. He also scored his first goal for the Club in a 2-1 win at Newcastle United.

Strong in the air with steely determination, extremely fit and with a good 'football brain' Foulkes was now first choice right-back, despite some critics claiming that he lacked real pace. In October 1954 he made his England début in that position with Roger Byrne at left-back and Ray Wood in goal as England beat Northern Ireland in Belfast. Amazingly only after gaining his cap did he decide to quit his job at the pit.

Foulkes won a Championship medal in 1955/56 but in February of that season, after playing 26 games, he lost his place to Ian Greaves. Some football correspondents wrote that this decision was taken by Matt Busby because the player had started his National Service duties and was finding it difficult to meet both requirements.

Foulkes' response was to work harder than anyone else in pre-season training and by the start of the 1956/57 season he was again first choice in the No. 2 shirt.

Last season he played 39 League games, 6 FA Cup, 8 European Cup and 1 Charity Shield game as United were again crowned Champions. He had to settle for an FA Cup loser's medal.

	Appearances	Goals
Football League	140	1
FA Cup	11	
European Cup	8	

****

Tommy Taylor – Centre-Forward

Born Barnsley 29th January 1932
Début for Man. U. 7th March 1953 v Preston N. E. (home) 5-2

Tommy Taylor played his first match for Barnsley aged 18 in October 1950 and the following month, in only his second game, he scored a hat-trick as Queens Park Rangers were hammered 7-0.

Over the next two seasons he scored a further 21 League and Cup goals for the Club and by March 1953 was hot property on the transfer market with his progress being monitored by a number of First Division clubs. It was Manchester United who made the decisive move signing him for £29,999. Matt Busby reportedly took £1 from his wallet and gave it to the tea lady, as Taylor did not want to become a £30,000 player.

Taylor immediately made a sensational début for the 'Red Devils' when, on 7th March 1953, he scored twice at Old Trafford as United beat Preston 5-2. His first goal, a trademark bullet header, made him an instant hit with the home supporters in the crowd of 54,397. The International selectors watched as he scored 7 goals in just 11 appearances and it was no surprise when he won his first cap on 17th May 1953 against Argentina in Buenos Aires. With the game goalless after 23 minutes a freak rainstorm caused the pitch to be unplayable and the game was abandoned. A week later he scored for England as they beat Chile 2-1 in Santiago. The goal had an element of luck about it as his cross into the penalty area was deflected into the net by the goalkeeper.

Taylor's bravery by putting his body into situations where he could be hurt and powerful shooting skills made up for what some critics felt was a lack of ability on the ground. He has dominated English football over the last four seasons scoring more than 100 League and Cup goals at a better rate than one every two games.

During this time he has won 2 Championship medals and an FA Cup loser's medal. Taylor has also been the first choice striker for England since 1953 having scored 14 goals in 16 games. The player scored a hat-trick for United in the 1956/57 European Cup 10-0 home win against Anderlecht.

	Appearances	Goals
Barnsley Football		
League	44	26
FA Cup	2	2
Man. U. Football		
League	141	96
FA Cup	7	5
European Cup	8	8

Duncan Edwards – Wing-Half

Born Dudley 1ˢᵗ October 1936
*Début **4ᵗʰ April 1953** v Cardiff City (home) 1-4*

Duncan Edwards was an outstanding schoolboy footballer and played for England Schools v Wales at Wembley on 1ˢᵗ April 1950 when aged just 13. After being appointed captain of the side he played for a further two seasons whilst a number of League sides monitored his progress.

The coach of the England Schools side, Joe Mercer, is reported to have brought the player's abilities to the attention of the United manager who duly signed him as an amateur in 1952. Stan Cullis, manager of Wolves, was apparently bitterly disappointed on missing out on the capture of this local lad.

Initially playing for United's Youth and Reserve sides, Edwards was given his début in April 1953, aged 16½, playing at left-half against Cardiff at Old Trafford. The same season he represented United in the FA Youth Cup helping them reach the final. In the first leg at home with a crowd of over 20,000 he gave an astonishing performance as United beat Wolves 7-1. The second leg at Molineux ended 2-2 giving United the first tenure of the new trophy much to the joy of Matt Busby.

The following season Edwards replaced Henry Cockburn in the first team and played 25 League and Cup games all at left-half.

At 5ft 11ins tall and weighing 13 stone he gained the nick-name 'Big Dunc' and his strength, stamina and confidence were apparent for all to see. Despite now being a first team player he still loved his role in the Youth Team and played in the side that beat Wolves in the Final for the second consecutive year. The first leg at Old Trafford ended in a dramatic 4-4 draw with Edwards scoring twice. Three days later United travelled to Molineux with a team that also included Charlton, Colman and Pegg. A penalty, scored by Pegg after Edwards, playing at centre-forward, had been fouled in the area, clinched the trophy.

On 1ˢᵗ January 1955 Edwards scored his first League goal in a 4-1 home win against Blackpool. After appearing for England 'B', England Under 23's and the Football League XI he finally made his much anticipated début at left-half for the full senior side on 2ⁿᵈ April 1955 against Scotland in a stunning 7-2 victory at Wembley.

Although now a full international, Edwards was still selected to play for United in the 1955 FA Youth Cup Final against West Bromwich Albion despite criticism from within the football world that an England International should not be playing at that level. Matt Busby would have none of it and on 27ᵗʰ April 1955 the first leg at Old Trafford was one way traffic as United won 4-0 with Edwards playing at centre-forward. In the return game at the Hawthorns the home side lost

3-0. This was his last appearance in the competition and over the two legs he scored once as did Bobby Charlton, with Eddie Colman netting four times.

In the summer of 1955 he was selected for England's European tour and played in each game against France, Portugal and Spain. His next appointment was to undertake his two years of National Service in the Royal Army Ordinance Corps but fortunately he was still given time off to play for Manchester United. He was also expected to represent the Army and to play in other forces games resulting in him playing almost 100 competitive games in the season.

The 1955/56 campaign saw Manchester United clinch the Football League Championship by 11 points and in May 1956 Edwards scored his first International goal as England beat West Germany 3-1 in Munich's Olympic Stadium. United won the title again in 1956/57 as Edwards played 34 games scoring 5 goals. At Molineux in December 1956 he scored twice against Denmark in a World Cup qualifier as England won 5-2.

An FA Cup and League double seemed an odds on certainty in the 56/57 season but things went horribly wrong in the final game with goalkeeper Wood injured. The handicap proved too much as the 'Red Devils' lost 2-1 to Aston Villa despite Edwards covering every blade of grass in an attempt to level up the numbers.

Off the field Duncan Edwards did not drink alcohol and led a quiet life, escaping publicity whenever possible preferring instead to play cards, go fishing and watch the latest films at the cinema.

At the end of last season Edwards had played 15 times for England and scored 4 goals.

	Appearances	Goals
Football League	125	14
FA Cup	10	1
European Cup	7	1

****

Dennis Viollet – Inside-Forward

Born Manchester 20th September 1933
Début 11th April 1953 v Newcastle United (away) 2-1

Dennis Viollet captained Manchester Schoolboys and represented England at that level before joining United in September 1948, turning professional on his seventeenth birthday.

His physical appearance, being very thin, meant that he did not look like the typical professional footballer, but appearances can deceive and Viollet's stunning pace and superb understanding of the game soon earned him a place in the First team. He made his début in April 1953 and in his next game scored as United drew 2-2 against West Bromwich Albion.

By November 1953 the player had made the inside-left position his own and from that time until the end of the 1956/57 season he has played at least 30 League and Cup games each season scoring almost 80 goals.

Viollet has been the perfect foil for Tommy Taylor developing a telepathic understanding with the 'big fellow' always in the right place to pick up the 'knock-ons'.

He has scored three hat-tricks for United in League games but his outstanding performance must be the European Cup game against Aderlecht last season when he netted four times in a 10-0 second leg victory.

	Appearances	Goals
Football League	127	68
FA Cup	10	2
European Cup	6	9

****

Colin Webster – Forward

Born Cardiff 17th July 1932
Début 28th November 1953 v Portsmouth (away) 1-1

Manchester Evening News

Colin Webster began his professional career with Cardiff City in 1950 but, despite playing regularly for the reserve side, he was unable to force his way into the First team.

Whilst undertaking his National Service his football ability was brought to the attention of Jimmy Murphy who duly signed him on a free transfer in May 1952. He had to wait until the end of November 1953 before making his début in a 1-1 draw at Fratton Park and made no more appearances that season.

His versatility, being able to play anywhere along the forward line, earned him 19 appearances scoring 11 goals in the 1954/55 season, including a hat-trick against Burnley.

Webster was still unable to establish himself in the First team but his blistering pace and quick feet were always a useful addition to the side. In 1955/56 he won a Championship medal after playing 15 games, scoring 4 goals. Last season he only managed 6 League and Cup appearances.

Despite his limited opportunities in the United side he still gained his first International Cap for Wales on the 1st May 1957 as the home side beat Czechoslovakia 1-0 in a World Cup qualifying game.

	Appearances	Goals
Football League	38	15
FA Cup	3	3

Ian Greaves – Full-Back

Born Shaw, Nr Oldham 26th May 1932
Début 2nd October 1954 v Wolves (away) 2-4

Ian Greaves joined United from Buxton United in May 1953 and made his début at Molineux in October 1954 playing at right-back in place of Bill Foulkes who was on international duty for England. This was the only game Foulkes missed during the season and Greaves returned to the reserve side.

He won a Championship medal in 1955/56 after a run of 14 consecutive league games from 4th February 1956 to the end of the season with United winning 10 and drawing 4. At six foot and weighing twelve stone four pounds Greaves is an imposing figure and his superb tackling ability and sureness of pass looked certain to have secured the full-back position in the team.

However, by the start of the 1956/57 season, Foulkes was once again the first choice right-back and Greaves only made 3 appearances during the season.

	Appearances	Goals
Football League	19	

****

Frederick Goodwin – Wing-Half

Born Heywood 28th June 1933
Début 20th November 1954 v Arsenal (home) 2-1

Freddie Goodwin joined United in 1953 and made his début the following year. A tall, talented ball player he has faced stiff competition for the wing-half berth in the First team from Colman, Edwards and Whitefoot which has limited his appearances over the last three seasons.

A talented cricketer, Goodwin has played 11 First Class matches for Lancashire having made his début at Old Trafford in June 1955, taking 5 wickets against Kent. Has a personal best of 5 for 35 and highest score of 21 not out. He has taken 27 wickets.

	Appearances	Goals
Football League	19	

Manchester Evening News

****

33

Albert Scanlon – Outside-Left

Born Manchester 10th October 1935
Début 20th November 1954 v Arsenal (home) 2-1

Albert Scanlon was spotted playing for Manchester Schoolboys and invited to join United as an amateur in 1950 before turning professional in December 1952.

His main assets, good ball control and blistering pace, have made him a difficult opponent to contain. In 1953 and 1954 he won FA Youth Cup winners medals playing at outside-left in the successful United side.

In November 1954 he made his League début against Arsenal and later in the season was picked for the final twelve games and then the opening six games of the following season. At that point in September 1955 he lost his place to David Pegg and has only made a handful of appearances since.

A dapper, charismatic individual, Scanlon has been nicknamed 'Joe Friday' by his team-mates because of his habit of talking out of the side of his mouth similar to the TV detective in the American cop series Dragnet.

	Appearances	Goals
Football League	25	7

****

Geoff Bent – Full-Back

Born Salford 27th September 1932
Début 11th December 1954 v Burnley (away) 4-2

At the age of 13 Geoff Bent was awarded a medal by the 'Humane Society' after rescuing a boy from the Salford canal. Less than two years later he won a second medal, this time as captain of the Salford Boys team that beat Leicester Boys over two legs to win the English Schools Trophy. United followed his progress at schoolboy level whilst playing mainly at wing-half or inside-forward and he joined the ground staff aged 15 before turning professional in May 1949.

He gained a few inches in height and at just under six foot tall was soon a regular member of the reserve side playing in the Central League but now at right-back.

His main attributes as a player are his pace, tenacious tackle, ability to read the game and an eye for a good pass.

In December 1954 he made his début at left-back at Turf Moor as United won 4-2 and made just one further appearance that season.

With Roger Byrne at full-back his opportunities have been limited and over the last two seasons he has made just ten appearances mainly as a stand-in for Byrne.

Many 'football experts' have stated that if he played for any other team he would be the regular first choice right-back. It has been reported that Bent asked for a transfer only to be told by Matt Busby that all the players were 'first team probables' and not 'first team players' and his request was refused.

	Appearances	Goals
Football League	12	

****

Liam 'Billy' Whelan – Inside-Forward

Born Dublin 1st April 1935
Début 26th March 1955 v Preston North End (away) 2-0

His outstanding ability as a schoolboy footballer came to the attention of United whilst he played at various age levels for Home Farm in Dublin.

United eventually made a move to sign the player when it was discovered that John Doherty would not be fit to play in the 1953 FA Youth Cup Final. Whelan played at inside-forward scoring one goal in each leg as United beat Wolves 9-3.

He settled into the reserve side playing in the Central League for the next two seasons and after scoring lots of goals at that level, finally made his début at Deepdale in March 1955. The following week he scored his first League goal in a 5-0 win against Sheffield United during a run of seven consecutive appearances.

When United won the Football League Championship in 1955/56, Whelan played just enough games to earn a medal whilst scoring 4 goals in his 13 matches. The end of the season saw him win his first cap for the Republic of Ireland in a 4-1 win in Rotterdam against Holland. He has since earned a further 3 caps in World Cup Qualifying games but has yet to score for his country.

At just over six feet tall he has developed into a difficult opponent who can show a defender a deceptive change of pace together with his close dribbling skills.

Billy Whelan made the No 8 shirt his own in the 1956/57 season scoring 33 goals in 50 League and Cup games, including his first career hat-trick against Burnley on Good Friday 1957 in a 3-1 away victory.

	Appearances	Goals
Football League	59	31
FA Cup	3	4
European Cup	8	3

Wilf McGuinness – Wing-Half

Born Manchester 25th October 1937
*Début 8th **October 1955** v Wolves (home) 4-3*

Wilf McGuinness played for Manchester and England schoolboys and, aged 17, made his début for United playing at left-half in a thrilling 4-3 home win against Wolves. He retained his place in the side and the following Saturday scored against Aston Villa in a 4-4 draw (his only goal for the club to date). He played one further game during the season.

Unusually he won three FA Youth Cup Winners medals in 1954, 1955 and 1956, captaining the team on his last appearances in the two-legged final.

His place in the First team has always been blocked by Duncan Edwards but, despite this obstacle, McGuinness still managed to play 15 League and Cup games last season.

As a defensive wing-half he possibly lacks some of the ball skill of other players, but his strength of tackle and fierce competitive edge have easily compensated making him a useful member of the squad.

	Appearances	Goals
Football League	16	1
FA Cup	1	
European Cup	1	

****

Eddie Colman – Wing-Half

Born Salford 1st November 1936
*Début 12th **November 1955** v Bolton Wanderers (away) 1-3*

Eddie Colman joined United straight from school after representing Salford Boys, turning professional on his seventeenth birthday by which time he had already won an FA Youth Cup Winners medal. The following season he again played in the side which retained the Cup and his growing reputation earned him the captaincy of the team for the 1954/55 competition. He led from the front driving the team forward as they once more won the coveted Trophy, this time beating West Bromwich Albion 7-1 on aggregate in April 1955 with Colman scoring 4 goals.

Matt Busby was reportedly astounded at his calmness on the ball and instinctive ability to make the right pass without ever having to strike the ball hard.

It was inevitable that his First Team début wouldn't be long in coming and in November 1955, having just turned 19, he played at Burnden Park but suffered the disappointment of a 3-1 defeat.

After his début he only missed one game during the season as United won the title.

He made the No 4 slot his own and only missed a handful of games during United's 56/57 Championship winning season. In November 1956 he scored his first League goal in a 2-2 draw at White Hart Lane. His body swerve has earned him the nickname 'Snake hips'.

	Appearances	Goals
Football League	61	1
FA Cup	7	
European Cup	8	

****

Ronald Cope – Centre-Half

Born Crewe 5th October 1934
Début 29th September 1956 v Arsenal (away) 2-1

Ronnie Cope was an England schoolboy international and one of the many fine youth players developed at Old Trafford. He captained the side that won the first ever FA Youth Cup Final in 1953.

He became a professional footballer in 1951 but had to wait five years before making his Football League début at Highbury.

His only other First Team appearance prior to the start of the 1957/58 season was on Easter Monday 1957 when United beat Burnley 2-0 at home.

	Appearances	Goals
Football League	2	

Bobby Charlton – Inside-Forward

Born Ashington, Northumberland 11th October 1937
Début 6th October 1956 v Charlton Athletic (home) 4-2

An outstanding schoolboy footballer, Bobby Charlton was on United's radar from an early age. He made his début whilst still undertaking his National Service duties in October 1956 scoring twice in a 4-2 victory against Charlton Athletic.

He has since made a further 13 League appearances scoring 8 goals whilst playing at inside-left, including a hat-trick in the away fixture at Charlton.

In the Cup he scored in the semi-final victory against Birmingham City and retained his place in the FA Cup Final defeat against Aston Villa. He also played in the European Cup second leg 2-2 draw against Real Madrid scoring once.

His speed, ability to shoot powerfully with either foot and good football brain have singled him out as a future star player.

	Appearances	**Goals**
Football League	14	10
FA Cup	2	1
European Cup	1	1

****

Anthony Hawksworth – Goalkeeper

Born Sheffield 15th January 1938
Début 27th October 1956 v Blackpool (away) 2-2

Tony Hawksworth played for England schoolboys and then helped United win the FA Youth Cup in 1954, 1955 and 1956.

With Ray Wood injured and having only played a handful of reserve games, Hawksworth made his only First Team appearance to date at Bloomfield Road.

	Appearances	Goals
Football League	1	

Gordon Clayton Goalkeeper

Born Wednesbury, Staffordshire 3rd November 1936
Début 16th March 1957 v Wolves (away) 1-1

A burly six-footer and weighing just under fourteen stone, Clayton has found his appearances limited for a place in the United reserve team due to the good form of Tony Hawksworth. He did however win an FA Youth Cup medal in 1953.

After making his début in the First Team against Wolves he played in the final game of the 1956/57 season in a 1-1 draw against West Brom. as United won the Championship.

	Appearances	Goals
Football League	2	

Alex Dawson Centre-Forward

Born Aberdeen 21st February 1940
Début 22nd April 1957 v Burnley (home) 2-0

Alex Dawson was a powerfully built young lad of seventeen when he made his First Team début scoring against Burnley at Old Trafford. He retained his place for the last two games of the season scoring in each match.

He played in both legs of the 1956 FA Youth Cup Final when United beat Chesterfield 4-3 on aggregate and scored 3 goals the following season as United retained the trophy beating West Ham 8-2 over the two legs.

	Appearances	Goals
Football League	3	3

David Gaskell Goalkeeper

Born Wigan 5th October 1940

Having just celebrated his sixteenth birthday two weeks earlier, David Gaskell was summoned from the crowd just before half-time to replace Ray Wood in goal in the FA Charity Shield game against Manchester City at Maine Road in October 1956.

Wood had injured his hip in a goalmouth scramble and the United physio decided not to risk any aggravation to the injury.

Gaskell, a schoolboy international, made two exceptional saves late in the game from Dyson and Johnstone helping United to win 1-0.

He is still not old enough to turn professional at the start of the 1957/58 season.

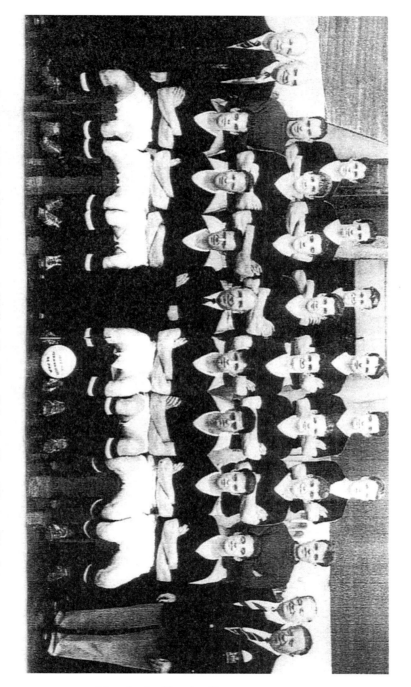

Back row left to right-McGuinness, Viollet, Charlton, Doherty, Blanchflower, Scanlon.
Middle row-T. Curry, B. Inglis, Wood, Greaves, Foulkes, Goodwin, Whelan, Jones, Edwards, Clayton,
E. Dalton, J. Murphy
Front row- Webster, Whitefoot, Berry, M. Busby, Byrne, Taylor, Colman, Pegg.

Manchester Evening News

41

July 1957

Wed. 10ᵗʰ July

The Football Association met in London to consider a report following an investigation into alleged breaches of rules and regulations by Sunderland Football Club.

Trevor Ford, the former Sunderland and Wales International who has now joined P.S.V. Eindhoven, was banned from playing as a professional footballer under the jurisdiction of the Football Association for the next three seasons. This follows the statement made by Mr Murray, the previous manager of Sunderland, that in August 1951 he handed Trevor Ford a parcel containing £250 in Treasury notes. Ford denied that this ever happened and was present at the hearing with Murray.

The Commission, having considered all the evidence, had no doubt that 'Murray was a witness of truth' and accordingly accepted his evidence and rejected Ford's denial.

A further eight Sunderland players who had received illegal payments - Aitken, Anderson, Bingham, Holden, Kemp, McDonald, Purdon and Shackleton, who had all asked for the Commission to deal with them in their absence, were informed that they would forfeit six month qualification for benefit or accrued share of benefits.

Replies from Hedley and Fleming had still not been received and therefore their cases will be dealt with separately.

Tues. 16ᵗʰ July

The press reported that Manchester United's share of the FA Cup Final receipts was £7,718. When the full profits for the season are announced it is expected that they will exceed the previous record of £50,810 in 1948/49.

Thurs. 18th July

A hearing in the Queen's Bench Division of the High Court was informed that the parties had agreed terms in the case of a claim for wrongful dismissal by Mr Hewitt, former secretary/manager of Millwall F. C.

One of the terms of the agreement was that the details would be announced in open court and accordingly Mr Justice Byrne stated that Mr Hewitt would receive £4,500 plus costs for the action.

Wed. 24th July
The European Cup Draw

Manchester United have been drawn against Shamrock Rovers of Dublin in the First Round of next seasons European Cup.

Following the acceptance of three late applications to enter the tournament, the total number of clubs in the draw was increased to 24, with the teams divided into three groups-Western Europe, Eastern and Central.

Real Madrid, the current holders, are exempt from the First Round. All the matches, both home and away, must be completed by 30th September.

Wed. 31st July

Sunderland announced that Mr A. Brown had been appointed as Manager having left Burnley to take up the post.

Everton issued a press release confirming that Eire International, Peter Farrell, has been appointed as captain for the tenth consecutive season.

Player Profile

Gil Merrick
Born 26th January 1922-Birmingham

After excelling at cricket and football at school, it was no surprise when Birmingham City spotted Gil Merrick playing in goal for a local junior team and offered him a contract in 1939.

As the War intervened, he served as a Physical Training Instructor in the Army but still appeared for the 'Blues' in over 170 competitive games helping the team win the 1945/46 Football League South title. The same season the FA Cup competition was reintroduced and Birmingham reached the semi-final before losing 4-0 in a replay to eventual winners Derby County.

On 31st August 1946 the crowds flocked to the opening games of the new season and, aged 24, Merrick finally made his League début for Birmingham in a Second Division game at Spurs. Standing at over six feet tall, his neat moustache made him easily recognisable. His calm approach to goalkeeping, preferring to make saves by positioning and anticipation rather than throwing himself around, have endeared him to football supporters. Merrick also prefers to catch crosses rather than punching the ball away like many of his fellow 'keepers.

In the second season after the War, Birmingham were promoted as Second Division Champions and also in 1947 Merrick made the first of eleven appearances for the Football League, his last being in 1954. The 'Blues' found life in the top flight difficult, finishing in 17th position and then bottom of the table in 1950. After five seasons in the Second Division Birmingham were eventually promoted as Champions in 1955. It was during this period that he won his first cap for England, playing in his home town at Villa Park on 14th November 1951 in the 2-0 win against Northern Ireland. His impressive, calm performance led the selectors to include him in a further 22 out of 23 internationals until June 1954.

Although only playing in five defeats, all whilst a Second Division player, he had the misfortune to face the Hungarians at Wembley in November 1953 as England lost 6-3, their first defeat at home to a Continental team. Worse was to follow when, the following year, England lost the return fixture 7-1 in Budapest. Over the two games Puskas and the rest of the Hungarian players had torn the England defence to shreds, playing a style of football completely alien to the English game. England manager, Walter Winterbottom, refused to make excuses preferring instead to congratulate the opponents on their wonderful ability. The press gave Merrick a hard time over conceding the 13 goals and, although he retained his place for the 1954 World Cup in Switzerland, he has not appeared for England since the 4-2 defeat against Uruguay in the Quarter Finals.

Back on the domestic scene, in 1956 Birmingham finished in 6th position on their return to Division 1 and reached the FA Cup Final losing 3-1 to Manchester City in a game remembered for the serious neck injury to Bert Trautmann.

In 1956/57 Birmingham finished in 12th position and reached the semi-finals of the Cup before losing 2-0 to Manchester United. Since 1951 Merrick has combined his professional football career with teaching Physical Training at Greenmore Private Secondary College in Birmingham.

Career Appearances (as at 31/07/1957)

League	421
FA Cup	49
Europe	4
England	23

AUGUST 1957

Thurs. 1st Aug.

The Football League Secretary, Alan Hardaker, issued a statement confirming the new arrangements for the creation of a Fourth Division from the start of the 1958/59 season.

The two clubs relegated from the Second Division in 1957/58 will go into the new Third Division and will be replaced by the top side in Division 3 North and South.

The top eleven clubs from each of the existing Division 3 North and South will form the remainder of the new Third Division.

The bottom eleven clubs from each North and South Division will create the new Fourth Division with the teams in the bottom position in each group having to apply for re-election.

Wed. 14th Aug.

Manchester United beat a Combined West Berlin side 3-0 under floodlights at the Olympic Stadium watched by a crowd of 60,000 including a large number of British Servicemen. Viollet scored in the 15th and 58th minutes whilst Taylor got the second in the 40th minute to give United a comfortable victory. The Berlin side did have the ball in the net only for the referee to disallow the effort for an infringement.

In Rotterdam a crowd of approximately 25,000 saw Blackpool beat Sparta-Rotterdam by 3-2. Blackpool led 3-1 at the interval following goals from Taylor, Mudie and Perry.

Fri. 16th Aug.

The FA announced that ticket prices for the England International games at Wembley against France and Ireland in November will be reduced. The top price seat falls from 50 shillings to 42s. With other seating reduced from 25s to 21s, 15s down to 12s 6d and 10s 6d to 10s and some to 7s 6d. However, general terrace prices will remain at 3s 6d.

Sat. 17ᵗʰ Aug.

In Hanover United won their second tour match by 4-2 after producing a superb performance. Fielding the same side in both games-Wood, Foulkes, Byrne, Colman, Blanchflower, Edwards, Berry, Whelan, Taylor, Viollet and Pegg-United thoroughly entertained the Servicemen and locals alike.

The goals were shared two apiece by Taylor and Viollet and the party headed home in great spirits ready for the new season.

The German officials were so impressed with the quality of football played by the 'Red Devil's' that they invited the Club to return next summer for a three week tour. Matt Busby and the directors considered their request but regretfully decided to decline the invitation as United would have a number of players involved in the World Cup in Sweden during the summer of 1958.

Sun. 18ᵗʰ Aug.

In a friendly in Amsterdam, Chelsea's left-winger Frank Blunstone, unfortunately broke his left leg in a 4-2 victory.

Wed. 21ˢᵗ Aug.

The Football League announced that a flu epidemic at Sheffield Wednesday had resulted in a decision to postpone their opening game of the season at Maine Road. It is also possible that their second fixture at Newcastle on the following Wednesday may also have to be re-arranged.

The Reserve team games against Manchester City at home on Saturday and Newcastle on Monday have also been postponed.

Originally seven players had reported unfit but the numbers were quickly doubled when Bingley, Cargill, Ellis, Fantham, Martin, O'Donnell and Young complained of feeling unwell and were told to stay away from the Club. In the end only six players from the First and Second team were able to train.

Mr Taylor, manager, confirmed that the situation would be monitored daily and that swabs and blood samples had been taken as well as the spraying and disinfecting of changing rooms.

Fri. 23ʳᵈ Aug.
Season Preview

Football League Champions Manchester United travel to newly promoted Leicester City for the opening game of the season, seeking a third consecutive title.

United have named the same side that won both games in Germany with Blanchflower preferred to Jones at centre-half.

Only two teams in football history, Huddersfield Town 1924-1926 and Arsenal 1933-1935, have won the Championship three seasons in a row.

Making their début in the 'top flight' are 17 years old Jimmy Greaves for Chelsea, Ray Crawford-Portsmouth and Mick Meagan for Everton at Goodison Park in place of club captain Farrell.

Wolves most expensive signing, £25,000 Harry Hooper, will start the season in the reserves. Last season he scored 19 goals in 39 appearances but his place has been taken by former schoolboy international Norman Deeley who cost a £10 signing-on fee. England International Bill Slater and Wilshaw are also in the reserve team to face Barnsley at Molineux.

Portsmouth manager, Eddie Lever, will not see his team's game against Burnley, instead he will be in Ireland to have a second look at Derek Dougan, the Distillery wing-half or inside-forward.

Last season's Division 2 runners-up, Nottingham Forest, have an attractive home fixture against Preston North End, captained by Tom Finney, with a crowd in excess of 30,000 expected. The two sides last met in Division 1 during the 1924/25 season when Preston won 1-0 at Nottingham.

Saturday 24th August

The new football season was heralded by warm sunshine in many parts of the country as almost one million spectators attended the forty-five games. The matches at Birmingham, Everton, Sunderland and Tottenham each attracted over 50,000 fans.

Newly promoted Nottingham Forest had a superb victory against a very experienced Preston side and took the lead after only two minutes through Barrett. A blistering drive from Taylor levelled the scores but after half an hour Gray netted the winner with a lofted shot which entered the net off a post.

Jimmy Greaves marked his début for Chelsea with a goal at White Hart Lane to earn the 'Pensioners' a point.

At Goodison Park a solitary goal from J. Harris gave Everton both points in a hard fought match against Wolves. The afternoon was marred by the news that two supporters collapsed and died during the game. They were later named as Mr Marr, aged 64 from Wednesbury and Mr Cottier 69 from Liverpool.

At Bloomfield Road a howling gale greeted the teams making attractive football very difficult. After a goalless first half Blackpool took control of the game. Matthews, now aged 42, playing at outside-right made the first goal with a cross which Durie headed into the net. Perry added a second and Ernie Taylor made it three after leaving his 'sickbed' to play in the game.

There was also a strong wind at Roker Park as Sunderland created a number of chances early in the game, including an amazing miss by Shackleton in front of an open goal. Arsenal eventually came more into the game and in the 41st minute Groves scored, what turned out to be the only goal, with a superb header. In the final minute Revie had a chance to equalise but blasted his shot over the crossbar.

Manchester City decided to arrange a public friendly game to give their first and reserve team players match practice following the postponement of the scheduled encounter against Sheffield Wednesday. Unfortunately Jack Dyson broke his leg and will be out of action for some considerable time.

SATURDAY 24TH AUGUST 1957

BIRMINGHAM C. 3   **ASTON VILLA** 1
Brown, Kinsey, Murphy   McParland
           Att. 50,780

BLACKPOOL 3   **LEEDS UNITED** 0
Durie, Perry, Taylor
           Att. 26,700

EVERTON 1   **WOLVES** 0
Harris J.
           Att. 58,229

LEICESTER CITY 0   **MANCHESTER U.** 3
     Whelan 3
           Att. 40,214

LUTON TOWN 1   **BOLTON W.** 0
Turner
           Att. 17,591

MANCHESTER C. v   **SHEFFIELD WED.**
(Postponed due to an influenza outbreak)

NOTTINGHAM F. 2   **PRESTON N.E.** 1
Barrett, Gray   Taylor
           Att. 33,285

PORTSMOUTH 0   **BURNLEY** 0
           Att. 30,134

SUNDERLAND 0   **ARSENAL** 1
     Groves
           Att. 56,493

TOTTENHAM H. 1   **CHELSEA** 1
Stokes   Greaves
           Att. 52,580

WEST BROM. ALB. 2   **NEWCASTLE U.** 1
Robson, Allen   White
           Att. 30,931

Leicester City	0	Manchester United	3

Whelan   3

Att. 40,214

Leicester City-*MacLaren, Milburn, Ogilvie, Morris, Froggatt, O'Neil, McDonald, McNeill, Hines, Rowley, Hogg.*

Manchester United-*Wood, Foulkes, Byrne, Colman, Blanchflower, Edwards, Berry, Whelan, Taylor, Viollet, Pegg.*

The Leicester City players and supporters had been looking forward to this game against the Champions, Manchester United, ever since the fixtures were released in the summer. Last season's Second Division winners made a bright start and Foulkes was forced to make a hasty clearance as the home side stormed forward. Within a few minutes Edwards was given a stern lecture by the referee following a wild challenge on Froggatt, who needed treatment from the trainer. Leicester held the upper hand for long periods as United took time to settle.

Hogg caused problems down the left flank but received poor support from his colleagues, especially Rowley who seemed strangely lethargic.

Despite having most of the possession the home side failed to really test Wood except for a powerful shot from Hines which the goalkeeper dealt with comfortably. At times their over-elaborate play lacked a cutting edge.

As United slipped up a gear an Edwards thunderbolt glanced over the crossbar and then Taylor and Viollet both missed heading opportunities. The game reached the interval goalless.

Leicester City

Back row – J. Morris, S. Milburn, J. Anderson, W. Webb, D. Ward, A. Rowley

Front row – T. McDonald, I. McNeill, J. Froggatt, W. Gardiner, D. Hogg

Inset – D. McLaren, J. Ogilvie

The second half began much the same as the first had ended with both defences being on top of their games but it was McLaren in the Leicester goal who was kept busier making three fine saves to keep the home side in the game. Eventually, after 70 minutes, the deadlock was broken. Byrne, Edwards and Pegg combined down the left wing to give Viollet a chance to shoot at goal. The ball was deflected by WHELAN into the net to give United the lead. The goal changed the game and within minutes United scored a second. Pegg, who had switched to the right wing for a short period following an injury to Berry, hit a perfect cross for WHELAN to score a simple goal.

After 78 minutes the game was over. Berry had returned to the pitch and from the right-wing hit a superb cross which WHELAN (pictured opposite) smashed beyond McLaren for his hat-trick. Leicester missed a late chance but could have no complaints as they were eventually well beaten by a determined United side who made the perfect start in their quest to gain a third consecutive Championship title.

****

United Reserves

A very strong United Reserves side were just too powerful for Blackburn Rovers at Old Trafford. Despite constant pressure the home side failed to score until the stroke of half-time when Whitefoot netted from a corner.

The goal opened the floodgates as the Rovers defence caved in and within 8 minutes of the restart United had added 3 more goals through Dawson 2 and Charlton. Although Smith pulled one back for Blackburn, Whitefoot scored his second and United's fifth in a 5-1 victory.

United team-Gaskell, Greaves, P. Jones, Goodwin,

M. Jones, McGuinness, Webster, Whitefoot, Dawson, Charlton and Scanlon.

Mon. 26ᵗʰ Aug.

ASTON VILLA	2	**LEEDS UNITED**	0
McParland, Sewell			

Att. 25,693

BLACKPOOL	1	**LUTON TOWN**	2
Perry		Turner x2	

Att. 21,099

Former 'Seasider' Alan Brown had a great game against his former club at Bloomfield Road helping Luton Town to maintain their perfect start to the season. Gordon Turner scored both goals with Brown playing a major role in the build up.

United Reserves

United made one change from the team that won easily on Saturday with Morgans playing at outside-right in place of Webster for the match at Goodison Park.

The 'Reds' gave a disappointing performance losing 3-1 with Dawson netting the consolation goal.

It was reported that thieves had broken into the Millwall grounds offices over the weekend and, using a drill, had managed to force the safe open. The gate money from Saturday's Division 3 South game against Southampton at 'The Den' amounting to approximately £1800 had been stolen.

Tues. 27ᵗʰ Aug

ARSENAL	2	**WEST BROM. ALBION**	2
Herd x2		Allen x2 (pen)	

Att. 45,988

BURNLEY	2	**PRESTON N E**	0
Shackleton x2			

Att. 27,804

Shackleton scored twice for Burnley at Turf Moor to ensure that local rivals Preston left the ground still pointless after two games.

Their win had much to do with a superb performance from centre-half Adamson who completely mastered Finney ensuring that the England International was unable to influence the game in his usual manner.

With the first half scoreless, Shackleton put the home side ahead within minutes of the restart with a terrific drive. He scored again with a header late in the game after good work from McIlroy.

Wed. 28ᵗʰ Aug.

CHELSEA	2	MANCHESTER CITY	3
Greaves, Lewis		Barlow, Hayes, McAdams	

Att. 43,722

LEICESTER CITY	4	SUNDERLAND	1
McNeill x3, O'Neil		Grainger	

Att. 34,164

MANCHESTER UNITED	3	EVERTON	0
Taylor, Viollet, Jones (OG)			

Att. 59,343

NEWCASTLE UNITED	P	SHEFFIELD WEDNESDAY	P
		Postponed due to influenza outbreak	

NOTTINGHAM FOREST	1	BIRMINGHAM CITY	1
Wilson		Brown	

Att. 29,705

PORTSMOUTH	5	TOTTENHAM HOTSPUR	1
Harris x3, Crawford x2		Smith	

Att. 33,479

WOLVES	6	BOLTON WANDERERS	1
Deeley x2, Murray x2, Booth, Broadbent		Lofthouse	

Att. 30,790

Leicester City, after suffering a home defeat against Manchester United on Saturday, recovered their composure and easily outplayed Sunderland-winning 4-1 including a hat-trick by Ian McNeill. Sunderland have now lost their opening two games.

There was another hat-trick in the game at Fratton Park where Portsmouth scored five times in the opening hour, eventually beating Spurs 5-1. Harris netted three with 21 years old Ray Crawford scoring twice.

Wolves were top scorers of the evening, hitting six against hapless Bolton.

Outside-right Norman Deeley, who is keeping Harry Hooper out of the team, scored twice to enhance his growing reputation.

Chelsea were two goals ahead within minutes of the start of the second half and appeared to be heading for a comfortable victory against Manchester City at Stamford Bridge. A Lewis header and a 'poachers' goal from Greaves seemed to have overcome the away side's off-side game. But in a fifteen minute purple patch City scored three times to secure the points. Matthews, in the Chelsea goal, had an uncomfortable game being at fault for two goals and then suffering a head injury which forced him to leave the field for a few minutes whilst Tindall donned the 'keeper's jersey.

Matthews returned for the final few minutes but was obviously not fully fit.

Manchester United   3   Everton   0

Taylor, Jones (og), Viollet

Att. 59,343

Manchester United-ic*Wood, Foulkes, Byrne, Colman, Blanchflower, Edwards, Berry, Whelan, Taylor, Viollet, Pegg.*

Everton-*Dunlop, Donovan, Tansey, Birch, Jones, Meagan, Harris J., Temple, Hickson, Fielding, Williams.*

After finishing their working day, thousands of United fans flocked to Old Trafford to see the first home game of the season. As kick-off approached at 7.30 p.m. almost 60,000 spectators were in the stadium ready for the action.

After only a few minutes United created the first chance as a neat passing move split the away defence but Viollet shot just wide.

United continued to dominate possession without really being able to penetrate the Everton defence but their four-pronged attack always looked dangerous. In the 35th minute Everton had an opportunity but a powerful header by Hickson was well saved by Wood. The crowd roared the home side forward and minutes before half time the deadlock was broken. Byrne hooked the ball up-field into the path of TAYLOR and the burly centre-forward used his strength to fend off defenders before his shot found the net.

Everton
Back row – K. Birch, W. Haughey, D. Donovan, A Dunlop, J. O'Neill
J. Gauld, P. Farrell, T. Jones. Seated – J. Tansey, J. Harris, D. Hickson, A.
McNamara, W. Fielding, B. Harris, D. Temple. Front row – M. Meagan, K. Rea.

As the second half got under way Byrne almost gifted Everton an equaliser.
For some reason he allowed Harris to race beyond him and the winger was
unfortunate to see his shot hit the post and rebound to safety.

The action swiftly moved to the other penalty area with Billy Whelan taking
the ball off a defender's toes before swinging a cross into the path of Taylor.
Everton centre-half JONES reached the ball first but in his haste to clear the danger
only managed to slice it into his own net.

Despite going two goals behind Everton were not beaten and Hickson in
particular continued to give Blanchflower a torrid time with his willingness to
chase every ball. But his colleagues were finding life more difficult and minutes
later United had a third.

Colman set up the chance for VIOLLET (below) who made no mistake with a
quick shot which surprised Dunlop in the Everton goal.

The ball went between the goalkeepers legs before nestling in the net. Four
points, six goals and none conceded continued United's perfect start.

56

Fri. 30th Aug.

Roger Duarte, aged 22, and Mrs Jeronima Duarte, both from different London addresses, were due to appear at Tower Bridge Court today charged with receiving £710-9s-0d each as part of the proceeds of the theft of £1,800 from Milwall F. C. at the weekend. Roger Duarte was also charged with breaking and entering.

Only two sides in the First Division, Manchester United and Luton Town have gained maximum points from their opening two games. United will again be unchanged for their local derby against City at Old Trafford tomorrow whereas Luton visit Highbury for a difficult encounter with Arsenal.

Len Shackleton, after playing in last Saturday's defeat against Arsenal has had an operation on his ankle and looks unlikely to return for Sunderland for some considerable time.

Preston, still to gain a point, have a difficult home fixture against Portsmouth who demolished Spurs 5-1 in mid-week.

Lythgoe will make his first League appearance for Blackpool for over two years in place of the injured Durie for the away game at Bolton.

Saturday 31st August

Manchester Utd	4	Manchester City	1

Edwards, Berry, Viollet
Taylor.

Barnes

Att. 63,347

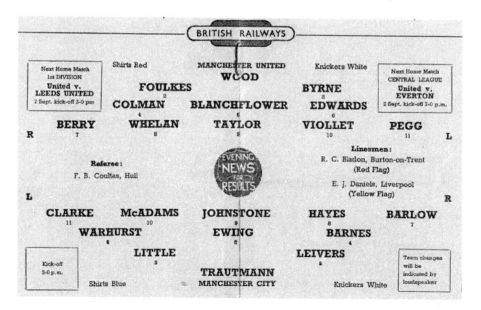

The 63rd derby meeting between United and City fittingly attracted a crowd of over 63,000 on a dry, calm day perfect for football.

Both sides set out to play in an attractive manner and the game quickly moved from one end of the pitch to the other. After 15 minutes the home side took the lead following a misunderstanding in the City defence which allowed EDWARDS to race through a gap and score.

Within a minute City should have equalised when a defence splitting pass from McAdams reached Clarke but he shot wide of the target. The miss proved costly as in the 20th minute BERRY put United further ahead with a powerful header from a Pegg corner.

Once again only 60 seconds later Clarke (pictured below) had a further opportunity to score. He intercepted a back-pass from Edwards meant for the goalkeeper but his shot missed the target and slammed into the half time scoreboard.

Edwards continued to power United forward giving a superb display at left-half but was also always available to help out in defence when needed. His wing-half partner Colman was guilty on at least two occasions of giving the ball away to an opponent. The game reached the interval with United sitting comfortably on a two goal lead.

The teams continued to provide splendid entertainment for the large crowd but City's off-side tactics were soon breached as United scored a third goal. Colman hit a long pass through the City defence and VIOLLET ran clear of three defenders before ramming home his shot.

Centre-forward TAYLOR, who was having one of his best games for some considerable time, tapped the ball beyond Trautmann for a fourth after the goalkeeper had initially blocked a shot from Pegg.

City were still able to create chances and BARNES pulled one goal back from a free-kick to become the first player to score against United this season. Late in the game Hayes had two half chances but failed to make either count.

Berry, on the right flank, had been a constant threat to the City defence who were never sure whether he would cross or pass to a colleague.

A great win to maintain United's one hundred percent record.

SATURDAY 31ST AUGUST

ARSENAL	2	LUTON TOWN	0
Groves, Holton			

Att. 49,914

ASTON VILLA	0	EVERTON	1
		Temple	

Att. 37,759

BOLTON W.	3	BLACKPOOL	0
Stevens, Allcock 2			

Att. 31,491

BURNLEY	2	WEST BROM. ALB.	2
Shackleton, Cheesebrough		Setters, Lee	

Att. 24,428

CHELSEA	5	BIRMINGHAM C.	1
Greaves 2, Brabrook		Brown	
Lewis, Allen			

Att. 43,806

LEEDS UNITED	2	LEICESTER CITY	1
Overfield, Baird(pen)		Rowley	

Att. 26,660

MANCHESTER U.	4	MANCHESTER C.	1
Edwards, Berry, Taylor		Barnes	
Viollet			

Att. 63,347

NEWCASTLE U.	3	TOTTENHAM H.	1
Eastham, Keeble,		Smith	
Mitchell			

Att. 37,742

PRESTON N.E.	4	PORTSMOUTH	0
Baxter, Thompson 2			
Finney			

Att. 24,422

SHEFFIELD WED.	1	NOTTINGHAM F.	2
McAnearney J.		Imlach, Barrett(pen)	

Att. 31,236

WOLVES	5	SUNDERLAND	0
Murray 2, Booth			
Deeley, Mullen			

Att. 38,645

	P.	W.	D.	L.	Goals F.	A.	Pts
Manchester U. ...	3	3	0	0	10	1	6
Arsenal	3	2	1	0	5	2	5
Notts. F.	3	2	1	0	5	3	5
Wolves	3	2	0	1	11	2	4
Burnley	3	1	2	0	4	2	4
Luton Town ...	3	2	0	1	3	3	4
W. Brom. A. ...	3	1	2	0	6	5	4
Everton	3	2	0	1	2	3	4
Chelsea	3	1	1	1	8	5	3
Birmingham	3	1	1	1	5	7	3
Portsmouth	3	1	1	1	5	5	3
North End	3	1	0	2	5	4	2
Newcastle U.	2	1	0	1	4	3	2
Aston Villa	3	1	0	2	3	4	2
Blackpool	3	1	0	2	4	5	2
Manchester C. ...	2	1	0	1	4	6	2
Leicester City ...	3	1	0	2	5	6	2
Bolton W.	3	1	0	2	4	7	2
Leeds United	3	1	0	2	2	6	2
Tottenham H. ...	3	0	1	2	3	9	1
Sheffield W. ...	1	0	0	1	1	2	0
Sunderland	3	0	0	3	1	10	0

Preston gained their first points of the season with an emphatic 4-0 home win against Portsmouth. Finney and Thompson kept the away defence at full stretch, scoring three of the four goals between them.

Birmingham City goalkeeper, Gil Merrick, was carried off the pitch on a stretcher after only four minutes of the game with Chelsea following a collision with Jimmy Greaves. He had five stitches to a cut under his jaw and suffered concussion. The ten men could not hold Chelsea at bay losing 5-1 with young Greaves scoring twice-he has now scored in every game.

Hugh Baird (pictured) scored his first goal in English football (a penalty) to help Leeds United beat Leicester City 2-1 at Elland Road. He had been the leading goal scorer in Scottish football over the last three seasons.

Sunderland, with three teenagers in their team, lost for the third game running at Molineux. Murray opened the scoring in the third minute with a fierce shot from the edge of the penalty area before Sunderland forced the pace for long periods of the first half.

Wolves eventually regained control in the second period and during a nineteen minute spell added four more goals to completely overpower their opponents.

A goal from Derek Temple after 23 minutes following good work from Brian Harris secured both points for Everton at Villa Park. The home side found Donovan and Jones unmovable in the visitors defence.

Jim Iley played the opening game of the season for Sheffield United, his 99th appearance for the Club despite only being 21, before transferring to Spurs for a fee of £16,000. His début ended in disappointment as he failed to inspire his new club at Newcastle.

Spurs chances were not helped by an injury to left-winger Robb after 25 minutes which left him as a passenger for the rest of the game. Eastham gave Newcastle the lead in the 11th minute after a mazy dribble by Mitchell. Keeble added a second in the 35th minute and although Bobby Smith reduced the arrears in the second half, Mitchell secured the game with a third goal.

Luton Town lost their 100 % record at Highbury as goals from Groves and Holton ensured a victory for Arsenal. Man of the match was Luton goalkeeper Baynham who looks certain to challenge for international honours.

After the first week of games Manchester United are now the only side with maximum points scoring 10 goals and conceding 1 in contrast to Sunderland at the foot of the table who have no points having scored 1 goal and let in 10.

United Reserves

In addition to the 63,000 spectators at Old Trafford, across the City at Maine Road almost 13,000 more watched the Reserve derby.

The first half gave no indication of the avalanche of goals which would follow the restart as the sides reached the interval level at 1-1 with Dawson scoring for United.

Charlton put them ahead, then City scored twice, and looked to have earned the points as the game reached the closing stages. Outside-left Scanlon had other ideas and after netting the equaliser, then scored the winner in the 89th minute to give United a 4-3 victory.

****

Player Profile

Robert Dennis Blanchflower
Born 10th February, 1926- Belfast

Danny Blanchflower was born in Bloomfield Belfast, the son of a shipyard worker. His mother played amateur football in a local ladies' team.

A bright pupil at school he was awarded a scholarship to Belfast College of Technology but left early to work at Gallagher's Cigarette Company as an apprentice electrician.

Blanchflower had impressed in school football with his ability to dictate the play from midfield making him stand out from the other youngsters. By falsely declaring his age, he was able to join the RAF and was posted to Scotland to train as a navigator and subsequently found himself in Canada before peace was declared.

On returning home his 'silky' skills were soon spotted by Glentoran and in 1946 he signed as a part-time professional whilst still working at Gallaghers. Within twelve months he had been selected for the Irish League against the Football League, alerting a number of clubs in England to show an interest in him.

In 1949 Angus Seed, the Barnsley manager, paid a transfer fee of approximately £6,500 to take Blanchflower to Barnsley and he made his début in the final game of the season. The 1949/50 season saw him firmly established in the team and he also won his first International Cap for Ireland against Scotland in Belfast. Unfortunately the Irish were hammered 8-2 and he was dropped for the next game. However, his strong and impressive performances for Barnsley soon convinced the selectors to pick him again and he played in the final home International Championship game against Wales in Wrexham.

He scored his first League goal for Barnsley in a drawn game against Hull City. Over a period of time reports suggested that he strongly objected to the training methods used at Oakwell and wanted more ball contact during the week rather than just running and exercising.

The following season saw him play almost every game for Barnsley until March when he once again disagreed with the system of training and was placed on the transfer list. After a disastrous 7-0 defeat at Deepdale against Preston (with Finney, Horton and Wayman sharing the goals) he was allowed to move to First Division Aston Villa for a fee of £15,000. It was later reported that the Club Chairmen had met in a hotel to finalise the details, leaving the player sat in the kitchens with a chauffeur.

The Villa Park fans were soon won over by the efforts of Blanchflower who always seemed to have the ability to be available in space to receive a pass whenever a team-mate was in trouble.

After making almost 150 League appearances he became disillusioned with life at Villa Park, disagreeing with the manager's tactics and he let other people know he was unhappy. It first appeared as though he would join Arsenal but eventually he signed for Tottenham Hotspur in December 1954 for £30,000.

In the early stages at White Hart Lane he formed a strong bond with manager Arthur Rowe and just as the partnership was working, Rowe was forced to retire due to ill health in 1955.

Mr Anderson took over as manager and made Blanchflower captain but the relationship was far from smooth and after Spurs lost an FA Cup Semi-final in 1956 to Manchester City, Blanchflower was not reappointed as captain for the following season. He was said to have changed the tactics during the game in contradiction to those outlined by the manager.

As the 1957/58 season unfolds, Blanchflower will still no doubt have a strong influence in the team.

His younger brother, Jackie, plays for Manchester United and is also an Irish International.

Career Appearances (as at 31st July 1957)

		League	Goals
1949/51	Barnsley	68	2
1951/54	Aston Villa	148	10
1954/57	Tottenham H.	101	1
1949/57	Northern Ireland	25	0

September 1957

Mon. 2nd Sept.

After Sheffield Wednesday were forced to postpone their opening two League games due to a flu epidemic the problem now seems to have crossed the city to Sheffield United. At least ten players, mainly in the second team, have contracted the bug and the Yorkshire league game scheduled for Saturday has had to be postponed.

Sheffield Transport have reported that over 300 drivers and conductors are off work causing havoc to the public transport system.

United Reserves

In the game against Everton at Old Trafford both sides played attractive football to enthral a crowd of almost 13,000 but it was the away side who gained their second victory over United in the space of a week.

Everton raced into a three goal lead before Webster pulled one back, but as the interval approached Everton scored a fourth. No matter how hard United pressed they only managed to reduce the deficit by one goal courtesy of the away team captain Peter Farrell who deflected the ball into his own net to make the final score United 2 Everton 4.

United reported that, at the first two home games of the season, they had sold almost 52,000 United Review programmes per game.

Tues. 3rd Sept.

Manchester United will again be unchanged for tomorrow's game at Goodison Park with a crowd of over 65,000 expected.

Blackpool have some major injury worries ahead of their game at Luton and intend to give a début to 22 year-old centre-forward Ray Charnley. The player was only signed from Morecambe in the Lancashire Combination three months ago and has played just two reserve team games. The side will also contain a South African left-wing partnership of Peterson and Perry.

Arsenal will make five changes, two of them positional, for their visit to the Hawthorns. Evans and Dodgin are fit again and return to the side, whilst Swallow will play at inside-left.

Sheffield Wednesday will give a début to 22 year-old Peter Baker who replaces Staniforth at full-back for the Newcastle match. The Walthamstow born player is a cousin of the Tottenham full-back with the same name.

Wed. 4th Sept.

BIRMINGHAM C.	0	NOTTINGHAM F.	2
		Barrett, Wilson	
		Att. 26,852	
BOLTON W.	1	WOLVES	1
Stevens		Deeley	
		Att. 25,845	
EVERTON	3	MANCHESTER U.	3
Temple 2, Harris J.		Viollet, Berry, Whelan	
		Att. 71,868	
LEEDS UNITED	4	ASTON VILLA	0
O'Brien, Baird 2, Brook		Att. 22,685	
LUTON TOWN	2	BLACKPOOL	0
Brown, Cullen		Att. 19,567	
MANCHESTER C.	5	CHELSEA	2
Barlow 2, Fagan 2,		Lewis, Brabrook	
McAdams		Att. 27,943	
PRESTON N.E.	2	BURNLEY	1
Finney, Thompson		McIlroy (pen)	
		Att. 31,267	
SHEFFIELD WED.	1	NEWCASTLE U.	0
Broadbent		Att. 22,067	
SUNDERLAND	3	LEICESTER CITY	2
O'Neill 2, Goodchild		Hines, McDonald	
		Att. 39,629	
TOTTENHAM H.	3	PORTSMOUTH	5
Dulin, Brooks,		Harris, Henderson 2,	
Harmer (pen)		Gordon, McClellan	
		Att. 35,813	
WEST BROM. ALB.	1	ARSENAL	2
Allen		Swallow, Bloomfield	
		Att. 25,983	

Greaves was missing from the Chelsea side for their visit to Maine Road following his collision with Gil Merrick on Saturday. After only two minutes the visitors took the lead when Trautmann misjudged a shot from Brabrook allowing it to run up his arm and over his shoulder into the net. City then attacked with a purpose but could not find a way through the resolute Chelsea defence. With less than 30 minutes played City were reduced to ten men as Johnstone was sent off following an altercation with an opponent.

The game deteriorated as the tackles became more ferocious and the numbers were evened up when, in the 36th minute, McFarlane was also sent off for a wild challenge on Hayes. In the next four minutes City incredibly scored three times to completely change the game and reach half time with a 3-1 lead.

In the second period Chelsea forced City onto the defensive but just when it seemed they may pull a goal back Barlow increased the lead and City eventually ran out easy winners 5-2.

The Portsmouth team coach arrived late at White Hart Lane following a road traffic accident and the game kicked off twenty minutes after the scheduled start. The delay did not seem to have hampered the away side who, within fifteen minutes, had raced into a three goal lead.

The first, by Harris, followed a dreadful back-pass by Ryden which never reached his goalkeeper. Although three goals in arrears Blanchflower urged his team-mates forward – Dulin scored with a header, Brooks volleyed in a second and Harmer equalised from the penalty spot. The crowd of over 35,000 applauded both teams from the pitch wondering what was in store in the second half.

Once again Spurs virtually gave a goal away within minutes of the restart. A harmless shot from McClellan somehow slipped through the grasp of Reynolds and into the net. A final goal by Henderson had no element of luck about it as his shot crashed into the Spurs net. Pompey had scored five goals against Tottenham for the second time in a week.

Sunderland gained their first win of the season thanks to two goals from 19 year-old Alan O'Neill as they beat Leicester City 3-2. The young player is also a part-time painter and decorator and was denied a hat-trick when the linesman flagged for off-side as he slammed the ball into the net.

Everton	3	**Manchester United**	3

Temple 2, J. Harris   Viollet, Berry, Whelan

Att. 71,868

Everton-*Dunlop, Donovan, Tansey, Birch, Jones, Meagan, Harris J., Temple, Hickson, Fielding, Harris B.*
Manchester United-*Wood, Foulkes, Byrne, Colman, Blanchflower, Edwards, Berry, Whelan, Taylor, Viollet, Pegg.*

United started the game at a blistering pace and completely overwhelmed the home side whilst racing into a two goal lead, much to the dismay of the Everton fans in the huge crowd.

With Pegg causing problems down the left flank and Whelan orchestrating everything from the right side, Everton appeared to be in for an evening of toil.

TEMPLE (above) did pull a goal back for the 'Toffees' only to see WHELAN score again for United who reached the interval with a 3-1 lead.

Everton never gave up the chase, fighting like tigers for every ball and then their luck changed. United centre-half, Blanchflower, suffered an injury and had to be moved into the attack solely for nuisance value.

Edwards switched to centre-half and Viollet moved back to left-half. All these changes destroyed the rhythm of the United side and Everton capitalised by slowly but surely clawing themselves back into the game.

Wood was at fault for the Everton second goal and the Liverpudlians' roared their team forward at every opportunity. Eventually the equaliser came and United dropped their first point of the season. There is little doubt that without the injury to Blanchflower the game would have ended completely differently. The challenge of beating the Champions in a competitive game certainly lifted the Everton players who gave everything for the full ninety minutes. Jimmy Harris (below) scored his second goal of the season to earn Everton a hard-fought point.

Manchester Evening News

Duncan Edwards

The player, who is approaching his twenty-first birthday, has already made almost
150 competitive appearances for Manchester United.

Thurs 5th Sept.

Newspapers reported that Len Shackleton, the Sunderland inside-forward (pictured) would never play again. His career was ended in the consulting rooms at Barnsley Hospital where he was informed that his ankle could no longer withstand the rigours of professional football.

Shackleton accepted the verdict philosophically stating that he was ready for the decision which had probably denied him a further two seasons.

So ends one of the most colourful careers in contemporary football. The player, aged 35, who christened himself 'The Games Clown Prince' was at one time an amateur on Arsenal's books. He turned professional with Bradford Park Avenue and moved onto Newcastle for £13,000 in 1946. Two years later he was transferred to Sunderland for a fee in the region of £20,000 and at his best was the greatest ball artist in the game. No inside-forward in recent years could match his spectacular control.

He only won five England caps scoring one goal with a chip shot against the then World Champions, West Germany, in December 1954. He played 348 League games for Sunderland scoring 101 goals.

Sunderland's Welsh international, centre-half Ray Daniel, has been placed on the transfer list at his own request after failing to make a first team appearance this season due to the good form of Aitken.

Manchester United assistant manager, Jimmy Murphy, has reportedly had four offers from League clubs to step into their vacant manager's position. The 'rumour mill' has once again started in respect of the post at Leyton Orient but it seems unlikely that Murphy will leave Old Trafford. United reported today that they had made a profit of £39,785 last season.

Wolves are in the process of installing their new floodlights which will be some of the best in the country.

Millwall centre-half, Charlie Hurley, is apparently attracting interest from a number of First Division clubs and manager Ron Gray now appears to be prepared to sell his main asset at the right price.

Manchester City have placed great faith in 21 years-old outside-right Colin Barlow, giving him his League début last week in the win against Chelsea. Having only signed as an amateur one year ago, his impressive performances in the Central League team have rocketed him into the first team and he made the perfect start scoring on his début.

Fri. 6th Sept.

United centre-half, Blanchflower has recovered from the concussion injury he suffered on Wednesday and should be fit to face Leeds at Old Trafford in an unchanged side. Jack Charlton is unfit for the visitors so Marsden will deputise at number five.

Nottingham Forest face Manchester City determined to keep their unbeaten record intact and have named an unchanged side for the fifth consecutive game. City have Trautmann and Leivers injured with Savage and Sear stepping in.

Blackpool will have Mudie and Taylor fit again to play against the third undefeated side, Arsenal, at Bloomfield Road. Groves will return to the Arsenal side at centre-forward.

Spurs, with only one point, face Burnley at home hoping to bounce back from their humiliating defeat on Wednesday but have been hampered by injuries to Smith and Brooks. Dunmore and Stokes will replace them in the attack.

Sat. 7th September

Manchester Utd.   **5**   **Leeds United**   **0**

Berry 2, Viollet, Taylor 2   Att. 50,842

Manchester United-Wood, Foulkes, Byrne, Colman, Blanchflower, Edwards, Berry, Whelan, Taylor, Viollet, Pegg.

Leeds United-Wood, Dunn, Hair, Ripley, Marsden, Kerfoot, Meek, O'Brien, Baird, Brook, Overfield.

In a largely uneventful first half neither side gained the upper hand. Leeds, at first, looked as though they would cause the United defence some problems and Meek in particular worked hard at trying to create an opening. Unfortunately he received poor support from his team-mates and the much heralded Baird was easily subdued by Blanchflower.

As United gained momentum it was Edwards who drove them forward. Looking every inch an international player his ferocious tackles, superb distribution of the ball and willingness to shoot on sight gave the opposing defence nightmares. Pegg hit the post, Taylor had a shot saved and another effort disallowed for offside. Eventually, after a succession of corners, the deadlock was broken. Pegg took a corner kick and as the ball reached BERRY at the far post the right-winger guided it into the net through a ruck of players with only a minute of the first half remaining (pictured below).

Berry

After ten minutes of the second half Leeds United left-back, Hair, suffered a knee injury and had to leave the field. Initially Leeds reorganised their defence and looked to be able to cope with the handicap of playing with 10 men. Meek hit the post with a long range shot but United, to a man, sensed they had the upper hand. The avalanche came within a devastating spell of nine minutes as the home team scored four times.

A glorious pass from Edwards gave VIOLLET the opportunity to net number 2. Then Whelan had a hand in laying on another for TAYLOR.

With the score at 3-0 the home fans roared their team forward and it was no surprise when BERRY and TAYLOR added further goals. There is no doubt that the injury to Hair (pictured below) had a detrimental effect on the Leeds defence.

After the fifth goal United took pity on the opposition and settled for the victory and continue in top position in the League.

SATURDAY 7TH SEPTEMBER 1957

BIRMINGHAM C.	1	**NEWCASTLE U.**	4
Hellawell,		Curry 2, Hill, Mitchell	
		Att. 29,784	
BLACKPOOL	1	**ARSENAL**	0
Taylor			
		Att. 31,486	
EVERTON	3	**CHELSEA**	0
Fielding, Hickson, Temple			
		Att. 45,066	
LEICESTER CITY	2	**BOLTON W.**	3
O'Neil, Rowley (pen)		Holden, Stevens Lofthouse	
		Att. 30,033	
LUTON TOWN	3	**WOLVES**	1
Turner 2, Cullen		Wilshaw	
		Att. 22,030	
MANCHESTER U	5	**LEEDS UNITED**	0
Berry 2, Taylor 2, Viollet			
		Att. 50,842	
NOTTINGHAM F.	2	**MANCHESTER C.**	1
Barrett, Wilson		Hayes	
		Att. 37,191	
PORTSMOUTH	3	**SHEFFIELD W.**	2
Mansell, Crawford McLellan		Ellis, McAnearney J.	
		Att. 29,141	
SUNDERLAND	1	**ASTON VILLA**	1
O'Neill		Chapman	
		Att. 43,901	
TOTTENHAM H.	3	**BURNLEY**	1
Dunmore 2, Dulin		Cheesebrough	
		Att. 40,108	
WEST BROM. ALB.	4	**PRESTON N.E.**	1
Allen, Kevan, Griffin Horobin		Docherty	
		Att. 29,768	

	P	W	D	L	F	A	Pts
Manchester United...	5	4	1	0	18	4	9
Nottingham Forest..	5	4	1	0	9	4	9
Luton Town........	5	4	0	1	8	4	8
Arsenal............	5	3	1	1	7	4	7
Everton............	5	3	1	1	8	6	7
Portsmouth........	5	3	1	1	13	10	7
West Bromwich A....	5	2	2	1	11	8	6
Wolverhampton W...	5	2	1	2	13	6	5
Bolton Wanderers...	5	2	1	2	8	10	5
Newcastle United....	4	2	0	2	8	5	4
Manchester City......	4	2	0	2	10	10	4
Preston North End...	5	2	0	3	8	9	4
Burnley............	5	1	2	2	6	7	4
Blackpool..........	5	2	0	3	5	7	4
Leeds United........	5	2	0	3	6	11	4
Chelsea............	5	1	1	3	10	13	3
Tottenham Hotspur..	5	1	1	3	9	15	3
Birmingham City....	5	1	1	3	6	13	3
Aston Villa.........	5	1	1	3	4	9	3
Sunderland.........	5	1	1	3	5	13	3
Sheffield Wednesday..	3	1	0	2	4	5	2
Leicester City........	5	1	0	4	9	12	2

Leicester City are finding life tough in the top Division and another defeat, this time 3-2 at home against Bolton Wanderers, leaves them rooted to the foot of the table. Newspaper reports have indicated that Leicester are monitoring the performances of Millwall centre-half Charlie Hurley.

Nottingham Forest, who accompanied Leicester into the First Division, have performed much better, making the best start of any promoted team since Spurs in 1951. Another victory against Manchester City leaves them in second place on goal average behind Manchester United and maintains their unbeaten record. Former Tottenham and England forward, Baily, was again in superb form, turning back the years and setting a perfect example for his younger team-mates.

David Dunmore, deputising for the injured Bobby Smith, was easily the best player on view at White Hart Lane. His lion hearted performance scoring twice and almost grabbing a hat-trick, as well as creating a goal for Dulin, certainly endeared him to the home fans. At times he appeared clumsy and unorthodox but this often worked in his favour. His strength and powerful shooting proved a handful for the Burnley defence as Spurs won their first match of the season after a run of three consecutive defeats.

Matthews created the only goal of the game for Ernie Taylor to score and earn Blackpool both points against Arsenal. It was no more than they deserved as earlier Kelsey had saved from Perry, Mudie and Matthews to keep the 'Gunners' in the game.

West Bromwich Albion raced into a three goal half-time lead against Preston playing some scintillating football with Ronnie Allen outstanding. They stretched the lead to four within three minutes of the restart but could not add to their total. Docherty scored a consolation goal for Preston.

Leading Scorers

5 Goals-Turner (Luton T.) ,   Allen (W.B.A.)
4 Goals-Greaves (Chelsea), Temple (Everton), Taylor, Viollet, Berry, Whelan (All Manchester United), Barrett (Nottingham Forest), Harris (Portsmouth), Deeley, Murray (Wolves).

United Reserves

United team-Gaskell, Cope, Jones P., Goodwin, Jones M., McGuinness, Webster, Doherty, Dawson, Charlton, Scanlon.

At Elland Road Leeds reserves made the better start to the game against United but Gaskell was in top form and determined to keep a clean sheet.

Scanlon posed the home defence problems and from one of his crosses Charlton shot wide of the post. It was no surprise when Scanlon created the opening two goals with accurate and perfectly weighted passes, making it almost impossible for Dawson and Goodwin to miss.

Just before half time United scored a third as Dawson smashed a shot into the roof of the net.

United failed to add to their total in the second half as Leeds dominated the play but were only able to pull back one goal.

Leeds United Reserves 1 Manchester United Reserves 3

Mon. 9th Sept.

Blackpool	**1**	**Manchester United**	**4**
Mudie		Whelan 2, Viollet 2	

Att. 34,181

Blackpool-*Farm, Armfield, Garrett, Kelly, Gratrix, Fenton, Matthews, Taylor, Mudie, Durie, Perry.*
Manchester United-*Wood, Foulkes, Byrne, Colman, Blanchflower, Edwards, Berry, Whelan, Taylor, Viollet, Pegg.*

Eighteen goals in the opening five games became twenty-two in six as unchanged United had little difficulty in beating Blackpool 4-1 to maintain their unbeaten record on a lovely evening at Bloomfield Road.

United had to face the early evening sunshine in the first half but Blanchflower and his fellow defenders coped easily with the Blackpool tactics of punting long balls down the field.

The away side were far more polished in their approach work and 'snake-hips' Colman was in majestic form dictating the play from mid-field. From one of his many searching passes, WHELAN received the ball and hammered it into the net.

The Blackpool defence struggled to stem the tide and within a minute Whelan almost had a second but his shot struck the post. Next it was the turn of Edwards who was unlucky to see his thunderbolt shot hit the crossbar and rebound to VIOLLET who steered the ball home for United's second. Blackpool finally regained some composure forcing United on the back foot. Mudie hit a lofted shot over Wood's head only to see Edwards race back into the goalmouth and clear the ball before it could cross the line. Little had been seen of Matthews down the right wing as he had been easily subdued by Byrne. The referee blew for half time with United two goals ahead.

United had an early scare in the second half when Ernie Taylor's shot was deflected goal-wards. Wood was alert to the danger and acrobatically dived in the opposite direction to catch the ball. In the 60th minute United scored a third after a perfectly placed centre from Pegg was headed into the net by WHELAN. The game was over for Blackpool who embarked on a damage limitation exercise as they tried to stem the flow of attacking football from United.

The white-shirted away side continued to pass the ball around with ease and soon it was FOUR, in a move involving three players. A long pass to Whelan was headed into the path of Pegg down the left side. The winger crossed the ball giving VIOLLET a simple tap in for his second goal.

Although Blackpool pulled a goal back late in the game from MUDIE it was the delightful football played by United that the spectators would remember.

Nottingham Forest lost for the first time this season despite playing some wonderful football that on another occasion could well have earned them at least a point. Two goals from Shackleton in the first half at Turf Moor gave Burnley the platform to go on and win the game 3-1.

United Reserves

The second team's topsy-turvy start to the season continued at Old Trafford with goals from Doherty and Scanlon earning a hard fought 2-2 draw against Blackpool Reserves in front of a crowd of 10,978.

Tues. 10th Sept.

Arsenal 2 **Everton** 3

Groves 2 Fielding, J. Harris, Hickson

Att. 42,013

Real Madrid, the European Cup holders have agreed to play Wolves in a friendly match at Molineux on Thursday 17th October.

John Charles of Juventus has been refused permission by the Italian Football Federation to play for Wales against East Germany in a World Cup qualifying match on 25th September. Apparently Juventus were prepared to allow him to play but the Federation issued the following statement 'Foreign players with Italian clubs are banned from taking part in games outside Italy during the Italian League season'.

Leeds United have been informed that they have been selected to host the Football League v League of Ireland game on Wednesday 9th October under floodlights at Elland Road.

Bolton Wanderers have had to cancel their friendly game scheduled to take place in Barcelona later this month because of fixture congestion.

Division 2 side, Rotherham United, have ten players suffering from influenza and the Football League have had no option but to cancel their away game against Liverpool tomorrow.

The bug has also struck in Bradford with over 2,000 youngsters reportedly absent from school. In Blackburn 50 Corporation bus drivers and conductors are off sick severely disrupting local bus services.

Wed. 11th Sept.

Only 17 goals in the seven Wednesday evening games proved just how difficult life in Division 1 can be. The best gate of the night was at St. James' Park where Newcastle beat Portsmouth 2-0.

Luton Town won their fifth game of the season 2-0 at Elland Road and despite the fact that Baird missed a first half penalty for the home side, Luton were always the better side.

Chelsea fought back after twice being behind against West Brom. and fully deserved to win a point.

Manchester United remain at the top of the table and are now the only side who have not lost a game in Division 1.

WEDNESDAY 11TH SEPTEMBER

BIRMINGHAM C.	0	TOTTENHAM H.	0
		Att.26,485	
BOLTON W.	2	SUNDERLAND	2
Parry, Allcock		Bingham, Goodchild	
		Att.17,647	
CHELSEA	2	WEST BROM. ALB.	2
Tindall 2		Allen, Horobin	
		Att.29,824	
LEEDS UNITED	0	LUTON TOWN	2
		Morton, Turner	
		Att.21,972	
MANCHESTER C.	2	PRESTON N.E.	0
Fagan, Hayes		Att.24,439	
NEWCASTLE U.	2	PORTSMOUTH	0
Davies, Mitchell		Att.39,027	
SHEFFIELD WED.	2	LEICESTER CITY	1
Ellis, McAnearney J.		Rowley	
		Att.17,472	

Thurs. 12th Sept.

It was reported that at yesterday's A.G.M. Mr Petherbridge, a Club Director of Manchester United, outlined initial plans to increase the crowd capacity to 100,000.

The proposals included the covering of the popular side of the ground and the building of a double-decker main stand. There are many potential obstacles facing the Club before this dream can become reality. Not least of which are-more car parking spaces, the ability to disperse such a large crowd safely and the provision of more trains and terminus points.

There is no doubt that Manchester United envisage Old Trafford as being a serious competitor to Wembley in respect of show-piece games.

Fri. 13th Sept.

Manchester United have not won at Burnden Park since 31st August 1949 and last season Bolton were the only side to complete the double over the 'Champions'.

Tommy Taylor has recovered from bruised ribs suffered at Bloomfield Road on Monday evening, allowing United to field an unchanged side for the seventh consecutive game.

Bolton have decided to move Nat Lofthouse back to centre-forward and Birch will play on the right-wing.

Preston will make their first change of the season with Derek Mayers, a summer signing from Everton, making his début at outside-right in place of Les Dagger for the visit of Spurs. The away side have been forced to make one change at outside-left as Dulin has dislocated his right knee and suffered ligament damage so Dyson will take his place.

Blackpool travel to Molineux in a game that appears a banker home win especially as 'The Seasiders' will be missing Ernie Taylor and Dave Durie.

Wilshaw, who scored the only goal for Wolves at Luton last Saturday, has been dropped and Mullen will replace him at outside-left. Mason will come into the side at inside-right in place of Booth.

Manchester City will have Trautmann and Leivers back in the side after missing the last two games for the visit of Portsmouth.

Saturday 14th September

Bolton Wanderers   4   Manchester U.   0

Stevens, Birch, Parry (pen),
Lofthouse   Att. 48,003

Bolton Wanderers-*Hopkinson, Ball, Edwards G. B., Hennin, Higgins, Bell, Birch, Stevens, Lofthouse, Parry, Holden.*

Manchester United-*Wood, Foulkes, Byrne, Colman, Blanchflower, Edwards D., Berry, Whelan, Taylor, Viollet, Pegg.*

United started slowly and Ray Wood had to save twice from Parry in the opening few minutes. The onslaught continued and after only 5 minutes STEVENS put Bolton ahead as he raced onto a long 'punt' up field by Hennin and smashed the ball beyond Wood's despairing dive. Both Duncan Edwards and Byrne were caught out of position as they had advanced up field to support a United attack.

On the half hour the goal scorer was injured after coming second best in a tussle for the ball with his cousin Duncan Edwards. He was carried off on a stretcher.

The large crowd roared each side forward in a battle for supremacy and the 'hell for leather' approach of both teams never wavered. United had a number of chances as Viollet twice and Taylor really should have scored but Hopkinson kept them at bay. He was lucky to see another shot from Whelan hit the crossbar just before half time.

Stevens returned for the second half but did not look fully fit and within minutes Bolton's problems increased when right-back, Ball, limped to the wing where he remained a passenger for the rest of the game.

With the wind in their favour United looked certain to draw level but a mistake cost them a second goal. Blanchflower, who had played superbly in the first half, tried to dribble the ball out of defence only to be tackled by BIRCH who stormed forward to score.

United decided to push everyone forward against the nine fit players of Bolton but paid the price when Lofthouse broke away and hit a fierce shot which struck Foulkes on the arm in the penalty area and PARRY scored from the spot. Stevens (pictured below), Parry and Birch were tireless in their efforts. Supporting the defence one minute then surging forward the next. From a late counter attack LOFTHOUSE added his name to the score sheet hitting Bolton's fourth and in the process shattering United's unbeaten record.

SATURDAY 14TH SEPTEMBER

ARSENAL	3	**LEICESTER CITY**	1
Groves 2, Herd		Froggatt	
		Att. 45,369	
ASTON VILLA	2	**LUTON TOWN**	0
McParland, Dixon			
		Att. 28,962	
BOLTON W.	4	**MANCHESTER U.**	0
Stevens, Lofthouse Parry (pen), Birch			
		Att. 48,003	
BURNLEY	3	**BIRMINGHAM C.**	1
Shackleton, Cheesebrough Pilkington		Neal	
		Att. 20,522	
EVERTON	3	**SUNDERLAND**	1
Hickson 2, Meagan		Revie	
		Att. 47,119	
LEEDS UNITED	1	**NOTTINGHAM F.**	2
Overfield		Barrett, Wilson	
		Att. 25,566	
MANCHESTER C.	2	**PORTSMOUTH**	1
Ewing, Johnstone		Harris	
		Att. 28,798	
NEWCASTLE U.	1	**CHELSEA**	3
Mitchell (pen)		Tindall 2, Block	
		Att. 44,560	
PRESTON N.E.	3	**TOTTENHAM H.**	1
Mayers, Thompson 2		Stokes	
		Att. 23,364	
SHEFFIELD WED.	1	**WEST BROM. ALB.**	2
Ellis		McEvoy(og), Allen (pen)	
		Att. 26,395	
WOLVES	3	**BLACKPOOL**	1
Broadbent, Mullen, Murray		Perry	
		Att. 38,496	

	Home			Goals			Away			Goals		
	P	W	D	L	F	A	W	D	L	F	A	Pts
Man Utd	7	3	0	0	12	L..	3	1	1	10	8	11
Everton	7	3	1	0	10	4..	2	0	1	4	5	11
Notm F	7	2	1	0	5	3..	3	0	1	7	5	11
Luton	7	3	0	0	6	1..	2	0	3	4	5	10
Arsenal	7	2	1	1	9	6..	2	0	1	3	2	9
W Brom	7	3	0	1	7	4..	1	3	0	8	7	9
Burnley	7	3	1	0	10	4..	0	1	3	2	5	8
Man City	6	3	0	0	9	3..	1	0	2	5	8	8
Bolton	7	2	2	0	10	3..	1	0	2	4	9	8
Wolves	6	3	0	0	14	2..	0	1	2	2	5	7
Prtsmth	7	2	1	0	8	3..	1	0	3	6	11	7
Nwcastle	6	2	0	1	6	4..	1	0	2	5	4	6
Chelsea	7	1	1	1	9	6..	1	1	2	6	10	6
Preston	7	3	0	0	9	2..	0	0	4	2	10	6
A Villa	6	2	0	1	4	1..	0	1	2	2	8	5
Sheff W	6	2	0	2	5	6..	0	0	1	2	3	4
Tottnhm	7	1	1	1	7	7..	0	1	3	3	11	4
Bckpool	7	2	0	2	6	6..	0	0	3	1	8	4
Leeds	7	2	0	2	7	5..	0	0	3	0	10	4
Sundrlnd	7	1	1	1	4	4..	0	1	3	4	14	4
Birmghm	7	1	1	2	4	7..	0	1	2	3	9	4
Leicester	7	1	0	2	6	7..	0	0	4	5	10	2

Arsenal went two goals up in four minutes at Highbury against bottom side Leicester City. Groves got the first as Anderson, in the Leicester goal, could only help the ball over the line whilst attempting to stop the shot. A few minutes later a superb pass by Bloomfield found Herd who scored with ease.

Against the run of play, Froggatt pulled a goal back with a low drive, but after the interval Groves added a third (his sixth of the season) to give Arsenal a conclusive victory.

Leslie Smith, the Aston Villa outside-right, fractured his collar bone in the first half against Luton Town but Villa still won 2-0.

Everton had a comfortable 3-1 home win against Sunderland to maintain their great start to the season. The victory could have been even more convincing if Tommy Jones had not missed from the penalty spot. The 'Toffees' now sit in second place in the table on equal points with United.

The game at Elland Road started slowly but Forest soon settled into a rhythm and Wilson headed a Barrett centre into the net. Leeds responded when Overfield scored from outside the penalty area. Leeds dominated the play and should have reached half time ahead as Overfield, Brook and Forrest all missed chances.

The home side paid the penalty for failing to take their chances when Wilson scored the winner for Forest.

Mayers scored the opening goal on his début for Preston in the 3-1 win at Deepdale against Spurs. Tommy Thompson added two further goals to bring his tally for the season to five as North End maintained their 100% home record. Spurs goalkeeper, Ron Reynolds, was not to blame for any of the goals. He is one of the first professional footballers to wear contact lenses whilst playing.

United Reserves

In the Central League game at Old Trafford the second team's indifferent start to the season continued as they drew against Bolton. Both sides had a number of lucky escapes before Bolton took the lead. Doherty equalised from the penalty spot following a foul on Scanlon. After only 60 seconds of the second half Doherty put United ahead with a well-placed shot. In the closing stages Bolton piled forward and eventually scored a second goal to gain a draw.

Barnsley R..	1	Everton Res.	1
Blackburn R	3	Wolves R...	1
Blackpool R.	0	Aston V. R.	1
Bury Res...	3	Man. C. R.	1
Chesterf'd R.	2	Sheff. W.R.	3
Hudd'sf'd R.	0	Leeds U. R.	3
Liverpool R.	3	Newc'stle R	2
Man. U. Res	2	Bolton Res.	2
Sheff. U. R.	1	Derby Res...	2
Stoke C. R.	1	Preston Res.	2
W. Brom R.	6	Burnley .Res.	1

	P.	W.	L.	D.	F.	A.	Pts
Bury Res.	6	5	0	1	15	3	11
Huddrsf'd Res.	7	4	2	1	14	9	9
Barnsley R.	7	3	1	3	15	9	9
Man. Utd Res.	6	3	1	2	19	14	8
Newcastle Res.	6	4	2	0	11	9	8
Everton Res.	7	3	2	2	20	14	8
Derby Res.	6	3	1	2	15	13	8
Wolves Res.	7	3	2	2	13	13	8
Aston Villa R.	7	3	3	1	12	12	7
Liverpool Res.	6	3	3	0	13	14	6
Sheff. Utd. Res.	7	2	3	2	11	10	6
Blackpool Res.	6	2	2	2	6	6	6
Bolton Res.	7	2	3	2	10	11	6
Leeds U. Res.	6	2	2	2	13	14	6
Burnley	7	2	3	2	8	14	6
Preston Res.	7	2	4	1	6	11	5
O'field R.	6	2	3	1	9	11	5
Shef Wed R.	4	2	1	1	4	3	5
Stoke Res.	7	1	4	2	9	12	4
Blackburn Res.	6	2	4	0	9	18	4
West B. Res.	6	1	4	1	10	15	3
Man. City Res.	6	1	5	0	9	16	2

Mon. 16th Sept.

Wolverhampton W.	2	Aston Villa	1
Murray, Deeley		McParland	

Att. 26,033

In a whirlwind start to the game at Molineux both sides scored in the opening five minutes. Thereafter the home side were always in control but had to wait until five minutes from time before Deeley scored the winner.

In the Inter Cities Fairs Cup Semi-Final First Leg, Lausanne beat London 2-1 with Haverty of Arsenal scoring for the visitors. The Second Leg will be at Highbury on 23rd October.

United Reserves

A disappointing crowd of only 1,458 at Bloomfield Road witnessed a superb performance by the 'The Red Devils' as they annihilated Blackpool Reserves 8-1.

Alex Dawson was unstoppable scoring five times with Scanlon, Charlton and Doherty also getting on the score sheet.

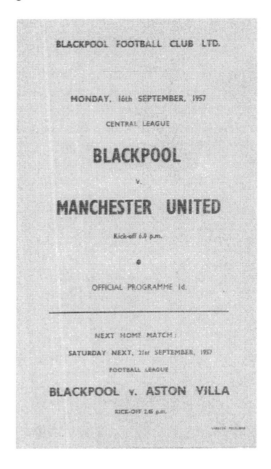

BLACKPOOL FOOTBALL CLUB LTD.

MONDAY, 16th SEPTEMBER, 1957

CENTRAL LEAGUE

BLACKPOOL

v.

MANCHESTER UNITED

Kick-off 6.0 p.m.

OFFICIAL PROGRAMME 1d.

NEXT HOME MATCH :
SATURDAY NEXT, 21st SEPTEMBER, 1957
FOOTBALL LEAGUE
BLACKPOOL v. ASTON VILLA
KICK-OFF 2.15 p.m.

Tues. 17th Sept.

Wales have named the following side for the important World Cup game against East Germany at Cardiff next week-KELSEY (Arsenal), THOMAS D. A. (Swansea T.), HOPKINS (Spurs), HARRIS (Middlesbrough), CHARLES M. (Swansea T.), BOWEN (Arsenal) (captain), ALLCHURCH L. (Swansea T.), VERNON (Blackburn R.), PALMER (Swansea T.), ALLCHURCH I.(Swansea T.), JONES (Swansea T.). Reserve-DAVIES (Newcastle U.).

John Charles, who has already been refused permission to play in the game, is expected to be included in the Juventus side for a friendly game against Leeds United at Elland Road on Wednesday 2nd October. Charles scored on his début for Juventus in a 3-2 home win against Verona.

Norbert Stiles, who has played five times for England schoolboys, has been signed by Manchester United. The youngster will not be 16 years old until May 1958.

Jimmy Greaves, at just 17 years of age, has been chosen for the England Under 23s match against Bulgaria at Stamford Bridge on 25th September following his superb early season form for Chelsea.

Wed. 18th Sept.

Manchester United	1	Blackpool	2
Edwards		Mudie 2	

Att. 41,003

Manchester United-*Wood, Foulkes, Byrne, Colman, Blanchflower, Edwards, Berry, Whelan, Taylor T., Viollet, Pegg.*

Blackpool-*Farm, Garrett, Wright, Kelly J., Gratrix, Kelly H., Harris, Taylor E., Mudie, Peterson, Perry.*

Blackpool, without a single point on their travels, upset the form book by beating United on their own ground to gain revenge for their humiliating 4-1 defeat at Bloomfield Road last week.

Without Matthews and Durie the selected eleven players 'worked their socks off' for ninety minutes and fully deserved the lucky breaks that came their way when United forced them back into their own half for long periods.

The game started with a dramatic mistake as Foulkes lost the ball in the opening minute allowing Peterson to gain possession. The South African pushed the ball to Perry who sent a precise cross which MUDIE headed into the net. Not long afterwards Ernie Taylor slammed a shot just over the cross bar.

United were stunned into action, Tommy Taylor hit the post then the same player should have scored with a header but missed the target. Next it was Whelan who drove the ball against the bar. Somehow Blackpool survived.

In the 31st minute Blackpool scored a second, again against the run of play, when Harris played an inch perfect pass into the path of Ernie Taylor. The little inside-forward pushed it onto MUDIE whose shot entered the net off the post.

The second half was just one-way traffic as United tried every possible way to break down 'The Seasiders'' defence. Blackpool's organisation and the willingness of the players to work for each other helped to nullify the effectiveness of United's game. Farm made an incredible one-handed save from Viollet as time began to run out for the home side. Ernie Taylor was everywhere, tackling, cajoling, encouraging and keeping possession of the ball whenever possible.

With only three minutes remaining EDWARDS pulled a goal back and the home fans screamed at their heroes to get a second. It almost happened with only seconds remaining but somehow Blackpool cleared the danger to win the game.

A second consecutive defeat for the home side was not something the supporters had expected but with Arsenal 'next up' at Old Trafford on Saturday the players have a great opportunity to put matters right.

Jackie Mudie

WEDNESDAY 18TH SEPTEMBER

LEICESTER CITY	4	**SHEFFIELD WED.**	1
Gardiner 2, Rowley 2		McAnearney T.	
		Att.22,449	
LUTON TOWN	1	**LEEDS UNITED**	1
Morton		Overfield	
		Att.16,887	
MANCHESTER U.	1	**BLACKPOOL**	2
Edwards,		Mudie 2	
		Att.41,003	
NOTTINGHAM F.	7	**BURNLEY**	0
Gray, Barrett, Imlach 2,			
Baily, Wilson 2.		Att.26,842	
PORTSMOUTH	2	**NEWCASTLE U.**	2
McClellan, Weddle		Hill, Curry	
		Att.32,093	
PRESTON N.E.	6	**MANCHESTER C.**	1
Dagger, Finney 2,		Fagan	
Taylor 2, Thompson		Att.22,034	
SUNDERLAND	1	**BOLTON W.**	2
Revie		Parry, Lofthouse	
		Att.30,021	
TOTTENHAM H.	7	**BIRMINGHAM C.**	1
Dyson, Stokes 5, Harmer		Brown	
		Att.35,292	
WEST BROM. ALB.	1	**CHELSEA**	1
Allen (pen)		Greaves	
		Att.36,680	

Nottingham Forest took full advantage of Manchester United's surprise home defeat to Blackpool by slamming seven goals without reply against Burnley and in the process moved to the top of the table. With Adamson and Seith missing from the heart of the defence, Burnley were completely overrun as all five Forest forwards got their name on the score sheet. Outside-right, Gray, who was a Burnley player until just before the start of the season, seemed to know all the weaknesses of his former colleagues and had a great game.

Tottenham Hotspur were another side to score seven on the evening as they brushed aside Birmingham City. Stokes scored five times as Spurs won only their second game of the season.

The home side were helped by the fact that Birmingham goalkeeper, Gil Merrick, had to have stitches for a cut eye during the first half and could only play as a passenger on the wing after the interval.

West Bromwich Albion had to settle for a draw against Chelsea under floodlights which were used for the first time in a League game at the Hawthorns. Albion stormed the Chelsea goal in the second half but could not beat Matthews who made many saves to help Chelsea avoid defeat.

Finney was the star at Deepdale as Preston hit six goals against Manchester City completely destroying the much discussed 'Marsden defensive plan'. The home side never allowed any City defender time on the ball and despite City having four players nearer their goal line than Finney, he was still able to slam home goal number two in the twentieth minute. He added the sixth late in the game and had a hand in at least two others.

The Scottish League beat the League of Ireland 5-1 in Dublin with Bobby Collins of Celtic scoring a hat trick. The other goals for the Scottish League were scored by Kelly of Raith and Bauld of Hearts. League of Ireland's consolation goal was scored by Tuohy of Shamrock Rovers in front of a crowd of around 23,000.

Thurs. 19th Sept.

Report of the proposals to amend the pay and conditions of Professional Footballers.

The Football League Management Committee, yesterday, published their suggested changes in the promised revision of regulations to eradicate 'under the counter' payments to players. The League President, Mr J. Richards, informed the press that "The committee are trying to find a solution to all the problems which will satisfy the majority of the clubs, players and the public so that the loyal player will receive a just reward for his efforts and the trouble-monger will not be able to gain financially at the expense of his loyal colleagues.

It will be necessary to have a clearly defined code of discipline and conduct to which all clubs and players will be expected to adhere."

The main points of the proposals which will be discussed by the Chairmen of Division 1 and Division 2 clubs and representatives of the Third Division in London on October 21st are as follows:

a) **The maximum weekly basic wage, irrespective of age, shall be £20 per week or £1,040 per annum.**

The present maximum wage is £17 in the playing season and £14 in the closed season at age 20 or over.

b) **The minimum weekly basic wage for a player, irrespective of age, shall be £8 per week or £416 per annum.**

The present rate varies between £4-10s. both winter and summer at age 17 to £8-10s. in the playing season at age 20.

If a player agrees to be transferred to another club then he can receive a payment not exceeding 2½% of the transfer fee.

A signing on fee when joining a new club will be increased from £10 to £20.

It is not proposed to increase the £4 bonus for a win and £2 for a draw.

The talent money payments for the top four clubs in the First and Second Divisions will remain the same.

Following the hearing regarding the illegal payments made by Sunderland, the League propose to strengthen the wording of the regulations to penalise the action of inducing a player to leave a club or make illegal payments.

It is also proposed that no player, official, referee or linesman shall contribute any article dealing with any game in which he or his club has taken part to any newspaper or journal, nor allow himself to be interviewed by, nor discuss with anyone on their behalf, any incident or reason for any decision arising during a game in which he or his club has taken part during the current season.

Nor shall they contribute any article, nor allow themselves to be interviewed on the administration of the League organisation without consent of the Committee.

It is recommended that referees' match fees should be raised from five guineas to seven guineas and linesmen from two and a half guineas to three and a half guineas.

Mr Hardaker, the League Secretary, stated that the £20 per week maximum wage or £1,040 per annum payout could be varied by Clubs to provide winter and summer payments provided the total amount did not exceed £1,040 during the year. The Secretary also gave an example of a player's remuneration on transfer after serving a club for five years. Under the suggested new scheme he
could receive, if transferred for a £20,000 fee, £1,270 made up of £750 benefit, £500 share of fee and £20 signing-on fee. This would be an increase of £510 on present scales.

Mr Hardaker said the Players' Union will be receiving a copy of the suggested alterations and will be asked to comment on them. His final words were "It will need a three-fourths majority of the clubs to become law".

Fri. 20th Sept.

Matt Busby stated that he was in full agreement with the wage increase proposals of the Football League. At the press conference he announced that despite two consecutive defeats he had decided to keep the same team that had played every game this season for the attractive home fixture against Arsenal.

The London club stated that their goalkeeper, Kelsey, had suffered a bruised knee in training and will be replaced by Sullivan.

Burnley's troubles continued when half-back Shannon was added to the list of flu victims and will miss the trip to London for the game against Chelsea. The departure of the club's coach was delayed whilst a taxi was sent for 18 years old inside-forward Robson to join the squad of thirteen making the journey.

Matthews is fit again and will return to the Blackpool side for the visit of Aston Villa in place of Harris. Durie is still under treatment and Peterson will continue at inside-left.

Dunn and Finney are both injured and will miss the trip to Birmingham with Milne and Hatsell deputising.

Saturday 21st September

Manchester United   4   Arsenal   2

Taylor, Whelan 2, Pegg   Tiddy, Herd

Att. 47,389

Manchester United-*Wood, Foulkes, Byrne, Colman, Blanchflower, Edwards, Berry, Whelan, Taylor, Viollet, Pegg.*

Arsenal-*Sullivan, Charlton, Evans, Holton, Dodgin, Bowen, Clapton, Herd, Groves, Bloomfield, Tiddy.*

The day's highest attendance, over 47,000, were at Old Trafford and witnessed a pulsating game against Arsenal. Six goals scored and twice as many misses kept the supporters on their toes from the first to the last minute.

United opened at a frantic pace with Berry, in particular, using his full repertoire of tricks down the Arsenal right flank. Despite this early pressure it was Arsenal who created the first opportunities. Herd should have scored from a few yards out and then minutes later Byrne was forced to head a shot off his own goal line.

After fifteen minutes United took the lead following a delightful move involving Berry and Whelan. The ball was eventually placed into the path of TAYLOR who slammed it into the net with a fierce drive.

Six minutes later and United had a second. There appeared to be no danger as WHELAN received the ball just outside the penalty area. He paused to look for support from his colleagues. Within a split second he decided to shoot for goal and, before Sullivan was aware of what was happening, the ball was nestling in the back of the net.

The home side, in complete control, looked as though they could score at will but Viollet and Taylor were both guilty of missing easy chances as Colman and Edwards drove the side forward.

Taylor scores United's first goal

In the 37th minute Arsenal pulled a goal back. Wood misjudged his attempt to punch the ball clear from a centre by Clapton and, despite the fact United had a packed defence, the ball arrived at the feet of TIDDY for a simple tap-in.

Amazingly, within 90 seconds, Arsenal were level following a long clearance out of the 'Gunners' defence. HERD collected the ball and ran clear of the defenders before needing two attempts to beat Woods. Foulkes, Byrne, Colman, Blanchflower and Edwards were all guilty of taking their eyes off the ball for a few seconds.

Just as the crowd were ready to take a break from the non-stop action with the half time whistle only two minutes away, United restored their lead. Berry took a free kick and from the cross WHELAN headed home unchallenged.

The second half was just as frenetic as the first and on three occasions Wood made superb saves to keep his side in front. This was in stark contrast to the difficulties he had encountered dealing with high cross-field balls in the first half.

Eventually United eased the tension by scoring a fourth goal to seal the points. Colman set off on an amazing run, beating four opponents before laying the ball off for PEGG to score.

Arsenal were still dangerous and Groves missed a chance from a beautiful pass from Herd when it looked easier to score.

The win maintained United's unbeaten home run against London sides dating back to 1938. The performance, no doubt, would have given any officials watching from Shamrock Rovers plenty to think about with the European Cup First Leg game scheduled for Wednesday.

		Home Goals					Away Goals					
	P	W	D	L	F	A	W	D	L	F	A	Pts
Nottm F	9	3	1	0	12	3	4	0	1	11	8	15
Man Utd	9	4	0	1	17	5	2	1	1	10	8	13
Everton	8	3	1	0	10	4	3	0	1	5	5	13
W Brom	9	3	1	1	17	7	1	3	0	8	7	12
Wolves	8	4	0	0	16	3	1	1	2	5	7	11
Luton	9	3	1	1	7	3	2	0	2	4	5	11
Bolton	9	2	2	0	10	3	2	0	3	7	12	10
Chelsea	9	2	1	1	15	7	1	2	2	7	11	9
Arsenal	8	2	1	1	9	6	2	0	2	5	6	9
Preston	9	4	0	0	15	3	0	0	5	3	13	8
Tottenhm	9	3	1	1	18	10	0	1	3	3	11	8
Portsmth	9	2	2	1	11	9	1	0	3	6	11	8
Man City	8	3	0	0	9	3	1	0	4	8	23	8
Burnley	9	3	1	0	10	4	0	1	4	3	18	8
Newcastle	8	2	0	1	6	4	1	1	3	7	8	7
Blackpool	9	2	1	2	7	7	1	0	3	3	9	7
Leeds U	9	3	0	2	9	6	0	1	3	1	11	7
A Villa	8	2	0	1	4	1	0	2	3	4	11	6
Sundrland	9	2	1	2	7	6	0	1	3	4	14	6
Brmngham	9	2	1	2	7	8	0	1	3	4	15	6
Leicester	9	2	0	3	12	11	0	0	4	5	10	4
Sheff Wed	7	2	0	2	5	5	0	0	3	5	11	4

SATURDAY 21st SEPTEMBER

BIRMINGHAM C. 3   PRESTON N. E. 1
Govan (pen), Neale   Thompson
Murphy   Att. 24,894

BLACKPOOL 1   ASTON VILLA 1
Taylor   McParland
  Att. 31,079

CHELSEA 6   BURNLEY 1
Nicholas 2, Brabrook   Cheesebrough
Greaves, Tindall, Block   Att. 42,449

LEEDS UNITED 2   BOLTON W. 1
Baird, Meek   Parry (pen)
  Att. 18,379

LEICESTER CITY 2   WOLVES 3
McNeill, Russell   Murray 2, Clamp
  Att. 35,496

LUTON TOWN 0   EVERTON 1
  Fielding
  Att. 19,797

MANCHESTER U 4   ARSENAL 2
Whelan 2, Pegg, Taylor   Tiddy, Herd,
  Att. 47,389

PORTSMOUTH 1   NOTTINGHAM F. 4
Weddle   Barrett 2,Gray,Wilson
  Att. 33,801

SUNDERLAND 2   NEWCASTLE U. 0
Grainger, Revie
  Att. 45,718

TOTTENHAM H. 4   SHEFFIELD WED. 2
Smith 2, Dyson, Medwin   Ellis, Hopkins (og)
  Att. 39,954

WEST BROM. ALB. 9   MANCHESTER C. 2
Griffin 3, Howe 2 (1 pen)   Clarke, Fagan
Robson, Horobin,
Whitehouse, Kevan (pen)   Att. 26,080

West Bromwich Albion overwhelmed Manchester City at the Hawthorns scoring nine goals in a game for the first time since 1906. The 'M' plan devised by City with Marsden, their No.10, playing as a second centre-half was well and truly demolished by an Albion side who passed the ball around at will. The strange thing about the plan was that at half time City were only 3-1 down and decided to move Marsden into the traditional forward role in the second half, only to concede six further goals.

Some cynics remarked that perhaps the plan had worked in the first half.

Six Albion players got their names on the score sheet with Griffin grabbing a hat trick. Stand in City 'keeper, Savage, could not be blamed and after the ninth goal kicked the ball into the crowd in anger. The same player had conceded six goals at Deepdale three days earlier.

Nottingham Forest maintained their superb start to the season with a stunning 4-1 victory at Portsmouth. Sitting at the top of the table with only one defeat in nine games, Forest have set the bench mark in the opening weeks.

It was not all one-way traffic as Portsmouth drew level early in the first half. However Wilson hit a left foot opportunist goal in the 36th minute from a carefully placed free kick to restore their lead. Barrett and Gray sealed the game with two second half strikes.

Sheffield Wednesday unexpectedly took the lead in the 16ᵗʰ minute at White Hart Lane when Hopkins lobbed the ball over Reynolds and into his own net whilst trying to make a back-pass. Spurs were still ahead by the interval as, first Smith headed an equaliser and then Medwin scored from close range. For the second time this season the visiting goalkeeper was forced to leave the pitch as Pilu dislocated a finger trying to save the opening goal.

In the second half the home side ran out easy winners by 4-2 as Smith and Dyson both scored and Ellis netted a consolation goal for the visitors.

With an average age of only nineteen, all five Chelsea forwards scored in the 6-1 rout of Burnley at Stamford Bridge. Brabrook was a constant threat to the away defence, scoring one but also having a hand in a number of goals and near misses. The goal of the game was scored by Greaves. He collected the ball in the Burnley half and beat two defenders before shooting beyond Blacklaw from the edge of the penalty area.

Preston failed to improve their away form and after five games on their travels have still to gain a point. Thompson gave them an early lead but Govan equalised from a disputed penalty. The scores were level with ten minutes to play but Birmingham scored twice with Fred Else in the Preston goal being partly at fault for both of them.

United Reserves

Goals from Doherty and Charlton gave United a deserved 2-1 victory away at Wolves. The win moves them into second place in the Central League table, one point behind Bury with both sides having lost only one game.

Mon. 23ʳᵈ Sept.

In the only Division 1 game of the evening Billy Wright, England's regular centre-half and captain, had a nightmare match at Villa Park scoring an own goal and then nearly repeated the act later in the game. Fortunately the other Wolves players were not as generous as the visitors beat Villa 3-2. Broadbent, Murray and Deeley scored for Wolves with McParland netting the second Villa goal from the penalty spot. This was Wolves' fourth successive win watched by a crowd of 20,904.

United Reserves

A third consecutive victory by 2-1 at home to Sheffield United moved United Reserves to the top of the Central League table. Scanlon and Charlton were the scorers.

Tues. 24th Sept.

United's preparations for the European Cup game in Dublin tomorrow have been slightly changed following the news that Eddie Colman is suffering from influenza. His place at right-half will be taken by Goodwin. A number of clubs have reported that the 'flu bug' has laid low players and it looks likely that at least two Football League games will be postponed on Saturday.

The Shamrock Rovers pitch has been drenched following heavy rain and, with the game scheduled to start at 6 p.m., there is a risk that the natural light may not be good enough to see the match to a conclusion.

Wales face East Germany at Ninian Park, Cardiff tomorrow in their final Group 4 game knowing that only a win can keep their slim hopes alive of qualifying for the 1958 World Cup Finals in Sweden next summer. The Cardiff City goalkeeper, Vearncombe, will win his first cap in place of Kelsey who is injured.

Wed. 25th Sept.

Leeds United	**2**	**Sunderland**	**1**
Baird, Gibson		O'Neill	
			Att.17,600
Newcastle United	**0**	**Sheffield Wednesday**	**0**
			Att.27,651

Although they failed to score at Newcastle, Sheffield Wednesday are now no longer bottom of the First Division. Their goalless draw enabled them to move above Leicester City.

European Cup Preliminary Round 1st Leg

Shamrock Rovers	**0**	**Manchester United**	**6**

Taylor 2, Whelan 2, Berry, Pegg

Att. 45,000

Shamrock Rovers-*D'Arcy, Burke, Mackey, Nolan, Keogh, Hennessy, Peyton, Ambrose, Hamilton, Coad, Tuohy.*
Manchester United-*Wood, Foulkes, Byrne, Goodwin, Blanchflower, Edwards, Berry, Whelan, Taylor, Viollet, Pegg.*

The day that football supporters from the Dublin area had been waiting for had finally arrived – a European Cup, First Leg tie against Manchester United at Dalymount Park.

With a 6 p.m. kick-off and no floodlights everyone hoped that the weather would be fine and bright. Unfortunately a dreary, dull, cold evening greeted the teams as they emerged onto the pitch. A strong wind threatened to spoil the game.

A crowd of over 40,000 watched as the part-timers of Shamrock Rovers, despite facing the wind, made a bright start causing United a number of problems.

The home crowd urged them forward and Tuohy was unlucky to see a shot cleared off the goal line by Byrne. Wood had to be alert and only just managed to divert a further attempt at goal with his foot. Shortly afterwards he saved a header from Ambrose.

As the first half reached the mid-point United, at last, found their feet. Taylor hit the post, then Viollet, Whelan and Pegg all missed good opportunities.

In the 36th minute the deadlock was broken as United struck the first blow. Pegg created the opening with a superb pass to TAYLOR who skilfully placed the ball over the head of the advancing goalkeeper and into the net.

This was the only goal of the first half and the Belgian referee instructed both teams to re-start the second period immediately without an interval. He was worried that the deteriorating light could force him to abandon the game before ninety minutes had been played.

The fitness, stamina and professional ability of the United side quickly dampened the home supporters enthusiasm as United scored twice within twelve minutes of the re-start. By a strange twist of fate it was the man from Dublin, WHELAN, who scored both goals. The first came in the 51st minute when he steered home a cross from Berry and six minutes later he headed the ball into the net from a centre from the opposite flank from Pegg.

The home side realised that they needed to pull a goal back quickly before United took complete control of the game. Peyton came closest when he hit the crossbar, but the Dubliners never again troubled the United defence as Goodwin and Edwards began to control the game.

In the final ten minutes United scored three more goals in a tremendous exhibition of football which even the home fans had to applaud.

TAYLOR scored the fourth with a header from a well-placed centre by Viollet. Minutes later Taylor laid on a chance which BERRY duly took and the right-winger, almost immediately after Shamrock had restarted play, passed the ball to PEGG who crashed it beyond D'Arcy for United's sixth.

The result almost certainly guarantees United a place in the next round but unfortunately the huge goal difference going into the second leg at Old Trafford will no doubt reduce the numbers through the turnstiles.

World Cup Group 4 Qualifying Match
Wales   4   East Germany 1

This important World Cup qualifying match at Ninian Park, Cardiff was played on a quagmire of a pitch with persistent rain throughout making the evening thoroughly miserable.

Wales adapted better to the conditions and three goals in the last seven minutes of the first half thoroughly deflated the Germans. Two opportunist goals came from Swansea Town centre-forward, Palmer, and a German own goal gave Wales a strong hold in the match. Although Mel Charles sliced one into his own net, the Germans never looked like adding to their total.

Palmer netted the fourth and his own hat-trick goal following a superb pass from Bowen and the game was won.

The qualifying group is now delicately poised as the table below shows. A win or draw for Czechoslovakia next month against East Germany will take them through to the finals, but if they lose, all three teams will have to replay for a place in Stockholm.

	P	W	D	L	F	A	Pts
Czechoslovakia	3	2	0	1	5	2	4
Wales	4	2	0	2	6	5	4
East Germany	3	1	0	2	4	8	2

Under 23's International at Stamford Bridge
England   6   Bulgaria   2

The England Under 23 side squandered a number of early opportunities against a packed Bulgaria defence. Eventually, in the 40th minute, Greaves scored with a simple tap in from an A'Court pass and within the next five minutes Haynes, from the edge of the penalty area, and Brabrook had also added their names to the score sheet.

Haynes was superb throughout with his masterful passing unlocking the away defence on many occasions.

Bulgaria pulled a goal back in the 47th minute but England were still in control. Greaves scored again and Haynes and A'Court added further goals. Greaves had a chance to get his hat-trick but missed from the penalty spot in the closing minutes.

The England defence was well marshalled by Crowther and Setters.

England team-**Hopkinson** (Bolton W.), **Howe** (W.B.A.), **Harris** (Wolves), **Setters** (W.B.A.), **Smith** (Birmingham C.), **Crowther** (Aston V.), **Brabrook** (Chelsea), **Greaves** (Chelsea), **Kevan** (W.B.A.), **Haynes** (Fulham) (captain), **A'Court** (Liverpool).

Thurs. 26th Sept.

After adopting the Italian style 'catenaccio tactics' with Marsden playing as a stopper centre-half behind the normal No.5, Manchester City manager, Mr

McDowall, has decided to return to a normal formation following conceding 15 goals in their last two games.

The 'bolt plan' looks as though it has seen its final day and with it Marsden who has been left out of the City team for the game at Maine Road against Spurs on Saturday. The home side have made six changes, two of them positional, with Johnstone given the No.9 shirt. Tottenham will be missing Hopkins and Smith through influenza and Dunmore will return to lead the attack.

Harry Gregg, who appeared in goal in all of Ireland's international matches last season, has requested permission NOT to be selected for the game against Scotland in Belfast on October 5th. He feels that his priority must be to help his club, Doncaster Rovers, gain more points and move away from the bottom of Division 2. His place will be taken by Uprichard of Portsmouth who has not appeared in the first team this season. Tommy Docherty of Preston will captain the Scotland side.

Charlie Hurley, the Millwall centre-half, has signed for Sunderland for a fee reported to be in the region of £20,000.

Fri. 27th Sept.

Everton have received permission from the Football League to postpone their home game against Blackpool on Saturday. Reserve players Leeder and Sanders are the latest influenza victims bringing the total number of players unavailable to eleven.

On Wednesday, Everton were informed by their forward, Brian Harris that he also has the bug and had been confined to bed by his Army Medical Officer.

The number of Football League matches postponed because of the flu epidemic now stands at eight with the Gateshead v Mansfield Town game also off tomorrow.

Chelsea goalkeeper, Matthews, has declared himself fit following a dose of influenza and will play at Deepdale tomorrow in an unchanged team from that which slammed Burnley 6-1 last Saturday. Finney is fit again and will lead the Preston attack with Mayers returning on the right wing following his bout of flu.

Manchester United have not escaped the virus with flu victims Byrne, Colman, Whelan and Viollet all unavailable for selection for tomorrow's important game at Wolves. Matt Busby will not name his team until the last minute on Saturday.

Wolves only have Stuart from the first team squad down with the bug and his place at right-back will be taken by Showell. Finlayson and Harris will return after injury.

Sat. 28th Sept.

Wolverhampton W	**3**	**Manchester U**	**1**
Deeley 2, Wilshaw		Doherty	

Att. 48,825

Wolverhampton W. *Finlayson, Showell, Harris, Clamp, Wright, Flowers, Deeley, Broadbent, Murray, Wilshaw, Mullen.*
Manchester United *Wood, Foulkes, McGuinness, Goodwin, Blanchflower, Edwards, Berry, Doherty, Taylor, Charlton, Pegg.*

Berry captained Manchester United in place of flu victim Roger Byrne, and four players McGuinness, Goodwin, Doherty and Charlton all made their first League appearances of the season. By a strange coincidence the four players had all appeared in the Reserve side, on the same ground, the previous Saturday.

There was little to choose between the two teams in the opening skirmishes. United looked lively and Berry shot over the crossbar as Charlton moved the ball around at pace. In the next attack Wood saved a header from Broadbent after good work by Wilshaw. Soon afterwards Wolves won a corner but McGuinness was on hand to clear the danger. Deeley looked menacing and Wood was forced to make a save from his shot. Moments later the same player slammed the ball just wide of the post after beating Blanchflower for pace.

99

At the opposite end Charlton easily brushed aside Wright but his shot was comfortably saved by Finlayson. Charlton was in action minutes later with a more powerful drive which again was kept out by the 'keeper.

The game was a great spectacle for the large crowd and chances continued to go begging at either end. As the interval approached both sides squandered opportunities. Firstly Deeley hit a superb pass to Broadbent who somehow shot wide from a good position. Then a pass from Doherty found Charlton who agonisingly sent the ball a few inches wide of the goal. The second half started with Wolves in the ascendency but the home side continued to waste some great opportunities. Edwards was everywhere, trying to support his forwards and assist the defence when danger prevailed. After 63 minutes Wolves grabbed the opening goal from a corner. Murray swung the ball across the goalmouth and Broadbent deceived the United defence by allowing the ball to pass through his legs. As it arrived at the feet of DEELEY (pictured below) he beat the goalie with a left foot shot. Five minutes later and Wolves added a second. Murray crossed the ball from the right wing and DEELEY headed home from close range. Two minutes later it was THREE and game over as WILSHAW dispossessed Blanchflower before shooting beyond Wood. United were shell-shocked and did well to prevent the home side adding to their total. As Wolves relaxed DOHERTY scored a consolation goal in the 89th minute.

It was a case of goals galore in Division 1 with the 10 games producing 42. Four home teams scored 5 goals but disappointingly three games in Lancashire, those at Bolton, Burnley and Preston, all had attendances of less than 20,000.

Despite losing for the first time at home this season, Nottingham Forest remain in first place on goal average, by one fiftieth of a goal from Wolves. Strikes in each half from Robson earned West Brom. the points but, for long periods, Forest were the better side with Eddie Baily turning back the years in midfield.

Arsenal made the best possible start at Highbury when Herd scored from a corner to put them ahead after only two minutes against Leeds United. Despite sustained Arsenal pressure, Brook scored an equaliser for the visitors. However, justice was done when Herd added a second for the 'Gunners' after good work by Tiddy and Bowen. The game was a disappointing spectacle for the large crowd.

Burnley suffered their third consecutive defeat going down to two goals from Curry of Newcastle, who incurred the wrath of the home fans after twice being reprimanded by the referee for bad fouls on Adamson. The Burnley skipper finally retaliated in the last minute, only to have his name taken to compound a miserable afternoon for the 'Clarets'.

After their humiliating defeat at West Brom. last Saturday, Manchester City abandoned their controversial 'M' defensive plan and immediately reaped the benefits by outplaying Spurs to win 5-1 at Maine Road. Johnstone was the architect of the victory, playing just behind the forwards whilst using his experience and skill to control the game. The crowd revelled in the goal feast and stood to applaud the players from the field at the final whistle.

The first half at Deepdale was evenly contested and ended with Chelsea level at 2-2. Finney and Thompson were outstanding for North End, creating chance after chance and eventually the home side ran out easy winners by 5 goals to 2.

Taylor scored a hat-trick with a shot, a penalty and a header, but it was the performances of 'The Preston Plumber' Tom Finney, who scored the first goal, and Tommy Thompson with the last which will remain in the memory of the home fans.

SATURDAY 28TH SEPTEMBER

ARSENAL	2	LEEDS UNITED	1	
Herd 2		Brook		
				Att. 39,538
ASTON VILLA	5	LEICESTER CITY	1	
Sewell 2, Southren		Morris		
McParland, Lynn (pen)				Att. 31,691
BOLTON W.	1	PORTSMOUTH	0	
Stevens				
				Att. 13,184
BURNLEY	0	NEWCASTLE U.	2	
		Curry 2		
				Att. 18,465
EVERTON	v	BLACKPOOL		
(Postponed due to influenza outbreak)				
MANCHESTER C.	5	TOTTENHAM H.	1	
Hayes 2, Johnstone 2		Branagan (og)		
Barlow				Att. 22,497
NOTTINGHAM F.	0	WEST BROM. ALB.	2	
		Robson 2		
				Att. 41,825
PRESTON N.E.	5	CHELSEA	2	
Finney, Taylor 3 (1pen)		Nicholas A. Tindall		
Thompson				Att. 17,944
SHEFFIELD WED.	5	BIRMINGHAM C.	3	
Ellis 2, Quixall 2		Orritt 2, Murphy		
Smith (og)				Att. 20,129
SUNDERLAND	3	LUTON TOWN	0	
Fleming 2 (1pen),				
O'Neill				Att. 36,724
WOLVES	3	MANCHESTER U.	1	
Deeley 2, Wilshaw		Doherty		
				Att. 48,825

		Home Goals					Away Goals					
	P	W	D	L	F	A	W	D	L	F	A	Pts
Nottm F	10	3	1	1	12	5..	4	0	1	11	6	15
Wolves	10	5	0	0	18	4..	2	1	2	8	9	15
W. Brom	10	3	1	1	17	7..	2	3	0	10	7	14
Man Utd	10	4	0	1	17	5..	2	1	2	11	11	13
Everton	8	3	1	0	10	6..	3	0	1	5	5	13
Bolton	10	3	2	0	11	3..	2	0	3	7	12	12
Luton	10	2	1	1	7	3..	2	0	3	4	8	11
Preston	10	5	0	0	20	5..	0	0	5	3	13	10
Nwcastle	10	2	1	1	v	4..	2	1	3	9	8	10
Man City	9	4	0	0	14	4..	1	0	4	8	23	10
Chelsea	10	2	1	1	15	7..	1	2	3	9	16	9
Leeds U	11	4	0	2	11	7..	0	1	4	2	13	9
A Villa	10	3	0	2	11	5..	0	2	3	4	11	8
Tottnhm	10	3	1	1	18	10..	0	1	4	4	16	8
Sundrlnd	11	3	1	2	10	6..	0	1	4	5	15	8
Burnley	10	3	1	1	18	6..	0	1	4	3	18	8
Sheff W	9	3	0	2	10	8..	0	1	3	5	11	7
Blackpool	9	2	1	2	7	7..	1	0	3	3	9	7
Brmngm	10	2	1	2	7	8..	0	1	4	7	21	6
Leicester	10	2	0	3	12	11..	0	0	5	6	15	4

9 goals – Barrett (Nottingham F.) Murray (Wolves)

8 Goals – Whelan (Manchester U.) Thompson (P.N.E.)

Allen (W.B.A.) Deeley (Wolves)

United Reserves

The Club reported that the opening four home Central League fixtures at Old Trafford had attracted a total of 46,354 spectators through the turnstiles. If the Reserve team continues to play the kind of attractive football which overwhelmed Aston Villa Reserves 6-1 today then these attendance figures will only increase.

The 'flu bug' which decimated the first team meant that the Reserve side had to make a number of changes to replace those players promoted for the game at Wolves.

An unfamiliar side of-Gaskell, B. Smith P. Jones, Whitefoot, M. Jones, Cope, Morgans, Webster, Dawson, Harrop and Scanlon were just too strong for Villa. Morgans had given United the lead from a Scanlon cross in the first half. After the interval United scored five more through Harrop 2, Dawson 2 and Scanlon for a great win.

CENTRAL LEAGUE

	P	W	D	L	F	A	Pts
Man. United....	10	6	2	2	31	19	14
Bury	8	6	1	1	18	6	13
Everton	9	5	2	2	27	14	12
Barnsley	9	4	4	1	19	12	12
Sheffield Wed.	7	5	1	1	17	6	11
Huddersfield T.	9	5	1	3	17	13	11
Liverpool	8	5	0	3	18	15	10
Aston Villa	10	4	2	4	18	17	10
Derby County	9	4	2	3	17	21	10
Bolton W.	10	3	3	4	15	14	9
Wolves	9	3	3	3	15	16	9
Newcastle Un.	8	4	0	4	12	12	8
Leeds	8	3	2	3	14	15	8
Stoke	9	3	2	4	13	14	8
Sheffield United	10	3	2	5	14	18	8
Preston N. End	9	3	1	5	9	14	7
Blackpool	9	2	3	4	10	18	7
Man. City	8	3	0	5	17	17	6
Burnley	9	2	2	5	8	18	6
West Brom A.	9	2	1	6	18	25	5
Chesterfield	8	2	1	5	10	19	5
Blackburn	9	2	1	6	11	26	5

Mon. 30th Sept.

Preston North End's outside-left, 33 year old Angus Morrison, moved to Millwall today and three hours later scored the first goal after only seven minutes of the game as he inspired his new club to a 5-0 victory against Queens Park Rangers.

Morrison's accurate crosses from the left-wing also contributed to a further two goals in a display that delighted his new Manager, Ron Gray and also the 12,000 home crowd. The player had travelled by train to London on the morning of the game and agreed personal terms as Millwall took the first steps in a re-building programme using some of the £20,000 they received from Sunderland following the transfer of Charlie Hurley. One week earlier, Q. P. R. had beaten Millwall 3-0 in the reverse fixture. Morrison had appeared in 261 League games for North End scoring 69 goals since signing form Derby County in December 1948. Last season he only played 6 games and this season had been unable to gain a first team place due to the outstanding form of Sammy Taylor.

Player Profile

Tom Finney
Born 5th April, 1922-Preston

Tom Finney is one of the most famous footballers in the country having, at the start of the season, played 67 games for England scoring 27 goals.

Although he played for Preston in the 1941 Cup Final against Arsenal at Wembley and subsequent replay at Ewood Park, he did not make his Football League début until August 1946 because of the Second World War. He wasted no time scoring in his first game in a 3-2 victory against Leeds United at Deepdale. The following month he made his International début in Belfast again scoring as England beat Northern Ireland 7-2.

In May 1950, Finney scored 4 goals for England in the 5-3 victory over Portugal in Lisbon but has not yet achieved a hat-trick in League or Cup games for Preston.

A month later in Belo Horizonte, Brazil Finney played for England in the, never to be forgotten, 1-0 World Cup defeat against the U.S.A.

After spending two seasons in the 2nd Division Preston won the title in 1951 to secure a return to the top flight. At the start of the 1952/53 season it was reported that Italian side Palermo had offered Tom Finney a £10,000 signing on fee plus a salary of £130 per week, a villa and free flights home if he agreed to join them. The

Preston Chairman, Nat Buck, had no hesitation in telling the player that 'If you do not play for North End then you don't play for anyone'. The matter was closed.

In one of the closest finishes in Division One history, Arsenal and Preston reached their final League game of the season level on points with identical playing records except for goal average. North End played at Derby on the Wednesday before the FA Cup Final and Finney scored the only goal of the game from the penalty spot. Arsenal did not play until the Friday evening and clinched the title with a 3-2 victory against Burnley.

Finney was chosen as The Footballer of the Year in 1954 but then had a nightmare game in the FA Cup Final, being unable to influence the match as Preston lost 3-2 to West Brom.

Disappointment was also to follow in the 1954 World Cup when, although Finney scored against Uruguay in the Quarter Final match in Basle, it was not enough as England lost 4-2, mainly due to two costly mistakes by goalkeeper Gil Merrick.

Tommy Thompson moved to Deepdale in 1955 from Aston Villa and stated that the reason for him joining the Club was the opportunity to play alongside Finney. The two players have already struck up a prolific partnership despite the fact that Finney has suffered from a chronic back problem which, at times, affects his fitness.

He was again Footballer of the Year in 1957, becoming the first player to receive the award on two occasions.

Such is his drawing power, Preston tend to announce the team as late as possible, as it is not unknown for fans to turn round and go home if they hear that Finney is not playing.

His ability to be as equally strong with his left or right foot has resulted in him being selected to play in all five forward positions. He has also appeared for England in three different positions. Although now aged 35, he is still the one player feared by the opposition and has recently been converted to centre-forward on a regular basis with his heading skills bringing him a number of goals.

A plumber by trade, he owns his own firm and can often be seen working around Preston, earning him the nickname 'The Preston Plumber'.

Career Appearances (As at 31st July 1957)

FOOTBALL LEAGUE	346	GOALS	138
INTERNATIONAL	67	GOALS	27

October 1957

Tues. 1st Oct.

England and Manchester United wing-half, Duncan Edwards, celebrated his 21st birthday today ill in bed suffering from influenza and will miss the European Cup game at Old Trafford tomorrow against Shamrock Rovers. Whelan also has 'the bug' and their places will be taken by McGuinness and Webster.

Byrne, Colman and Viollet are fit again and expected to be named in the starting eleven.

West Brom. Alb.   **0**   **Birmingham C.**   **0**

Att. 39,738

Wed. 2nd Oct.

Wolves played their first evening fixture since the installation of the new £25,000 floodlighting system and enjoyed the occasion by beating Spurs 4-0. The victory was their sixth consecutive League win and deservedly moved them to the top of the table.

The opening goal was the best of the game as Wright found Murray with a long pass. The ball was played onto Deeley and Murray then raced down the wing, received the return pass and beat Reynolds with a powerful drive from the edge of the penalty area. Flowers and Clamp were outstanding for the home team.

Arsenal   **4**   **Aston Villa**   **0**
Swallow, Tiddy, Bloomfield, Herd   Att. 18,482

Wolves   **4**   **Tottenham H.**   **0**
Murray, Flowers, Broadbent 2.   Att. 36,024

Denmark	0	Eire	2
		Cummins, Curtis	

With England having already won the Group, there was only pride at stake in Copenhagen as Eire won a bad tempered encounter 2-0. The Danes made life difficult for the Republic and after the game accused the Irish of 'dirty tactics' as they conceded 35 free kicks. The home supporters pelted the Irish team with apples at the final whistle.

European Cup-Preliminary Round 2nd Leg

Manchester U	3	**Shamrock Rovers**	2
Viollet 2, Pegg		McCann, Hamilton	

Att. 33,754

(Manchester United win 9-2 on aggregate)

Manchester United-*Wood, Foulkes, Byrne, Colman, Jones M., McGuinness, Berry, Webster, Taylor, Viollet, Pegg.*
Shamrock Rovers-*D'Arcy, Burke, Mackey, Nolan, Keogh, Coad, McCann, Peyton, Ambrose, Hamilton, Tuohy.*

With a six goal advantage from the first leg, United supporters obviously felt that this return game at Old Trafford was a forgone conclusion which resulted in a reduced gate of less than 34,000. The smallest for any European match at the ground.

What a pity for the missing fans, for both teams provided a wonderful, entertaining encounter.

United stormed into a two goal lead inside the first quarter of the game. VIOLLET, after missing an early opportunity through dwelling on the ball too long, soon made amends after five minutes when he smashed the ball home from a centre by Pegg.

Both Berry and Pegg down the flanks caused the Irish problems. Only great defending by Coad and acrobatic saves by D'Arcy kept the 'Red Devils' at bay.

In the 22nd minute Viollet returned the compliment laying on a pass for PEGG who fended off two defenders before striking the ball into the net.

At this stage United put the away defence under extreme pressure and appeared as though they would add to their total at any time.

The Shamrock Rovers team continued to work hard and almost pulled a goal back before the interval when Peyton outran Byrne but just failed to prevent the ball going out for a goal-kick when well clear of the United captain.

In the 55th minute the visitors scored. Inside-forward, Peyton, found space beyond the United defence and laid the ball across for McCANN who netted from a few yards. For just a few minutes the home side 'wobbled' but after 60 minutes United increased their lead as Webster played the ball into the path of VIOLLET who let fly an unstoppable shot.

The away team had no intentions of allowing United to build up an even bigger margin of lead and in the 68th minute HAMILTON (pictured below) hit the ball under the diving Wood to make the score 3-2. The home crowd were generous in their applause and within a few minutes the same player forced Wood to make a fine save.

The final act of the game was a one-handed save by D'Arcy from a Pegg header.

Former Leeds United favourite, John Charles, returned to Elland Road with his new club Juventus for a 'friendly' game. The gentle giant, who had cost Juventus £65,000, was made captain for the night and did not disappoint the large crowd of 41,000 scoring twice in a very rough game.

His first, a header, went into the net off Jack Charlton's shoulder to level the scores 2-2 at half time. Four minutes from time he hit the ball into the roof of the net to secure a 4-2 victory for his new team which maintained their unbeaten start to the season.

The other big money signing of Juventus, Argentinian Enryco Sivori (on his 22nd birthday), scored the other two goals.

Charles left the field to rapturous applause from the Leeds supporters who also sang 'Auld Lang's Syne' to complete a wonderful evening for the Welshman.

Thurs. 3rd Oct.

Football League Secretary, Alan Hardaker, issued a stern warning to officials of foreign clubs against approaching Football League players.

Italian clubs have already spent £65,000 on John Charles and £40,000 on Tony Marchi and appear willing and able to splurge more money on British players.

Mr Hardaker said, "If any offer is made by anybody to any player without his club first having been approached then immediate action will be taken through the FA and FIFA on the ground of irregular approach to players".

Fri. 4th Oct.

After scoring for Manchester United last Saturday in the 3-1 defeat against Wolves, his first game of the season, John Doherty has decided that his future lies elsewhere. The player signed today for Leicester City for a fee in the region of £6,500 and will play at inside-right tomorrow against Everton.

He made his début for United in 1952 and has played 26 League and Cup games scoring 7 goals.

United will be without Jackie Blanchflower tomorrow for the game against Aston Villa as he has been selected for Ireland against Scotland at Windsor Park Belfast. Villa player, McParland is also in the Irish side. Whelan has recovered from flu and will return to lead the United attack.

The Football Association announced a strong England 'B' team to play a Combined Sheffield side at Hillsborough on 23rd October. The game will form part of the Centenary celebrations of the Sheffield Amateur Club.

*The team will be-**Else** (P.N.E.), **Bond** (W.H.U.), **Evans** (Arsenal), **Colman** (Manchester U.), **Gratrix** (Blackpool) (Capt.), **Flowers** (Wolves), **Douglas***

(Blackburn R.), **Robson** *(W.B.A.),* **Allen** *(W.B.A.),* **Barrett** *(Nottingham F.),* **Perry** *(Blackpool). Reserve-***Stokes** *(Tottenham H.)*

Peter Farrell (below), the former Everton Captain and Irish International, joined Tranmere Rovers today and will captain his new club against Southport tomorrow. He has failed to make a first team appearance this season for the 'Toffees' and reportedly has been given an assurance that he will be appointed as manager of Tranmere in the future.

Farrell, aged 35, made 421 League appearances for Everton scoring 14 goals.

SATURDAY 5ᵀᴴ OCTOBER 1957

BIRMINGHAM C. 4   MANCHESTER C. 0
Murphy 3, Brown
Att. 28,059

BLACKPOOL 7   SUNDERLAND 0
Durie 2, Charnley 2,
Taylor 2, Perry
Att. 33,172

BOLTON W. 0   ARSENAL 1
Herd
Att. 20,212

CHELSEA 1   SHEFFIELD WED. 0
Tindall
Att. 38,722

LEEDS UNITED 1   WOLVES 1
Baird   Deeley
Att. 28,635

LEICESTER CITY 2   EVERTON 2
Gardiner, Hogg   Fielding, Hickson
Att. 28,922

LUTON TOWN 3   BURNLEY 2
Turner 2, Brown   Pilkington 2
Att. 15,179

MANCHESTER U. 4   ASTON VILLA 1
Taylor 2, Pegg,   Pace
Dugdale (og)
Att. 43,332

NEWCASTLE U. 0   PRESTON N.E. 2
Taylor, Finney
Att. 36,131

TOTTENHAM H. 3   NOTTINGHAM F. 4
Medwin, Harmer   Gray, Imlach, Quigley
Brooks   Wilson
Att. 51,429

WEST BROM. ALB. 3   PORTSMOUTH 1
Allen 2, Robson   Harris
Att. 31,882

		Home			Goals		Away			Goals		
	P	W	D	L	F	A	W	D	L	F	A	Pts
Wolves	13	6	0	0	23	4	2	3	2	9	10	18
W Brom	13	4	2	1	20	8	2	3	0	10	7	17
Nottm F	11	3	1	1	12	5	5	0	1	15	9	17
Man Utd	11	5	0	1	21	6	1	2	1	11	11	15
Arsenal	11	4	1	1	15	7	3	0	3	6	16	15
everton	9	3	1	0	10	4	3	1	1	7	7	14
Luton	11	4	1	1	10	5	2	0	3	4	8	13
Preston	11	5	0	0	20	5	1	0	5	5	13	12
Bolton	11	3	2	1	11	4	3	0	3	7	12	12
Chelsea	11	3	1	1	16	7	1	2	3	9	16	11
Nwcastle	11	2	1	2	6	6	2	0	3	8	10	10
Man C	10	4	0	0	14	4	1	0	5	8	27	10
Leeds U	11	4	1	2	12	8	0	1	4	2	13	10
Blackpl	10	3	1	1	14	7	1	0	3	3	9	9
Bnghm	12	3	1	2	11	8	0	2	4	7	21	9
Portsmth	11	2	2	1	11	9	1	0	5	7	15	8
Tottnhm	12	3	1	2	21	14	0	1	5	4	20	8
A Villa	12	3	0	2	11	5	0	2	5	5	19	8
Burnley	11	3	1	1	10	6	0	1	5	5	21	8
Sunderld	12	3	1	2	10	6	0	1	5	5	23	8
Sheff W	10	3	0	2	10	6	0	1	4	5	13	7
Leicester	11	2	1	3	14	13	0	0	5	6	13	5

Norman Deeley earned Wolves a point at Leeds with his ninth goal of the season to maintain their position at the top of the table. It would appear that Harry Hooper will have to bide his time in the reserves with little chance of gaining his first team place back.

At Kenilworth Road both teams wore black armbands as a show of respect following the death of Mr Richardson, a Luton Town Director, earlier in the week. Cumming made his first appearance of the season in the Luton forward line and together with Adam on the wing, totally destroyed the Burnley defence in the first half.

Turner opened the scoring after 17 minutes and twenty minutes later Brown headed the second goal from a cross by Adam. Burnley pulled two goals back, both scored by Pilkington, but a further goal from Turner ensured a well-deserved victory for the home side.

A crowd of over 51,000 witnessed a pulsating game at White Hart Lane in the sunshine, as Forest emerged victorious in a seven goal thriller.

Former Spurs favourite, Eddie Baily, (pictured) was made captain for the day and received a rousing reception from the home fans. Throughout the game the experienced player, who had made almost 300 League appearances for Spurs, allowed the ball to do the work for him showing his former colleagues what they were missing. Spurs raced into a two goal lead in the opening thirty minutes and should have had a third, but Thompson made a wonderful save from Smith. Forest eventually settled down and swift passing movements began to unsettle the defence.

Wilson scored a header from a corner to reduce the arrears before half time. After the interval Imlach scored the goal of the game with a thirty yard pile-driver which gave Reynolds no chance. Gray then put the away side ahead for the first time in the game only to see Brooks equalise. Late in the game justice was served when Quigley scored the winner for Forest.

Manchester Utd	**4**	**Aston Villa**	**1**
Taylor 2, Dugdale (og), Pegg		Pace	

Att. 43,332

Manchester United-*Wood, Foulkes, Byrne, Colman, Jones M., McGuinness, Berry, Whelan, Taylor, Charlton, Pegg.*

Aston Villa-*Sims, Lynn, Aldis, Crowther, Dugdale, Saward, Hinchcliffe, Sewell, Pace, Crowe, Myerscough.*

Bobby Charlton was intercepted on his way to Derby to play for United reserves and given the No. 10 shirt at Old Trafford as a late replacement for Viollet who was yet another victim of the influenza bug.

United were hell bent on revenge for the heartbreak caused by the defeat against Villa at Wembley in the Cup Final. This manifested itself in a whirlwind start with the home side storming forward at every possible occasion, and after only 15 minutes they were ahead. A superb pass from Whelan found TAYLOR who ran clear of the defence, evading a tackle from Dugdale, before slamming the ball beyond Sims into the net.

Sims was soon in action again making a fine save from Berry, but after 32 minutes he had no chance when DUGDALE sliced the ball into his own net. The defender was trying to stop Berry's cross reaching Taylor, who was in a dangerous position, but in attempting to intercept the ball his miss-kick proved fatal.

As the teams left the field at half time it appeared it would only be a matter of time before the home side added to their total because of their complete dominance in the first half. Surprisingly, with the second half only ten minutes old, Villa pulled a goal back. Hinchcliffe, making his début at outside-right, crossed the ball into the path of PACE who hit an unstoppable volley past Wood. The goal only served to spur United into more frantic efforts, driven by Colman who was always in the thick of the action, and after 62 minutes the two goal advantage was restored.

PEGG received the ball in the penalty area and, seeing the 'keeper off his line, delicately and with great precision, lobbed the ball over his head to put United 3-1 ahead.

The much changed Aston Villa side were not good enough to provide any response and, only six minutes later, United scored a fourth. Again it was TAYLOR who steered the ball at head height to the left of the Villa goalkeeper. His two goals crowned a superb display which answered some of his critics who had begun to question his ability on the ball. He ran at defenders, retained possession of the ball when needed and looked a perfect all round player to 'lead the line'.

It could have been more as Lynn stopped one shot on the line and Crowther, in another desperate situation, hit the ball hard into the stomach of his own goalkeeper. The United defence had easily coped with the Villa attack and McGuinness, deputising for Edwards, proved what a good player he is by always being in the right place at the right time. Overall this was an easy victory for the home side who will again face the same opposition at Old Trafford later this month in the FA Charity Shield.

Centre-half, Charlie Hurley, made his début for Sunderland at Bloomfield Road following his transfer from Millwall. What a nightmare he encountered as Blackpool overran their visitors to win 7-0. Alan Spence, a sixteen year old grammar schoolboy, also made his début at centre-forward for Sunderland.

In the first home International match of the season Ireland drew 1-1 with Scotland at Windsor Park Belfast in a game watched by 58,000 fans. Ireland created numerous opportunities in the opening 45 minutes but failed to capitalise on their superiority as the game reached half time goalless.

McIlroy and Simpson were over anxious in front of goal, opting to snatch at chances rather than placing shots at goal.

In the 48th minute Simpson finally put Ireland ahead following a pass from Bingham. Ten minutes later Scotland equalised when Mudie caused confusion in the home defence and McMichael could only partially clear the ball before Leggat pounced to score.

United Reserves

After an unbeaten run, spanning seven games, the reserve side surprisingly lost 4-2 away to Derby County. Scanlon and Morgans scored the goals but, despite the result, United remain top of the Central League table.

Mon. 7th Oct.

It was reported that representatives from three English and three Scottish clubs had met in Newcastle and decided to proceed with the creation of an Anglo-Scottish floodlit tournament.

The clubs-Manchester City, Newcastle United, Tottenham Hotspur, Hearts, Hibernian and Partick Thistle also decided on a provisional list of fixtures with games scheduled to be played on Monday evenings from October 14th to December 9th 1957.

Newcastle United reported a trading profit of £3,367 for the year ending 31st July 1957.

Tues. 8th Oct.

The flu epidemic, which has caused the postponement of a number of Football League games this season, is still causing havoc throughout the country. Newspapers report that there have been almost 1200 deaths this year but, more significantly, 442 of those deaths occurred in the week ending 5th October.

Wed. 9th Oct.

Everton became the latest team to install floodlighting at their Goodison Park home and celebrated the event with a 2-0 friendly match victory against Liverpool. The lights, costing £40,000, are the highest in the country with the pylons standing at 185 feet.

The match was held on the 9th October to celebrate the 75th anniversary of the Liverpool County FA's foundation. Thomas, who replaced Fielding at half time, scored both the Everton goals.

Manchester City	**2**	**Sheffield Wednesday**	**0**
McAdams, Barlow		Att. 24,016	

Full-back Don Howe was pronounced unfit for the Football League game v The League of Ireland at Elland Road and his place was taken by Jimmy Armfield.

The Football League won easily 3-1 with the goals from Ray Parry (pictured below) who scored twice and Peter Broadbent. Ronnie Nolan from Shamrock Rovers scored the consolation goal.

In the other Inter League match at Ibrox Park the Scottish League defeated the Irish League resoundingly 7-0. Leggat scored 3, Bauld 2, Collins a penalty and one from McColl.

Despite conceding 7 goals the Irish goalkeeper, Rea of Glenavon, had an outstanding game.

A Football Association X1 beat the Royal Air Force 5-2 under floodlights at Nottingham. Durie, the Blackpool inside-left scored four goals with Clough from Middlesbrough netting the other. The scorers for the R.A.F. were Birch and Thomson.

FA X1-Wakeham (Torquay U.), Carberry (Ipswich T.), Langley (Fulham), Clamp (Wolves), Stokoe (Newcastle U.), Burkitt (Notts. Forest), Clapton (Arsenal), Newsham (Notts. County), Clough (Middlesbrough), Durie (Blackpool), Burbeck (Middlesbrough).

R.A.F.X1-Wren (Hibernian), Tether (Wolves), Baird (Partick T.), Kay (Sheffield W.), Scott (Newcastle U.), Williams (Bristol C.), Campbell (P.N.E.), Brabrook (Chelsea), Nicholas (Chelsea), Thomson (Wolves), Birch (Bolton W.)

European Cup Competition

The draw for the First Round proper of the European Cup took place in Madrid today.

Manchester United were drawn against Dukla Prague of Czechoslovakia and both legs must be played by November 30th 1957 with United hosting the First leg at Old Trafford.

Thurs. 10th Oct.

The England team to meet Wales at Cardiff on 18th October was announced today and includes three new caps-Hopkinson (Bolton W.), Howe (W.B.A.) and Douglas (Blackburn R.). Finney of Preston will switch to the left wing to accommodate Douglas on the right flank. The side will also include Byrne, Edwards and Taylor of Manchester United.

England captain, Billy Wright, will make his 86th international appearance.

In Lisbon the Portuguese Army beat the British Army 3-1 in a game played at 10 p.m. G.M.T. Despite the score line the British Army had a number of scoring opportunities with Hitchens in particular guilty of two missed chances. Jones scored the only goal for the away side with a twenty yard pile-driver.

BRITISH ARMY-Barnett, Parker, Whelan, Curry, Ferguson, Appleton, Harris, Charlton, Hitchens, Melia, Jones.

Fri. 11th Oct.

Manchester United will visit the County Ground tomorrow to face third place Nottingham Forest. The visit of the 'Champions' has been eagerly awaited since the fixtures were released and the game will mark the opening of a new stand with seating for 2,500 spectators.

Tickets for the game were sold out weeks ago and the ground record attendance of 44,166, set up 27 years ago for an FA Cup game against Sheffield Wednesday, is expected to be broken.

United have Edwards and Viollet fit again in a full strength side. In the Forest team Quigley will continue to deputise for Barrett who has recovered from an injury but is now suffering from influenza.

After losing 7-0 at Blackpool last Saturday Sunderland travel to Turf Moor to face a Burnley side who have suffered four consecutive defeats. With Sunderland occupying 19th position and Burnley 20th the game is vital to both teams.

In an intriguing clash at the Hawthorns, West Bromwich Albion, who have not lost for eight games, face Bolton Wanderers whose form fluctuates from one game to another.

Albion will be aware that Bolton inflicted the heaviest defeat of the season to date against Manchester United, beating them 4-0 last month, and will treat their opponents with utmost respect.

Saturday 12th October

In the London Derby at White Hart Lane Bobby Smith put Spurs ahead after only four minutes. Although Arsenal played some good football they allowed the home side to increase their lead after 27 minutes when Harmer created a goal for Medwin.

Shortly afterwards Tottenham goalkeeper Ditchburn and Arsenal forward Groves, collided with each other and Groves had to leave the pitch with a knee injury.

Just before half time the home fans in the crowd of over 60,000, thought Spurs had scored again when Kelsey appeared to save a header from Brooks behind the line. The referee ruled otherwise.

SATURDAY 12TH OCTOBER

BIRMINGHAM C. 1   WOLVES 5
Astall   Clamp 2, Deeley, Murray, Wilshaw
   Att. 43,005

BURNLEY 6   SUNDERLAND 0
Shannon 2, Newlands 2, Pointer, Cheesebrough
   Att. 22,868

CHELSEA 4   ASTON VILLA 2
Tindall 2, Nicholas 2   Sewell, McParland
   Att. 40,769

MANCHESTER C. 4   LEICESTER CITY 3
Hayes 2, Barlow, McAdams   Rowley 2 (1pen), McDonald
   Att. 29,884

NEWCASTLE U. 2   EVERTON 3
Curry, Davies   Harris B., Hickson, Keith (og).
   Att. 30,472

NOTTINGHAM F. 1   MANCHESTER U. 2
Imlach   Viollet, Whelan
   Att. 47,804

PORTSMOUTH 1   LEEDS UNITED 2
Newman   Baird, Brook
   Att. 23,534

PRESTON N.E. 1   LUTON TOWN 0
Finney (pen)   Att. 25,403

SHEFFIELD WED. 0   BLACKPOOL 3
   Mudie, Peterson, Durie
   Att. 30,332

TOTTENHAM H. 3   ARSENAL 1
Medwin 2, Smith   Holton
   Att. 60,671

WEST BROM. ALB. 2   BOLTON W. 2
Kevan, Allen (pen)   Sanders (og), Stevens
   Att. 31,370

	P	W	D	L	F	A	W	D	L	F	A	Pts
Wolves	13	6	0	0	23	4	3	2	2	14	11	20
W Brom	13	4	3	1	22	10	2	3	0	10	7	18
Man Utd	12	5	0	1	21	6	3	1	2	13	12	17
Nottm F	13	3	1	2	13	7	5	0	1	15	9	17
Everton	10	3	1	0	10	4	4	1	1	10	9	6
Arsenal	12	4	1	1	15	7	3	0	3	7	9	15
Preston	13	6	0	0	21	5	1	0	5	13	14	
Man City	12	6	0	0	20	7	1	0	5	8	27	14
Chelsea	12	4	1	1	20	9	1	2	3	9	16	13
Bolton	12	3	2	1	11	4	3	1	3	9	14	13
Luton	12	4	1	1	10	5	2	0	4	4	9	12
Leeds U	13	4	1	2	12	8	1	1	4	4	14	12
Blckpool	11	3	1	2	14	7	2	0	3	6	8	11
Nwcastle	12	3	1	3	8	9	2	1	3	9	8	10
Spurs	13	4	1	2	24	15	0	1	5	4	20	10
Burnley	12	4	1	1	16	6	0	1	5	5	21	10
Bmnghm	13	3	1	3	12	13	0	2	4	7	21	9
Portsmth	12	2	2	2	12	11	1	0	5	7	15	8
A Villa	13	3	0	2	11	5	0	2	6	7	23	8
Sundrlnd	13	3	1	2	10	6	0	1	6	5	29	8
Sheff Wd	12	3	0	3	10	11	0	1	5	5	14	7
Leicester	12	2	1	3	14	13	0	0	6	2	19	5

In the second half Spurs added a third goal in the 65th minute when Medwin scored from a few yards in a build-up that included Harmer and Stokes. Arsenal's consolation was scored by Holton. Herd had been fouled in the penalty area and

118

Holton took the spot kick only to see the ball strike Ditchburn. Fortunately he was able to tap home the rebound.

Another derby game, this time in the Midlands, saw Wolves completely overpower Birmingham City in a devastating first half at St Andrews. Wilshaw put Wolves ahead after ten minutes from a pass by Deeley. Against the run of play Astall equalised four minutes later, but by the half hour mark further goals from Murray and Deeley had put the game beyond Birmingham.

In the second half Wolves added two more, both scored by Clamp to win comfortably.

Blackpool were too good for Sheffield Wednesday at Hillsborough and Taylor in particular ran the home defence ragged with his trickery and superb distribution of the ball.

Peterson, Blackpool's South African forward, scored his first League goal for the club. Wednesday were disappointing and offered little threat to the Blackpool goal.

Following the game the Blackpool team coach was in collision with a car at Stocksbridge on the outskirts of Sheffield. Fortunately no one was seriously injured and after about half an hour the coach was able to resume its journey north.

The flu epidemic forced Aston Villa to make five changes to their team and the reshuffled side were well beaten by Chelsea. Nicholas scored the opening two goals with a header and shot, both from moves involving Brabrook.

Tindall increased Chelsea's lead in the second half following a defensive mistake, but Villa never gave up, eventually losing 4-2.

Nottingham F.	**1**	**Manchester Utd.**	**2**
Imlach		Whelan, Viollet	

Att. 47,804

Nottingham Forest-*Thomson, Whare, Thomas, Morley, Watson, Burkitt, Gray, Quigley, Wilson, Baily, Imlach.*

Manchester United-*Wood, Foulkes, Byrne, Colman, Blanchflower, Edwards, Berry, Whelan, Taylor, Viollet, Pegg.*

This was the first meeting of the two sides in the top division since 1907 and the occasion was marked by a beautiful sunny day. The opening of a new stand had, as anticipated, resulted in a new record crowd for the ground of almost 48,000.

United, playing in an all-white strip, were soon in their stride and took the lead after only four minutes. Wood threw the ball out to Pegg on the left wing and the player quickly advanced down the touchline towards the Forest penalty area. He crossed the ball for WHELAN to volley into the net.

Despite the early setback Forest soon settled into their rhythm with Baily, as always, the main schemer-in-chief. Burkitt also provided some beautifully placed passes to drive Forest forward as United were forced to defend. Edwards blocked a shot on the line and Wilson should have done better than see his header go over the crossbar.

Late in the first half Imlach had a great chance to score following a mistake by Blanchflower. Unfortunately the player squandered the opportunity with the goal at his mercy.

Within one minute after the interval the home side drew level when IMLACH headed a high cross-ball from Quigley into the net. Wood then made a great save to prevent Baily giving Forest the lead. In the 60th minute United regained the lead. Berry was the architect of a move finished sublimely by VIOLLET. Once United were in front they had no intention of letting the home side back into the game for a second time.

Nottingham Forest

Back row L to R – T. Graham (Trainer), G. Thomas, W. Morley, W. Whare, C. Thomson, H. Nicholson, P. Watson, J. Hutchinson, R. McKinlay, R. Davies (Physiotherapist).
Middle Row – P. Higham, T. Wilson, W. Gray, Mr W. H. Walker (Manager), J. Burkitt, E. Baily, D. Alexander.
Front Row – J.Barrett, F. Knight (Assistant Trainer), S. Imlach.

United controlled the game for the last twenty minutes as Colman drove them forward. Taylor and Whelan should have increased their advantage but failed to find the net.

In the end a comfortable victory for the away side in a great match enjoyed by everyone present and played in a superb spirit by all twenty-two players.

United Reserves

After suffering a defeat last week at Derby, the reserves side got back to winning ways with a 3-0 victory at home to nearest rivals Sheffield Wednesday. Goals from Harrop 2 and Morgans gave them a comfortable win.

Mon. 14ᵗʰ Oct.
Press reports from Saturday's game

TIMES- *"Yet one man stood out above all others. He was Edwards now more than usual guarding the backward areas around Blanchflower. His was a massive performance."*

MANCHESTER GUARDIAN *"A continuous bombardment of the United goal with only the broad bulk of the peripatetic Edwards and occasionally the safe hand of Woods intervening to save their side from disaster."*

DAILY EXPRESS *"Forest's swift well drilled forward routine demanded only the best from the goalkeeper and that hunk of excellence Duncan Edwards, the most effective one-man performer in British football."*

TOURNAMENT BANNED-The proposed floodlight competition involving three English and three Scottish sides now looks like it will not take place. The Scottish League have informed Hearts, Hibernian and Partick Thistle that, if they proceed with the Anglo-Scottish tournament they may face expulsion from the League.

The Football League has advised Spurs, Newcastle United and Manchester City that they should not take part. As the final decision is awaited, Spurs have announced that they will go ahead with the fixture against Hibs. in Edinburgh but this will be classed as a friendly match.

Tues. 15ᵗʰ Oct.

In the Youth International match played at White Hart Lane, England beat Rumania 4-2. Chelsea duo, Block and Bridges, shared three goals between them with Temple from Everton also netting.

Wed. 16ᵗʰ Oct.

Ray Daniel from Sunderland today signed for Cardiff City. The twenty-eight year old centre-half made 87 League appearances for Arsenal and 137 for Sunderland.

England Under 23's 3 Rumania Under 23's 2

England- Hodgkinson (Sheffield U.), Armfield (Blackpool), Harris (Wolves), Setters (W.B.A.), Smith (captain) (Birmingham C.), Crowther (Aston V.), Brabrook (Chelsea), Greaves (Chelsea), Curry (Newcastle U.), Parry (Bolton W.), A'Court (Liverpool).

The England under 23's team made heavy weather of defeating Rumania at Wembley on a pitch saturated by persistent rain which had left it waterlogged in places.

Jimmy Greaves was the outstanding player on view and opened the scoring in the first minute after a defensive mistake left him the simple job of tapping the ball into the net.

The Rumanian goalkeeper, Utu, then made two great saves to prevent Greaves from adding to his total. This was only short-lived and as the half progressed he scored a second goal following a cross from Crowther. England then eased off allowing the away side to score twice and reach the interval on level terms.

Early in the second half Curry scored with a powerful shot and, despite constant pressure, England failed to add to their total.

In the re-arranged Football League game at Goodison Park, watched by a crowd of 34,345, Arsenal dominated the game but, in the end, had to be satisfied with a point in a 2-2 draw.

Bloomfield had given them the lead after 28 minutes when he spectacularly hooked the ball over his shoulder into the net. The 'Gunners' failed to capitalise on their superiority and 13 minutes from time Thomas equalised. Within two minutes, Herd with a header, restored their advantage but in injury time Kelsey failed to catch the ball cleanly allowing Harris to score.

In a friendly match played at Ayresome Park, 2nd Division Middlesbrough easily beat Sunderland from the top tier 2-0. The game marked the first occasion that floodlights had been used at the stadium.

At Villa Park goals from Hitchens (Cardiff City), Robinson (Bury) and Newman (Portsmouth) were not enough to give the British Army victory. Aston Villa scored four times to win the game in a very entertaining match.

Thurs. 17th Oct.

The European Champions, Real Madrid, visited Molineux for a floodlit friendly game against Wolves. The match caught the imagination of the footballing public in the Midlands and the crowd of 55,000 witnessed a pulsating encounter.

The two differing styles of football were obvious for all to see. The home side, strong, forceful and eager to attack with Mullen and Wilshaw outstanding on the left flank. Real Madrid providing a more controlled, passing, slow build up but very dangerous in the penalty area. With minutes remaining the game was locked at 2-2 and the draw seemed inevitable. Wilshaw had other ideas and after inter passing with Mullen drove the ball into the net for the winner.

As a result of three players being away on international duty with England, Manchester United will give a début to 19 year-old Peter Jones at left-back in the home game against Portsmouth. The Salford born youngster played for England at Youth level and was a member of the side that won the Youth Cup in 1955 and 1956. McGuinness will play at left-half and 17 year-old Alex Dawson at centre-forward.

Dougan will make his début for Portsmouth in the No. 9 shirt.

Saturday 19th October

ARSENAL	1	BIRMINGHAM C.	3
Swallow		Orritt, Neal 2	
		Att. 39,031	
ASTON VILLA	4	NEWCASTLE U.	3
Dixon, Pace, Myerscough		Curry 2, Eastham	
Scott (og)		Att. 29,395	
BLACKPOOL	2	MANCHESTER C.	5
Mudie 2		Hayes 2, Barlow,	
		Barnes, McAdams	
		Att. 28,322	
BOLTON W.	3	TOTTENHAM H.	2
Lofthouse 2, Parry		Smith, Robb	
		Att. 20,381	
EVERTON	1	BURNLEY	1
Temple		Cheesbrough	
		Att. 45,024	
LEEDS UNITED	1	WEST BROM. ALB.	1
Forrest		Allen	
		Att. 24,614	
LEICESTER CITY	3	NOTTINGHAM F.	1
Gardiner, McDonald		Wilson (pen)	
Whare (og)		Att. 36,836	
LUTON TOWN	2	SHEFFIELD WED.	0
McLeod, Brown			
		Att. 14,473	
MANCHESTER U.	0	PORTSMOUTH	3
		Harris, Henderson	
		Newman	
		Att. 39,423	
SUNDERLAND	0	PRESTON N.E.	0
		Att. 34,676	
WOLVES	2	CHELSEA	1
Deeley, Wilshaw		Nicholas	
		Att. 37,524	

		Home			Goals		Away			Goals		
	P	W	D	L	F	A	W	D	L	F	A	Pts
Wolves	14	7	0	0	25	5	3	2	2	14	11	22
W Brom	14	4	3	1	22	10	2	4	0	11	8	19
Everton	12	3	3	0	13	7	4	1	1	10	9	18
Man Utd	13	5	0	2	21	9	3	1	2	13	17	17
Nottm F	13	3	1	2	13	7	5	0	2	16	12	17
Arsenal	14	4	1	2	16	18	3	1	3	9	11	16
Man City	13	6	0	0	20	7	2	0	5	13	29	16
Preston	13	6	0	0	21	5	1	1	5	5	13	15
Bolton	13	4	2	1	14	6	2	1	3	8	14	15
Luton	13	5	1	1	12	5	2	0	4	4	9	15
Chelsea	13	4	1	1	20	9	1	2	4	10	18	13
Leeds U	14	4	2	1	13	9	1	1	4	4	14	13
Blckpool	12	3	1	3	16	12	2	0	3	6	9	11
Burnley	13	4	1	1	16	6	0	2	5	6	22	11
Brmghm	14	3	1	3	12	13	1	2	4	10	22	11
Newcstle	13	2	1	3	8	9	2	1	4	12	12	10
Portsmth	13	2	2	2	12	11	2	0	5	10	15	10
Tottnhm	14	4	1	2	24	15	0	1	6	6	23	10
A Villa	14	4	0	2	15	8	0	2	6	7	23	10
Sundrlnd	14	3	2	2	10	6	0	1	6	5	29	9
Leicester	13	3	1	3	17	14	0	0	6	9	19	7
Shef Wed	13	3	0	3	10	11	0	1	6	5	16	7

League leaders Wolves found themselves one goal down after only eight minutes when a through ball from Greaves was netted by Nicholas. Two minutes later they were level, Wilshaw scoring with a well-placed header from a Broadbent pass.

Although Wolves took control of the game for long periods, it was Chelsea who came nearest to regaining the lead when Greaves hit a shot against the foot of the post just before the interval.

Wolves went ahead in the 49th minute. Deeley powered a shot goal-wards, the ball hit Saunders and deflected beyond Matthews and over the line. The win enabled Wolves to maintain their one hundred percent home record.

Second place West Brom. conceded a goal after five minutes at Leeds. Forest, who scored the goal with a header, almost increased their advantage a few minutes later but Setters just managed to clear the ball off the line.

In the second half the away side eventually equalised through Ronnie Allen to gain a hard earned point. The goal was Allen's twelfth strike of the season.

The performance of the day must surely have been Manchester City's demolition of Blackpool 5-2 away from home. Since abolishing their controversial M plan following a 9-2 hammering at West Brom. last month, City have won four of their last five games.

A Barlow header in the first minute gave City the lead but following good work from Perry and Taylor, 'Pool' equalised through Mudie. In the 24th minute Hayes restored their lead from a Fagan centre and nine minutes later Barnes converted a penalty. Within a minute Hayes ran through the home defence to score a fourth. In the second half McAdams added a fifth for Manchester City whilst Mudie scored a consolation goal.

Leading Goalscorers

ALLEN-West Brom.	**12**
DEELEY-Wolves	**11**
MURRAY-Wolves	**11**
BARRETT-Nott'm. F.	**9**
HAYES-Man. City	**9**
HERD-Arsenal	**9**
TINDALL-Chelsea	**9**
WHELAN-Man. Utd.	**9**
WILSON-Nott'm. F	**9**
CURRY-Newcastle U.	**8**
McPARLAND-Aston V.	**8**
THOMPSON-P.N.E.	**8**
TURNER-Luton T.	**8**

Manchester United   0   Portsmouth   3

Henderson, Harris, Newman.

Att. 39,423

Manchester United-*Wood, Foulkes, P. Jones, Colman, Blanchflower, McGuinness, Berry, Whelan, Dawson, Viollet, Pegg.*

Portsmouth-*Uprichard, Gunter, Wilson, Albury, Rutter, Dickinson, Harris, Gordon, Dougan, Henderson, Newman.*

An astonishing first half at Old Trafford saw Portsmouth score three times without reply against a below par United. Even allowing for three regulars being away on international duty, the home fans expected that the incoming reserve players would be good enough to overcome a side sitting fifth from the bottom of the table with only three wins this season.

Jackie Henderson and Norman Uprichard

Making his début for Portsmouth, slim, tall centre-forward, Derek Dougan, created the first opportunity of the game which, Scottish International HENDERSON (pictured above), took with ease.

United then stormed forward and bombarded the 'Pompey' goal without being able to beat Uprichard who dealt with everything thrown at him. A few minutes before the interval NEWMAN added a second and a minute later Dougan was again involved as HARRIS scored a third.

Half time Man. United 3-0 down at home with many of their supporters never having witnessed such a score after 45 minutes.

Both sides strived to score in the second half without success and United lost their second home game of the season.

United wing-halves, Colman and McGuinness, both left huge gaps in defence which Portsmouth exploited. Dougan, in particular, gave Blanchflower a torrid time, both in the air and on the ground.

As the United fans left the ground the talk was of whether Mark Jones should be recalled at centre-half to replace Jackie Blanchflower who seems to have lost his way.

F.A. Youth Cup Competition (1st Round)
at Turf Moor, Burnley

BURNLEY v. MANCHESTER UNITED
SATURDAY, 19th OCTOBER, 1957 (Kick-off 10.30 a.m.)

B U R N L E Y

P. ROBINSON

M. HENNAGHAN   F. McLEAN

R. BALDWIN   J. TALBUT   J. BRIER

FENTON   McAULEY

I. TOWERS   HART   T. LIGHTBOWN

J. ELMS   N. LAWTON   T. SPRATT

PEARSON   J. GILES

H. BRATT   HOLLAND   J. HENNESSEY

D. YEOMANS   B. SMITH

D. GASKELL

MANCHESTER UNITED

Referee: Mr. G. W. HILL.   Linesmen: Mr. A. DAY (Red Flag)
(Newchurch-in-Rossendale)   Mr. E. GREENWOOD (Yellow Flag)

PRICE — ONE PENNY

United's Youth team defeated Burnley 2-0 in a 10 30am kick-off at Turf Moor in the 1st round of the FA Youth Cup. Elms put United ahead in the first half and, despite strong Burnley pressure, the away side held out until the interval. A goal by Lawton in the second half put the game beyond Burnley.

The win earned United an away tie at Blackpool in the next round.

United Reserves

Also at Turf Moor with an afternoon kick-off the reserve side were always too strong for Burnley reserves, easily winning the game 3-0 to retain top position in the table.

Harrop, Charlton and Scanlon scored the goals.

Wales   **0**   **England**   **4**

With the match played in pouring rain for long periods, England had no trouble overcoming a poor Welsh team in front of their own fans at Ninian Park. The hopes of the 60,000 crowd were dashed after only 5 minutes when Wales left-back HOPKINS turned and put the ball into his own net beyond the bemused Kelsey. England took control with the half-back line of Clayton, Wright and Edwards outstanding.

In the 39th minute HAYNES added a second goal when he hit a low shot into the net from a Taylor pass.

The goal of the game came in the 64th minute when outside-left FINNEY received the ball, dummied beyond two defenders before scoring with a right foot shot. Minutes later HAYNES took aim and scored from the edge of the penalty area for number four.

Bowen never gave up for Wales and Kelsey made some superb saves to keep the score respectable.

In the England side Taylor and Kevan surprisingly had little impact on the game.

Mon. 21st Oct.

Following a three hour meeting in London of Football League 1st and 2nd Division Chairmen together with representatives from the 3rd Division it was reported that some financial changes could be introduced next season. Amongst the subjects considered were:

a) **£20 maximum weekly wage payable to players throughout the year.**
b) **2½% share of transfer fees for players.**
c) **Doubled signing on fees.**
d) **Increased fee for referees.**

The Management Committee would now consider further suggestions and amendments for consideration at a future meeting.

Tues. 22nd October
FA Charity Shield at Old Trafford

Manchester United 4   Aston Villa 0

Taylor 3, Berry

Att. 27,293

Manchester United-*Wood, Foulkes, Byrne, Goodwin, Blanchflower, Edwards, Berry, Whelan, Taylor, Viollet, Pegg.*
Aston Villa-*Sims, Lynn, Aldis, Crowther, Dugdale, Saward, Smith, Sewell, Pace, Myerscough, McParland.*

The game did not catch the imagination of the Manchester public and a surprisingly low attendance of just over 27,000 saw United take to the field with their three England regulars back on duty.

As Colman will be playing for the England 'B' side tomorrow in Sheffield, Goodwin deputised at right-half.

Supporters were surprised to see Wood and McParland appear together on the centre-spot to shake hands as rival captains for the night, in an attempt to draw a line under the events from the FA Cup Final.

United dominated the game for long periods during the opening hour without being able to make their superiority pay dividends.

Berry and Pegg, on the flanks, were a constant menace and Taylor led the line with skill and purpose. After only a few minutes he beat Lynn and crossed to Viollet who was unlucky to see his shot hit Sims. Viollet then laid on an opportunity for Berry who carefully placed his shot only to see it hit the post.

Despite United's pressure, Villa were always dangerous on the breakaway and Wood had to be alert to save a strong drive from Saward.

The Aston Villa half-back line of Crowther, Dugdale and Saward were determined to keep United out but eventually, after sixty minutes, the deadlock was broken. Pegg shot only to see the ball deflect off a defender and crawl along the goal-line. TAYLOR was awake to the opportunity and dashed forward to score from close range whilst, at the same time, colliding with the post.

Four minutes later Edwards hit a pinpoint cross giving TAYLOR the simplest of chances to put United two ahead.

After being fouled just outside the penalty area Berry took the free kick himself hitting a forceful ground shot through a ruck of bodies. Sims was unsighted and at the last minute made a desperate save but the ball rebounded off his chest into the path of TAYLOR who completed his hat-trick with ease.

Aston Villa
Back row l. to r. Aldis, Saward, Lynn, Crowther, Sims, Dugdale, Pace, Birch.
Front row E. Houghton (manager), Smith, Sewell, Myerscough, Dixon,
McParland, W. Moore (trainer).

BERRY scored a fourth goal from the penalty spot late in the game to finish the scoring.

United captain and England full-back Roger Byrne had a wonderful game, breaking up the Villa attacks whilst having time to push United forward down the left wing. Many in the press box were of the opinion that Tommy Taylor had just played his best game in a United shirt.

Viollet turns to congratulate Taylor on his hat-trick

The Cup winners have now failed to beat the League Champions in the Charity Shield since 1936. United had gained sweet revenge for the bitter disappointment of their Cup Final defeat against the same opposition.

Wed. 23rd Oct.

Scotland Under 23's	4	Holland Under 23's	1

Inter City Fairs Cup

London	2	Lausanne	0
Birmingham City	4	Barcelona	3

Sheffield Centenary Game

SHEFFIELD. 4. Colours : Red Shirts, Black Shorts.

A. HODGKINSON
(Sheffield United)

2 I. SHORT 3 G. SHAW
(Barnsley) (Sheffield United)

4 D. GIBSON 5 D. W. McEVOY 6 K. KEYWORTH
(Sheffield Wednesday) (Sheffield Wednesday) (Rotherham United)

7 A. FINNEY 8 A. QUIXALL 1. 9 D. M. HAWKSWORTH 2. 10 R. HOWITT. 1. 11 R. WALKER
(Sheffield Wed.) (Sheffield Wed.) (Sheffield United) (Sheffield United) (Doncaster Rov.)

Referee :
R. J. LEAFE,
Nottingham.

KICK OFF
WITH
Bassetts
LIQUORICE
ALLSORTS

Linesmen :
G. McCABE (Red Flag) :
R. RYALLS (Yellow Flag).

11 W. PERRY 10 J. BARRETT 9 R. ALLEN. 2. 8 R. ROBSON 3. 7 B. DOUGLAS
(Blackpool) (Nottingham Forest) (West Brom. Alb.) (West Brom. Alb.) (Blackburn Rovers)

6 R. FLOWERS 5 R. GRATRIX 4 E. COLMAN
(Wolverhampton Wanderers) (Blackpool) (Manchester United)

3 D. EVANS 2 I. BOND
(Arsenal) (West Ham United)

F. ELSE
(Preston North End)

ENGLAND 'B'. 5. Colours : White Shirts, Blue Shorts.

In an amazing first half at Hillsborough seven goals were scored as England 'B' eventually defeated a Sheffield XI by 5-4 in a game to mark the Sheffield Centenary.

Robson was outstanding for the England side, scoring a hat trick and he could have had more. Allen netted the other two goals.

For the Sheffield XI Quixall scored one and had a hand in two others taken by Hawksworth with Howitt making it four. Finney from Sheffield Wednesday showed his skills for the home side and was the best winger on display.

Fri. 25ᵗʰ Oct.

United's clash at West Brom. tomorrow is undoubtedly the match of the day. Albion have only lost once this season whereas United have already suffered four defeats and are losing their look of invincibility.

Viollet will be missing through injury and Charlton takes his place at No.10. Goodwin will again play at right-half with Colman rested. Byrne, Edwards and Taylor will return from international duty.

For Albion full-back, Williams, has a heavy cold and Setters will switch to his position with Howe returning at right-back. A fascinating struggle is in store between Albion's forwards Robson, Kevan and Allen against the United half-back line of Goodwin, Blanchflower and Edwards.

Sat. 26ᵗʰ Oct.

SATURDAY 26ᵀᴴ OCTOBER

BIRMINGHAM C. 5   BOLTON W. 1
Brown 2, Orritt, Murphy   Parry
Watts   Att. 26,225

BURNLEY 3   ASTON VILLA 0
Pilkington 2, Newlands
                  Att. 20,860

CHELSEA 0   ARSENAL 0
                  Att. 66,007

MANCHESTER C. 2   LUTON TOWN 2
Barlow, McAdams   Pearce, Turner
                  Att. 30,654

NEWCASTLE U. 1   WOLVES 1
Curry   Deeley
                  Att. 44,361

NOTTINGHAM F. 1   BLACKPOOL 2
Barrett (pen)   Perry, Durie
                  Att. 41,586

PORTSMOUTH 2   LEICESTER CITY 0
Mansell, Gordon
                  Att. 25,949

PRESTON N.E. 3   EVERTON 1
Mayers 2, Finney   Harris J.
                  Att. 31,449

SHEFFIELD WED. 3   SUNDERLAND 3
Froggatt, Quixall   Grainger, O'Neill
Young   Spencer
                  Att. 21,168

TOTTENHAM H. 2   LEEDS UNITED 0
Medwin, Smith
                  Att. 33,860

WEST BROM. ALB. 4   MANCHESTER U. 3
Robson 2, Allen,   Taylor 2, Whelan
Kevan   Att. 52,664

	P.	W.	L.	D.	F.	A.	Pts.
Wolverhampton Wanderers	15	10	2	3	40	17	23
West Bromwich Albion	15	7	1	7	37	21	21
Everton	13	7	2	4	24	19	18
MANCHESTER UNITED	14	8	5	1	37	25	17
Manchester City	14	8	5	1	35	38	17
Nottingham Forest	14	8	5	1	30	21	17
Preston North End	14	8	5	1	29	19	17
Arsenal	15	7	5	3	25	21	17
Luton Town	14	7	5	2	18	16	16
Bolton Wanderers	14	6	5	3	24	25	15
Chelsea	14	5	5	4	30	27	14
Blackpool	13	6	6	1	24	22	13
Burnley	14	5	6	3	25	28	13
Birmingham City	15	5	7	3	27	36	13
Leeds United	15	5	7	3	17	25	13
Tottenham Hotspur	15	5	8	2	32	38	12
Portsmouth	14	5	7	2	24	26	12
Newcastle United	14	4	7	3	21	22	11
Aston Villa	15	4	9	2	22	34	10
Sunderland	15	3	8	4	18	38	10
Sheffield Wednesday	14	3	9	2	18	30	8
Leicester City	14	3	10	1	26	35	7

West Brom. Alb	4	Manchester Utd	3

Robson 2, Kevan, Allen   Taylor 2, Whelan

Att. 52,664

West Brom. Alb. *Sanders, Howe, Setters, Dudley, Kennedy, Barlow, Griffin, Robson, Allen, Kevan, Horobin.*
Manchester Utd. *Wood, Foulkes, Byrne, Goodwin, Blanchflower, Edwards, Berry, Whelan, Taylor, Charlton, Pegg.*

A light rain was falling as Albion kicked off in front of a crowd in the region of 50,000. In the first incident of the game Allen was brought down before he scarcely crossed the half-way line.

He resumed after attention from the trainer and the referee gave a bounce up. Albion were the first to make headway but Allen and then Robson failed to make contact on the slippery surface.

Manchester, however, were the first to make real headway and, after 7 minutes took the lead.

TAYLOR seized on a pass from Whelan to put the ball beyond Sanders. United continued to keep on top and once again Taylor nearly broke through, Sanders clearing in the nick of time.

When Albion equalized after 16 minutes it came as rather a surprise, so much had they been on the defensive. Horobin crossed the ball from the left touchline to Allen who pushed it forward to **ROBSON**. He lobbed the ball over Woods' head from about 12 yards range-a finely taken goal. This goal put new life into Albion and they swung into attack.

First Allen was just wide with a long shot and then, following a free kick awarded against Edwards, he tested Wood.

After 22 minutes however, United went in front again. A free kick was awarded against Setters when he brought Berry down near the touchline. Berry placed the free kick well and **TAYLOR** soared above the Albion defenders to deflect the ball neatly past Sanders.

United at this stage looked the more direct and purposeful side and their attack carried the greater threat. Robson, following a free kick just outside the penalty area, well placed by Allen, saw his glancing header
go a foot or so wide.

After 27 minutes Robson again put Albion on level terms. Horobin's accurate cross beat two defenders for **ROBSON** to pick up the ball a few yards from goal and slam it past Wood.

With defenders finding it difficult to gain a footing on the slippery turf, chances were fairly frequent.

KEEN TACKLING

So far the game had not been the classic expected, keen tackling by both sides breaking up attacks before they could properly get in motion.

Barlow set the crowd gasping when taking a pass from Horobin in his stride, he raced through and caused Wood to dive across goal to gather the ball. Then Allen saw a first-timer rebound off Edwards.

At the other end, Dudley came dangerously near to putting a right wing cross through his own goal.

While this was going on, Allen was lying knocked out in a collision in the other half of the field. He quickly resumed, though in a dazed condition. Albion stepped up the intensity of their attack.

Four minutes before the interval Albion went in front. Horobin flung a beautiful long cross-field pass to Griffin on the opposite wing.

The right winger took the ball up to the by-line before screwing it accurately into the goalmouth, where **KEVAN** was beautifully positioned. His head did the rest. Half time **W.B.A. 3 MAN. UTD. 2**

United began the second half determined to get back on level terms. First Kennedy charged down a dangerous looking shot from Edwards and then Whelan again put Charlton through. For the second time the inside left's shot was wide of the mark.

Once again Charlton got clean through. He took the ball a little too far when Sanders advanced but Whelan, gaining possession, screwed it towards the empty goal. It appeared certain to pass the line but Setters appeared from nowhere and handed it out.

The referee did not appear to see the incident but, after consulting with a linesman, awarded the penalty. Berry waited patiently as Sanders spoke to Setters but when the penalty was eventually taken Berry hit it low to the left and Sanders made a great save.

Albion went further ahead in the 60th minute and what a goal!

Manchester United were pressing hard when a long, accurate clearance from Setters put Kevan, who had moved out to the left touchline, in possession. United appealed unsuccessfully for offside.

Kevan raced almost half the length of the field, taking the ball almost to the by-line before crossing accurately to **ALLEN** who tapped home.

Albion had now really turned on the heat and were making splendid use of the through ball.

United fought back hard and **WHELAN** made it 4-3 in the 77th minute. Receiving from the right, he crashed home a hard drive which Sanders appeared to have covered, but the goalkeeper slipped on the wet turf and the ball shot past him into the net.

The final action was a tremendous drive from Barlow which Wood did well to turn round the post.

(Newspaper report of unknown source)

Headlines:

'Spanking for the babes'

'This was a worthy exhibition'

'I'll save it,' says Sanders

Here was a game that, for once, lived up to expectations. One which had the crowd on tip-toe with excitement from start to finish.

West Bromwich Albion and Manchester United, probably the two best footballing sides in the country today, gave an exhibition worthy of their high reputation.

Albion were just about worthy of their victory in a game of thrills, goals and rarely a dull moment.

Blackpool had the better of the opening exchanges in their game at Forest and Thompson was forced to make good saves from Durie and Mudie. Just before half time Armfield prevented a shot from Baily going into the net by using his arm and from the resulting penalty Barrett gave the home side a fortunate lead. Blackpool piled on the pressure in the second half and deservedly equalised in the 50th minute. Matthews created the goal by running half the length of the field before crossing for Perry to score with his head. Durie headed a second goal from a corner and the points were won.

The gates were closed at Stamford Bridge shortly before the kick-off against Arsenal with 66,000 spectators present. Many climbed onto advertisement hoardings for a better view, while others clambered onto the lower platforms of a 200 foot floodlight pylon. Despite both sides having opportunities, the best two players on view were goalkeepers Matthew and Kelsey who repelled everything thrown at them as the game ended in a goalless draw.

Wolves got off to a flier at St James' Park when Deeley gave them the lead in the 2nd minute with a brilliant shot. The home side poured forward in search of an equaliser and after 17 minutes Finlayson could only parry a shot and Curry scored.

Wolves remained the better side throughout the game but missed chances cost them a point as the game ended all square.

At Deepdale, Mayers scored twice against his former team-mates to help Preston beat Everton 3-1. The goal of the game was the second, scored by Finney in the 60th minute. 'With centre-half Jones ever the vigilant watchdog, Finney was too clever for him. A quick shuffle and sidestep and he was through to beat the goalkeeper with a perfectly timed right foot shot into the bottom corner for his eighth goal of the season.'

United Reserves

Manchester United reached the interval only one goal ahead against Preston reserves at Old Trafford in a keenly contested encounter. The goal was scored by Scanlon after 12 minutes, who beat Knowles with a low driven shot. Five minutes after half time Dagger equalised with a splendid goal.

This stirred United into action as they steam-rolled the North End defence scoring five times to win the game at ease 6-1.

Bobby Harrop, playing as a forward instead of his usual role in the half-back line, scored a hat-trick with Dawson netting the other two.

Mon. 28th Oct.

Manchester United announced that the First leg of the European Cup 1st Round game against Dukla of Prague will take place at Old Trafford on November 13th with the return match in Prague the following Wednesday.

Tues. 29th Oct.

England have announced the same side that beat Wales 4-0 for the next game against Ireland at Wembley on November 6th. Chelsea forward, 17 year old Jimmy Greaves, is named at 12th man after having only played 14 first team games. Many shrewd people in the game consider that it will not be long before he makes his International début.

Wed. 30th Oct.

The Football League were rather fortunate to beat the Irish League by 4-2 in Belfast in a game watched by 18,000 spectators. Haynes gave them the lead with a header from an A'Court centre after 15 minutes. The Irish League equalised on the half hour but Murray scored a second for the Football League in the 40th minute after running half the length of the field. Within two minutes the home side equalised once more.

A'Court was a constant threat down the left wing and both Stevens and Haynes hit the woodwork. In the last 15 minutes the Football League scored twice to win the game 4-2. Brabrook netting from a Murray pass and A'Court, deservedly getting his name on the score sheet for the fourth.

Old Trafford hosted the friendly match between an FA XI and an Army XI and those present witnessed a feast of nine goals.

Brian Clough from Middlesbrough scored five times for the FAXI in a perfect example of awareness and marksmanship as his side won 6-3.

Cliff Jones of Swansea was outstanding for the Army XI with his dribbling, speed off the mark and powerful shooting a highlight of the evening.

Thurs. 31ˢᵗ Oct.

Leicester City announced that they had granted the transfer requests of Froggatt, Moran and Morris.

Jeff Whitefoot of Manchester United has been in discussion with Nottingham Forest regarding a possible transfer.

Furnival cartoon from the Lancashire Evening Post

Player Profile

James 'Jimmy' Scoular
Born Livingston, Scotland, 11th January 1925

Jimmy Scoular served in the Royal Navy on HMS Dolphin in Gosport during the Second World War. Whilst playing for Gosport he was spotted by Portsmouth and joined the Club in 1945, making his Football League début in the 1946/47 season.

At Portsmouth he formed a brilliant partnership with his wing-half colleague Jimmy Dickinson and their styles of play could not have been more different. Dickinson, was cultured, cool and graceful whereas Scoular was a tireless worker, fierce tackler with a competitive edge that at times bordered on the reckless.

Portsmouth won the First Division title in the 1948/49 and 1949/50 seasons earning the popular player two Championship medals. Unusually Scoular was sent off and missed the final two games of the successful 49/50 season and his actions were severely criticised in the national and local press.

In May 1951 he was awarded his first International Cap for Scotland in a 3-1 victory against Denmark and won a further eight caps during 51/52. He has not appeared for the national side since with some cynics citing his over-exuberance as being the reason.

After being dropped from the Portsmouth side for two games, Scoular asked for a transfer and in the summer of 1953 moved to Newcastle United for a transfer fee of £22,250 and was immediately made captain of the side. He made his début for his new club against bitter rivals Sunderland in August 1953 and his robust, all action style soon won him over to the Newcastle fans. In 1955 he led Newcastle United to an FA Cup triumph at Wembley when Manchester City were defeated 3-1. His performance was outstanding and he helped to nullify the threat of the City forward line.

Career Appearances (as at 31st July 1957)

		League	Goals
1945/53	PORTSMOUTH	247	8
1953/57	NEWCASTLE UNITE	133	6
1951/52	SCOTLAND	9	

NOVEMBER 1957

Fri. 1st Nov.

Charlton has been left out of the United side to play Burnley at home tomorrow with his place at inside-left being taken by Webster. Viollet is still missing with an ankle injury. Goodwin will remain at right-half in preference to Colman.

Table-topping Wolves will have to be at their best at home to Nottingham Forest if they are to maintain their 100% home record. Forest have impressed since their return to the top flight.

Finney will be absent from the North End side to play Leeds as he has not recovered from the groin injury he suffered last Saturday. He must also be regarded as very doubtful for the England International against Ireland at Wembley on Wednesday.

Third Division South side Bournemouth and Boscombe Athletic have been forced to postpone their game at Gillingham as they have 19 first team players suffering from influenza.

Sat. 2nd Nov.

Wolves increased their lead at the top of the table with a fine 2-0 win against Midland rivals Nottingham Forest whereas nearest challengers West Brom. dropped a point in a hard fought draw at Everton. Albion are the only side in the country who remain unbeaten away from home. Robson could have given them the victory just before the interval but could only watch as his header hit the post and rebounded to safety.

Although Luton beat Birmingham City by 3-0, the score could easily have been doubled had it not been for the superb form of Gil Merrick. In the first half the City 'keeper made three astonishing saves from Pearce, Turner and Brown to keep the score down to a respectable total.

In a game of penalties at Elland Road. Baird scored two from the spot for the home side and Baxter one for the visitors as Preston eventually emerged winners beating Leeds 3-2.

SATURDAY 2nd NOVEMBER 1957

ARSENAL	2	**MANCHESTER C.**	1
Tapscott, Bloomfield		McAdams	
		Att. 43,692	
ASTON VILLA	2	**PORTSMOUTH**	1
Southren, Pace		Stenhouse	
		Att. 28,773	
BLACKPOOL	2	**CHELSEA**	1
Durie, Peterson		Greaves	
		Att. 17,817	
BOLTON W.	5	**SHEFFIELD WED.**	4
Holden, Lofthouse 2		Shiner 2, Finney	
Parry, Birch		Quixall	
		Att. 18,072	
EVERTON	1	**WEST BROM. ALB.**	1
Harris J.		Griffin	
		Att. 53,579	
LEEDS UNITED	2	**PRESTON N.E.**	3
Baird 2 (2pens)		Alston, Baxter (pen),	
		Mayers	
		Att. 23,832	
LEICESTER CITY	2	**NEWCASTLE UTD.**	1
Gardiner, Russell		Batty	
		Att. 32,884	
LUTON TOWN	3	**BIRMINGHAM C.**	0
Turner 2, McLeod			
		Att. 17,316	
MANCHESTER U.	1	**BURNLEY**	0
Taylor			
		Att. 49,689	
SUNDERLAND	1	**TOTTENHAM H.**	1
Bingham		Brooks	
		Att. 36,091	
WOLVES	2	**NOTTINGHAM F.**	0
Broadbent, Deeley			
		Att. 47,858	

At Bloomfield Road in the early exchanges, Chelsea goalkeeper, Matthews, made good saves from Perry, Durie and Mudie whilst Whittaker also cleared off the line.

Completely against the run of play Greaves scored an opportunist goal from a cross by Block to send the away side into the interval ahead 1-0.

Ernie Taylor, who has been left out of the Blackpool side and has asked for a transfer, could only watch as his replacement, Peterson, had a great match scoring the second goal to win the game (Durie having equalised earlier) as Blackpool eventually capitalised on their superiority.

142

Manchester United   1   Burnley   0

Taylor   Att. 49,689

Manchester United-*Wood, Foulkes, Byrne, Goodwin, Blanchflower, Edwards, Berry, Whelan, Taylor, Webster, Pegg.*

Burnley-*McDonald, Smith, Winton, Seith, Adamson, Shannon, Newlands, McIlroy, Pointer, Cheesebrough, Pilkington.*

United returned to winning ways with a hard earned one goal victory against a tireless, hard-working Burnley side who never gave up the chase. The encounter was not a classic with chances few and far between but United always looked as though they would just 'shade the game'.

The goal, when it finally arrived, was worth the wait and inevitably Edwards was involved in the build-up. Upon receiving the ball Edwards played a quick pass to Taylor. The centre-forward played the ball back to Edwards at head height and, quick as a flash, the No.6 headed it back into the path of TAYLOR. The England centre-forward ran onto the perfectly placed ball unleashing a powerful shot from just outside the penalty area giving the Burnley 'keeper no chance.

Edwards was back at his best, pushing his side forward at every opportunity. His strength, eye for a pass and non-stop work-rate kept the Burnley defenders on their toes from start to finish.

The only criticism of his play was that at times Goodwin looked a little exposed as the left-half neglected his defensive duties.

Taylor worked hard for his team but was never given much room or opportunity by Adamson to extend the lead. Berry was also dangerous down the right flank and with a little luck could have got his name on the score sheet.

Burnley also had their moments, none more so than in the final few minutes, when Wood made a brilliant save from a shot by Pilkington. Then from the resulting corner Seith won the ball in the air only to see his header clear the cross-bar.

The silky skills of Viollet were badly missed by United and his replacement, Webster, had a disappointing game.

Burnley never allowed the United forwards any time on the ball and their tight marking and tigerish tackling upset the rhythm of the home side.

A hard earned win was a reminder to United that sometimes results have to be grafted for and cannot always just be achieved with fast flowing football.

Burnley

Back row l to r- L. Shannon, D. Smith, C. McDonald, D. Winton, R. Seith. Front row- D. Newlands, J. McIlroy, A. Shackleton, J. Adamson, A. Cheesebrough, B. Pilkington.

United Reserves

After hitting 6 goals against Preston last week, United reserves almost repeated the performance but had to settle for one goal less as they defeated Newcastle United reserves 5-0 at St James' Park.

Scanlon, Charlton and a McMichael own goal and two from Harrop completed the scoring.

Harrop has now scored 8 goals in the last four reserve games.

TOP OF THE TABLE

	P	W	D	L	F	A	Pts
Man. Utd.	16	11	2	3	56	25	24
Sheff. W.	15	10	2	3	31	15	22
Everton	14	9	3	2	41	19	21
Wolves	15	8	3	4	35	26	19
Bury	15	8	2	5	34	27	18
Liverpool	14	8	1	5	41	25	17

Burnley Res.	2	Bolton Res..	1
Bury Res....	1	Everton Res.	2
Chesterf'd R	3	Barnsley R.	0
Hudd'sf'd R	4	Derby Res. .	2.
Liverpool R.	9	Blackburn R.	1
Man. C. R.	5	Aston V. R.	0
Newcastle ᴖ	0	Man. U. R.	5
Preston Res.	2	Leeds U. R. .	0
Sheff. W. R.	1	Wolves R...	0
Stoke C. R.	2	Blackpool R.	0
W. Brom R.	2	Sheff. U. R.	1

Mon. 4ᵗʰ Nov.

A crowd of over 34,000 flocked to Burnden Park to see the floodlit friendly match between Bolton Wanderers and C. D. S. A. (Moscow) also known as The Red Army.

The main difference between the two sides in the opening half hour was Nat Lofthouse who gave an outstanding exhibition of how to 'lead the line'. Parry gave Bolton the lead in the 28ᵗʰ minute from the penalty spot following a foul by the goalkeeper on Stevens and two minutes later Lofthouse scored with a towering header. Lofthouse was then taken off suffering from concussion. His place was taken by Gubbins who added his name to the score sheet almost immediately.

The Russian side committed a number of petty fouls in the second half in an attempt to 'mix it up' but it made no difference to the final result as Bolton won comfortably 3-1.

Tues. 5ᵗʰ Nov.

It was reported that Tom Finney had failed a fitness test following his groin injury and will miss the game against Ireland at Wembley tomorrow. His place at outside-left will be taken by Alan A' Court from Liverpool who has previously played four times for the England Under 23's.

This is only the eighth time in twelve seasons that Finney has missed a game for England, the player having now won 68 caps.

Tommy Taylor from Manchester United will also face a late fitness test but is expected to play. Jimmy Greaves from Chelsea is on standby just in case he is needed.

Wed. 6ᵗʰ Nov.

Ernie Taylor of Blackpool has been placed on the transfer list at his own request.

In the first round of the Lancashire Senior Cup, United beat Bolton Wanderers 3-1. Scanlon, Brennan and Hunter were the scorers.

Scotland beat Switzerland 3-2 at Hampden Park, watched by a crowd of 56,811, to qualify for the Finals of the 1958 World Cup Competition in Sweden. They were rather fortunate to win the game as the Swiss played some delightful football.

Robertson gave the home side the lead after half an hour, following an inch perfect pass from Docherty. Then the Scottish captain made a mistake as his misplaced pass was seized upon by Riva to equalise.

Mudie restored Scotland's lead and Scott added the third from, what looked like, an off-side position.

The Swiss pulled a goal back but Scotland hung on for an important victory.

SCOTLAND TEAM-*Younger* (Liverpool), **Parker** (Falkirk), **Caldow** (Rangers), **Fernie, Evans** (Celtic), **Docherty** (captain) (Preston), **Scott** (Rangers), **Collins** (Celtic), **Mudie** (Blackpool), **Robertson, Ring** (Clyde).

ENGLAND	2	IRELAND	3

A'Court, Edwards   McIlroy (pen.), McCrory, Simpson.

Att. 40,000

What a pity such an exciting encounter on a Wednesday afternoon at Wembley was only seen by 40,000 football fans.

After a run of 16 unbeaten games England finally lost a match most critics said that they would win easily.

The main reasons for the defeat were: a) The magnificent performance of Harry Gregg of Doncaster Rovers in the Irish goal, b) The poor finishing of the English forwards, c) The sheer determination of the Irish to win against England for the first time since 1927.

England dominated the early stages of the game and Douglas was desperately unlucky not to score when his header hit the cross-bar and rebounded to safety.

Shortly afterwards A'Court out-sprinted the full-back down the left wing and hit a high cross into the penalty area. Gregg came off his line but Taylor beat him to the ball only to see his header cleared by a defender.

The Irish sprang into life and after 32 minutes McILROY received the ball in the England penalty area and was unceremoniously brought down by a combination of Wright and Hopkinson. The player brushed himself down and took the penalty, placing it to the right of the 'keeper. He was rather fortunate that the ball hit the post and then the shoulder of Hopkinson before nestling in the net.

Edwards and Clayton both had shots at goal but half time was reached with England one goal down.

Early in the second half England were finally rewarded for their pressure when A'COURT scored a début goal from an acute angle following a pass from Kevan.

On the hour mark a tangle in the England defence allowed McCRORY (again on International début) to shoot home from just inside the penalty area. The ball going into the net off the post.

In the 71ˢᵗ minute Ireland scored a third when Bingham crossed and SIMPSON headed into the net from a suspiciously looking off-side position. England pushed forward in earnest with Douglas outstanding on the right flank, causing the Irish defence problems with his probing runs.

Eventually ten minutes from time England pulled a goal back from a flowing move. Douglas placed the ball to the edge of the penalty area for EDWARDS to slam home a right foot shot.

The Irish half-back line was then fully tested as, first Clayton had a shot and a Kevan header were brilliantly saved by Gregg. McMichael then dived full-length to prevent a shot from Kevan crossing the line.

The Irish side hung on for a famous victory and hundreds of green clad supporters invaded the pitch in celebration.

ENGLAND-Hopkinson (Bolton W.), **Howe** (W.B.A.), **Byrne** (Manchester U.), **Clayton** (Blackburn R.), **Wright** (Wolves) (Capt.), **Edwards** (Manchester U.) **Douglas** (Blackburn R.), **Kevan** (W.B.A.), **Taylor** (Manchester U.), **Haynes** (Fulham), **A'Court** (Liverpool).

IRELAND-Gregg (Doncaster R.), **Keith** (Newcastle U.), **McMichael** (Newcastle U.), **Blanchflower D.** (Tottenham H.), (Capt.), **Blanchflower J,**

147

(Manchester U.), **Peacock** *(Celtic)*, **Bingham** *(Sunderland)*, **McCrory** *(Southend U.)*, **Simpson** *(Rangers)*, **McIlroy** *(Burnley)*, **McParland** *(Aston V.)*.

Fri. 8ᵗʰ Nov.

A full house is expected at Deepdale for the visit of 'Champions' Manchester United.

North End have won all their seven home games this season and have not lost on home soil since 20ᵗʰ August 1956 when Manchester United beat them 3-1.

The teams presently occupy third and fourth places in the table with identical playing records except Preston have a superior goal average.

Finney is again regarded as doubtful with his groin strain and will face an early morning fitness test. If he does not pass, Alston will play at centre-forward.

Viollet is still unfit and United have named an unchanged side that defeated Burnley last Saturday. Goodwin (the Lancashire cricketer) retains his place at right-half in preference to Colman who will play in the reserve team against Liverpool.

Top of the table Wolves face Portsmouth at Fratton Park having not lost a League game since 7ᵗʰ September. The away side have been forced to make a change as goalkeeper Finlayson is unfit and his place will be taken by Dwyer.

England 'B' outside-right, Harry Hooper, has been placed on the transfer list at his own request. He has not made a first team appearance this season due to the brilliant form of Norman Deeley.

There is an interesting encounter in the Midlands as West Bromwich Albion face Aston Villa. The Albion have only lost one game this season and should have no difficulty in overcoming a Villa side who have a number of injury problems and flu victims.

Cunliffe, a twenty-one-year-old part-time player, will make his début for Bolton at No.6 in the game against City at Maine Road. The youngster works at the Colliery in Hindley.

Two players will make their débuts following mid-week transfers. Newman joined Leicester City from Birmingham City for £12,000 and Fogarty moved from Glentoran to Sunderland for £3,000.

Saturday 9ᵗʰ November

PRESTON N. E.   **1**   **MANCHESTER UNITED**   **1**

Finney   Whelan   Att. 39,066

Preston North End-*Else, Cunningham, Walton, Docherty, Dunn, O'Farrell, Mayers, Thompson, Finney, Baxter, Taylor.*

Manchester United-*Wood, Foulkes, Byrne, Goodwin, Blanchflower, Edwards, Berry, Whelan, Taylor, Webster, Pegg.*

Roger Byrne leads the United side out at Deepdale

Fine seasonable weather with a frosty nip in the air, came opportunely to swell the 'gate' for Preston North End's attractive visitors Manchester United, whose major aim this season is the hat-trick of League Championship triumphs.

The outcome of recent meetings of these Lancashire rivals was encouraging to Manchester enthusiasts, for the United are credited with six wins in their last seven games at Deepdale.

Against this impressive record may be set Preston's feat of having won all their seven home League games this season, and by their convincing goal figures. This sequence falls into a pattern of invincibility in League and Cup games since August of last year.

It may be an ominous coincidence that Manchester United were the last English side to beat them on August 20th 1956. Preston in the meantime, have won 23 and drawn three of 26 League matches at home.

Two of the more noted contestants in an array sparkling with big names-Finney, and his England full-back colleague Byrne- were doubtful starters this morning. Happily, both were able to play.

Finney passed a fitness test, and Byrne put up with pain and irritation of a boil under an armpit. It troubled him so much at one period that United sent post-haste for his understudy, Greaves, who joined the party at Bolton.

Not the least potent magnate for the 39,000 crowd was the appearance on opposite sides of England's two most recent centre-forwards Taylor and Finney. The game afforded an opportunity to study their sharply contrasted styles.

The pitch was showing the effects of wear and weather, and looked on the heavy side. The sun was obscured and there was only a slight breeze when Manchester United kicked off towards the Town end.

The game had a dramatic opening. Taylor opened up play for Preston with a cross field pass to Mayers, who responded with a first-rate centre. It was wasted through his colleagues becoming hopelessly involved in the middle through making too many moves. In the next attack Taylor repeated his defence splitting move, and it resulted in North End being awarded a first-minute penalty – as harsh a one as I have seen, although Mr Luty had not the slightest hesitation in giving it.

Mayers smartly centred backwards from the by-line, and the ball hit Edwards' left arm. I saw no sign of intent. He could not get out of the way of it. The referee ruled otherwise.

It was poetic justice that Finney, back in the role of penalty taker, should fail to score. His spot kick had little power behind it, and it was almost straight. Wood parried it out to Baxter, who would not risk a first time drive. He moved forward, determined to pick his spot, and Wood beat out his slanting shot. The ball travelled to Thompson, whose effort to score at the third attempt was frustrated by an intervening defender.

Manchester United have won several matches this season by striking an early blow. They believe in getting a quick one in first.

They tried to do this at Preston's expense. The only tangible outcome of their striving was a well taken short range opportunist shot, by Pegg which Else caught a foot from the ground. Preston were terrier like in their tackling. Even Baxter chipped in with a timely obstructing foot. Dunn watched Taylor closely, Walton clung-not literally-to Berry. Cunningham met Pegg's threats at the source.

Nevertheless, North End owed their avoidance of a setback to a superb save by Else from a 25-yard power-drive by Webster. The forward took his chance splendidly. He hit the ball accurately with all his strength. The force of it almost caused the ball to bounce out of Else's grasp as he took it expertly.

Soon afterwards Else was called upon for a repeat performance which he achieved to the discomfiture of Taylor, who showed that he too knew how to find the target when given a yard of latitude.

Else was in action again, gathering long balls, when Walton and Cunningham, in turn passed back to him at some distance. North End's forwards could not make headway, whereas United were constantly assertive and thrustful. Cunningham stopped Pegg with a brilliant tackle, and Docherty came away with the ball from Webster. Walton was less successful with a similar spoiling effort. Berry beat him, and Preston followers were relieved when Dunn and Docherty between them scrambled the ball away.

North End's first chance since the start came when Taylor ran into the middle and tried to beat Wood with a first time shot from a corner kick placed along the ground by Mayers. His aim was well wide, and O'Farrell was also out of direction with a long range shot.

Byrne handled a foot outside the penalty area when Thompson, who had lost a chance of breaking in through hesitating a second, tried to redeem his failure by passing to Mayers. North End's elaborate strategy of 'dummying' when Docherty took this free-kick and passed back instead, was a fiasco. While the idea was good, the execution did not match it.

Manchester came through a harassing five minutes without a rebuff, although they had an escape when a short centre from the line by Finney led to a struggle in the goal area. A packed defence prevailed.

United seized every chance to get in a shot, with Pegg particularly persistent. Rising drives by him from the right, then the left wing, cleared the bar by a foot.

A neat bout of triangular passing involving Finney, Docherty and Mayers ended with, I thought, a mistaken off-sided decision against Mayers, who appeared on-side when Finney thrust the ball forward for the wing man to chase it. It was an instance of intelligent anticipation being penalised.

A breakaway by Taylor looked ominous. Dunn chased him after losing a yard of ground through turning in the expectation of offside. Too far ahead to be caught, Taylor advanced and narrowly missed with a well taken drive which he intended to pass across Else and over his head.

North End replied with a delightful clear-cut effort by Mayers and Finney. Mayers' perfect pass found Finney in a scoring position, and only a great save by Wood prevented a goal.

Another choice pass by Finney presented a capital chance to Thompson. Again he dallied, and good scheming went to waste through his inability to attempt a scoring shot without hesitation.

Another alarm to United occurred when Taylor judiciously placed a centre to the far side of goal. Thompson was going for it when the ball glanced off Edwards for a corner. It only just missed scraping in off the near post.

The football was fulfilling everyone's hopes of a fine game between two accomplished teams.

Taylor and Whelan were dangerous for United. Preston fought off the challenge, and retaliated with a well-designed attack, which culminated in Mayers being adjudged offside from a through pass by Thompson. North End then had a fright when Else only partially cleared a corner kick by Berry. He was out of his goal by eight yards when the ball was headed over him. Sound covering prevented a goal, although Else had to fling himself at Taylor's feet before the peril was finally liquidated.

Finney tricked Blanchflower out on the left wing by deft footwork and from his pass Taylor brought Wood to his knees with a grand shot. More spoon feeding of Thompson by Finney was unrewarded owing to a too forceful pass by Thompson when Mayers was running in for the ball. A back header by Baxter from Else's goal kick put North End in trouble. United gained possession to force a corner.

North End's defence resolutely repelled the danger without gaining much relief. United came again, and Else was out of goal when Cunningham cleared off the line. During this assault Dunn suffered a severe shaking and had his shoulder hurt. He required attention before he could resume.

Docherty's worrying of Pegg forced the menacing left winger to shoot wide after promisingly working his way forward. Cunningham enjoyed his tussles with Pegg, whom he beat again close on the interval, to finish with a rousing clearance.

Manchester were a more threatening side. They could not find any loopholes, even though Else had to make a spectacular punched-out clearance.

Half-time: Preston North End 0 Manchester United 0

The game maintained its high pitch of interest and excitement. Manchester United resumed bent upon making good their isolated lapses of the first half. Twice in the opening minutes Whelan received good passes when in a position to shoot. His first effort passed wide. His second, which he really meant to go in, was gloriously beaten out by Else, who flung himself sideways to meet it.

Twice, when North End replied, Finney was overpowered by two opponents. He came again, and defeated Blanchflower, to cut in and centre to the far side of goal. Mayers had a good chance of scoring at short range. He missed it by shooting into the side netting, and hung his head in shame.

Preston North End

Standing – T. Docherty, W. Cunningham, F. Else, J. Dunn, J. Walton, F. O'Farrell

Seated – D. Mayers, T. Thompson, T. Finney, J. Baxter, S. Taylor.

Although a hard game, with the contestants all keyed up to make a supreme effort, as befits a challenge match, it was fought out in a sportsmanlike way by both teams. There were periodic fouls through an excess of zeal, of course. They were mainly of a technical character. The play was never dirty.

It was hardly possible to fault one player in either defence. All gave of their best. Yet I would single out Dunn for his steadiness against Taylor, and O'Farrell too, earned praise for curbing Whelan, one of the best opportunists in the game. No one on the home side worked as tirelessly as Docherty. Cunningham still thoroughly relished his duels with Pegg and Walton, anxious to shine against his old club, allowed Berry little scope.

Finney did his best to inspire his colleagues in attack. Only he could really be said to have the beating of United's powerful rear-guard. He made an opening for Mayers, who had suddenly appeared on the left wing by an adroit feint and perfect pass. Mayers' dangerous oblique shot was swept aside by Wood, who throughout, had kept goal confidently and well.

Wood was there again to make a timely, if desperate, stop when Baxter shot hard after running onto a beautiful far-flung centre by Taylor.

The lights were now on to heighten the game's own illuminated features.

Play still surged on either goal, pendulum fashion, to give the excited crowd full value. Else, stretching himself an extra inch, thrillingly finger-tipped a good attempt by Taylor over the bar. In the next minute Taylor beat him, and

Cunningham, though still feeling the effects of a nasty knock he had received, was composed enough to clear off the goal-line.

If only North End's forwards had been able to match the defenders in general effectiveness, the crowd might not have been still sighing for a 'taste of blood'.

Their share of the laurels was scanty by comparison they were not incisive enough to cut through United's well-drilled defence. Even when a cross drive by Mayers was luckily parried aside, the tall Foulkes got his foot to the ball to concede a corner before Taylor could pounce upon it. Mayers beat the advancing Wood but Byrne cleared from Thompson's feet as he rushed in to score.

United's response was a left wing raid and a cross shot by Pegg which Else fielded cleanly.

North End renewed their efforts and won credit for persistence in spite of many rebuffs. They came again, and in the 71st minute FINNEY had the Preston followers in the 39,066 crowd roaring with delight by scoring. It was a spectacular climax to a persevering bid for supremacy. When Docherty lobbed the ball to the far side of goal Finney was up with it, and his unerring header gave Wood no chance of saving. For almost a minute the exulting partisans cheered frantically.

Thus encouraged, Preston attacked hotly. Finney almost got through. An outstretched foot foiled him at the last second when he had beaten two defenders. Wood saved a slanting drive by Mayers without clearing. The ball was despatched to safety after a scramble for possession.

United rallied. Walton stopped Webster, who had gone on the right wing on one of United's many interchanging moves. Cunningham frustrated Pegg and Dunn got a foot in a second before Taylor.

Twelve minutes from time United got the ball into the net, and if it had counted as a goal there would have been the biggest uproar on this ground for years. United attackers had all been played offside and the linesman's flag was up. Referee Luty ignored his signal.

United pressed on with the defenders having lost position and Edwards beat Dunn, to shoot into the far corner. **The referee gave a goal, then he consulted the linesman, and much to the relief of North End and their supporters the goal was disallowed.**

Byrne, the United captain, was so annoyed that he knocked the referee's arm down as they passed. I saw this and was surprised Mr Luty did not pause to admonish him. Still, it was excusable to some extent in the heat of the game and the bitterness of frustration.

Six minutes from time United got their due. In a good and, this time valid, equalising goal. Edwards nodded a left wing centre onto WHELAN who instantly hooked it through, a fine piece of opportunism.

Mayers was given offside from Thompson's pass when North End fought back. Right to the finish this gripping match maintained its pulsating character.

Result: Preston North End 1 Manchester United 1

SATURDAY 9TH NOVEMBER

BIRMINGHAM C. 2	SUNDERLAND 3	
Murphy, Govan	Revie 2, Bingham	
	Att. 25,315	
BURNLEY 7	LEICESTER CITY 3	
McIlroy 3,Cheesebrough 3	Doherty 2, Hogg	
Pointer	Att. 20,978	
CHELSEA 1	LUTON TOWN 3	
Block	Turner 3	
	Att. 34,102	
MANCHESTER C. 2	BOLTON W. 1	
Hayes, McAdams	Birch	
	Att. 34,147	
NEWCASTLE U. 1	BLACKPOOL 2	
Gratrix (og)	Mudie 2	
	Att. 36,410	
NOTTINGHAM F. 4	ARSENAL 0	
Wilson 2, Barrett, Imlach		
	Att. 34,366	
PORTSMOUTH 1	WOLVES 1	
Dougan	Clamp	
	Att. 38,430	
PRESTON N.E. 1	MANCHESTER U. 1	
Finney	Whelan	
	Att. 39,066	
SHEFFIELD WED. 3	LEEDS UNITED 2	
Froggatt 2,	Forrest, Ripley	
McAnearney J.	Att. 21,469	
TOTTENHAM H. 3	EVERTON 1	
Brooks, Smith,	Temple	
Harmer (pen)	Att. 39,999	
WEST BROM. ALB. 3	ASTON VILLA 2	
Robson, Allen (pen)	Hazelden, Crowther	
Horobin	Att. 41,307	

		Home Goals					Away Goals					
	P	W	D	L	F	A	W	D	L	F	A	Pts
Wolves	17	8	0	0	27	5	3	4	2	16	13	26
W Brom	17	6	3	1	29	15	2	5	0	12	9	24
Man Utd	16	6	0	2	32	9	3	2	3	17	17	20
Preston	16	7	1	0	25	7	2	1	5	8	15	20
Luton	16	6	1	1	15	5	3	1	4	9	12	20
Nottm F	16	4	1	3	18	9	5	0	3	16	14	19
Everton	15	3	4	0	14	8	4	1	3	12	15	19
Arsenal	17	5	1	2	18	11	3	2	4	9	15	19
Man C	16	7	1	0	24	10	2	0	6	14	31	19
Blackpl	15	4	1	3	18	13	4	0	3	10	11	17
Bolton	16	5	2	1	19	10	2	1	5	11	21	17
Burnley	16	6	1	1	26	9	0	2	6	6	23	15
Tottnhm	17	6	1	2	29	16	0	2	6	7	24	15
Chelsea	16	4	2	2	21	12	1	2	5	11	20	14
Portsmth	16	3	3	2	15	12	2	0	6	11	17	13
Birmghm	17	4	1	4	19	17	1	2	5	10	25	13
Leeds U	17	4	2	3	15	12	1	1	6	6	19	13
Sundrlnd	17	3	3	2	11	7	1	2	6	11	34	13
A Villa	17	5	0	2	17	9	0	2	8	9	29	12
Newcstle	16	2	2	4	10	12	2	1	5	13	14	11
Sheff W	16	4	1	3	16	16	0	1	7	9	21	10
Leicestr	16	4	1	3	19	15	0	0	8	12	28	9

Wolves, in a confident mood, headed to the south coast to face a depleted Portsmouth side. What the players in the 'Old Gold' shirts had not allowed for was a 19 year-old, lanky, Irish forward by the name of Derek Dougan.

Young Dougan led Billy Wright a merry dance and, after Clamp had given Wolves the lead early in the second half, the 'Pompey' centre-forward equalised a few minutes later. He received the ball in the penalty area and turned to hammer it beyond Dwyer to earn Portsmouth a point.

After scoring he stood with both arms outstretched above his head as if to acknowledge the cheers of the home fans.

Neither side deserved to lose an enthralling game played in a great spirit.

Another youngster to score a goal, this time on his début, was 16 year-old Walter Hazelden who gave Aston Villa the lead at West Brom. The same player also had a part to play in the move for the second goal but still ended up on the losing side as Albion won 3-2 to gain a point on Wolves at the top of the table. An unusual occurrence happened during the game when Allen scored from the penalty spot and, whilst doing so, burst the ball.

Furnival Cartoon and Match Report from The Lancashire Evening Post

In a quite amazing match at Turf Moor, Leicester City twice took the lead but eventually lost the game 7-3. Two players in the Burnley side scored hat-tricks, McIlroy and Cheesebrough.

United Reserves

Bobby Charlton opened the scoring after 5 minutes in the Central League game at Old Trafford against Liverpool. He was fortunate as his shot was deflected into the net off Bickershaw.

Liverpool pulled a goal back through Arnell to reach the interval level. United missed the sharpness of Alex Dawson in front of goal as he was playing for the Youth side in the FA Youth Cup at Blackpool.

There was little between the two sides in the second half but fortunately Scanlon scored to give United the points. Eddie Colman had an outstanding game.

UNITED TEAM-Clayton, Cope, Jones P., Colman, Jones M., McGuinness, Morgans, Harrop, Brennan, Charlton, Scanlon.

UNITED YOUTH TEAM

In the FA Youth Cup 2nd Round tie at Blackpool United were just too powerful for their opponents, storming into a three goal lead in the first half. All the goals came from Alex Dawson.

In the second half United added four more goals to make the final score 7-0 with Dawson scoring two more and Pearson netting twice.

Tues. 12th Nov.

Manchester United face a difficult match tomorrow against Dukla Prague knowing that they need to establish a lead to take to Prague next week for the return leg.

United don't have any new injury worries and should be able to choose a settled eleven. Dukla have Czechoslovakian internationals throughout the spine of the team.

Wed. 13th Nov.

A crowd of 42,918 at Hampden Park, Glasgow witnessed a rather tepid Home International match between Scotland and Wales which ended in a 1-1 draw.

Scotland took the lead after only 14 minutes and the Welsh supporters feared the worst following their recent heavy defeat against England. The goal came when Gardiner headed the ball down to Collins whose shot was deflected into the net by Mel Charles.

Medwin and Jones were a constant threat to the home defence and, if Vernon had taken the chances offered to him, Wales could have been two goals clear by half time.

Just as it looked as though Scotland would hang on for a 1-0 victory Wales equalised 15 minutes from time.

Jones hit a shot towards goal and Medwin smartly clipped it into the net as it came across in front of him. Two minute from time Jones almost scored the winner with a header from a corner but, fortunately, Younger palmed the ball against the post and the danger was cleared.

The European Cup match between Manchester United and Dukla Prague scheduled for this evening has been postponed following the death of Czechoslovakian President Zapotocky. The Czech Army side have returned home and new dates will be arranged as soon as possible.

In the Inter Cities Fairs Cup match Barcelona beat Birmingham City 1-0 to make the aggregate scores 4-4. A replay date will have to be arranged.

Fri. 15th Nov.

The match of the day tomorrow will be at Molineux where top of the table Wolverhampton Wanderers will face second placed West Bromwich Albion.

Albion are unbeaten away and Wolves have won every home game so an intriguing encounter lies ahead.

Manchester United utility wing-half Jeff Whitefoot yesterday joined Grimsby Town for a fee of £11,500. He made 93 League appearances for United but had not featured in the first team this season.

Colman returns to the side tomorrow in place of Goodwin for the home game against Sheffield Wednesday.

The European Cup tie between United and Dukla will now take place at Old Trafford next Wednesday 20th November with the return match in Czechoslovakia on December 4th.

The 58,000 tickets sold for the original date (13th November) will now be valid for the new date.

Sat. 16th Nov.

Manchester Utd   2   Sheffield Wed. 1

Webster 2   Finney

Att. 41,066

Manchester United-*Wood, Foulkes, Byrne, Colman, Blanchflower, Edwards, Berry, Whelan, Taylor, Webster, Pegg.*
Sheffield Wednesday-*Pllu, Martin, Curtis, McAnearney T., O'Donnell, Hill, Wilkinson, McAnearney J., Shiner, Froggatt, Finney.*

A strangely lethargic United side, perhaps with one eye on Wednesday's European Cup match, just did enough to defeat Sheffield Wednesday with all the goals coming in the first half.

The opening goal came as Wednesday centre-half O'Donnell 'blocked off' Taylor in the penalty area. Referee, Mr Callaghan from Merthyr Tydfil, awarded United an indirect free kick approximately twelve yards from goal. The away defence created a 'human wall' in front of goal and Whelan side-footed the ball to WEBSTER. The inside-forward miss-hit his shot and, with Pllu unsighted, the ball slowly rolled between his legs into the net.

Within five minutes Wednesday were level. A good high cross from the wing was headed home superbly by FINNEY, giving Wood little chance to save.

This equaliser spurred United into action and it was Colman, playing his first league game since 19th October, who started the move after robbing Froggatt of the ball. Colman then found Taylor who laid it wide for Berry. The winger placed his cross beautifully into the path of WEBSTER who met it perfectly with his head. Pllu managed to get both hands to the ball but could only palm it into the roof of the net.

United had an opportunity to seal the game when Whelan was tripped in the penalty area but Berry's effort from the spot was easily saved by the 'keeper.

In the closing minutes Wednesday could have equalised but Wilkinson blasted his shot over the crossbar.

Both goalkeepers had excellent games but Pllu in particular shone with his saves from Pegg, Webster and Edwards remaining in the memory.

The representatives from Dukla Prague in the stands, including the trainer K. Kolskoy, did not see a true reflection of the real United side.

Sheffield Wednesday

Back row – *R. Froggatt, T. McAnearney, A. Broadbent, D. McIntosh, W. Bingley, D. Gibson, R. O'Donnell.*

Seated – *W. Finney, A. Quixall, R. Staniforth, R. Shiner, D. McEvoy, N. Curtis.*

SATURDAY 16TH NOVEMBER 1957

ARSENAL	3	PORTSMOUTH	2
Herd 2, Clapton		Mansell, Gordon	
		Att. 40,532	
ASTON VILLA	1	TOTTENHAM H.	1
Sewell		Smith	
		Att. 28,390	
BLACKPOOL	2	BURNLEY	4
Mudie, H. Kelly (pen)		Shackleton 2,	
		Cheesebrough,	
		Pilkington	
		Att. 21,641	
BOLTON W.	2	NOTTINGHAM F.	0
Holden, Lofthouse			
		Att. 24,562	
EVERTON	0	BIRMINGHAM C.	2
		Murphy 2	
		Att. 34,875	
LEEDS UNITED	2	MANCHESTER C.	4
Baird, Kerfoot		Hayes 2, Barnes,	
		McAdams	
		Att. 23,855	
LEICESTER CITY	1	PRESTON N. E.	3
McDonald		Finney, Thompson	
		Taylor	
		Att. 27,319	
LUTON TOWN	0	NEWCASTLE U.	3
		White 2, Bell	
		Att. 19,703	
MANCHESTER U.	2	SHEFFIELD WED.	1
Webster 2		Finney	
		Att. 41,066	
SUNDERLAND	2	CHELSEA	2
Bingham, Fogarty		Stubbs, Lewis	
		Att. 32,678	
WOLVES	1	WEST BROM. ALB.	1
Clamp		Kevan	
		Att. 55,618	

			Home Goals				Away Goals				
	P	W	D	L	F	A	W	D	L	F	A	Pts
Wolves	18	8	1	0	28	6	3	4	2	16	13	27
W Brom	16	8	3	1	29	13	2	6	0	13	10	25
Preston	17	7	1	0	25	7	3	1	5	11	16	22
Man Utd	17	7	0	2	24	10	3	2	3	17	17	22
Arsenal	18	6	1	2	21	13	3	2	4	9	15	21
Man City	17	7	1	0	24	10	3	0	6	18	33	21
Luton	17	6	1	2	15	8	3	1	4	9	12	20
Nottm F	17	4	1	3	18	9	5	0	4	16	16	19
Everton	16	3	4	1	14	10	4	1	3	12	15	19
Bolton	17	6	2	1	21	10	2	1	5	11	21	19
Blackpool	16	4	1	4	20	17	4	0	3	10	11	17
Burnley	17	6	1	1	26	9	1	2	6	10	25	17
Tottnhm	18	6	1	2	29	16	0	3	6	8	25	16
Chelsea	17	4	2	2	21	12	1	3	5	13	22	15
Birmghm	18	4	1	4	19	17	2	2	5	12	25	15
Sundrlnd	18	3	4	2	13	9	1	2	6	11	34	14
Newcstle	17	2	2	4	10	12	3	1	5	16	14	13
Portsmth	17	3	3	2	15	12	2	0	7	13	20	13
A Villa	18	5	1	2	16	10	0	2	8	9	29	13
Leeds U	18	4	2	4	17	16	1	1	6	6	19	13
Sheff W	17	4	1	3	16	16	0	1	8	10	23	10
Leicester	17	4	1	4	20	18	0	0	8	12	28	9

160

The Midlands derby at Wolverhampton lived up to its pre-match hype as the top two sides strove for the ascendancy in a pulsating game.

Although both teams had chances in the opening forty-five minutes the game reached the interval goal-less.

As the second half began, the crowd of over 55,000, roared both sides forward in a cacophony of noise and it was the Albion who struck first on the hour. Slack marking in the home defence allowed Kevan to slam the ball into the net following a quick throw-in by Griffin.

Just as it looked likely that West Brom. would secure both points and with only five minutes remaining, Wolves were awarded a dubious penalty.

Broadbent appeared to stumble as he dribbled passed Barlow in the penalty area but the referee thought otherwise and Clamp made no mistake from the spot to level the scores.

The outstanding player on view was Albion's centre-forward Ronnie Allen who gave England captain Billy Wright a testing game. He seemed to be involved in all the attacking moves of the away side and his touch was at times majestic.

Many newspaper 'scribes' considered his inclusion in the England team for the game against France to be almost a foregone conclusion on this performance.

FA Cup First Round

The highest scorers in the opening round of the FA Cup were Gillingham who scored 10 against non-league Gorleston with Saunders helping himself to 5. Workington scored 8 against Crook Town.

Non-league Wigan had a great 2-1 win at Southport in a game watched by over 14,000. Wisbech and Bath City also defeated their Football League opposition. The Wisbech side contained three players who had previously appeared in an FA Cup final. Pye, who scored the goal that beat Colchester, played for Wolves in 1949. Crosland appeared for Blackpool in 1948 and Langton for Bolton in 1953.

United Reserves

Manchester United reserves had little problem in winning their sixth consecutive game at Stoke.

The 3-0 victory with goals from Scanlon, Dawson and Charlton maintained their position at the top of the Central League.

Tues. 19th Nov.

The re-arranged European Cup clash between Manchester United and Dukla of Prague will take place at Old Trafford tomorrow evening. With the Dukla side containing a number of Czech. Internationals, United look to be facing a tough encounter. The delay may have helped as Viollet could possibly be fit to play his first game for a month following an ankle injury.

Luton Town have cancelled their friendly game against Athletico Madrid in Spain on Sunday 24th November. The Luton players were due to fly to Spain immediately after their game in London against Spurs on Saturday. The Football League asked that Luton should cancel the game as it was not in the best interests of the League competition and Luton agreed to the request.

It would appear that there is concern that too many friendly matches are being arranged abroad during the season and the Football League Management Committee will discuss the problem at a future meeting.

Charlton are in Milan for a game against the Italian National side on Wednesday and Wolves are in Brussels for a match against Anderlecht. Neither side have had any communication from the Football League.

England have announced two changes for the game against France at Wembley on November 27th. Finney will return at outside-left in place of A'Court and West Brom. forward Robson will replace his team mate Kevan at inside-right.

Wales, after failing to qualify for the World Cup Finals in Sweden, have now been given a second chance. They accepted an invitation to enter a draw of runners-up in the European groups for a chance to play Israel over two legs. The World Cup Organising Committee decided it would be unfair to allow Israel to qualify for the finals without playing a game after the withdrawal of a number of countries in the Asian group.

Wed. 20th Nov.
European Cup First Round 1st Leg

Manchester Utd   **3**   **Dukla of Prague**   **0**

Webster, Taylor, Pegg   Att. 60,000

Manchester United-Wood, Foulkes, Byrne, Colman, Blanchflower, Edwards, Berry, Whelan, Taylor, Webster, Pegg.

Dukla-Pavlis, Jecny, Novak, Pluskal, Cader, Masopust, Vacenovsky, Dvorak, Borovicka, Safranek, Dobal.

During the first half under the floodlights at Old Trafford United failed to create any clear-cut opportunities. In contrast the Czech side played in a calm controlled manor and should have reached the interval ahead.

Outside-left, Dobal, could have done better than see his drive hit the side netting with the goal at his mercy. Dvorak and then Vacenovsky also missed great opportunities through poor finishing.

Taylor and Webster at least tested the goalkeeper as Edwards and Byrne drove the 'Reds' forward.

In the early stages of the second half Edwards started to influence play more and more. His driving runs, superb distribution and boundless energy spurred on his colleagues and on the hour he almost opened the scoring. Receiving the ball just outside the penalty area he crashed a shot goal wards bringing a superb save from Pavlis in the Dukla goal.

Three minutes later United were ahead following a dreadful mistake in the away defence. Colman avoided two defenders in the Czech half before passing the ball to Whelan. The inside-forward placed it into the path of Webster. Pluskal seemed to gain possession but then decided to leave the ball to his goalkeeper. During the melee WEBSTER stuck a foot out and prodded the ball home.

The crowd roared United forward and in the 67th minute they scored again. Webster crossed the ball and TAYLOR met it perfectly on his forehead, the ball crossing the line after hitting a post. The away side now embarked on a damage limitation exercise but in the 75th minute United added a third. Whelan found PEGG unmarked in front of goal and the winger had the simple task of passing the ball into the net.

During the final quarter of an hour the Czech defence was constantly under pressure but despite the promptings of Colman and Edwards United could not add to their total.

Dukla of Prague

Headlines:

Busby Boys Rip Back with Old 1, 2, 3.

Manchester United's Great Victory

Defensive Error Opens the Way for Manchester United

Hugh Kelly, the Blackpool captain (pictured below) had a great game at Goodison Park whilst making his 350th League appearance for the Club. The game ended in a 0-0 draw with both goalkeepers having excellent games in front of a crowd of 47,765.

The player has never been a goal- scoring wing-half and his penalty goal against Burnley last Saturday was his first for Blackpool since August 1950 when he scored against Spurs in a 4-1 victory at White Hart Lane. Incidentally, the Blackpool players stated after the game, that the floodlights were the best they had ever played under-they cost £40,000.

Charlton Athletic drew with the Italian National side in Milan. Ayre put them ahead in the 65th minute with a powerful shot from twenty yards. Nicole equalised for Italy four minutes later.

The match was intended as a trial game to help the Italian selectors pick a side for the important World Cup match against Northern Ireland in Belfast in two weeks' time.

In the other friendly match Wolves lost for the first time under floodlights in Belgium by 2-0 against Anderlecht. They were guilty of missing a number of easy chances.

Thurs. 21st Nov.

The draw for the 3rd Round of the FA Youth Cup has been made and Manchester United have been drawn away to Leeds United.

The game will be played on Saturday December 14th.

Newspapers reported that Eddie Hapgood, the former Arsenal and England captain, had been awarded £1,500 in damages and £10 for slander at Bristol Assizes. Hapgood had been dismissed from his post of Secretary/Manager of Bath City in February 1956.

The award was made against Bath City Chairman Arthur Mortimer who was quoted in a newspaper as saying, "During the past five years the club has done absolutely nothing. Little wonder our gates have dropped as low as 1,200. Our new board is dedicated to putting Bath back in the limelight and that means no Hapgood."

Mr Justice Salmon told the jury that Hapgood had a lifetime of experience in football having played at the highest level for England on 43 occasions. The statement issued to the press by the Bath City Chairman had tarnished his reputation and the jury were advised that the award of the sum would show the world that there was no truth in the imputation.

Fri. 22nd Nov.

Vastly improved Manchester City, after earlier in the season conceding 15 goals in two games, face League leaders Wolves at home. Trautmann faces a late fitness test and, if he fails, his place in goal will be taken by Salford-born Steve Fleet.

In the Wolves side Wilshaw is unfit and Mason will play at inside-right with Broadbent switching to the No.10 slot.

Berry suffered an injury in Wednesday's European Cup victory and will miss the trip to Newcastle tomorrow. His place at outside-right will be taken by Scanlon in an otherwise unchanged team.

Sat. 23rd Nov.

BIRMINGHAM C. 0   BLACKPOOL 0

Att. 32,178

BURNLEY 3   LEEDS UNITED 1
McIlroy, Pilkington,   Baird (pen)
Shackleton

Att. 24,144

CHELSEA 4   LEICESTER CITY 0
Lewis 2, McNichol,
Tindall

Att. 27,757

MANCHESTER C. 3   WOLVES. 4
McAdams, Barnes 2 (1pen)   Murray 2, Mason,
   Broadbent

Att. 45,121

NEWCASTLE U. 1   MANCHESTER U. 2
Mitchell   Edwards, Taylor

Att. 53,950

NOTTINGHAM F. 4   ASTON VILLA 1
Barrett, Quigley,   Crowther
Wilson. Whare

Att. 30,382

PORTSMOUTH 3   EVERTON 2
Mansell, Dougan, Gordon   Temple, Thomas

Att. 27,015

PRESTON N.E. 3   BOLTON W. 0
Stevens (og), Finney,
Thompson

Att. 28,036

SHEFFIELD WED. 2   ARSENAL 0
Quixall (pen), Froggatt

Att. 23,904

TOTTENHAM H. 3   LUTON TOWN 1
Brooks, Medwin 2   Cummins

Att. 41,242

WEST BROM. ALB. 3   SUNDERLAND 0
Kevan, Robson, Setters

Att. 32,522

	P.	W.	L.	D.	F.	A.	Pts.
Wolverhampton Wanderers	19	12	2	5	48	22	29
West Bromwich Albion ...	19	9	1	9	45	25	27
MANCHESTER UNITED...	18	11	5	2	43	28	24
Preston North End	18	11	5	2	39	23	24
Nottingham Forest	18	10	7	1	38	26	21
Manchester City	18	10	7	1	45	47	21
Arsenal	19	9	7	3	30	30	21
Everton	18	7	5	6	28	28	20
Luton Town	18	9	7	2	25	23	20
Burnley	18	8	7	3	39	35	19
Bolton Wanderers ...	18	8	7	3	32	34	19
Blackpool	18	8	7	3	30	28	19
Tottenham Hotspur ...	19	7	8	4	40	42	18
Chelsea	18	6	7	5	38	34	17
Birmingham City ...	19	6	9	4	31	42	16
Portsmouth	18	6	9	3	31	34	15
Sunderland	19	4	9	6	24	46	14
Aston Villa	19	5	11	3	28	43	13
Newcastle United	18	5	10	3	27	28	13
Leeds United·	19	5	11	3	24	38	13
Sheffield Wednesday ...	18	5	11	2	28	39	12
Leicester City	18	4	13	1	32	50	9

As expected Manchester City fielded 19 year old Stephen Fleet in goal for his début at home against League leaders Wolves and he certainly encountered a baptism of fire.

The youngster made a confident start and, although Murray gave the visitors the lead after 25 minutes, goals from McAdams and Barnes sent City into the interval with a 2-1 lead.

In the second half the debutant had to pick the ball out of the net on three occasions as Wolves eventually won a thrilling game 4-3.

The game at White Hart Lane was virtually decided in the opening ten minutes as Spurs galloped into a two goal lead against Luton Town. The first came in the third minute as a quick throw in from Hopkins caught the Luton defence flat-footed and Brooks took his chance to score. Then on ten minutes the same player was involved again playing a through ball to Medwin who shot into the net from just inside the penalty area.

Medwin netted again mid-way through the half when he beat his marker before hitting a precise shot between Baynham and the near post.

Luton scored a consolation goal in the second half through Cummins.

McIlroy put Burnley ahead after only three minutes against Leeds at Turf Moor. The away side fought back but poor finishing let them down and Burnley increased their lead through Pilkington, following a free kick by Seith.

Just before the interval Baird, who was the only Leeds forward to retain his place in the team from the previous game, scored from the penalty spot.

The second half was delayed for six minutes to enable medical staff to assess the referee who was unable to take any further part in the game following a sprained ankle. The senior linesman took over his duties. Burnley were easily the better side after the interval and in the 84th minute Shackleton secured the points after McIlroy had played him through with a defence splitting pass.

Newcastle Utd. 1   Manchester Utd.   2

Mitchell   Edwards, Taylor

Att. 53,950

Newcastle United-*Simpson, Keith, McMichael, Scoular, Stokoe, Franks, Hughes, Eastham, White, Bell, Mitchell.*

Manchester United-*Wood, Foulkes, Byrne, Colman, Blanchflower, Edwards, Scanlon, Whelan, Taylor, Webster, Pegg.*

Everyone wanted to see the League Champions in action at St. James' Park and it was no surprise that the ground hosted the highest attendance of the day, almost 54,000.

Newcastle United gave a home league debut to eighteen-year-old local lad Jackie Bell at inside-left.

Manchester United had much of the early play on a cold but fresh afternoon. Simpson did well to save a header from Taylor and then Scanlon opened up the home defence with a dazzling run but unfortunately his pass to Webster was wasted.

Despite having more of the ball, United found themselves a goal down after 28 minutes. A right-wing centre from Hughes was netted by MITCHELL from just inside the penalty area.

After forty minutes White had a wonderful chance to increase Newcastle's lead but shot wide of an empty net. The teams reached half time with Newcastle having the advantage of a slender lead and the earlier miss was to prove costly.

The second half continued in much the same vein as the first with United well on top but unable to penetrate the steadfast Newcastle defence. Just when it was looking like the home side would hang on to gain the two points United finally struck when, with five minutes remaining, EDWARDS took advantage of the tiring back line to equalise.

The 'Red Devils' threw everything into attack in an onslaught on the Newcastle goal and in the 88th minute got their reward when TAYLOR scored the winner.

The result still leaves them adrift by six points from League leaders Wolverhampton Wanderers albeit that United have one game in hand. Newcastle remain only one point away from the relegation places.

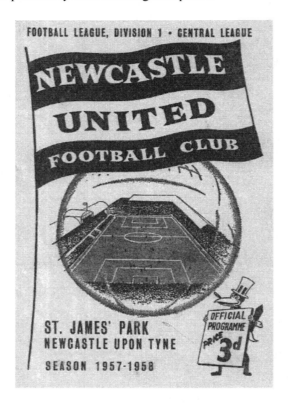

United Reserves

A crowd of approximately 12,000 at Old Trafford had to wait only three minutes for the first goal as Dawson scored from close range. West Brom replied strongly and Gaskell was forced to save from Lee and Whitehouse.

Harrop increased United's lead after 29 minutes and then added another on the stroke of half time. The powerful reserve side were just too strong for their opponents and goals from Dawson and Charlton gave them a comfortable 5-1 victory. They retain top position in the Central League.

Team – Gaskell, Cope, Greaves, Goodwin, M. Jones, McGuinness, Morgans, Harrop, Dawson, Charlton, Hunter.

TOP OF TABLE	P	W	D	L	F	A	Ps
MANCHESTER UNITED	**19**	**14**	**2**	**3**	**66**	**27**	**30**
EVERTON	17	11	3	3	50	24	25
WOLVES	18	11	3	4	49	30	25

NEWCASTLE UNITED 1957-58.

Standing: J. Scoular, R. Batty, R. Stokoe, R. Simpson, A. McMichael, T. Casey.

Seated: J. Hill, R. Davies, W. Curry, G. Eastham, R. Mitchell.

Sports Shorts

The local newspaper reported that Blackpool's Jackie Mudie had received a letter from the Scottish Football Association asking him to return the shirt that he wore in the international against Wales.

Barrett made his one hundredth League appearance for Nottingham Forest and celebrated by giving them the lead in the 4-1 victory against Aston Villa.

Out of the 92 Football League clubs only 6 have not changed their manager since the war – Blackpool, Manchester United, Nottingham Forest and Sheffield Wednesday of the First Division, together with Gillingham and Southport.

TV FOOTBALL DIARY FOR SPORTS FANS

Sat. 23rd November

BBC-Today's Sport 5.45 p.m., Sports Special 10 p.m.

ITV-Sport's Results 5.40 p.m.

Wed. 27th November

BBC-England v France at Wembley 2.30 p.m., Sportsview 9.30 p.m.

ITV-Sport's Outlook 10.30 p.m.

Thurs. 28th November

BBC-Sheffield Wednesday v Juventus 8 p.m.

Mon. 25th Nov.

United wing-half, Freddie Goodwin, was informed today that his request to be placed on the transfer list had been refused.

A BBC spokesman said that they had been asked by the FA to only televise the second half of the England game against France at Wembley on Wednesday. Originally the full game was scheduled to be shown from 2.30 p.m. but the 'unsatisfactory sale of tickets so far for this match' had led to the request with the programme now due to start at 3.25 p.m.

Tues. 26th Nov.

Nine of the side that lost to Northern Ireland earlier in the month have been named in the England team to face France at Wembley tomorrow afternoon. With the World Cup just over six months away it is important that England find a settled side over the last few remaining international fixtures in readiness for the main event.

In the Inter Cities Fairs Cup semi-final play-off in Basle, Barcelona beat Birmingham City 2-1 in a drab game. The winners will now play London in the final.

Wed. 27th Nov.

Rangers lost 4-1 at home to Milano in the 2nd round first leg of the European Cup. Murray had given Rangers the lead in the thirty-first minute after Buffon had initially parried his shot. After the interval the Italians were just too powerful and look to have already cemented their spot in the next round.

Eros Beraldo, the Milano left-back who has a fear of flying, travelled by train and boat to reach Glasgow approximately 36 hours after the rest of the team who flew in on Monday.

European Cup holders Real Madrid qualified for round three after beating Royal Antwerp 6-0 at home.

In Rotterdam Bolton Wanderers beat Feyenoord 3-0 in a friendly match.

England   4   France   0

Despite the mid-week afternoon kick-off and the fact that the second half was live on TV, a crowd in the region of 50,000 still turned out at Wembley to see this friendly game.

They had to wait only three minutes for the first goal as Bryan Douglas beat the full-back on the outside before floating the ball to the edge of the six yard box. Despite the attention of a French defender, TAYLOR reached the ball first and deftly glanced a header into the far top corner of the net. It was Douglas again who tore the French defence to shreds, pulling the ball back from the by-line into the path of ROBSON (pictured below) who had the simple task of slotting home for his first international goal on his début.

The third followed a beautiful through pass from Haynes to TAYLOR, who held off the challenge from two defenders before striking the ball into the net to give England a 3-0 half time lead.

In the second half, Finney hit the cross-bar with a header and then was involved in the fourth goal. Receiving the ball deep in the French half he played it out to Douglas on the right flank. Once more the Blackburn winger proved too tricky for the opposition and laid the ball back for ROBSON to score his second goal of the game.

An easy victory for the home side to help wipe out the memory of the defeat against Ireland.

England Team – Hopkinson (Bolton W.), Howe (W.B.A.), Byrne (Manchester U.), Clayton (Blackburn R.), Wright (Wolves), Edwards (Manchester U.), Douglas (Blackburn R.), Robson (W.B.A.), Taylor (Manchester U.), Haynes (Fulham), Finney (P.N.E.)

Fri. 29th Nov.

League leaders Wolves will have Finlayson back in goal for the home game against Burnley after missing the previous three games.

Bottom club, Leicester City, have recalled transfer listed Morris at right-half, nine weeks since his last appearance, for the game at home against West Brom. Albion have not lost away from home this season.

South African Francis, who paid his own fare to travel to England to play professional football, will make his début for Leeds United at outside-right in the home game against Birmingham City.

Manchester United have been forced to make a change following Tommy Taylor suffering an injury against France on Wednesday. Webster will play at centre-forward with Charlton taking the No. 10 shirt for the home game against Spurs.

Sat. 30th Nov.

SATURDAY 30TH NOVEMBER 1957

ARSENAL	2	NEWCASTLE U 3
Holton, Clapton		Hughes,
		Mitchell 2(1 pen)
		Att. 41,697
ASTON VILLA	2	PRESTON N. E. 2
Lynn (pen)		Thompson, Taylor
McParland		Att. 25,847
BLACKPOOL	2	PORTSMOUTH 1
Mudie, Harris A.		Dickinson
		Att. 14,722
BOLTON W.	3	CHELSEA 3
Parry, Stevens 2		Brabrook, Stubbs
		Lewis J.
		Att. 18,815
EVERTON	1	SHEFFIELD WED. 1
Temple		Dunlop (og)
		Att. 31,011
LEEDS UNITED	1	BIRMINGHAM C. 1
Cush		Orritt
		Att. 21,358
LEICESTER CITY	3	WEST BROM. ALB. 3
Rowley 2, Doherty		Robson 2, Allen
		Att. 33,755
LUTON TOWN	3	NOTTINGHAM F. 1
Turner 3		Gray
		Att. 18,391
MANCHESTER U.	3	TOTTENHAM H. 4
Pegg 2, Whelan		Smith 3,
		Blanchflower J. (og)
		Att. 43,307
SUNDERLAND	2	MANCHESTER C. 1
Revie, Anderson		McAdams
		Att. 35,442
WOLVES	2	BURNLEY 1
Murray, Broadbent		McIlroy
		Att. 32,888

Wolves	20	13	5	2	50	23	31
West Brom. A.	20	9	10	1	48	28	28
Preston N. E.	19	11	3	5	41	25	25
Manchester Utd.	19	11	2	6	46	32	24
Luton Town	19	10	2	7	28	24	22
Nottingham F.	19	10	1	8	39	29	21
Blackpool	19	9	3	7	32	29	21
Everton	19	7	7	5	29	29	21
Arsenal	20	9	3	8	32	33	21
Manchester C.	19	10	1	8	46	49	21
Tottenham H.	20	8	4	8	44	45	20
Bolton W.	19	8	4	7	35	37	20
Burnley	19	8	3	8	40	37	19
Chelsea	19	6	6	7	41	37	18
Birmingham C.	20	6	5	9	33	43	17
Sunderland	20	5	6	9	26	47	16
Newcastle U.	19	6	3	10	30	30	15
Portsmouth	19	6	3	10	32	36	15
Leeds United	20	5	4	11	25	39	14
Aston Villa	20	5	4	11	30	45	14
Sheffield Wed.	19	5	3	11	29	40	13
Leicester City	19	4	2	13	35	53	10

Wolves maintained their top spot with a hard earned 2-1 home victory against Burnley. The away goal had a number of early escapes but in the 8th minute Murray shot Wolves into the lead following some intricate build up play.

McDonald, in the Burnley goal made three brilliant saves to keep his side in the game but in the 48th minute he conceded a further goal. Murray hit a long pass into the Burnley penalty area, where Broadbent neatly flicked it over the head of the advancing goalkeeper and into the net.

The second goal stirred Burnley into action and, mid-way through the second half, McIlroy scored with a ground shot. Wolves withstood some strong pressure to hold on for victory.

Although missing Stanley Matthews, who was suffering from a heavy cold, Blackpool just about deserved their victory over Portsmouth.

Fifteen minutes prior to kick-off on a dank, grey afternoon, only about 8,000 spectators were in the ground. The total eventually swelled to just under 15,000.

Young Sandy Harris created the first goal after seven minutes with a superb cross which Mudie met with a diving header giving Uprichard no chance in the Pompey goal.

Dickinson (pictured below) equalised with a header from a Peter Harris corner five minutes from the interval. Two minutes later Harris was in the right place to score a second for the 'seasiders' from just under the crossbar.

Portsmouth were the better side in the second half but could not force an equaliser.

Sunderland belied their lowly league position with some delightful football in the opening half at home to Manchester City. With only four minutes played they took the lead when Revie lifted the ball over the advancing Trautmann. Anderson added a second with a thunderous shot.

McAdams reduced the arrears early in the second period but City lacked the penetration to score again.

Gordon Turner scored a hat trick, taking his seasons total to 17 as Luton Town beat Nottingham Forest 3-1 to move into fifth place.

Manchester Utd.   3   Tottenham H.   4

Pegg 2, Whelan   Smith 3, Blanchflower J. (Og)

Att. 43,307

Manchester United-*Gaskell, Foulkes, Byrne, Colman, Blanchflower J., Edwards, Scanlon, Whelan, Webster, Charlton, Pegg.*
Tottenham Hotspur-*Ditchburn, Baker, Hopkins, Blanchflower D. Norman, Ryden, Medwin, Brooks, Smith, Harmer, Robb.*

David Gaskell, aged 17, made his League debut in goal for United at Old Trafford as a late replacement for Wood. Irish International colleagues, the Blanchflower brothers, were in opposition to each other.

Five goals were scored in an astonishing first half, but it was United who found themselves 4-1 down.

It had all started so well with PEGG giving the home side the lead in the 18th minute with a clever low drive. Charlton had hit a series of accurate passes to Pegg and it was no surprise when the winger finally scored from one.

The home fans joy was short lived as two minutes later Jackie Blanchflower failed to control the ball and SMITH took full advantage to smash it home. In the 25th minute came goal number 3. Danny Blanchflower received the ball from a throw-in down the left flank and whipped a cross into the penalty area. SMITH reached the ball first and cleverly flicked it over his head and beyond Byrne before driving a shot into the net.

United's woes were compounded when JACKIE BLANCHFLOWER scored an own goal. His brother had played a ball from the right wing into the path of Smith. The United centre-half got to it first but found himself under pressure from the burly No. 9. He turned to pass the ball back to Gaskell only to see that the young goalkeeper had moved from his goal just as he kicked it and could then only watch in horror as it trickled into the net.

Tottenham Hotspur

Back row l to r – Mel Hopkins, Danny Blanchflower, Ted Ditchburn, Maurice Norman, Terry Medwin.

Front row – Johnny Brooks, Tommy Harmer, Johnny Ryden, Bobby Smith, Peter Baker, George Robb.

Unbelievably with half-time approaching Spurs scored a fourth. SMITH was too strong in the air for Blanchflower and easily out-jumped him, before heading the ball into the net for his hat-trick.

The United forward line had been ineffective in the opening 45 minutes and only Pegg looked lively enough to cause Spurs any problems.

A more determined United side emerged for the second half and amazingly the 'Red Devils' had reduced the arrears to one goal with over 20 minutes left to play. In the 63rd minute PEGG scored his second goal and five minutes later WHELAN got United's third.

Duncan Edwards was now influencing the game more and Webster started to dart from one side of the pitch to the other in an attempt to upset the away side's half-back line. Ditchburn was determined to prevent United getting an equaliser and twice saved from Webster.

Despite all their efforts United were unable to add to their total and suffered their first defeat at home to a London club since 1938.

United Reserves

The second team were given a fright at lowly Chesterfield as the determined home side pushed them all the way.

United eventually emerged winners by 3-2 with two goals from Cope and one from Pearson extending their winning sequence to eight games.

Player Profile

Royston James Clarke
Born Newport, Monmouthshire 1ˢᵗ June 1925

Roy Clarke excelled at sport whilst at school, playing table tennis and baseball as well as football. After leaving school Clarke worked down the mines and played recreational football in the local amateur leagues. During The War years he was 'spotted' by Cardiff City and joined the club as an amateur in 1942.

He helped Cardiff win promotion from Division 3 (South) in the 1946/47 season before joining Second Division Manchester City for a fee of £12,000 in May 1947, just before the conclusion of the season. Clarke played in City's final game, a 5-1 win, against Newport County as the Club secured promotion to the First Division.

On the opening day of the following season, Clarke played for City in a Division 1 game against Wolves scoring his first goal for the club. In the process he delighted all 'football anoraks' by achieving the rare feat of playing three consecutive League games at three different levels of football.

His early achievements in the game were soon spotted by the Welsh selectors and he appeared in an unofficial victory international against Ireland in May 1946. He won his first cap against England in November 1948 and at the start of the 1957/58 season had made 22 appearances on the left-wing scoring five international goals. His last game being in April 1956, since when he found his place in the side taken by flying winger Cliff Jones.

At Maine Road, Clarke honed his skills proving a tricky customer down the left flank, head down and with the ability to change his pace when needed, whilst possessing a thunderous left foot shot. Following relegation in 1950 and then an immediate return to the top flight the following season, City became a middle of the table team.

In 1955 he scored the winning goal against Sunderland in the semi-final of the FA Cup at Villa Park before suffering the devastation of missing the Final against Newcastle United as a result of a knee injury. The following season City again reached Wembley and this time Clarke was in the side that beat Birmingham City 3-1 to lift the trophy.

At the start of the current season it appeared that Clarke would be allowed to leave City but an injury to Jack Dyson changed the manager's mind.

Career Appearances (As at 31st July 1957)

		League	Goals
1946/47	CARDIFF CITY	39	11
1947/57	MANCHESTER CITY	343	72
1948/56	WALES	22	5

December 1957

Mon. 2nd Dec.

During last month Stan Cullis, the manager of League leaders Wolves, sold three players. Joe Bonson moved to Cardiff City, Harry Hooper to Birmingham City and Dennis Wilshaw to Stoke City for a combined total of £40,000.

It is interesting to note that in the present Wolves squad only Malcolm Finlayson and Peter Broadbent cost a transfer fee.

Leeds United reported a record profit of £59,966 for the 1956/57 season. The majority of this profit came as a result of the sale of John Charles to Juventus for £65,000.

A fourteen strong Manchester United party arrived in Prague today for their European Cup match on Wednesday only to be greeted by snow, heavy winds and freezing temperatures.

Viollet and Berry were not fit enough to travel but Wood has recovered to take his place in goal. Taylor is expected to resume his role at centre-forward. Mark Jones will play his third senior game of the season at centre-half in place of Jackie Blanchflower who is on international duty with Northern Ireland.

Tues. 3rd Dec.

In Belfast Northern Ireland have a crucial World Cup qualifying match against Italy tomorrow. If they win the game they have a great chance of joining England in the World Cup Finals in Sweden.

The Italians won the game in Rome 1-0 earlier in the year and will provide stern opposition.

The United players had a training session at the stadium this morning in poor conditions. The ground was bone hard with a covering of water and mud due to a slight thaw in temperatures. It was decided that the players would wear normal studs in their boots at a length decided by each individual, unless the conditions change again by tomorrow.

Wed. 4ᵗʰ Dec.
European Cup 1ˢᵗ Round 2ⁿᵈ Leg

Dukla of Prague   1   **Manchester Utd**   0

Dvorak   Att. 35,000

(Manchester United win 3-1 on aggregate)

Dukla of Prague-_Pavlis, Novak, Jecny, Masopust, Cadek, Pluscal, Safranek, Dvorak, Urbun, Borovicks, Vacenovsky._

Manchester United-_Wood, Foulkes, Byrne, Colman, Jones, Edwards, Scanlon, Whelan, Taylor, Webster, Pegg._

After a period of overnight rain the pitch was heavy on the surface but then bone hard underneath making playing conditions far from ideal.

There was little to choose between the two sides in the opening fifteen minutes with both goalkeepers called upon to make good saves to prevent a goal. In the 19ᵗʰ minute Dukla took the lead following good work by Pluskal. He played the ball into the path of DVORAK who scored with a well-placed shot from just inside the penalty area.

The home side played some intricate football that was not really suited to the conditions but the United defence, with Byrne and Colman in particular, outstanding in keeping them at bay.

With half time approaching, Pegg beat a number of defenders in a mazy dribble before the goalkeeper dived at his feet and then Scanlon had a stunning drive well saved.

Duncan Edwards was involved in an ugly clash of heads but appeared to be none the worse as he came out for the second half. Dukla were stronger in the second period and strove manfully to reduce the arrears but the United defence remained resolute, preventing any clear cut opportunities. On one occasion Byrne made a superb interception to prevent Dvorak from shooting for goal.

Little was seen of the United forwards although Taylor headed the ball into the net from a Pegg cross only to have it disallowed for off side. Jones had a powerful game at centre-half and Foulkes was difficult to beat down the left flank.

In the closing minutes Borovicks and Webster had their names taken by the German referee following a nasty challenge and subsequent scuffle, but the game overall was not a dirty one.

Mark Jones emerged at the end with a black eye following an aerial tussle for the ball.

The English newspapers were critical of the United performance and Busby expressed himself as 'disappointed with the result'. Nevertheless United had achieved their objective to reach the last eight of the European Cup.

Later in the day, in Paris, the draw for the next round was made pairing Manchester United with Belgrade Red Star. As United were the first team to be drawn in the pairing they will have the option to play at home or away in the first leg. The two legs must be completed by 28th February.

NORTHERN IRELAND   2   ITALY   2

Cush 2   Ghiggia, Montuori

Att. 40,000

Northern Ireland-Gregg (Doncaster R.), Keith (Newcastle U.), McMichael (Newcastle U.), Blanchflower D. (Spurs), Blanchflower J. (Manchester U.), Peacock (Celtic), Bingham (Sunderland), McIlroy (Burnley), McAdams (Manchester C.), Cush (Leeds U.), McParland (Aston V.).

What was supposed to be a vital World Cup qualifying match ended in a farce following the non-appearance of Hungarian referee Istvan Zsolt and his two linesmen, left fog-bound in London. The Italian officials would not agree to an Irish referee taking charge of a World Cup match and the game was re-classified as a friendly.

The gates were opened at 12.15 p.m. and the crowd began to gather, many of them having taken the day off work. At approximately 2 p.m. the crowd were informed that the game would have to go ahead as a 'friendly' match. Slow hand

183

clapping, booing and angry shouting greeted the players as they emerged and this set the tone for the behaviour of the fans for the next ninety minutes.

The game itself was a bad tempered affair with the Italians guilty of some crude challenges and the Irish not slow to 'get stuck in' with shoulder charges to the Italian 'keeper Bugatti at every possible opportunity.

What of the match itself? Ghiggia gave the Italians the lead in the 23rd minute and Cush equalised four minutes later. Montuori put the away side ahead again after 50 minutes but once more Cush equalised ten minutes later.

Irish official, Tommy Mitchell, must have regretted ever agreeing to officiate the game as twice in the final ten minutes Italian players manhandled and pushed him away. In the final minute Chiapelle was sent off following a horrendous challenge on an Irish forward.

As the final whistle blew, thousands of Irish fans invaded the pitch and attacked any Italian player they could reach. Ferrari (pictured) was punched, kicked and stamped upon before a group of policemen batten charged the mob and, with the help of the Irish players, managed to help the Italians to the safety of the dressing rooms.

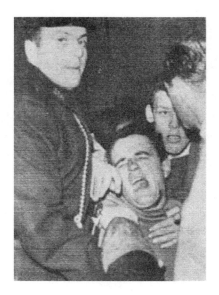

Fortunately the injured players only received minor cuts and bruises in the fracas.

Behind closed doors it was decided that the World Cup match would be re-scheduled for Belfast in January 1958. The Irish officials also agreed to play a future friendly match in Italy.

Ironically the draw would have guaranteed the Italians qualification for the World Cup finals in Sweden.

Thurs. 5th Dec.

The Manchester United squad had a disrupted journey by air following their game in Prague yesterday. Fog caused various delays and eventually their flight was diverted to Liverpool airport where they arrived late in the evening-almost 24 hours behind schedule. Not ideal preparations for their important game at Birmingham City on Saturday.

Fri. 6th Dec.

The match of the day tomorrow will be at Deepdale where Wolves, unbeaten in their last 15 games, face Preston who have not lost at home since August 1956. Unfortunately Finney will miss the game with a groin injury and Mullen is unavailable following the death of his mother. Hatsell and Lill will take their places.

For their game at St. Andrews tomorrow, United have made a number of changes. Berry and Viollet are both fit again and return to the starting line-up to replace Scanlon and Charlton. Mark Jones, after a stirring display on Wednesday retains his place at centre-half at the expense of Irish international Jackie Blanchflower.

Birmingham have made four changes and include Harry Hooper at outside-right following his move from Wolves.

Sat. 7th Dec.

United Reserves were just too strong for Bury at Old Trafford, easily winning 4-0. Pearson opened the scoring in the first half with a powerful shot and shortly afterwards Scanlon missed from the penalty spot. The player made amends by scoring twice before the interval. In the second half Cope added a fourth to help the side maintain top spot.

The top of the table clash at Deepdale saw Wolves extend their unbeaten run to 16 games with a narrow 2-1 victory against Preston. Debutant, Lill, made a dream start to first team football by scoring in the opening minute. Else, in the North End goal, dropped a simple cross at his feet and the outside-left quickly took his chance.

In the 40th minute Preston drew level when Hatsell scored from a Thompson pass. Both sides had opportunities in the second half but only Murray took advantage after 72 minutes from a through pass by Clamp to give the visitors both points.

The shock result of the day was at White Hart Lane where bottom placed Leicester City beat Spurs 4-1 to record their first away win of the season. The home side failed to capitalise on a number of goal scoring situations and Leicester were flattered by the three goal margin.

Former 'Busby Babe', John Doherty, scored twice and transfer listed right-half, John Morris, had a superb game.

At Moss Side Manchester City right-half, Ken Barnes, created a piece of history by scoring a hat trick of penalties in the 6-2 victory against Everton. Giving a master-class in how to take a penalty, Barnes placed each kick wide of the 'keeper giving him no chance to save.

In the second half Everton centre-forward, Dave Hickson, was sent off by referee, Mr Leafe, for expressing too strongly his views of the official's performance. City are in sixth position in the table.

Following the 20 Second Round FA Cup games only three non-league sides will be in the draw for the 3rd Round to be made on Monday. **Hereford United** who had an outstanding 6-1 win against Queens Park Rangers watched by over 10,000 spectators. **Yeovil Town**, who knocked out fellow non-league side Bath 2-0 and **Wigan Athletic** who drew with Mansfield and now face a difficult replay on Wednesday.

Birmingham C.	3	**Manchester Utd**	3
Murphy, Astall, Kinsey		Viollet 2, Taylor	

Att. 35,191

Birmingham City-Merrick, Hall, Farmer, Larkin, Smith, Neal, Hooper, Kinsey, Brown, Murphy, Astall.
Manchester United-Wood, Foulkes, Byrne, Colman, Jones, Edwards, Berry, Whelan, Taylor, Viollet, Pegg.

Birmingham kicked off and, almost immediately, won a corner but the United defence easily dealt with the danger. The home side had a slight advantage in the opening exchanges and looked stronger in midfield.

Centre-forward Brown was sent flying by a wild challenge from Jones and from the free kick won a corner. Hooper took the kick and Neal was unfortunate to see his header graze the crossbar.

After 14 minutes United took the lead when VIOLLET scored with a header from Berry's corner kick. Perhaps United relaxed as straight from the restart Astall laid the ball to MURPHY who hammered it beyond Wood.

This goal stirred the crowd and the 'Blues' stormed forward again, taking the lead in the 16th minute. ASTALL received the ball on the left side of the penalty area and hit a shot into the net with his right foot.

In the 18th minute United drew level. Berry crossed the ball for TAYLOR to score with his head.

FOUR GOALS IN FOUR MINUTES and once again the game 'all square', with 72 minutes remaining.

The match continued at a frenetic pace with Birmingham always dangerous in front of goal. Astall blasted the ball over the bar and then Brown just failed to get his shot away as United defenders closed around him.

In the 36th minute Birmingham retook the lead following a corner.

Murphy won the ball in the air but Wood appeared to have it covered. The 'keeper failed to reach the ball as he was hampered by Brown allowing KINSEY to take full advantage of the situation scoring with ease.

Just before the interval Foulkes headed a shot off the line and then Wood finger-tipped a header from Larkin over the crossbar.

As spectators were still returning to their places after the interval, United equalised in the 46th minute. A neat move involving Byrne and Taylor lead to VIOLLET shooting into the corner of the net.

SATURDAY 7TH DECEMBER

BIRMINGHAM C.	3	MANCHESTER U.	3	
Murphy, Astall,		Viollet 2, Taylor		
Kinsey				Att. 35,191
BURNLEY	2	ARSENAL	1	
Newlands, Cheeseborough		Holton		
				Att. 18,563
CHELSEA	2	LEEDS UNITED	1	
Stubbs, McNichol		Baird		
				Att. 17,038
MANCHESTER C.	6	EVERTON	2	
Barnes 3 (3pens),		J. Harris 2		
McAdams 2, Hayes				Att. 20,912
NEWCASTLE U.	1	BOLTON W.	2	
Eastham		Lofthouse, Parry		
				Att. 29,886
NOTTINGHAM F.	2	SUNDERLAND	0	
Wilson 2				Att. 24,262
PORTSMOUTH	5	LUTON TOWN	0	
Crawford 2, Harris 3 (1pen)				
				Att. 17,782
PRESTON N.E.	1	WOLVES	2	
Hatsell		Lill, Murray		
				Att. 22,771
SHEFFIELD WED.	2	ASTON VILLA	5	
Ellis 2		Hazelden 2,		
		Crowther 2,		
		McParland		
				Att. 15,411
TOTTENHAM H.	1	LEICESTER CITY	4	
Brooks		Doherty 2, McDonald		
		Rowley		
				Att. 27,855
WEST BROM. ALB.	1	BLACKPOOL	1	
Robson		Durie		
				Att. 28,085

	P.	W.	L.	D.	F.	A.	Pts.
Wolverhampton Wanderers	21	14	2	5	62	24	33
West Bromwich Albion	21	9	1	11	49	29	29
Preston North End	20	11	6	3	42	27	25
MANCHESTER UNITED	20	11	6	3	49	35	25
Nottingham Forest	20	11	8	1	41	29	23
Manchester City	20	11	8	1	60	51	23
Bolton Wanderers	20	9	7	4	37	28	22
Blackpool	20	9	7	4	33	30	22
Luton Town	20	10	8	2	28	29	22
Burnley	20	9	8	3	42	38	21
Arsenal	21	9	9	3	33	35	21
Everton	20	7	6	7	31	33	21
Chelsea	20	7	7	6	43	38	20
Tottenham Hotspur	21	8	9	4	45	49	20
Birmingham City	21	6	9	6	35	46	18
Portsmouth	20	7	10	3	37	36	17
Aston Villa	21	6	11	4	35	47	16
Sunderland	21	6	10	4	26	49	16
Newcastle United	20	6	11	3	31	32	15
Leeds United	21	6	12	4	26	41	14
Sheffield Wednesday	20	5	12	3	31	45	13
Leicester City	20	5	13	2	39	54	12

Birmingham City

Back row left to right – Newman, Allen, Green, Fairhurst (physio), Merrick, Watts, Orritt.

Middle row – Mr Turner (Manager), Murphy, Govan, Neal, Smith, Kinsey, Hall, Shaw (Trainer).

Front row – Farmer, Astall, Brown, Larkin.

Both teams pushed forward to try to score a fourth and winning goal but despite a number of near misses the game ended level at 3-3. Both 'keepers made late saves. Merrick holding a fierce drive from Taylor and then Wood blocking a shot from Murphy with his body.

Sun. 8th Dec.

The British Army team played the Belgian Army in Brussels in the Kentish Cup-a triangular tournament that includes France. The British Army won the game 2-1 with goals from Curry and Hitchens.

Goalkeeper, Willie Duff of Charlton Athletic, had to miss his first League game of the season yesterday in order to play in this match. He will be released from the Forces in June at the end of his National Service. A number of other first team players including Bobby Charlton, Cliff Jones and Gerry Hitchens were also unavailable to their club sides.

The British Army have won five and lost four of their games this season.

British Army team-Duff (Charlton A.), Parker (Falkirk), McIntosh (Falkirk), Williams (Plymouth A.), Spiers (Reading), Sharpe (Spurs), Harris

B. (Everton), Hitchens (Cardiff C.), Curry (Newcastle U.), Charlton (Manchester U.), Jones (Swansea T.).

Mon. 9th Dec.

The FA Cup draw made in London today produced its usual assortment of intriguing Third Round ties.

Third Round Draw

West Bromwich Albion	V	Manchester City
Portsmouth	V	Aldershot
Leyton Orient	V	Reading
Hereford United	V	Sheffield Wednesday
York City	V	Birmingham City
Crystal Palace	V	Ipswich Town
Norwich C *or* Brighton and H. A	V	Darlington
Scunthorpe United	V	Chester *or* Bradford City
Port Vale *or* Hull City	V	Barnsley
Stockport County	V	Luton Town
Doncaster Rovers	V	Chelsea
Tottenham Hotspur	V	Leicester City
Workington	V	Manchester United
West Ham United	V	Blackpool
Plymouth Argyle	V	Newcastle United
Northampton Town	V	Arsenal
Sunderland	V	Everton
Sheffield United	V	Grimsby Town
Carlisle United *or* Accrington Stanley	V	Bristol C.
Liverpool	V	Torquay United *or* Southend United
Bristol Rovers	V	Wigan Athletic *or* Mansfield Town
Notts County	V	Tranmere Rovers
Stoke City	V	Aston Villa
Lincoln City	V	Wolverhampton Wanderers
Rotherham United	V	Blackburn Rovers
Leeds United	V	Cardiff City
Preston North End	V	Bolton Wanderers
Nottingham Forest	V	Millwall *or* Gillingham
Fulham	V	Yeovil Town
Huddersfield Town	V	Charlton Athletic

Burnley V Swansea Town
Middlesbrough V Derby County

Matches to be played on 4th January 1958

Non-league Hereford United were handed a 'plum' home game against First Division Sheffield Wednesday.

There are four all First Division clashes including Tottenham Hotspur drawing Leicester City at White Hart Lane for the second season running. Amazingly Leeds United will play Cardiff City at home for the third successive season – what odds would the bookies have given for that happening?

Thurs. 12ᵗʰ Dec.

The Republic of Ireland and Wales will be included in the eight non-qualifiers given the opportunity to enter a draw on Sunday to play Israel in the World Cup. The winner of the game, played over two legs, will earn a place in the 1958 Finals.

Fri. 13ᵗʰ Dec.

Mike Pinner, the 23 year old England Amateur International goalkeeper, will make a surprise appearance for Sheffield Wednesday tomorrow against Wolves. All three of Wednesday's regular 'keepers – Charlie Pllu, Bryan Ryalls and Dave McIntosh are injured and the club made a late attempt to sign Harry Gregg from Doncaster Rovers only to be quoted a hefty transfer fee.

Pinner, who has previously made four appearances for Aston Villa, could not face a sterner test. By a strange coincidence his last league appearance for Villa was against Wolves at Molineux on 23ʳᵈ April 1957 when the home side won 3-0.

The player was named in the Great Britain squad at the 1956 Olympic Games in Melbourne but had to withdraw following an injury. He has played amateur football for Pegasus and Corinthian Casuals.

Manchester United will field an unchanged side for the game at home against Chelsea. There is still no Jimmy Greaves in the Chelsea side as the 'Pensioners' have decided to keep the same team for the third consecutive game and have not lost a match since 9ᵗʰ November.

Leeds United, who have not won in their last eight games, failed in their efforts to sign Ernie Taylor from Blackpool. They have made one change for the match with Forest replacing the unfit Baird at centre-forward for the visit of Newcastle United.

Saturday 14th December

Second placed West Bromwich Albion were torn apart at Kenilworth Road as Luton Town stormed into a 4-1 half time lead. An early goal from Adam was cancelled out by Bobby Robson in the 29th minute. Thereafter it was one way traffic as the home side scored through Brown and Turner. Then, on the stroke of half time, Kennedy, whilst trying to clear from Brown, put the ball into his own net.

In the second half Turner added a fifth as Albion suffered their first away defeat of the season. Some experts felt that the muddy conditions had hindered West Brom's attacking style of football but in reality on the day Luton's half-back line were just outstanding.

Mike Pinner's début for Sheffield Wednesday saw him having to pick the ball out of the net on four occasions as Wolves won 4-3. Despite the scoreline he had a brilliant game and saved Wednesday on numerous occasions. Wolves forward Norman Deeley commented after the game 'It was like trying to beat a slippery eel'.

At Filbert Street both Rowley of Leicester City and Murphy of Birmingham City missed from the penalty spot in the 2-2 draw.

Bobby Smith, the Spurs centre-forward, has now scored 14 League goals following the two he notched in the 2-0 win against Blackpool. The first was hotly disputed as he appeared to be offside when heading the ball into the net following a superb cross field pass from Blanchflower after 8 minutes.

There was no doubt about his second goal after 25 minutes. Blanchflower again lofted the ball into the penalty area and Smith leapt to nod it down and over the line.

At that point Blanchflower turned his attentions to defence and helped his side resist the promptings of Perry and Matthews.

Sunderland included Maltby at centre-forward, the player having flown from Germany on Friday. He made the perfect start scoring following a move involving Anderson, Bingham and Fogarty.

SATURDAY 14th DECEMBER 1957

ARSENAL	4	**PRESTON N.E.**	2
Nutt, Herd, Dunn (og)		Thompson, Mayers	
Bloomfield		Att. 31,840	
ASTON VILLA	1	**MANCHESTER C.**	2
McParland		Aldis (og), Hayes	
		Att. 24,767	
BLACKPOOL	0	**TOTTENHAM H.**	2
		Smith 2.	
		Att. 14,938	
BOLTON W.	2	**BURNLEY**	1
Stevens, Parry		Newlands	
		Att. 20,197	
EVERTON	1	**NOTTINGHAM F.**	1
Harris J.		Gray	
		Att. 29,099	
LEEDS UNITED	3	**NEWCASTLE U.**	0
Crowe, Forrest			
Overfield		Att. 23,363	
LEICESTER CITY	2	**BIRMINGHAM C.**	2
Rowley 2.		Astall, Kinsey	
		Att. 28,680	
LUTON TOWN	5	**WEST BROM. ALB.**	1
Adam, Brown, Turner 2,		Robson	
Kennedy (og)		Att. 15,365	
MANCHESTER U.	0	**CHELSEA**	1
		Tindall	
		Att. 37,073	
SUNDERLAND	1	**PORTSMOUTH**	1
Maltby		Harris (pen)	
		Att. 25,920	
WOLVES	4	**SHEFFIELD W.**	3
Murray, Broadbent		Finney, Wilkinson	
Mason, Clamp (pen)		Shiner	
		Att. 28,082	

			Home			Goals			Away			Goals		
	P	W	D	L	F	A		W	D	L	F	A	Pts
Wolves	22	10	1	0	34	10	..	5	4	2	22	17	35
W Brom	22	7	4	1	33	16	..	2	7	1	17	18	29
Preston	21	8	1	1	29	9	..	3	2	6	15	22	25
Man Utd	21	7	0	4	27	15	..	4	3	3	22	21	25
Man City	21	8	1	2	33	15	..	4	0	7	21	36	25
Nottm F	21	6	1	3	24	10	..	5	1	5	18	20	24
Luton	21	8	1	2	23	10	..	3	1	6	18	20	24
Bolton	21	7	3	1	26	14	..	3	1	6	13	23	24
Arsenal	22	7	1	3	27	18	..	3	2	6	18	19	23
Chelsea	21	6	2	2	27	13	..	2	4	5	17	25	22
Blackpl	21	5	1	5	22	20	..	4	3	3	11	12	22
Tttnhm	22	7	1	3	33	21	..	2	3	6	14	26	22
Everton	21	3	7	1	16	12	..	4	1	5	16	24	22
Burnley	21	8	1	1	31	11	..	1	2	8	12	29	21
Brmghm	22	4	3	4	22	20	..	2	4	5	13	28	19
Prtsmth	21	5	3	2	23	14	..	2	1	8	16	23	18
Sndrlnd	22	4	5	2	16	11	..	1	2	8	11	39	17
A. Villa	22	5	2	3	21	14	..	1	2	9	15	35	16
Leeds	22	5	3	4	21	17	..	1	1	8	8	24	16
Nwcastle	21	2	2	6	12	16	..	4	1	6	19	19	15
Leicester	21	4	3	4	25	23	..	1	0	9	15	33	13
Sheff W	21	5	1	4	30	21	..	0	2	9	14	28	13

Manchester United   0   Chelsea   1

Tindall

Att. 37,073

Chelsea achieved their first victory at Old Trafford since winning 2-0 in the 1919/20 season but just how they managed to gain the two points remains a mystery. United 'battered' them from start to finish with some skilful football but could not get the ball into the net. The reasons-some woeful finishing, over-elaborate play and the brave defending of the whole Chelsea team.

At times every member of the away side were camped in their own half trying to disrupt the rhythm of the United players by giving them no time to settle on the ball.

Chelsea created very few chances and in the second half had only two attempts at goal. It was from the second of these in the 84th minute that they won the game.

The United defenders relaxed as they had virtually been spectators for much of the game and Chelsea caught them napping. A quick throw in and Brabrook took advantage with a burst of speed that left Byrne stranded before playing the ball into the danger area. TINDALL was onto it in a flash, evading the clutches of Jones, and a split second later the ball was in the net.

Matthews catches the ball to deny Taylor

United had opportunities as, first Whelan's hook shot beat Matthews but Pegg just failed to reach the ball. Then Berry grazed the crossbar with all defenders stranded. Later in the game an effort by Taylor was cleared off the line and then Matthews saved a pile-driver from Whelan.

United had the excuse that Colman was virtually 'walking wounded' for the last thirty minutes after being kicked on the leg, but despite this credit must be given to Chelsea, especially the half-back line of Casey, Mortimore and Saunders. These three players tackled, blocked shots, tracked back and threw their bodies in the way to ensure 'a clean sheet' was achieved.

What now for United as their fourth home defeat of the season leaves them in fourth position, ten points behind top placed Wolves, albeit with one game in hand. The goal of a third successive Championship title appears to now be a dream.

Manchester United-_Wood, Foulkes, Byrne, Colman, Jones, Edwards, Berry, Whelan, Taylor, Viollet, Pegg._

Chelsea-_Matthews, Sillet, Bellett, Casey, Mortimore, Saunders, Brabrook, McNichol, Tindall. Stubbs, Lewis._

LEADING SCORERS

TURNER (Luton)	19
MURRAY (Wolves)	16
ALLEN (W.B.A.)	15
HAYES (Manchester C.)	14
SMITH (Tottenham H.)	14
WILSON (Nottingham F.)	14
DEELEY (Wolves)	13
McADAMS (Manchester C.)	13
ROBSON (W.B.A.)	13

United Reserves

The second team stormed into an early two goal lead at Huddersfield with goals from Morgans and Cope and appeared well on their way to maintaining their winning sequence.

Unfortunately injuries to Blanchflower and Greaves hampered the side as Huddersfield scored three times to lead at the interval.

United pushed forward at every opportunity in the second half but eventually left too much space at the back allowing the home side to score a fourth to clinch the game 4-2.

Mon. 16th Dec.

Around 100 spectators were injured at Shawfield Park, Glasgow on Saturday when part of a retaining wall collapsed during the Clyde v Celtic match.

Celtic scored in the 7th minute and the crowd swayed forward forcing the wall to buckle and in the process injure many schoolboys who were sitting on and in front of it.

The game was stopped as ambulance men raced to the scene but unfortunately a twelve year old boy from Glasgow died in the ambulance on his way to hospital. During a twenty minute delay in the match firemen, police and spectators worked amongst the rubble to rescue the boys.

Doctors in the crowd assisted the injured and eleven ambulances were needed to take them to hospital.

Tues.17th Dec.

It was reported that Doncaster Rovers had rejected an offer from Manchester United for Harry Gregg, the Northern Ireland international goalkeeper.

Wed. 18th Dec.

Newspapers reported that Grimsby Town had been asked by the Football League to clarify a number of points regarding the recent transfer of Whitefoot from Manchester United following a series of rumours.

Mr Hardaker, the League Secretary, confirmed that Grimsby had informed the League that Whitefoot did not have another job and was still living in Manchester until a house was obtained for him.

The League Committee were satisfied with the responses.

United Youth Team

The Manchester United Youth team were just too strong for Leeds United under floodlights at Elland Road in the FA Youth Cup 3rd Round.

Spratt gave them the lead after only three minutes. Dawson playing at centre-forward scored a hat trick as the Leeds defence could not deal with his strength.

Leighton scored a consolation goal for the home side in the 4-1 defeat.

Thurs. 19th Dec.

Doncaster Rovers goalkeeper Harry Gregg (pictured) signed for Manchester United today after the two clubs finally agreed on a fee believed to be in the region of £23,500. If correct this now makes the player the most expensive goalkeeper in football history.

After initial negotiations had failed earlier in the week, Doncaster issued this statement today. "In view of the expressed desire of our player Gregg, to move to Manchester United, we contacted United and negotiations were re-opened and the player was transferred at a fee satisfactory to both parties."

The transfer fee beats the previous record for a goalkeeper when Reg Matthews moved from Coventry City to Chelsea for £20,000 in 1956.

Gregg had made his début for Doncaster in the 1952/53 season and has played 99 League and Cup games. The goalkeeper has also appeared for Northern Ireland on 8 occasions, gaining his first cap against England in 1956.

Fri. 20th Dec.

Manchester Evening News

Matt Busby has decided to make major changes to the United side for the visit of Leicester City tomorrow. A disappointing return of only one point from the last three games has left United a mountain to climb if they are to challenge for League honours. Wood, Berry, Whelan and Pegg are all dropped and their places are taken by new signing Gregg plus Charlton and Scanlon. On the right-wing 18-year-old, Welsh schoolboy international, Ken Morgans (pictured above) will make his début after some outstanding performances in the Reserves.

The fixture is the reverse of the opening game at Leicester which United won 3-0 and marks the half way stage of the season.

Sat. 21st Dec.

SATURDAY 21st DECEMBER 1957

ARSENAL	3	SUNDERLAND	0
Herd 2, Groves			Att. 28,156
ASTON VILLA	0	BIRMINGHAM C.	2
		Brown, Kinsey	
			Att. 41,118
BOLTON W.	1	LUTON TOWN	2
Hennin		Groves, Turner	
			Att. 16,754
BURNLEY	3	PORTSMOUTH	1
Pointer, Newlands 2		Gordon	
			Att. 19,761
CHELSEA	2	TOTTENHAM H.	4
McNichol, Bellett		Smith 2, Medwin	
		Harmer	Att. 39,747
LEEDS UNITED	2	BLACKPOOL	1
Cush, Forrest		Taylor	
			Att. 32,411
MANCHESTER U.	4	LEICESTER CITY	0
Scanlon, Charlton			
Viollet 2			Att. 41,860
NEWCASTLE U.	3	WEST BROM. ALB	0
White 2, Davies			Att. 31,699
PRESTON N.E.	2	NOTTINGHAM F.	0
Thompson, Mayers			Att. 20,945
SHEFFIELD W.	4	MANCHESTER C.	5
Froggatt, Shiner		Hayes 2, Kirkman 2	
Wilkinson, Quixall		Johnstone	
			Att. 22,042
WOLVES	2	EVERTON	0
Clamp, Mullen			Att. 29,447

	Pl	W	D	L	F	A	W	D	L	F	A	Pts
Wolverhampton Wdrs	23	11	1	0	36	10	5	4	2	22	17	37
West Bromwich Albion	23	7	4	1	33	16	2	7	2	17	21	29
Preston North End	22	9	1	1	31	9	3	2	6	15	22	27
Manchester United	22	8	0	4	31	15	4	3	3	22	21	27
Manchester City	22	8	1	1	33	16	5	0	7	26	40	27
Luton Town	22	8	1	2	23	10	4	1	6	12	21	26
Arsenal	23	8	1	3	30	18	3	2	6	10	19	25
Nottingham Forest	22	6	1	3	24	10	5	1	6	18	22	24
Tottenham Hotspur	23	7	1	3	33	21	3	3	6	18	30	24
Bolton Wanderers	22	7	3	2	27	16	3	1	6	13	26	24
Burnley	22	9	1	1	34	12	1	2	8	12	29	23
Chelsea	22	6	2	3	29	17	2	4	5	17	25	22
Blackpool	22	5	1	5	22	20	4	3	4	12	14	22
Everton	22	3	7	1	15	12	4	1	6	16	26	22
Birmingham City	23	4	3	4	22	20	3	4	5	17	28	21
Portsmouth	22	5	3	2	23	14	2	1	9	16	26	18
Leeds United	23	6	3	4	23	18	1	1	8	8	24	18
Newcastle United	22	3	2	6	15	16	4	1	6	19	19	17
Sunderland	23	4	5	2	16	11	1	2	9	11	42	17
Aston Villa	23	5	2	4	21	16	1	2	9	15	36	16
Sheffield Wednesday	22	6	1	5	24	26	0	2	9	14	28	13
Leicester City	22	4	3	4	25	23	1	0	10	16	37	13

The London derby at Stamford Bridge produced a six goal thriller with Spurs emerging victorious 4-2. The man of the match was Chelsea goalkeeper Reg Matthews who made two superb saves late in the game from Smith and Dyson. It was only in the final minute that Spurs sealed the game with a fourth goal scored by Smith. The crowd of almost 40,000 applauded both teams at the final whistle.

Top of the table Wolves continued their amazing run by registering their eighteenth consecutive game without defeat when they beat Everton 2-0 at home. In contrast Midlands rivals West Bromwich Albion lost for the second week running-this time by 3-0 at Newcastle United and now find themselves eight points behind the leaders.

At Deepdale Preston, with Finney fit again, faced Nottingham Forest for the first time since 1934. Fred Else failed a fitness test and his place in goal, on début, was taken by local lad, 23 year old, James Knowles. On a lovely afternoon Finney soon made his presence felt when, in the thirteenth minute, he was involved in the move that lead to Thompson scoring.

The 'Whites' had to wait until the last minute for their second goal, a brilliant solo effort by Mayers, after a pass from Thompson.

Gerry Hitchens made his début for Aston Villa in the local derby against Birmingham but found himself on the losing side as City won 2-0. The player, who *had scored three goals in sixteen appearances this season for Cardiff City, reportedly cost Villa over £20,000.*

Stan Lynn, the Villa full-back, missed his first penalty for three years when Merrick punched his spot kick away.

Manchester United 4 Leicester City 0

Scanlon, Charlton, Viollet 2 Att. 41,860

Manchester United-*Gregg, Foulkes, Byrne, Colman, Jones, Edwards, Morgans, Charlton, Taylor, Viollet, Scanlon.*

Leicester City-*MacLaren, Cunningham, Baillie, Morris, Newman, Walker, McDonald, Doherty, Gardiner, Rowley, Hogg.*

Matt Busby's decision to reinvigorate the forward line with youngsters paid full dividends as United easily defeated Leicester City 4-0. In truth the scoreline could have been more as the 'Red Devils' tore into the Leicester defence at every possible opportunity only to find goalkeeper, MacLaren, in outstanding form.

Former United players, Morris and Doherty, were helpless in preventing the tidal waves of attack. Gregg, on his début, had little to do but his promptings kept the defenders alert to any danger.

Little was seen of Rowley as he was well policed by Edwards who still found time to try his luck at goal but some of his shots endangered the crowd rather than the City net.

SCANLON   **VIOLLET**

United led 1-0 at the interval after SCANLON scored from an acute angle after first beating Cunningham.

Scanlon then turned provider, laying on the chance which CHARLTON took with ease. VIOLLET then scored twice to put the game out of Leicester's reach after an afternoon of toil.

The crowd revelled in the team performance, particularly Ken Morgans' outstanding contribution down the right flank. He never wasted a ball, always had time to select the right pass and caused problems with his ability to change pace when faced with a defender.

The 'stand out' moment from the game was when Duncan Edwards hit one of his thunderbolt shots at goal only for MacLaren to somehow get in the way as the ball rebounded off his knee leaving the 'keeper in some discomfort.

United Reserves

The second team emulated the first XI as they also scored four goals in defeating Blackburn Rovers 4-1 at Ewood Park. Tommy Spratt, who celebrated his sixteenth birthday yesterday, scored twice on his début, with the other goals scored by Colin Webster as United retained top spot.

In an astonishing game at The Valley, Charlton Athletic found themselves 5-1 down with thirty minutes to play in the Division 2 game against Huddersfield Town. Centre-half and captain, Derek Ufton, had suffered a dislocated shoulder and was unable to take any further part in the game as Charlton fought manfully with ten fit players.

Outside-left Summers then decided to attack the Town defence at every available opportunity and amazingly Charlton scored five times to lead 6-5. The away side equalised with five minutes remaining but Ryan scored the winner in the last minute to give Charlton a remarkable 7-6 victory with Summers having scored five.

Sun. 22nd Dec.

In Milan Italy beat Portugal 3-0 in a World Cup qualifying match to set up a do or die game against Northern Ireland in Belfast on January 15th.

The Italians only need a draw to qualify for the Finals in Sweden.

Mon. 23rd Dec.

With a number of games scheduled to be played on Christmas Day it is interesting to note that some players have refused to play because of their religious beliefs.

At Blackpool, Dave Durie will miss the home fixture against Leicester City whilst Mike Tiddy of Arsenal has also indicated that he will not play.

Rather surprisingly Phil Gunter, the Portsmouth right-back who is also a Sunday school teacher, had originally asked not to be considered for the fixture at Stamford Bridge, but it now appears that he will play in the game.

Tues. 24th Dec.

United expect to be unchanged for the visit of Luton Town tomorrow with Morgans, Scanlon and Charlton retaining their places. The two teams then travel south for the return match at Kenilworth Road on Boxing Day with a 2.15 p.m. kick-off.

Christmas Day

Manchester United 3   Luton Town 0

Edwards, Charlton, Taylor   Att. 39,594

Manchester United-_Gregg, Foulkes, Byrne, Colman, Jones, Edwards, Morgans, Charlton, Taylor, Viollet, Scanlon._

Luton Town-_Baynham, Dunne, Hawkes, Pacey, Kelly, Pearce, Adam, Gregory, Brown, Groves, McLeod._

It was a depleted Luton side which visited Old Trafford with half-backs Morton and Owen injured together with leading scorer Turner.

In contrast United named an unchanged team which proved to be just too strong for the opposition. EDWARDS scored from the penalty spot with a thunderbolt shot giving Baynham no chance to save. The other goals came from CHARLTON and TAYLOR to give the home fans another Christmas present.

The United Review programme gave the following Christmas message from Roger Byrne, "As United's skipper, it is my privilege to wish you, on behalf of all my colleagues at Old Trafford, a very happy Christmas! Already we are midway through the season and a testing time lies before us. But we are determined to be worthy of your loyalty and encouragement and shall strive our utmost to make 1958 both happy and successful!"

The game of the day was undoubtedly Chelsea's 7-4 home win against Portsmouth. After being 'rested' for the last six games, young Jimmy Greaves was restored to the side scoring four goals. The match was over at the interval with Chelsea leading 5-1 but, to their credit, Portsmouth never gave up and scored three second half goals to make the score more respectable.

There were eight goals at Hillsborough as Sheffield Wednesday and Preston shared the points in a thrilling 4-4 draw. North End were twice two goals behind during the game but a brace from Finney and Thompson put them 4-3 ahead. Wilkinson then equalised but in the final minute Preston could have won the game. Thompson crashed a shot at goal only to see Pinner palm the ball over the crossbar.

CHRISTMAS DAY WED. 25TH DECEMBER

BLACKPOOL	5	**LEICESTER CITY**	1
Peterson 2, Perry 2		Gardiner	
Mudie			Att.16,696
BURNLEY	2	**MANCHESTER C.**	1
Pilkington		Fagan	
Cheesebrough			Att. 27,666
CHELSEA	7	**PORTSMOUTH**	4
Greaves 4, Tindall		Mortimore (og),	
Rutter (og), Sillett P.		Barnard, Harris,	
		Gordon	
			Att. 27,036
EVERTON	1	**BOLTON W.**	1
Kirkby		Birch	
			Att. 29,584
MANCHESTER U.	3	**LUTON TOWN**	0
Edwards, Charlton			
Taylor			Att. 39,594
NEWCASTLE U.	1	**NOTTINGHAM F.**	4
Hughes		Wilson, Imlach 2,	
		Baily	
			Att. 25,214
SHEFFIELD WED.	4	**PRESTON N. E.**	4
Froggatt, Finney A. 2,		Finney T. 2,	
Wilkinson		Thompson 2	
			Att. 25,525

Boxing Day

United Reserves

The second eleven, despite having a number of first team regulars in their side, made heavy weather of their home game against Barnsley and, in the end, only managed to achieve a 3-3 draw.

The goals were scored by Pegg 2 and Whelan but the point gained was sufficient to maintain United's position at the top of the Central League table.

Luton Town	**2**	**Manchester United**	**2**

Groves, Brown   Scanlon, Taylor

Att. 26,478

Luton Town-*Marsh, Dunne, Hawkes, Pacey, Kelly, Pearce, Adam, Groves, Brown, Cullen, McLeod.*

Manchester United-*Gregg, Foulkes, Byrne, Colman, Jones, Edwards, Berry, Charlton, Taylor, Viollet, Scanlon.*

United brought in Berry for Morgans on the right wing and Luton gave goalkeeper Marsh his first start of the season.

LUTON TOWN Team Group 1957/58
Back row l to r – Groves, Dunne, Baynham, Jones, Pearce.
Front row – Cullen, Turner, Owen, Brown, Morton, McLeod.

As the match unfolded it looked as though it would be a re-run of yesterday's game with United once again two goals ahead at the interval through SCANLON and TAYLOR.

The second half found Luton in a far more determined mood and it was no surprise when GROVES pulled a goal back.

As tempers became frayed Viollet had his name taken and, for once, United began to look 'leg weary'. In the last minute BROWN equalised for the home side to earn them a deserved point.

A million football supporters attended the 46 League games throughout the country as the Boxing Day results threw up their usual quirky surprises.

Teams that had been easily beaten the day before then won against the same opponents 24 hours later. The most astonishing result was surely at Fratton Park as Portsmouth beat Chelsea 3-0 and should have won by an even bigger margin. This, after Chelsea had beaten them 7-4 on Christmas Day.

Another amazing result occurred at Burnden Park where Everton, after not winning since October 12th, beat the home side 5-1. This coming after only achieving a draw in the home game against Bolton.

BOXING DAY THURS 26TH DECEMBER

ASTON VILLA	3	ARSENAL	0
Evans (og), Lynn			
Hitchens		Att. 38,383	
BIRMINGHAM C.	3	WEST BROM. ALB.	5
Brown, Neal		Robson 2, Kevan 2,	
Hooper (pen)		Allan Att. 48,396	
BOLTON W.	1	EVERTON	5
Lofthouse		Keeley, Harris B. 2,	
		Harris J., Hickson	
		Att. 23,462	
LEICESTER CITY	2	BLACKPOOL	1
Walsh, Gardiner		Durie	
		Att. 33,052	
LUTON TOWN	2	MANCHESTER U.	2
Groves, Brown		Scanlon, Taylor	
		Att. 26,478	
MANCHESTER C.	4	BURNLEY	1
Barlow, Hayes		Pointer	
Fagan, Kirkman		Att. 47,285	
NOTTINGHAM F.	2	NEWCASTLE U.	3
Baily, Wilson		Mitchell, Casey, White	
		Att. 32,509	
PORTSMOUTH	3	CHELSEA	0
Gordon, Barnard			
Sillett (og)		Att. 32,236	
PRESTON N.E.	3	SHEFFIELD W.	0
Thompson 2, Finney		Att. 28,053	
SUNDERLAND	2	LEEDS UNITED	1
Revie, Godbold		Crowe	
		Att. 34,875	
TOTTENHAM H.	1	WOLVES	0
Smith		Att. 58,393	

The match of the day was at White Hart Lane where 58,000 fans saw Tottenham Hotspur inflict the first defeat on Wolves after a run of 18 unbeaten games. The only goal came in the tenth minute when Blanchflower crossed the ball into the Wolves penalty area and Smith dived full length to head it into the corner of the net. Both sides had further chances to score but on the day the one goal was just rewards for Tottenham's efforts.

All the Spurs players deserved praise for their performances but Blanchflower was majestic and easily the best player on view. Wolves centre-half and captain, Billy Wright, ended the game with a black eye.

West Brom beat Birmingham City 5-3 to reduce Wolves lead at the top of the table to six points.

Fri. 27th Dec.

Manchester United will now play Red Star Belgrade at Old Trafford on Tuesday 14th January 1958 instead of Wednesday 15th. The game will then not clash with the 'B' International between England and Scotland at Goodison Park, part of which will be televised on BBC.

Also, it is now possible for ITV to televise the full game which should net United in the region of £2,500.

It also means that Irish internationals Harry Gregg and Jackie Blanchflower will be able to play for United and the following day turn out for Ireland against Italy in the vital World Cup qualifying match in Belfast.

United have been forced to make a change at centre-forward for the local derby against City tomorrow as Taylor has failed to recover from knee and thigh injuries. Webster will now get a further opportunity to lead the attack.

The other change is the return of Morgans on the right wing in place of Berry.

Johnstone is fit again and will take the No. 9 shirt for City replacing Phoenix.

Sat. 28th Dec.

Manchester C. 2   Manchester U   2

Hayes, Foulkes (Og)   Viollet, Charlton

Att. 70,483

Manchester City-Trautmann, Leivers, Little, Barnes, Ewing, Warhurst, Barlow, Kirkman, Johnstone, Hayes, Fagan.
Manchester United-Gregg, Foulkes, Byrne, Colman, Jones, Edwards, Morgans, Charlton, Webster, Viollet, Scanlon.

A crowd of over 70,000 Mancunians witnessed a pulsating derby at Moss Side with honours equally divided.

The young United forward line proved more than a match for the vastly experienced City rearguard and if it hadn't been for Trautmann the 'Reds' would surely have won.

In the opening five minutes the City 'keeper made two breathtaking saves from Edwards and Scanlon but a minute later was beaten by VIOLLET. The inside-left placed his shot just too wide for the goalkeeper to reach following good work from Colman and Webster.

As the United following were still cheering City drew level through a simple goal. Johnstone hit a long ball beyond the United defence and into the path of HAYES who pushed it beyond the advancing Gregg before darting around the 'keeper to tap the ball in.

After fifteen minutes United restored their lead after Webster had initially missed a golden opportunity. Receiving a pass from the same player CHARLTON made no mistake with a powerful shot. The remainder of the half was all United as they powered forward looking for a third goal only to waste a number of opportunities or to find Trautmann blocking their path. Colman in particular was a constant thorn in the side of the City defence.

In the closing minutes of the half Morgans had two great chances to increase United's lead but wasted both. The second period started much as the first had ended with United giving the City defence a torrid time, but in the 65th minute they did score a third goal but not in the manner they wanted. Barlow outpaced Byrne down the right wing and hit the ball across the penalty area. Gregg had advanced from his line and FOULKES, fearing that the ball would reach a City forward, blasted it into the net instead of over the crossbar. Up to this point he had been outstanding and did not deserve this ill piece of luck.

Both sides went for a winner but United could not find a way around the City defence and Trautmann. In the end the final chance of the game fell to Barlow but he lifted his shot over the bar when it looked easier to score.

Overall the draw was a fair result leaving the fans from both sides of the City satisfied. It leaves United sitting in fourth place in the table eight points behind Wolves and one point ahead of Manchester City.

Wolves captain, Billy Wright, missed the game at Roker Park through injury. His place was taken by Showell. The League leaders soon went in front through Murray who scored with a beautiful header after only six minutes. A few minutes later Wolves were awarded a penalty but Clamp shot over the bar.

Sunderland were seldom in the game and Broadbent increased Wolves lead in the second half.

Luton Town centre-forward, Brown, was in brilliant form against Arsenal scoring a hat trick, his final goal coming on the stroke of full time. The home side gave their best performance of the season to win easily. A sad note from the game was that two spectators collapsed and died during the match.

The first half at the Hawthorns gave no indication as to what was to follow as Burnley took the lead after 18 minutes. Pointer, who had been selected in preference to Shackleton, played a perfect pass to left-winger Pilkington who scored a lovely goal on the run.

Setters hit a post and Kevan was close with a header but the away side reached the interval ahead. Roared on by the home fans 'Albion' destroyed Burnley in the second half scoring five times, with four of the goals coming in a purple nine minute patch from the 75th to 84th minute.

For the first time in his career Bobby Robson netted four goals in a match to bring his seasons total to nineteen.

Goalkeeper George Farm picked up an injury and missed his first game for Blackpool since February 1955, a sequence of 124 successive games. His place in goal was taken by 21 year-old Brian Caine who was at fault for the first Bolton goal in the 3-2 defeat.

SATURDAY 28TH DECEMBER 1957

BIRMINGHAM C.	3	CHELSEA	3
Murphy 2, Brown.		Brabrook, Greaves	
		Sillett P. Att. 37,436	
BLACKPOOL	2	BOLTON W.	3
Mudie, Harris.		Armfield (og)	
		Lofthouse, Parry	
		Att. 19,858	
EVERTON	1	ASTON VILLA	2
Harris J.		Hitchens 2	
		Att. 41,195	
LEICESTER CITY	3	LEEDS UNITED	0
Rowley 2 (1pen)			
Walsh		Att. 31,747	
LUTON TOWN	4	ARSENAL	0
Brown 3, Groves			
		Att. 27,493	
MANCHESTER C.	2	MANCHESTER U.	2
Hayes, Foulkes (og)		Viollet, Charlton	
		Att. 70,483	
NOTTINGHAM F.	5	SHEFFIELD W.	2
Wilson, Gray, Baily		Wilkinson, Shiner	
Imlach 2.		Att. 31,903	
PORTSMOUTH	0	PRESTON N. E.	2
		Thompson, Mayers	
		Att. 31,735	
SUNDERLAND	0	WOLVES	2
		Murray, Broadbent	
		Att. 46,479	
TOTTENHAM H.	3	NEWCASTLE U.	3
Norman, Stokes		White 2, Mitchell (pen)	
Harmer (pen)		Att. 51,649	
WEST BROM. ALB.	5	BURNLEY	1
Robson 4, Kevan		Pilkington	
		Att. 38,183	

	Pl	W	D	L	F	A	W	D	L	F	A	Pts
Wolverhampton Wdrs	25	11	1	0	36	10	6	4	3	24	18	39
West Bromwich Albion	25	8	4	1	38	17	3	7	2	22	24	33
Preston North End	25	10	1	1	34	9	4	3	6	21	26	32
Manchester United	25	9	0	4	34	15	4	5	3	26	25	31
Manchester City	25	9	2	1	39	19	5	0	8	27	42	30
Luton Town	25	9	2	2	29	12	4	1	7	12	24	29
Nottingham Forest	25	7	1	4	31	15	6	1	6	22	23	28
Tottenham Hotspur	25	8	2	3	37	24	3	3	6	18	30	27
Bolton Wanderers	25	7	3	3	28	21	4	2	6	17	28	27
Chelsea	25	7	2	3	36	21	2	5	6	20	31	25
Burnley	25	10	1	1	36	13	1	2	10	14	38	25
Everton	25	3	8	2	18	15	5	1	6	21	27	25
Arsenal	25	8	1	3	30	18	3	2	8	10	26	25
Blackpool	25	6	1	6	29	24	4	3	5	13	16	24
Birmingham City	25	4	4	5	28	28	3	4	5	17	28	22
Portsmouth	25	6	3	3	26	18	2	1	10	20	33	20
Newcastle United	25	3	2	7	16	20	5	2	6	25	24	20
Aston Villa	25	6	2	4	24	16	2	2	9	17	36	20
Sunderland	25	5	5	3	18	14	1	2	9	11	42	19
Leeds United	25	6	3	4	23	18	1	1	10	9	29	18
Leicester City	25	6	3	4	30	24	1	0	11	17	42	17
Sheffield Wednesday	25	5	2	5	28	30	0	2	11	16	36	14

United Reserves

The second team easily accounted for neighbours Manchester City in the reserves local derby at Old Trafford. Dawson scored twice to bring his seasons total to 21 and Pegg, together with Blanchflower, got the others.

Mon. 30th Dec.

It was reported that hooligans had caused trouble on the British Railways Football Excursion returning to Liverpool on Boxing Day following Everton's game at Bolton.

The communications cord was pulled and six windows were smashed as 600 supporters travelled home.

British Railways police were waiting for the train as it arrived in Liverpool but no arrests were made. A spokesman for British Railways said that, "there was no intention to stop these special excursions as the majority of the supporters are well behaved".

The draw for the 4th round of the FA Youth Cup has paired Manchester United with Newcastle United with the game having to be played at Old Trafford by no later than 8th February 1958.

Tues. 31st Dec.

Newspapers reported that the Italian Football Federation had today fined all the players of Florentina the sum of 10,000 Lire (£6 each) for **hiding the ball for a short time** during the game in Milan last Sunday.

Dense fog had descended during the second half and, with Milan leading 2-1, Florentina missed a penalty. The goalkeeper made a great save and from this moment, for some reason, the away side wanted the game to be stopped. The referee attempted to restart the match but the ball could not be found. A new ball was provided but immediately was taken by a Florentina player who then moved into a group of his team mates who refused to allow the game to continue.

The referee decided to abandon the match which has now been awarded to Milan. One Florentina player, the Argentinian Michaelangelo Monthori was fined an extra 50,000 Lire (nearly £30) because he was identified as the man who actually went off twice with the ball.

John Charles of Juventus and Ivor Allchurch of Swansea Town have been named in the Welsh side to play Israel in the World Cup in Tel Aviv on 15th January 1958.

Juventus have also stated that Charles will be allowed to play in the return match in Cardiff on 5th February. This approval is subject to Wales obtaining insurance for the player of £50,000 in case of serious injury at a premium projected to be between £50 and £100.

Referees' Association Secretary, Cyril Jackson, criticised the manor of Tommy Harmer's penalty against Newcastle on Saturday. Mr Jackson, who was at the game, stated, "Twice he feinted as if to kick the ball so that Simpson, Newcastle's goalkeeper, moved before it was actually hit. On the third time he scored.

If I had been refereeing I would have told him to take the kick properly. Had he persisted in this method I would have reported him for ungentlemanly conduct then ordered him off."

Harmer was then quoted as saying, "I have scored three goals like this so far this season and, until a referee says something about it, I shall go on taking penalties in the same way whenever I think it will pay off."

Player Profile

Manchester Evening News

Ernest Taylor
Born 2nd September 1925-Sunderland

Ernie Taylor signed for Newcastle United in 1942 aged seventeen whilst serving in the Royal Navy, having previously played for Hylton Colliery. He made his debut for Newcastle in the two-legged FA Cup Third Round defeat against Barnsley in January 1946.

He then played eight games for the Club during 1947/48 when Newcastle finished runners-up to Birmingham City to secure promotion from Division 2.

Listed at either 5'4" or 5'5" and 10st 6lb in the football annuals and wearing size 4 boots, Taylor soon established himself at inside-forward and in the 1950/51 season scored 8 goals in 40 games.

In the same season 'Tom Thumb' as he is nicknamed played at inside-right at Wembley for United in the FA Cup Final against Blackpool as part of this forward line-Walker, Taylor, Milburn, G. Robledo and Mitchell. Newcastle won the game 2-0 with both goals scored by Milburn, the second of which was partially created by a clever back-heel from Taylor.

Despite his small physique Taylor is very strong and powerful, possessing a deceptive turn of speed and bravery to face the lunging tackles of defenders. Stanley Matthews played in the Blackpool side that lost in the Final and is reported to have advised his manager, Joe Smith, to sign Taylor for the 'Seasiders'.

In October 1951 Taylor signed for Blackpool for a fee reported to be £25,000 and won a second FA Cup Winners medal less than two years later when 'Pool beat Bolton Wanderers 4-3 in what became known as the Matthews Final.

A regular in the side and partnering Matthews on the right wing, Walter Winterbottom decided to give him his England debut on 25th November 1953 in the ill-fated 6-3 defeat at Wembley against Hungary-his only International appearance to date. Three Blackpool colleagues also played with him that day-Johnston, Matthews and Mortensen.

Taylor has remained a regular in the Blackpool team playing over 200 League games and scoring 51 goals. Over recent months he has not always seen eye to eye with the manager and has been left out of the side on a number of occasions.

Career Appearances (as at 31st December 1957)

	League	Goals
1947/51 NEWCASTLE UNITED	107	19
1951/57 BLACKPOOL	214	51
1953 ENGLAND	1	0

January 1958

Fri. 3rd Jan.

United are expected to have England centre-forward Tommy Taylor fit again to face Workington tomorrow in the FA Cup, with Webster stepping down in an otherwise unchanged team.

Cup holders Aston Villa face a stiff task away to Second Division Stoke City and will be without recent signing Hitchens who has influenza.

Finney will return to the Preston side to play local rivals Bolton at Deepdale. Hatsell retains his place at No. 9 with Finney playing at No. 11.

Blackpool will be without Taylor, Mudie and Perry for the difficult away trip to West Ham United but Matthews is fit.

Sat. 4th January
FA Cup Third Round

As usual the FA Cup produced a number of shock results, the most significant being that of mighty Arsenal losing 3-1 at Northampton Town.

The home side took the lead after only 6 minutes when inside-right Tebbutt scored from a free-kick. Arsenal missed a number of opportunities to equalise before eventually drawing level through Clapton. The heavy pitch hindered both sides but in the main it was Arsenal who were unable to play their normal passing game.

In the second half mist reduced the visibility making it difficult for the spectators to follow the action. Northampton restored their lead on the hour and from that point it was Kelsey in the Arsenal goal who was the busier of the 'keepers. Despite his heroic efforts he could not prevent a third goal from Leek twelve minutes from time.

As the game finished in the gloom the crowd swarmed onto the pitch to acclaim the victors.

Second Division leaders West Ham United found themselves a goal down after two minutes against Blackpool at Upton Park. Wright handled the ball in the penalty area and Hughie Kelly smashed the ball into the net from the spot. After twenty minutes West Ham drew level following a mistake by Armfield. His attempted header back to the goalkeeper was intercepted by Keeble who gleefully tapped the ball over the line. Seven minutes later West Ham took the lead with a header from Dick after he had out-jumped two defenders.

The scoreline remained the same until the 65th minute when the 'Hammers' increased their lead. The ball was floated over from the left and Dick again scored with a header, placing it wide of the falling Farm. Worse was to follow for Blackpool when in the 74th minute Keeble scored from close range with the away defenders claiming for offside.

West Ham scored a fifth five minutes from time when Keeble was given too much space. The game was over with the home fans shouting, "We want Six!"

The quickest goal of the day came at snowbound Huddersfield where Law put the home side ahead after twenty seconds against Charlton. There were three more goals in the opening fifteen minutes but that was the end of the scoring as the game finished level 2-2.

Non-league teams Yeovil Town and Hereford United both exited the Competition with neither side able to register a goal.

Division 3 North side Stockport County easily accounted for Luton Town winning 3-0 with goals from Holden 2 and Jackson. Ex England international, 35 years old Neil Franklin, had an outstanding game at the heart of the County defence.

ACCRINGTON STANLEY	2	**BRISTOL CITY**	2
Stewart, Byron		Hinshelwood, Curtis	
H.T. 1-1		Att.12,276	
BRISTOL ROVERS	5	**MANSFIELD TOWN**	0
Hooper 2, Biggs, Ward,			
Petherbridge			
H.T. 3-0		Att.20,446	
BURNLEY	4	**SWANSEA TOWN**	2
Newlands, Cheesebrough		Charles, Lewis	
McIlroy 2.			
H.T. 3-0		Att.26,593	
CRYSTAL PALACE	0	**IPSWICH TOWN**	1
		McLuckie	
H.T. 0-1		Att.21,939	
DONCASTER ROVERS	0	**CHELSEA**	2
		McNichol 2.	
H.T. 0-1		Att.19,888	

FULHAM	4	YEOVIL TOWN	0
Hill 2, Key, Doherty			
H.T. 0-0		Att.24,820	
HEREFORD UNITED	0	SHEFFIELD WED.	3
		Froggatt 2, Shiner	
H.T. 0-1		Att.18,114	
HUDDERSFIELD TOWN	2	CHARLTON ATHLETIC	2
Law, Massie		Summers, Ryan	
H.T. 2-2		Att.20,227	
HULL CITY	1	BARNSLEY	1
Bradbury		Smith	
H.T. 1-1		Att.21,868	
LEEDS UNITED	1	CARDIFF CITY	2
Forrest		Harrington, Nugent	
H.T. 1-2		Att.30,374	
LEYTON ORIENT	1	READING	0
Johnston			
H.T. 1-0		Att.20,781	
LINCOLN CITY	0	WOLVERHAMPTON W.	1
		Mullen	
H.T. 0-0		Att.21,741	
LIVERPOOL	1	SOUTHEND UNITED	1
Smith (og)		McGuigan	
H.T. 1-0		Att.43,454	
MIDDLESBROUGH	5	DERBY COUNTY	0
Day, Holiday, Peacock 2,			
Clough			
H.T. 2-0		Att.29,530	
NORTHAMPTON TOWN	3	ARSENAL	1
Tebbutt, Leek, Hawkings		Clapton	
H.T. 1-1		Att.21,344	
NORWICH CITY	1	DARLINGTON	2
Gavin		Harbertson, Moran	
H.T. 0-1		Att.24,340	
NOTTINGHAM FOREST	2	GILLINGHAM	0
Quigley, Imlach			
H.T. 2-0		Att.24,546	
NOTTS COUNTY	2	TRANMERE ROVERS	0
Tucker (pen), Jackson			
H.T. 2-0		Att.13,394	
PLYMOUTH ARGYLE	1	NEWCASTLE UNITED	6
Carter (pen)		White 3, Mitchell, Eastham 2.	
H.T. 0-2		Att.38,129	
PORTSMOUTH	5	ALDERSHOT	1
Gordon 2, Newman 2, Barnard		Lacey	
H.T. 3-0		Att.33,171	
PRESTON NORTH END	0	BOLTON WANDERERS	3
		Parry 2, Stevens	
H.T. 0-0		Att.32,641	
ROTHERHAM UNITED	1	BLACKBURN ROVERS	4
Stephens		Douglas, Dobing 3	
H.T. 1-2		Att.11,716	

SCUNTHORPE UNITED	1	BRADFORD CITY	0
Haigh			
H.T. 0-0		Att.11,586	
SHEFFIELD UNITED	5	GRIMSBY TOWN ``	1
Summers, Howitt, Hawksworth		Evans	
Lewis 2			
H.T. 4-0		Att.27,459	
STOCKPORT COUNTY	3	LUTON TOWN	0
Jackson, Holden 2.			
H.T. 1-0		Att.18,158	
STOKE CITY	1	ASTON VILLA	1
Kelly.		McParland	
H.T. 0-1		Att.45,800	
SUNDERLAND	2	EVERTON	2
Bingham, Fogarty.		Hickson 2.	
H.T. 1-1		Att.34,602	
TOTTENHAM HOTSPUR	4	LEICESTER CITY	0
Smith 2, Stokes, Medwin			
H.T. 1-0		Att.42,716	
WEST BROMWICH ALB.	5	MANCHESTER CITY	1
Allen 2, Barlow, Griffin, Ewing (og)		Hayes	
H.T. 1-0		Att.49,669	
WEST HAM UNITED	5	BLACKPOOL	1
Keeble 3, Dick 2.		H. Kelly (pen).	
H.T. 2-1		Att.34,000	
WORKINGTON	1	MANCHESTER UNITED	3
Colbridge.		Viollet 3	
H.T. 1-0		Att.21,000	
YORK CITY		BIRMINGHAM CITY	

Postponed until Wednesday

Workington   1   **Manchester United**   3

Colbridge   Viollet 3.

Att. 21,000

Workington-*Newlands, Brown, Rollo, Kinloch, Aitkin, Burkinshaw, Mitchell, Robson, Purdon, Chisholm, Colbridge.*

Manchester United-*Gregg, Foulkes, Byrne, Colman, Jones, Edwards, Morgans, Charlton, Taylor, Viollet, Scanlon.*

The topic of conversation in Cumberland since the draw was made has been the visit of Manchester United and it was no surprise when a ground record attendance of 21,000 of which about 5,000 had travelled from Manchester, awaited the arrival of the teams.

There had been a light fall of snow earlier in the day leaving the pitch soft on top but bone hard underneath.

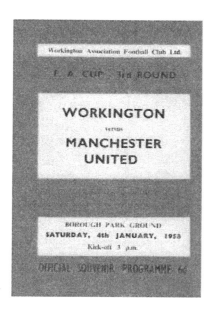

Workington Association Football Club Ltd.

F. A. CUP 3rd ROUND

WORKINGTON

versus

MANCHESTER UNITED

BOROUGH PARK GROUND
SATURDAY, 4th JANUARY, 1958
Kick-off 3 p.m.

OFFICIAL SOUVENIR PROGRAMME 6d

The away side should have taken the lead in the third minute after a Scanlon cross from the left wing. Taylor met the ball but somehow shot wide of the open target. In the sixth minute Workington scored. Chisholm had slotted the ball down the middle to Robson who shot only to see the ball parried away by Gregg, but COLBRIDGE was on hand to tap home the rebound.

Gregg then made a save from Chisholm as Workington grew in confidence. Jones slipped on the surface allowing Purdon a clear run to shoot but again Gregg made a wonderful one-handed save.

On two rare sorties forward Scanlon hit the post and Viollet had a shot saved by Newlands. The icy surface had caused the United defence all sorts of problems in the opening half and only Colman had looked at ease.

Matt Busby's half time talk obviously had the desired effect because United immediately stamped their authority on the game from the restart. First Newlands saved from Edwards but in the 55th minute he had no chance when VIOLLET met the ball from a cross by Taylor and steered it into the net. Only one minute later, with the Workington defence still reeling, VIOLLET scored again to put United in the lead.

In the 63rd minute VIOLLET got a third and hat-trick goal from a pass by Scanlon- three goals in eight minutes. The United following roared their team forward and, although Taylor hit the post and the 'keeper saved from Edwards and Scanlon, they could not add to their lead.

Workington fought to the end. They never stopped running, chasing and harassing their more accomplished opponents and were somewhat unfortunate when Robson hit the cross-bar, but the players had given United a great game of Cup football.

United Reserves

Despite some players being required for the FA Youth Cup tie at Old Trafford it was still a strong reserve side that suffered an embarrassing defeat in the Central League fixture at Barnsley despite scoring five goals.

Webster 2, Whelan 2 and Berry scored for the second team but Barnsley hit six in reply to win an amazing game 6-5.

FA YOUTH CUP FOURTH ROUND

A crowd of almost 20,000 at Old Trafford witnessed a pulsating performance by United's youth team as they beat Newcastle United 8-0 to progress to the fifth round of the competition. Goals from Dawson 4, Pearson 3 and Giles ensured the opposition were comprehensively beaten.

United will not know their next opponents until the draw is made in early February but once again look strong contenders to retain the trophy.

Mon. 6th Jan.
FA CUP 4TH ROUND DRAW

York City *or* Birmingham City	Vs	Bolton Wanderers
Tottenham Hotspur	Vs	Sheffield United
Stoke City *or* Aston Villa	Vs	Middlesbrough
Wolverhampton Wanderers	Vs	Portsmouth
Sunderland *or* Everton	Vs	Blackburn Rovers
Chelsea	Vs	Darlington
Bristol Rovers	Vs	Burnley
West Bromwich Albion	Vs	Nottingham Forest
Newcastle United	Vs	Scunthorpe United
Sheffield Wednesday	Vs	Hull City *or* Barnsley
Manchester United	Vs	Ipswich Town
West Ham United	Vs	Stockport County
Liverpool *or* Southend United	Vs	Northampton Town
Cardiff City	Vs	Leyton Orient
Fulham	Vs	Huddersfield Town *or* Charlton Athletic
Notts County	Vs	Accrington Stanley *or* Bristol City

Tues. 7ᵗʰ Jan.

United's FA Cup 4ᵗʰ Round tie with Ipswich Town on January 25ᵗʰ will kick-off at 2.45 p.m., but is unlikely to be an all-ticket match.

Hugh Baird, who was dropped from the Leeds side for last Saturday's Cup match, now looks certain to return for the game against United on Saturday.

F. A. CUP 3RD ROUND REPLAY

BRISTOL CITY	3	ACCRINGTON STANLEY	1
Atyeo 2, Curtis		Sowden	Att. 32,196

Wed. 8ᵗʰ Jan.

F. A. CUP 3RD ROUND

YORK CITY	3	BIRMINGHAM CITY	0
Bottom, Wragg, Wilkinson			Att. 19,750

F. A. CUP 3RD ROUND REPLAYS

ASTON VILLA	3	STOKE CITY	3
Sewell, Lynn, Hitchens		Coleman, Kelly, Oscroft	
(after extra time-score at 90 mins 3-3)			Att. 38,939

BARNSLEY	0	HULL CITY	2
		Clarke, Bulless	Att. 20,890

CHARLTON ATH.	1	HUDDERSFIELD TOWN	0
Ryan			Att. 26,637

EVERTON	3	SUNDERLAND	1
Keeley 2, Hickson		Fleming	
(after extra time-score at 90 mins 1-1)			Att. 56,952

SOUTHEND UNITED	2	LIVERPOOL	3
Molyneux (og), McCrory		Molyneux, White, Rowley	
			Att. 16,655

First Division Birmingham City were well beaten by Third Division opponents York City in this re-arranged game following the postponement of Saturday's fixture.

York took the lead after 13 minutes when Bottom raced through to score. Two minutes later and Merrick was once again collecting the ball from the back of the net as Wragg scored from a Spence free-kick. Birmingham were rattled and *continued to concede free-kicks enabling York to score a third in the 28th minute to seal the game.*

At Everton, with the scores level at 1-1 and just before the match went into extra time, Ambrose Fogarty of Sunderland was sent off by referee Arthur Ellis for carrying out a rugby tackle on Alan Sanders. The ten men of Sunderland could not withstand the Everton pressure and eventually lost 3-1.

Manchester United confirmed that they had received a transfer request from goalkeeper Ray Wood who was now playing in the reserve side following the arrival of Harry Gregg. The Directors considered the request at a meeting last night but decided to reject it, as Wood was needed to deputise should Gregg suffer any injury or be selected on international duty.

Thurs. 9th Jan.

The Football League Disciplinary Committee suspended Everton centre-forward Dave Hickson for 21 days following remarks he made to the referee in the game against Manchester City on 7th December. The player will now miss the Cup match against Blackburn Rovers.

The England Under 23's side to face Scotland at Goodison Park on 15th January will be – **Hopkinson (Bolton W.), Howe (W.B.A.), Harris (Wolves), Setters (W.B.A.), Smith (Birmingham C.), Crowther (Aston V.), Brabrook (Chelsea), Greaves (Chelsea), Murray (Wolves), Haynes (Fulham) (captain), A'Court (Liverpool).**

The Football League issued a press statement confirming that they had barred League players from taking part in the eight-nation indoor football tournament at the Empire Pool, Wembley on 11th February. Mr Hardaker stated, "The Management Committee considers that competitions of this nature are against the best interests of the League and the clubs, which have been asked not to give consent to any of their players taking part in it."

Fri. 10th Jan.

United have named an unchanged team to meet Leeds United on Saturday. As expected Baird will return to the Leeds side at centre-forward. The player has scored twelve goals in twenty-two League games and is the clubs leading scorer.

The top game in Division 1 will be at Deepdale where Preston play West Bromwich Albion. Preston's manager has decided to revert Tom Finney back to his role at centre-forward with Taylor, who is on the transfer list, restored to the left-wing position.

Sat. 11th Jan.

ARSENAL	2	**BLACKPOOL**	3
Herd 2.		Charnley 2, Dodgin(og)	
		Att. 43,447	
ASTON VILLA	5	**SUNDERLAND**	2
Lynn 3 (2 pens)		Grainger, Fleming	
Myerscough, Sewell		Att. 22,645	
BOLTON W.	2	**LEICESTER C.**	3
Parry, Stevens		Higgins (og), Walsh,	
		Cunningham	
		Att. 17,884	
BURNLEY	2	**TOTTENHAM H.**	0
McIlroy 2		Att. 25,927	
CHELSEA	3	**EVERTON**	1
Greaves 2, McNichol		J. Harris	
		Att. 29,490	
LEEDS UNITED	1	**MANCHESTER U.**	1
Baird		Viollet	
		Att. 39,401	
MANCHESTER C.	1	**NOTTINGHAM F.**	1
Johnstone		McKinlay	
		Att.34,837	
NEWCASTLE U.	1	**BIRMINGHAM C.**	2
White		Kinsey, Brown	
		Att. 34,825	
PRESTON N. E.	3	**WEST BROM. ALB.**	1
Thompson, Farrall		Kevan,	
Finney (pen).		Att.25,262	
SHEFFIELD W.	4	**PORTSMOUTH**	2
Quixall (pen), Shiner		Harris, Gordon	
Wilkinson, Froggatt		Att. 20,804	
WOLVES	1	**LUTON TOWN**	1
Mason		Brown	
		Att.30,805	

There were SEVEN goals in the opening 45 minutes at Villa Park with Aston Villa right-back Stan Lynn scoring a hat-trick. His first goal came from the penalty spot in the 5th minute and Myerscough then made it 2-0 after 11 minutes. Sunderland stormed back scoring twice through Grainger and Fleming to draw level. Villa centre-half, Dugdale, was carried off after 25 minutes, but with ten men Lynn soon converted another spot kick to restore their lead.

Sewell added a fourth shortly after and 3 minutes before half time Lynn completed his hat-trick after a short corner by Smith. Dugdale returned to the field just before the interval and bravely played on the left wing until 20 minutes from time when he had to withdraw. It was later reported that he had fractured two ribs and will be out for at least a month.

Preston came out on top in the match of the day with a great fight-back. Kevan put Albion ahead after 13 minutes when he tapped the ball home after Else could only parry a fierce drive from Horobin.

Albion continued to press forward but failed to capitalise on their pressure. In the 40th minute Thompson headed home (his 19th goal of the season) from a Taylor corner-kick. North End gained control and 15 minutes from time Farrall hit a rising shot beyond Sanders. In the 80th minute Barlow brought Finney down in full flight and the North End captain scored from the spot to give his side a superb victory which moved them into second place in the table, six points behind Wolves.

Wolves' manager, Stan Cullis, missed his team's home draw against Luton Town as he was at home in bed suffering from flu. He was apparently kept informed of the details of the game by a colleague who provided a running telephone commentary.

Brown had given Luton the lead in the 3rd minute with a spectacular overhead kick which Finlayson could only watch open mouthed as it passed over his head into the net.

Mason levelled after 15 minutes, but from then on it was all Wolves as Baynham single-handedly kept them at bay with some breathtaking saves.

Reports from the Press Box at Stamford Bridge claimed that the late goal scored by Jimmy Greaves was one of the best seen this season. The player received the ball in his own half before beating two defenders, then he body-swerved around two more before smashing a 25 yard shot beyond Dunlop to seal the game 3-1.

Leeds United   1   Manchester United   1

Baird   Viollet

Att. 39,401

Leeds United-*Wood, Dunn, Hair, Gibson, J. Charlton, Kerfoot, Meek, Cush, Baird, Forrest, Overfield.*

Manchester United-*Gregg, Foulkes, Byrne, Colman, Jones, Edwards, Morgans, R. Charlton, Taylor, Viollet, Scanlon.*

On a cold blustery day at Elland Road Leeds won the toss and decided to play with the wind behind them. In the opening few minutes it was all Leeds as, first Forrest watched as his shot hit the post and then Gregg managed to clear the ball away from the advancing Baird.

The pitch was very heavy and prevented both sides from playing attractive football along the ground. United gradually established supremacy with Colman and Edwards in particular directing proceedings. With one eye on the impending European Cup match on Tuesday, United seemed to be playing well within themselves, but this was still enough to cause the Leeds defence problems and in the 39th minutes VIOLLET shot them ahead. In the second period United sat back on their lead, giving Leeds the opportunity to take something from the game. Gregg was forced to make three fine saves but had no chance when BAIRD, playing in preference to Crowe, equalised for the home side. Taylor was seldom in the game leaving Charlton as easily the best forward on view. Unfortunately his shot direction was somewhat wayward otherwise Manchester United would have won the game comfortably. Mark Jones was dominant at centre-half, once again demonstrating why he was keeping Blanchflower out of the side.

The game ended level with United increasing their unbeaten run to five League games.

United Reserves

The second team took the lead after only six minutes in the fixture against Leeds United at Old Trafford when a Berry cross was headed into the net by Pegg. Twelve minutes later Whelan was fouled in the penalty area and Pegg converted the spot kick. In the 20th minute Pegg completed his hat-trick following a great pass from Webster.

Leeds never gave up and scored three second half goals but United also scored twice through Dawson and Berry to win an entertaining encounter 5-3.

Mon. 13th Jan.

Newspapers reported that Mark Jones has an ankle injury and is doubtful for the European Cup match tomorrow. If he fails to pass a late fitness test Blanchflower will deputise. In this event Gregg and Blanchflower will then fly to Belfast on Wednesday morning to play for Northern Ireland against Italy in the vital World Cup qualifying match.

F. A. CUP 3RD ROUND 2ND REPLAY

ASTON VILLA	**0**	**STOKE CITY**	**2**
		Coleman, Cairns	
At Wolverhampton			**Att. 36,584**

Tues. 14th Jan.
European Cup Quarter Final 1st Leg
Manchester U. 2   Red Star Belgrade   1

Charlton, Colman   Tasic   Att. 60,000

Manchester United-*Gregg, Foulkes, Byrne, Colman, Jones, Edwards, Morgans, Charlton, Taylor, Viollet, Scanlon.*

Red Star Belgrade-*Beara, Tomic, Zekovic, Mitic, Spajic, Popovic, Borozan, Sekularac, Toplak, Tasic, Kastic.*

With Mark Jones passing a late fitness test, Jackie Blanchflower was released to fly to Belfast for the World Cup game tomorrow. The early chances fell to United in front of a boisterous 60,000 crowd, peering through the mist for a better view of the game. Charlton slammed a shot inches wide of the left-hand post with the Red Star 'keeper stranded. Edwards saw his effort cleared over the crossbar and Beara made a stunning save from Charlton.

Red Star Belgrade
Standing l. to r. Popovic, Mitic, Sekularac, Toplac, Spajic, Kostic, Tasic, Rudinski.

Front row-Stankovic, Beara, Zekovic.

The Red Star team passed the ball accurately and with purpose on the bone hard pitch which had been made slippery by a heavy shower just before kick-off. Halfway through the first half the mist lifted as Red Star looked more dangerous. Mitic tried his luck from long range but Gregg dealt with it comfortably. In the 35th minute TASIC also decided to try his luck from a distance having seen Gregg had moved forward off his line. The ball from twenty-five yards out sailed over the 'keeper's head and into the net watched by a hushed crowd.

United launched wave after wave of attack in the opening minutes of the second half but Beara in the Red Star goal, who reportedly was a former ballet dancer, dealt with everything thrown at him. Three times Charlton looked certain to score but somehow Beara blocked his path. In the 64th minute United finally equalised thanks to the power of Edwards. The left-half gathered the ball before bulldozing his way forward, eventually laying off a pass for Scanlon. The winger played the ball to CHARLTON who hooked it into the net.

Only minutes later a superb pass by Byrne put Charlton clean through on goal but the young striker missed a simple chance. At last, with only nine minutes remaining, United took the lead. Viollet, who had rarely been involved in the game, received the ball and played it square to COLMAN who dashed forward and steered a left foot shot into the net.

Only a narrow lead to take to Belgrade for the return leg next month but Matt Busby in a press conference said that he was confident that United could also win the second leg.

The Management Committee of the Football League outlined a number of proposals which Club representatives will consider at a meeting in London on 27th January.

Included in the proposals is the payment of £300 to a player if he is asked to accept a transfer.

It would appear that the Committee have now had second thoughts on their initial proposal for a maximum wage of £20 throughout the year. Instead they now suggest that a maximum wage of £17 per week plus £3 appearance money if in the first team (including 12th man) be made, with a payment of £17 if a player is out of the team through injury and during the summer months.

Wed. 15th Jan.

Ireland   2   Italy   1

Ireland were forced to make a late change to their line-up when Harry Gregg was left 'fog bound' at Manchester airport. The goalkeeper, who played for United last night, could not fly to Belfast this morning and ended up watching the game on TV. His place was taken by Uprichard of Portsmouth.

In a dour, tough struggle for supremacy the two sides were evenly matched with the Italians the better ball players.

Cool, scheming Irish skipper Danny Blanchflower caused the attacking movements to flow from his twinkling feet. Oh what a roar when Ireland went one up through McIlroy after 18 minutes. Bugatti, the Italian goalkeeper, made a desperate attempt to save his cannonball shot.

Then Cush scored number two twelve minutes later at the second attempt as his first effort had been partially saved.

There was no stopping the Irish now and the Italians, despite a promised £800 a man bonus, were not inspired. Their cause was not helped when right winger Chiggia was sent off for a seemingly trivial offence. Da Costa pulled a goal back with thirty minutes to play but Ireland easily held their lead to reach the World Cup Finals for the first time.

Israel	**0**	**Wales**	**2**

In the First Leg of this World Cup eliminator in Tel Aviv, Wales were just too good for the plucky Israelis who had no competent answer to the magnificence of burly, big John Charles and back to top form Ivor Allchurch.

The happy band of Welsh troops who had flown in especially from Cyprus had plenty to roar about in the crowd of 55,000.

Allchurch brought the first big cheer with his well taken goal and then Bowen added a second. This 2-0 lead certainly looks as if it means that England, Scotland, Ireland and Wales will play in the World Cup Finals.

The Second Leg is in Cardiff in the first week of February.

England Under 23's	**3**	**Scotland Under 23's**	**1**

Mist prevented the 19,327 fans at Goodison Park from seeing some of the more skilful movements in this 'shop window for the selectors' game. Two goals in four minutes by Jimmy Greaves and Jimmy Murray virtually settled things in the first half.

England deserved to win with Haynes scoring the third goal and Young a consolation for Scotland.

Thurs. 16th Jan.

The Press reported that Matt Busby had accepted an invitation to become Team Manager of Scotland, on a part-time basis, subject to the agreement of the United directors.

Doncaster Rovers signed goalkeeper McIntosh from Sheffield Wednesday as a replacement for Harry Gregg. The player will make his début away to Stoke City on Saturday.

Fri.17ᵗʰ Jan.

United have named an unchanged team for the local derby against Bolton Wanderers at Old Trafford tomorrow. Wanderers have made changes on both wings with Birch returning at No.7 in place of Gibbins and Riley playing in the No. 11 shirt in place of Holden.

United will be keen to avenge the 4-0 drubbing suffered at Burnden Park earlier in the season.

League leaders Wolves have a difficult trip to Blackpool where they have lost four times in the last six seasons. With the 'Seasiders' back at full strength an interesting encounter looks in prospect.

Sat. 18ᵗʰ Jan.

United Reserves

In a hard fought game at Burnden Park Whelan scored twice for United within the space of a minute in the first half to give the reserves a 2-1 lead at the interval. Although 18 points behind United in the Central League table, Bolton deservedly equalised to gain a point.

SATURDAY 18TH JANUARY 1958

BIRMINGHAM C.	2	BURNLEY	3
Murphy, Hooper		White 2, Pilkington	
		Att. 22,281	
BLACKPOOL	3	WOLVES	2
Taylor, Durie, Perry		Deeley, Murray	
		Att. 17,953	
CHELSEA	2	NEWCASTLE U.	1
Lewis J., Greaves		White	
		Att. 37,327	
LEICESTER CITY	0	ARSENAL	1
		Groves	
		Att. 31,778	
LUTON TOWN	3	ASTON VILLA	0
Adam, Turner, McLeod			
		Att. 16,619	
MANCHESTER U.	7	BOLTON W.	2
Charlton 3, Viollet 2,		Stevens, Lofthouse	
Scanlon, Edwards		Att. 41,360	
NOTTINGHAM F.	1	LEEDS UNITED	1
Baily.		Baird	
		Att. 23,368	
PORTSMOUTH	2	MANCHESTER C.	1
Crawford 2.		Sambrook	
		Att. 26,254	
SUNDERLAND	1	EVERTON	1
Revie		Thomas	
		Att. 26,507	
TOTTENHAM H.	3	PRESTON N. E.	3
Medwin, Smith		Thompson 2,	
Brooks (pen)		Ryden (og)	
		Att. 43,941	
WEST BROM. ALB.	3	SHEFFIELD WED.	1
Griffin 2, Setters		Shiner	
		Att. 28,819	

Wolves	27	17	6	4	63	32	40
Preston N. E.	27	15	5	7	61	39	35
West Brom. A.	27	12	11	4	64	45	35
Manchester U.	27	14	6	7	68	43	34
Luton Town	27	14	4	9	45	37	32
Manchester C.	27	14	3	10	68	64	31
Notts Forest	27	13	4	10	55	40	30
Chelsea	27	11	7	9	61	54	29
Burnley	27	13	3	11	55	53	29
Blackpool	27	12	4	11	48	44	28
Tottenham H.	27	11	6	10	58	59	28
Arsenal	27	12	3	12	43	47	27
Bolton W.	27	11	5	11	49	59	27
Everton	27	8	10	9	41	46	26
Birmingham	27	8	8	11	49	60	24
Portsmouth	27	9	4	14	50	54	22
Aston Villa	27	9	4	14	46	57	22
Newcastle U.	27	8	4	15	43	48	20
Leeds United	27	7	6	14	34	49	20
Sunderland	27	6	8	13	32	62	20
Leicester City	27	8	3	16	50	69	19
Sheffield Wed.	27	6	4	17	49	71	16

Wolves took the lead after only six minutes at Bloomfield Road through Deeley, who hit his shot with such power that it rebounded from the back of the net almost to the edge of the penalty area.

Twelve minutes from half time Blackpool drew level with Matthews the architect. He raced twenty yards with the ball before passing for Taylor to score with the Wolves defenders claiming for off-side. On the stroke of half time Taylor centred the ball and Durie rose to head it wide of Finlayson to give 'Pool the lead. Within three minutes of the restart the Wolves 'keeper failed to catch the ball cleanly and Perry took advantage to score.

Wolves fought for every ball and after 65 minutes Murray pulled one back from a Broadbent pass.

Blackpool had a goal disallowed four minutes from time as Charnley's effort was ruled out for off-side. In the final minute Farm made a great save from Harris who hit a cannonball shot from forty yards. This was the final action of the game as Blackpool dented Wolves title aspirations with a 3-2 victory.

At the foot of the table Sheffield Wednesday were three goals down at half time at high flying West Brom. Griffin scored twice within the space of three minutes and, as the referee was about to signal half time, Setters netted a third. Wednesday never gave up and scored a consolation goal through Shiner.

Spurs and Preston drew 3-3 at White Hart Lane but the main talking point for the home supporters was the decision to drop Tommy Harmer and Alf Stokes. Stokes is now reported to have asked for a transfer.

Manchester U.	7	Bolton W.	2

Charlton 3, Viollet 2 Scanlon Edwards (Pen).

Stevens, Lofthouse

Att. 41,360

Manchester United-_Gregg, Foulkes, Byrne, Colman, Jones, Edwards D., Morgans, Charlton, Taylor, Viollet, Scanlon._

Bolton Wanderers-_Hopkinson, Hartle, Banks, Hennin, Higgins, Edwards G., Birch, Stevens, Lofthouse, Parry, Riley._

Early afternoon rain and strong winds left the pitch very heavy in places and certainly affected the gate as only around 35,000 were on the ground as the teams emerged.

The crowd did not have to wait long for the first goal. In only the third minute Byrne found CHARLTON with an inch perfect pass.

The inside-forward beat three opponents in a thirty yard dash before unleashing a powerful drive which hit the back of the net with a thud.

BOLTON WANDERERS F.C. 1957-58

Standing: Mr. G. Taylor (Coach), E. Bell, J. Ball, T. Banks, E. Hopkinson, D. Hennin, B. Edwards, J. Higgins, H. Webster, Mr. B. Sproston (Trainer). Seated: Mr. W. Ridding (Manager), T. Allcock, D. Holden, D. Stevens, N. Lofthouse, R. Parry, R. Gubbins, R. Hartle.

United drove forward but somehow the Bolton defence withstood the onslaught. After 20 minutes they even drew level. STEVENS received a pass from Parry and from outside the penalty area beat Gregg with a glorious strike. Edwards was partially to blame for the goal through losing the ball in midfield after being too casual.

The equaliser stirred United into even greater efforts and within a five minute period they scored three times.

CHARLTON just beat Hopkinson to the ball to score his second of the afternoon and then almost immediately VIOLLET pounced onto a poor clearance to make it 3-1. Worse was to follow for the away side when Hopkinson miss-kicked the ball to SCANLON who lobbed it into an empty net to give the 'Reds' a 4-1 half-time lead.

Within two minutes of the restart Bolton pulled a goal back. Gregg and Lofthouse jumped to meet the ball in the air, then landed in a tangled heap on the turf with the ball in the back of the net. The referee did not see anything wrong with the challenge and the goal was awarded to LOFTHOUSE.

United remained in control of the midfield and Charlton, in particular, looked dangerous every time he received the ball. It was hard to believe that he had played twice for his Army unit since the game against Red Star Belgrade on Tuesday.

Bolton's second goal had once again lighted the blue touch paper and United's frantic attacks soon brought a further goal from CHARLTON, for his hat-trick, following a pass from Viollet.

Taylor then brushed aside a number of robust challenges before scoring only to see the referee bring the play back and award him a free-kick instead.

The sixth goal came via some astute play between Taylor and Morgans. The latter laying the ball into the path of VIOLLET for him to side-foot into the net. Goal number SEVEN came from the penalty spot.

Higgins unceremoniously dumped Scanlon on his face leaving EDWARDS to blast his penalty into the net.

Despite conceding two goals United's defence provided a strong backbone to the team performance allowing the forwards the room and freedom to attack Bolton at will.

Mon. 20th Jan.

Tommy Taylor suffered a shoulder injury on Saturday but is hopeful that with treatment during the week he should be fit to play against Ipswich Town in the FA Cup.

Wed. 22nd Jan.

Alf Ramsey, the Ipswich Town manager stated that he was 'not concerned' when he heard that Taylor should be fit to play against his team on Saturday. Ramsey also stated that Dai Rees, who has recovered from an injured knee, will be fit to play directly opposite Taylor at centre-half.

Thurs. 23rd Jan.

Matt Busby has had a minor operation on his leg but is expected to be able to take charge of team affairs by Saturday.

Meanwhile heavy snow in Lancashire has resulted in the Old Trafford pitch being covered in a blanket of snow, which in some places is nearly a foot deep. The Club have wasted no time in taking action under the guidance of groundsman Joe Royle and are confident that the FA Cup tie will go ahead.

Over 100 men are taking part in the 'clear up' and provided there is no sudden drop in temperatures then everything should be fine with the work continuing around the clock.

Snow in other parts of the country has also caused concern with the game at Everton rated as doubtful.

Fri. 24th Jan.

It was estimated that 500 tons of snow had been removed from the Old Trafford pitch overnight. A final clearing up exercise was now under way to compress any soil that had been disturbed by the bulldozers.

The top surface is soft and will be playable tomorrow provided there is no more frost overnight.

At the moment all the other 15 Cup-ties are expected to take place on snow covered pitches although a number of League games have been postponed.

Second Division Ipswich Town are expected to give United a tough game having gone eight League and Cup games without defeat, which includes achieving a win and draw against league leaders West Ham United over the Christmas period.

Sat. 25ᵗʰ Jan.

FA Cup 4ᵗʰ Round

Manchester United 2   Ipswich Town 0

Charlton 2   Att. 53,550

(Match Receipts £7,286)

Manchester United-Gregg, Foulkes, Byrne, Colman, Jones, Edwards, Morgans, Charlton, Taylor, Viollet, Scanlon.

Ipswich Town-Bailey, Acres, Malcolm, Pickett, Rees D., Elsworthy, Reed, Millward, Garneys, Rees W., Leadbetter.

Matt Busby made a late appearance at Old Trafford following his varicose vein operation earlier in the week. He decided not to watch the game from his usual seat in the stand, opting instead to see the action through the window of Club Secretary Walter Crickmer's office.

The ground staff had done a superb job in clearing the snow from the pitch and during the morning had forked the ground to help remove any surface water. A crowd of 50,000 were already in the ground as Roger Byrne won the toss and decided to attack the Stretford end.

United attacked strongly at the start, but found the Ipswich defence in good form. The away side had one good move in which Leadbetter and Garneys combined cleverly but the danger was averted.

The 'Reds' should have taken the lead in the tenth minute when Taylor drew the goalkeeper, but Charlton somehow shot over the crossbar from less than ten yards. Ipswich moved the ball freely whereas United attempted a close passing game which was unsuited to the conditions. Gregg made a brilliant one-handed save from a shot by Leadbetter pushing the ball away for a corner.

Ipswich goalkeeper Bailey made good saves from Charlton and Colman. United almost scored when a back pass from centre-half, Rees, stuck in the mud allowing Viollet to dribble round two defenders only to see his shot deflected.

231

EDDIE COLMAN   **TOMMY TAYLOR**

In the 40th minute United eventually took the lead when CHARLTON beat the goalkeeper with a rising left-footed drive from thirty-five yards which hit the underside of the crossbar before entering the net. The home side reached the interval with a narrow lead whereas the game should really have been over but for wasted opportunities.

Early in the second half Leadbetter was unfortunate to see his shot hit the post with Gregg stuck in the mud. United continued to press forward putting the Ipswich defence under long periods of pressure. Taylor had a shot and header saved by Bailey then the keeper did remarkably well to grasp the ball from Scanlon's feet as he was about to shoot.

A twenty yard free kick by Edwards just grazed over the cross-bar. A drive from Taylor from outside the penalty area struck the upright. Ipswich had their chances also, but there was a slowness and lack of punch in the forward line at the decisive moment.

Elsworthy was outstanding for the visitors, helping to combat the United thrusts but still finding time to initiate attacking moves down the left flank. In the 86th minute CHARLTON scored again, somewhat fortuitously as it took a deflection off a defender to wrong foot the goalkeeper.

Ipswich Town

Back row l to r – B. Acres, W. Grant, N. Miles, W. Reed, L. Carberry, G. McLuckie.

Centre row – A. Ramsey (manager), T. Parker, K. Malcolm, R. Bailey, T. Garneys, D. Milward, J. Forsyth (trainer).

Front row – J. Leadbetter, E. Phillips, J. Elsworthy, D. Rees, R. Blackman, T. Deacon.

Sat on ground V. Snell, G. Macrow.

Ipswich kept going and two minutes from time Leadbetter raced away from the United defenders, but this time his shot hit the other goalpost to the relief of Gregg.

Third Division North side, Scunthorpe United raised a few eyebrows by beating First Division Newcastle United on their own ground to progress to the Fifth round for the first time in their history. The away side led 1-0 at the interval thanks to Haigh who scored with a down ward header. Although Newcastle equalised from a corner early in the second half, Scunthorpe were still the better side. They regained the lead through a Davis header and then the same player scored again to seal the game.

Only two Division One sides, Manchester United and Wolverhampton Wanderers are safely through to the next round.

Three other top flight sides face difficult replays against York City, Darlington and Bristol Rovers.

BRISTOL ROVERS	2	**BURNLEY**	2
Hale, Shannon (og)		Connelly, Pointer	
H.T. 1-0		Att. 34,229	
CARDIFF CITY	4	**LEYTON ORIENT**	1
Bishop (og), Walsh, Bonson 2.		Julians.	
H.T. 2-1		Att. 35,849	
CHELSEA	3	**DARLINGTON**	3
Lewis J., Tindall, McNichol		Harbertson, Carr,	
H.T. 0-2		Morton.	
		Att.40,759	
EVERTON	P	**BLACKBURN R.**	P
FULHAM	1	**CHARLTON ATH.**	1
Hill.		Ryan.	
H.T. 0-1		Att. 39,586	
LIVERPOOL	3	**NORTHAMPTON T.**	1
LiddelL, Collins(og), Bimpson.		Hawkins	
H.T. 1-1		Att. 56,939	
MANCHESTER UNITED	2	**IPSWICH TOWN**	0
Charlton 2.			
H.T. 1-0		Att. 53,550	
NEWCASTLE UNITED	1	**SCUNTHORPE U.**	3
Paterson.		Haigh, Davis 2.	
H.T. 0-1		Att. 39,234	
NOTTS COUNTY	1	**BRISTOL CITY**	2
Pritchard.		Etheridge, Hinshelwood	
H.T. 0-0		Att. 18,395	
SHEFFIELD WED.	P	**HULL CITY**	P
STOKE CITY	3	**MIDDLESBROUGH**	1
Wilshaw 3.		Clough.	
H.T. 2-1		Att. 43,756	
TOTTENHAM H.	0	**SHEFFIELD UTD.**	3
		Pace, Russell,	
H.T. 0-2		Hawksworth	
		Att. 51,136	
WEST BROM. ALB.	3	**NOTTINGHAM F.**	3
Robson, Kevan, Allen.		Imlach, Wilson 2 (1 pen)	
H.T. 0-0		Att. 58,763	
WEST HAM UTD.	3	**STOCKPORT CTY.**	2
Lewis 2, Keeble.		Holden, Finney.	
H.T. 0-0		Att. 36,084	
WOLVERHAMPTON W.	5	**PORTSMOUTH**	1
Mason, Broadbent 2, Mullen		Crawford.	
Rutter (og).			
H.T. 2-1		Att. 43,522	
YORK CITY	0	**BOLTON W.**	0
		Att. 23,460	

As the all First Division tie at the Hawthorns reached the half way stage goalless, the huge crowd of almost 60,000 could not have anticipated what was in store for the second period.

In an amazing scoring sequence West Brom. and Nottingham Forest both scored three goals each in a fourteen minute period from the 58th minute. Albion cruised into a 3-1 lead and the game appeared won but Forest would not concede defeat as Wilson scored twice, including a penalty after Barlow had handled in the area, to earn a replay next Wednesday.

London fans witnessed an upset at White Hart Lane as Sheffield United stunned the home side with a goal in the first minute after Pace had shrugged off *the challenge of two defenders to slam the ball into the net. Worse was to follow as in the 8th minute the Yorkshire side scored again through a header by Russell.*

Spurs threw everyone forward in the second half but could not pull a goal back, with the away side eventually adding a third with seven minutes remaining.

Mon. 27th Jan.
FA Cup 5th Round draw

Manchester United	Vs	Sheffield Wednesday *or* Hull City
Wolverhampton Wanderers	Vs	Chelsea *or* Darlington
Bristol City	Vs	Bristol Rovers *or* Burnley
York City *or* Bolton Wanderers	Vs	Stoke City
Scunthorpe United	Vs	Liverpool
West Ham United	Vs	Fulham *or* Charlton Athletic
Cardiff City	Vs	Everton *or* Blackburn Rovers
Sheffield United	Vs	West Bromwich Albion *or* Nottingham Forest

United had the luck of the draw after being handed another home tie in the 5th round. The winners of the postponed game between Sheffield Wednesday and Hull City will visit Old Trafford on Saturday 15th February.

Scunthorpe United and Sheffield United have both been rewarded for their excellent victories on Saturday with attractive home games.

Tues. 28th Jan.

The Football League Management Committee held its second meeting with Chairman of First and Second Division clubs and representatives of the Third Division in London yesterday. The proposals which were outlined at the previous meeting were again considered but no agreement was reached.

It is understood that the Clubs would prefer a flat weekly wage for players rather than one which includes appearance money.

F. A. CUP FOURTH ROUND REPLAY

BURNLEY	2	**BRISTOL ROVERS**	3
McIlroy, Pointer		Sykes, Ward 2	

Att. 41,113

Another First Division side was knocked out of the Cup at Turf Moor. The home side fought hard to lead 2-1 with 15 minutes remaining before conceding a fluke equalising goal. A right-wing centre struck Ward on the side of his head and the ball flew into the net. In the 85th minute Ward scored again with a powerful shot to win the game for Bristol Rovers.

Wales have omitted Len Allchurch, the Swansea outside-right, from the team to face Israel in the 2nd leg of the World Cup eliminator on 5th February. Medwin will switch from the No. 8 shirt to No. 7 and Hewitt of Cardiff City will make his début at inside-right.

Wed. 29th Jan.
F. A. CUP FOURTH ROUND

EVERTON	1	**BLACKBURN ROVERS**	2
J. Harris.		Dobing, Meagan (og)	
			Att.75,818
SHEFFIELD WEDNESDAY	4	**HULL CITY**	3
Wilkinson, Durham (og) Shiner		Stephens, Bullens, Bradbury	
Froggatt			
			Att.47,119

Replays

BOLTON WANDERERS	3	**YORK CITY**	0
Birch, Allcock 2.			
			Att.34,062
CHARLTON ATHLETIC	0	**FULHAM**	2
		Bentley, Stevens.	
			Att.43,097
DARLINGTON	4	**CHELSEA**	1
Moran 2, Carr, Harbertson		McNichol	
			Att.15,150

(After extra time, score at 90 minutes 1-1)

NOTTINGHAM FOREST	1	**WEST BROM. ALBION**	5
Wilson		Robson, Griffin, Whitehouse,	
		Kevan, Howe (pen).	
			Att.46,477

Two more First Division sides were knocked out of the Cup by lower graded clubs with the biggest shock being at Darlington. The replay kicked off at 2 p.m. and the home side held Chelsea to 1-1 in the opening 90 minutes. With extra time only 9 minutes old Darlington had already scored three more goals to shock their lofty opponents.

The side that had cost £4,000 to assemble, presently sat 4th from the bottom of Division 3 North and including six part-time players, thoroughly deserved their victory.

They now face table-topping Wolves in a lucrative tie. Darlington have only once before reached the fifth round in the 1910/11 season when they were still a non-league club.

A huge 75,000 crowd at Goodison Park witnessed Blackburn Rovers 2-1 win against Everton. Unfortunately events off the pitch made the headlines as 100 supporters were hurt, including women and children, when two crush barriers buckled. The injured were passed over the heads of the crowd to the edge of the pitch before receiving treatment from ambulance personnel.

It was estimated that 5,000 fans were locked out of the ground, many of whom claimed to hold reserved stand tickets for the game. More than 150 officers and mounted police were called to usher fans away down side streets to prevent them from swarming the gates.

The final attendance figure of 75,818 was only 2,000 less than the record attendance for the ground, generating receipts of £10,575.

A crowd of over 46,000 somehow made excuses to miss work for 2.15 p.m. kick-off at Nottingham Forest. Despite scoring the first goal after 12 minutes, the home side were brushed aside in the replay as West Brom. hammered them 5-1. The winning margin was even more astonishing as Albion only had ten fit players for 65 minutes of the game following an ankle injury sustained by Setters.

Sheffield United manager, Joe Mercer, took his team to watch the match as his side will now face Albion in the next round. The manager is quoted as saying, "This Albion performance is the greatest thing I have ever seen in football."

Thurs 30th Jan.

With the 16 survivors in the FA Cup now known it is interesting to see that only five First Division teams are still left in the competition. This is the lowest number in the history of the Cup at this stage, beating the previous low record of six in 1927.

Manchester United have announced that they will be using the programme token system for the FA Cup Fifth Round tie against Sheffield Wednesday on February 15th. Groundside, paddock and terrace tickets will be sold to those with 18 tokens or more next Sunday. Then the minimum will drop to 14 tokens or more on Monday, 12 or more on Tuesday and no fewer than 10 on Wednesday, Thursday and Friday. Season ticket holders can purchase their ticket at the office.

Match prices will be-Stands B and C Reserved 7s 6d

Stands A and D Reserved 6s 0d

Covered Paddock and Terrace 3s 6d

Groundside 2s 0d

Boys 9d

United's out of favour winger, Johnny Berry, has decided to ask for a transfer and his request will be considered by the Directors at their next meeting. Although the player seemed to be settled again following his recent meeting with Matt Busby, he has now decided that at 31 years of age he needs regular first team football.

The outstanding form of teenager Morgans has resulted in Berry being consigned to the reserve team with several other former first team regulars. The local newspapers have reported that it is unlikely that his request will be granted. Goodwin and Wood have both had transfer requests refused and Busby is quoted as saying, "The position is that we just cannot allow any of our players to go at the moment, but it is for the Directors to decide."

Fri. 31st Jan.

Blackpool wing wizard, Stanley Matthews, will celebrate his 43rd birthday tomorrow with a trip to Villa Park. In the opposition side 16 years old inside-forward, Walter Hazelden, will make his fifth league appearance. The player was born ten years after Matthews first appeared in league football for Stoke City.

Nottingham Forest goalkeeper, Thomson, is unfit for tomorrow's clash with Portsmouth and his place will be taken by Bishop Auckland and England amateur international Harry Sharratt (pictured). During the 1950's Sharratt has made one emergency appearance in goal for Blackpool and one for Oldham Athletic.

The Bishop Auckland custodian decided against turning professional because the money he earned from teaching together with his wages from playing amateur football was more than he could earn as a full time player.

Manchester United have named an unchanged team for the seventh consecutive game for the away trip to London to face Arsenal. During those last six games four have been won and two drawn.

Arsenal will be hoping to avenge the 4-2 defeat suffered at Old Trafford in September. Bloomfield is fit again after missing two games and Ward will replace Goring at right-half.

Player Profile

Richard Peter Tudor Sillett
Born Southampton 1ˢᵗ February 1933

The son of Charlie Sillett who played full-back for Southampton in the 1930's, Peter followed in his father's footsteps joining his home town club in 1949.

He made his debut for Southampton aged 18 in September 1951 in a Division 2 game against Cardiff City, gaining a regular place in the team the following season. Unfortunately he could not prevent Southampton from being relegated to Division 3 (South).

In the summer of 1953 the strong, powerful, muscular youngster attracted the attention of the top flight clubs and Ted Drake paid £12,000 to acquire him for Chelsea. His younger brother John who was also at Southampton followed him to Stamford Bridge.

Peter gradually established himself in the Chelsea side and his versatility enables him to play in either full-back position. During the 1954/55 season he played 21 League games scoring 6 goals as Chelsea won the First Division title. Towards the end of that season Chelsea met Wolves in a vital top of the table clash at 'The Bridge' on Easter Saturday. With the game scoreless and 15 minutes remaining Billy Wright handled the ball in the penalty area and up stepped Sillett to take the spot kick. With the hushed crowd of over 75,000 waiting anxiously Sillett crashed the ball into the net leaving Bert Williams helpless. This feat established his name in Chelsea folklore as the 1-0 victory followed by other good results gave Chelsea the Championship.

As a reward for his outstanding performances at Club level Peter Sillett won the first of three England Caps against France in Paris in May 1955. In contrast to a month earlier, Sillett gave away a penalty in this game allowing France to win 1-0. He retained his place for the other tour games against Spain and Portugal.

Sillett has wonderful ball control and the vision to pick the right pass as well as sound positional play, never allowing himself to be flustered by opponents. It has been reported that Stanley Matthews stated that he is one of the best full-backs he has ever played against.

His powerful shooting from outside the penalty area has earned him many goals together with his penalty kicks. He is a natural captain and an ideal leader of 'Drakes Ducklings'.

	Appearances	Goals	
SOUTHAMPTON	1950-53	59	4
CHELSEA	1953 to 31/01/58	129	12
ENGLAND	1955	3	0

FEBRUARY 1958

Saturday 1st February

The visit of Blackpool to Villa Park and the fact that it was Stanley Matthews 43rd birthday seemed to stir the imagination of football fans in the Midlands and over 47,000 turned out to watch the game, easily Villa's best attendance of the season. A special recording of 'Happy Birthday to You, Stanley' was played as the teams emerged and the whole crowd joined in, finishing with a tremendous cheer.

Cup holders Villa opened the scoring in the 21st minute. Sewell hit the ball into the penalty area and Hitchens just failed to make contact. The ball rolled across to McParland who scored easily from close range. Blackpool were always in the game and midway through the second half equalised through Taylor after good work by Charnley.

Despite the best efforts of both teams the game ended level and Matthews (pictured above) was given a great ovation from the crowd as he left the field. His superb close ball control and eye for an opening could easily have earned his side both points.

In a postscript after the match Blackpool manager, Joe Smith, announced that he had been given notice to terminate his contract with the club at the end of the season. The 68 year old had been asked to retire at a board meeting last Thursday, but refused and as a consequence was sacked by registered letter received by his wife at his family home.

Preston destroyed Birmingham City at Deepdale, eventually winning the game 8-0, although only being two goals ahead at the interval. Finney opened the scoring with a header in the 4th minute and soon afterwards scored a second following a blistering 35 yard run. The away side then found their feet and caused Else one or two anxious moments.

Early in the second half Thompson scored the third and Taylor netted number four with a header. Then, in a purple period of eleven minutes from the 70th to 81st minute, Thompson and Taylor both scored twice each to complete their hat-tricks to give Preston their biggest win of the century.

Wolves maintained their run of form with a convincing 5-1 home win against Leicester City and remain five points clear of Preston at the top of the table. West Brom. suffered a 4-1 defeat at Manchester City and are now in fourth place behind Manchester United. Amazingly the hero of the game was City goalkeeper, Bert Trautmann, who made a string of outstanding saves to prevent Albion from adding to their early goal.

Arsenal   4   Manchester United   5

Herd, Bloomfield 2,   Edwards, Charlton, Taylor 2, Viollet
Tapscott.

Att. 63,578

Arsenal-*Kelsey, Charlton S., Evans, Ward, Fotheringham, Bowen, Groves, Tapscott, Herd, Bloomfield, Nutt.*

Manchester United-*Gregg, Foulkes, Byrne, Colman, Jones, Edwards, Morgans, Charlton R., Taylor, Viollet, Scanlon.*

The visit of League Champions Manchester United to Highbury resulted in the highest attendance on the ground this season, a full house of over 63,500, all looking forward to see the 'Busby Babes' in action.

A few minutes before the game began, Duncan Edwards in his all white kit, still found time to sign autographs for youngsters by the touchline. Both sides wore black armbands as a sign of respect following the sudden death of United Director 82-years old, George Whittaker at the team's hotel earlier in the day.

After a quiet opening ten minutes United broke the deadlock through EDWARDS. The left-half received a pass from Morgans and, from just outside the penalty area, hit a fierce low drive into the bottom corner of the net. Kelsey, wearing gloves, made a valiant attempt to save the shot but only succeeded in parrying the ball into the net.

Arsenal defended resolutely and at times threatened the United goal but their finishing lacked conviction and it was no surprise when the away side increased their lead after 33 minutes. Gregg saved a header from Groves and threw the ball out to Scanlon on the left wing. The youngster sprinted seventy yards down the touchline with Tapscott in pursuit before crossing the ball into the path of CHARLTON. A split second later a fierce drive nestled in the Arsenal goal (pictured below).

The home side then had a goal disallowed for offside in a rare sortie forward. Their opponents, playing some majestic football with swift counter attacks, scored again two minutes before the interval. Morgans crossed the ball for TAYLOR to smash home goal number three.

The second half started more sedately, possibly with United having one eye on their European Cup match in Belgrade on Wednesday. Arsenal took advantage and after 58 minutes pulled a goal back when HERD volleyed the ball into the net from a pass by Bowen. Two minutes later it was 2-3 as Groves headed the ball into the path of BLOOMFIELD who scored from close range.

A further minute later Arsenal were level as BLOOMFIELD scored with a diving header from a pass by Nutt. Poor Harry Gregg in the United goal, who had made the decision not to wear gloves, could do nothing about any of the three goals which had been scored in the space of 150 seconds.

The home crowd found their voices at last and the stadium vibrated to a wall of sound. United seemed to re-awake from their slumbers and stepped up a gear. Within three minutes of the equaliser they were ahead again. Charlton laid the ball to Scanlon who crossed it into the penalty area for VIOLLET to head number four. In the 71st minute it was 5-3. Colman sent Morgans away down the right flank. The winger pushed the ball to TAYLOR who scored from an acute angle.

Roger Byrne seemed to be suffering from a knock which was causing him problems and became a passenger. After 76 minutes Arsenal scored a fourth. Edwards somewhat lethargically lost the ball in midfield allowing Bowen, Groves and Nutt to move it forward quickly for TAPSCOTT to score just inside the post.

Late in the game Evans prevented a certain United goal with a soaring header and despite their best efforts neither side were able to add to their tally.

The crowd applauded both teams from the field at the final whistle having witnessed an amazing game of football.

SATURDAY 1ST FEBRUARY

ARSENAL	4	MANCHESTER U.	5
Herd, Bloomfield 2,		Edwards, Charlton	
Tapscott.		Taylor 2, Viollet.	
		Att. 63,578	
ASTON VILLA	1	BLACKPOOL	1
McParland.		Taylor.	
		Att. 47,499	
BOLTON W.	0	LEEDS UNITED	2
		Forrest, Cush.	
		Att. 18,558	
BURNLEY	2	CHELSEA	1
Pilkington, McIlroy.		Allen	
		Att. 20,599	
EVERTON	0	LUTON TOWN	2
		Gregory, Turner	
		Att. 26,908	
MANCHESTER C.	4	WEST BROM ALB.	1
McAdams 3, Barlow		Kevan.	
		Att.38,702	
NEWCASTLE U.	2	SUNDERLAND	2
Tait, Curry.		Elliott (pen), O'Neill	
		Att. 47,739	
NOTTINGHAM F.	2	PORTSMOUTH	0
Imlach (pen), Baily.		Att. 23,344	
PRESTON N. E.	8	BIRMINGHAM C.	0
Finney 2,Thompson 3,			
Taylor 3.		Att.21,511	
SHEFFIELD W.	2	TOTTENHAM H.	0
Wilkinson, Shiner			
		Att. 22,966	
WOLVES	5	LEICESTER CITY	1
Murray 2, Broadbent,		Walsh.	
Deeley, Mason		Att.36,400	

Team	P	W	D	L	F	A	W	D	L	F	A	Pts
Wolverhampton Wdrs.	28	12	2	0	42	12	6	4	4	26	21	42
Preston North End	28	12	1	1	45	10	4	4	6	24	29	37
Manchester United	28	10	0	4	41	17	5	6	3	32	30	36
West Bromwich Albion	28	9	4	1	41	18	3	7	4	24	31	35
Luton Town	28	10	2	2	32	12	5	2	7	15	25	34
Manchester City	28	10	3	1	44	21	5	0	9	28	44	33
Nottingham Forest	28	8	2	4	34	16	6	2	6	23	24	32
Burnley	28	12	1	1	40	14	2	2	10	17	40	31
Chelsea	28	9	2	3	41	23	2	5	7	21	33	29
Blackpool	28	7	1	6	32	26	5	4	5	17	19	29
Tottenham Hotspur	28	8	3	3	40	27	3	3	8	18	34	28
Arsenal	28	8	1	5	36	26	4	2	8	11	26	27
Bolton Wanderers	28	7	3	5	30	26	4	2	7	19	35	27
Everton	28	3	8	3	18	17	5	2	7	23	31	26
Birmingham City	28	4	4	6	30	31	4	4	6	19	37	24
Aston Villa	28	7	3	4	30	19	2	2	10	17	39	23
Portsmouth	28	7	3	3	28	17	2	1	12	22	39	22
Leeds United	28	6	4	4	24	19	2	2	10	12	30	22
Newcastle United	28	3	3	8	19	24	5	2	7	26	26	21
Sunderland	28	5	6	3	19	15	1	3	10	15	49	21
Leicester City	28	6	3	5	30	25	2	0	12	21	49	19
Sheffield Wednesday	28	7	2	5	34	32	0	2	12	17	39	18

United Reserves

In the top of the table Central League game at Old Trafford, United drew first blood when Webster gave them the lead after 12 minutes. Wolves fought back strongly and, after being awarded a free-kick from outside the penalty area, Flowers scored with a powerful drive.

Just before the interval Middleton gave the visitors the lead but their advantage was short lived as, within a minute of the restart, Dawson scored a header and with it the second teams 100th goal for the season.

United then stormed into the lead as Pegg scored twice, including a penalty, to make the score 4-2. Wolves were still dangerous and it was no surprise when Durindt scored to reduce the arrears but United held out for a 4-3 victory. They are now three points clear at the top of the table with Wolves in second place.

Mon. 3rd Feb.

The United party travelled from Ringway airport this morning bound for Belgrade with a stop-over in Munich. Following problems with the scheduled flights in the previous round, United decided to charter a plane for both legs of the journey to Belgrade and back.

The eleven players who beat Arsenal on Saturday have been joined by Bent, Berry, Blanchflower, Pegg, Whelan and Wood.

Cope was originally going to travel with the team but was replaced by Bent at the last minute when it was discovered that Byrne was struggling with a thigh injury.

United Assistant Manager, Jimmy Murphy, was not with the party as, in his role of Welsh Team Manager, he will be in Cardiff on Wednesday for the vital World Cup qualifying match against Israel. His place on the plane was taken by Bert Whalley.

Tues. 4th Feb.

The United team group had a training session this afternoon at the Red Star Stadium and then travelled to the Stadium of The People's Army of Yugoslavia for a careful inspection of the pitch.

The freezing conditions in Belgrade had relented and a gradual thaw was under-way leaving the pitch rock solid underneath but with a couple of inches of melting snow on top. The game was expected to go ahead as planned with all 60,000 tickets sold, but conditions underfoot for the players will be testing to say the least.

The players and officials are expected to attend a cocktail party given by the British Ambassador.

Wed. 5th Feb.

In Cardiff, Wales became the 16th and final side to qualify for the 1958 World Cup when they beat Israel 2-0 to complete a 4-0 aggregate victory. A crowd of 38,000 had to wait until the 78th minute for the first goal in a strangely lacklustre encounter.

Their path had been blocked by Israel goalkeeper Jacob Chodorov who, single-handedly, kept them at bay at a cost of a broken nose and concussion. The 30 year old truck driver and amateur captain of his country received generous applause at the end of the game. Ivor Allchurch gave Wales the lead, hooking the ball home. A few minutes from time Cliff Jones, also of Swansea, fired a right foot shot into the net from a Medwin pass.

The 'scribes of the press' all agreed that Wales will need to up their game if they are to have any impact in Sweden.

The form of outside-left Jones, valued at £35,000, was monitored by a number of club representatives including Jack Crayston (Arsenal), Ted Drake (Chelsea), Jimmy Anderson (Tottenham), Arthur Rowe (West Brom.) and Stan Cullis (Wolves).

European Cup Quarter Finals 2nd Leg

Red Star Belgrade   3   Manchester U. 3

Kostic 2, Tasic (Pen)   Viollet, Charlton 2.
(Manchester United Win 5-4 On Aggregate) Att. 55,000

Red Star Belgrade-_Beara, Tomic, Zekovic, Mitic, Spajik, Popovic, Borozan, Sekularic, Tasic, Kostic, Coklic._

Manchester United-_Gregg, Foulkes, Byrne, Colman, Jones, Edwards, Morgans, Charlton, Taylor, Viollet, Scanlon._

Prior to the game the approach roads to the ground were packed with fans, some without tickets, but all desperate to see the game. The police had set up five check-points at which tickets were examined and those without a valid one were turned away.

Both teams emerged side by side, jogging onto a pitch mottled by white areas of snow and very soft on top. The Army Stadium was packed to its capacity of 55,000.

United made the best possible start to the game taking the lead after only 90 seconds. VIOLLET evaded a tackle just outside the penalty area and glided along the surface before beating the goalkeeper with a right foot shot into the corner of the net.

On the quarter of an hour mark Charlton had a goal disallowed for off-side but didn't have to wait long until he scored one that counted. After 30 minutes 'The Red Devils' advanced at pace with five players being involved in the move before the ball reached CHARLTON just outside the penalty area. He pulled the trigger and his left foot shot whizzed into the left hand corner of the goal. Kostic had a chance to pull a goal back but shot just wide of the post.

Two minutes later it was 3-0 and 5-1 on aggregate, as United appeared to have the game won. The ball had been pulled across the penalty area before being partially cleared by a defender. It rolled gently towards CHARLTON near the penalty spot and in a flash it was in the net. The home side were completely demoralised as the teams left the field at half time to a hushed atmosphere. All was to change two minutes after the restart as Red Star pulled a goal back. KOSTIC struck the ball inside Gregg's right hand post. Three minutes later the Yugoslavs should have had a second goal but this time Kostic's shot was too high.

In the 55th minute TOSIC scored a second from the penalty spot following a dubious decision by the Austrian referee. A Red Star player appeared to fall over Foulkes but the referee thought otherwise. At 2-3 the home supporters found their voices and roared their side forward. At times the atmosphere was hostile and supporters pushing forward threatened to burst over the concrete walls.

Although under pressure United still found time to counter attack and Morgans, despite obviously struggling with an injury, was unlucky to see his shot hit the post. As the game drew towards the close it looked as though the away defence would hold out. The referee had not helped matters by awarding over 20 free kicks against United during the second period.

With minutes remaining the game was levelled. Gregg had gathered the ball near the edge of his penalty area but his momentum carried him beyond the line. From the resulting free kick KOSTIC hit the ball to the left hand side of goal and, despite getting both hands to it, Gregg was unable to stop it entering the net. Luckily for Red Star the ball had glanced off Viollet's head on its way to goal.

Soon afterwards the game ended and United had once again reached the European Cup Semi-Finals.

That evening the players of both teams attended a banquet at the British Embassy and after the formalities were complete some of the United players received permission from Matt Busby to go out for a drink.

Thurs. 6th Feb.

The United party were in good spirits at breakfast after securing a place in the semi-final of the European Cup for the second consecutive season. On Saturday they will face League leaders Wolves at Old Trafford and are desperate for a win which would reduce the gap between the two teams to four points.

They began the first leg of their return journey on a chartered twin-engined British European Airways aircraft at 9 a.m., arriving at Munich airport at 12 noon to be greeted by snow, strong winds and freezing temperatures. The 38 passengers and 6 crew members disembarked and had a two hour break before the final boarding call at 2 p.m. hurried them back together for the return leg to Manchester.

The Elizabethan aircraft, 'Lord Burghley', had been refuelled and was ready for take-off. Captain Rayment, the co-pilot, was at the controls and at 14.19 GMT received clearance to proceed down the runway. When full power was reached his colleague in the cockpit, Captain Thain noticed the engines did not sound right and the port boost pressure gauge was fluctuating. At this point Captain Rayment abandoned the take-off.

A few minutes later a second attempt was made, but this time the engines seemed to be running too fast and take-off was once again aborted. The passengers returned to the airport lounge. Snow was falling heavily and with a further attempt to get airborne seemingly unlikely, Duncan Edwards decided to send a telegram to his landlady, "All flights cancelled, flying tomorrow. Duncan."

William Blake, the station engineer, came to the cockpit to find out exactly what had happened. He said that the engines could be re-tuned which would delay the flight until the following day. After further discussions it was agreed that a third attempt to take-off should be made, but this time the throttles should be opened more slowly.

After only a matter of minutes the passengers returned to the plane and some of the players decided to change seats, moving to the back of the plane which they felt was safer. Sports Journalist, Alf Clarke, was the last person to board the plane after making a phone call home.

The aircraft began its journey down the runway just after 3 p.m. GMT and gathered speed, but the port engine began to surge again. There was no time to abandon the take-off but the aircraft had not reached the minimum speed needed to lift it off the ground.

It was too late. The plane crashed into a fence before hitting a house causing the port wing to be torn off. The left side of the cockpit hit a tree and the plane's tail ripped away. Still moving, the plane hit a wooden hut following which there was an explosion as the building had housed a truck filled with tyres and fuel.

Captain Thain ordered his crew to evacuate the plane and move away from the area fearing more explosions.

Still in a part of the plane, Harry Gregg came round and found himself lying on his side with blood on his face and a splitting headache. He immediately headed for a shaft of light coming through a hole in the side of the plane which he kicked through to make larger. Captain Thain saw him and told him to run for it, but Gregg had heard a cry. Clambering back into the wreckage he found a baby under some debris, amazingly still alive. He passed the baby to crew member George Rogers who had returned to the plane and then went back in and found a woman, the baby's mother, very badly injured. He managed to manoeuvre her through the hole to safety.

His colleague, Bill Foulkes, had momentarily lost consciousness and came round as Captain Thain shouted at him to get out. He ran across a snow covered field, fearing that the plane would explode at any second.

On looking back at the crash scene he saw the plane was scattered over a wide expanse and flames lit up an area in the distance. The front of the plane had broken away and skidded into the fields but the rear had exploded.

Fellow players, Bobby Charlton and Dennis Viollet, were alive but dazed and injured when Gregg somehow managed to drag them away from what was left of the front of the aircraft.

Although it seemed an eternity it was only a few minutes before local people began to arrive at the scene followed by the airport emergency services. Someone arrived in a vehicle, a sort of converted wagon, and implored passengers to get in. Johnny Berry, Jackie Blanchflower and Matt Busby were carried on board. Bill Foulkes, Harry Gregg, Bobby Charlton and Dennis Viollet were able to climb on. The man at the wheel set off at speed, heading for the hospital with Bill Foulkes pleading with him to slow down fearing they would all be killed. The driver ignored his pleas and in desperation Foulkes struck him on the back of the head but it made little difference.

The scene at the Rechts der Isar hospital resembled a war zone and the dead and injured continued to arrive with the staff doing everything possible to treat the injured.

Eventually, after helping with the identification of survivors and bodies, Bill Foulkes and Harry Gregg were told to leave for the Stathus Hotel where rooms had been arranged for them together with newspaper staff Ted Ellyard and Peter Howard.

It was a bitterly cold day in Manchester and the weather forecast was for snow in the north-west. The early afternoon editions of the Manchester Evening News had a 'Stop Press' insert-'United Plane Held Up in Munich Blizzard.' As the telegraph wires continued to relay the horrendous news, the later editions headlined 'UNITED CUP XI CRASH, "28 DIE".'

With still no definitive information, United fans could only wait for the late news on the BBC radio and TV. Whilst the information was still unconfirmed and with differing stories emerging, one thing was clear – players had been killed or injured.

People began to gather at Old Trafford, waiting in silence for more news. Somehow hoping that the bulletins from Munich were inaccurate. The six o'clock news on the radio had failed to add anything to the story already conveyed in the papers and throughout the country people waited anxiously to hear the next main bulletin at 9 p.m.

The newsreader gave out the names of the players and officials who it was known had survived – Berry, Blanchflower, Busby, Charlton, Edwards, Foulkes, Gregg, Morgans, Scanlon, Viollet and Wood. He then used the words, "The following players and officials are unaccounted for" and read out a list of names. All those listening were fearful of what this meant.

Fri. 7th Feb.

As the people of Manchester awoke from the little sleep they had managed, they were suddenly made aware of the extreme gravity of the situation. The newspapers were now able to report the true extent of the tragedy with 21 out of the 44 passengers and crew on board killed in the disaster.

The list of those who died were as follows:

Players-Geoffrey Bent, Roger Byrne, Eddie Colman, Mark Jones, David Pegg, Tommy Taylor and Bill Whelan.

Club officials-Walter Crickmer (Secretary), Tommy Curry (Trainer) and Bert Whalley (Coach).

Sports Writers-Alf Clarke (Manchester Evening Chronicle), Don Davies (Manchester Guardian), George Follows (Daily Herald), Tom Jackson (Manchester Evening News), Archie Ledbrooke (Daily Mirror), Henry Rose (Daily Express), Frank Swift (News of the World) and Eric Thompson (Daily Mail).

Crew and other passengers-William Cable (B.E.A. Steward), Bela Miklos (Travel Agent), Willie Satinoff (Director of several Manchester Companies).

The wives and girlfriends of the United players and officials began to arrive in Munich today with their first stop being the hospital. They had encountered treacherous journeys on the two aircraft from Manchester, flying through snowstorms and were fortunate that the planes were allowed to land at Munich airport which had been closed earlier in the day due to the bad weather.

Mrs Busby saw her husband and stated that he was resting, and there was some slight improvement in his condition. Molly Leach arrived to see Duncan Edwards, who she intends to marry next year, knowing that his injuries will make it almost impossible for him to play again as a professional footballer.

United Assistant Manager, Jimmy Murphy, saw his boss, Matt Busby and the players. Personally he obviously felt the grief of the situation but stubbornly proclaimed, "Manchester United will live on" and, "The Red Devils will survive this".

Messages of condolence were received at the Club, including one from the Queen and the Duke of Edinburgh, Prime Minister, Harold MacMillan (in Australia) and other foreign dignitaries and royalty.

A spokesperson for B.E.A. said that the Company will pay compensation to family members of all those killed and to those injured subject to proof of loss. The

Airline can only pay a maximum of £3,000 as decreed by International Law. It is understood that all the Manchester United party were insured for at least £10,000.

After confirming that the United v Wolves game had been postponed, the Football League decided to go ahead with all the other scheduled fixtures tomorrow despite some strong criticism from clubs.

They also decreed that players will wear black armbands and observe a period of silence before kick-off. All flags at football stadiums will also be flown at half-mast.

Bert Tann, the Bristol Rovers Manager, was scathing of the decision to go ahead with the games, stating that, "The matches should be postponed out of respect for Manchester United and the wives and relatives of those killed or injured."

With the weather forecasters predicting snow or heavy rainfall for the weekend, Manchester City decided to travel to London today in plenty of time for tomorrow's game at White Hart Lane.

Preston will also be in the capital to meet Chelsea at Stamford Bridge. The game at Portsmouth against Bolton Wanderers is also expected to go ahead.

Sat. 8ᵗʰ Feb.

The morning papers carried the following reports on the condition of the United players and officials still in hospital:

Matt Busby – Shock, fracture of right foot, open wound on right knee, chest injuries-condition a little worse.

John Berry – Shock, head lacerations, fractured cheek bone, condition-unchanged.

Duncan Edwards – Shock, fractured ribs on the right side, compound fracture of the right leg, condition-better.

Jackie Blanchflower – Fracture of right lower arm, shock, suspected internal injuries, condition-unchanged.

Dennis Viollet – Concussion, head lacerations, condition-good.

Ken Morgans – Concussion, shock, condition-good.

Albert Scanlon – Shock, skull fracture, condition-satisfactory.

Ray Wood – Bruises and flesh wounds, condition-good.

Bobby Charlton – Slight head injuries, condition-good.

Professor Maurer, at the Isar Hospital, stated that five of the injured are critically ill – Matt Busby, Duncan Edwards and John Berry, together with Captain Rayment and Frank Taylor of the News Chronicle. He also stated that in the case of Duncan Edwards it could be years before he would regain full use of his legs.

The first survivors of the crash arrived at London Airport today. They were Mr Peter Howard, a photographer of the Daily Mail, his assistant Mr Ellyard and four members of the crew, Captain James Thain, Wireless Officer G. W. Rodgers, and the stewardesses, Miss Margaret Bellis and Miss Rosemary Cheverton.

The Chairman of Manchester United, Harold Hardman, issued the following statement, "Even if it means being heavily defeated, we will carry on with the season's programme. We have a duty to the public and a duty to football to carry out."

The Lord Mayor of Manchester, Alderman Leslie Lever, has organised the creation of a 'Disaster Fund'. The fund immediately received the donation of £1,000 guineas from Great Universal Stores and £1,000 from the Manchester Evening Chronicle. He has also contacted multi-denominational clergymen throughout Manchester in order to arrange to hold memorial services for those who died.

The Evening Chronicle reported that, after visiting the hospital today, Mrs Busby told reporters, "The lads still need your prayers."

Tonight the Evening Chronicle asks all who go to church tomorrow to add them to their prayers.

Mr Louis C. Edwards has been appointed as a Director of Manchester United in succession to Mr George Whittaker, who died in London last week. Mr Edwards, 43, is the proprietor of a firm of meat manufacturers and contractors and owner of a number of butcher's shops in the Manchester area.

SATURDAY 8TH FEBRUARY 1958

BIRMINGHAM C.	P	SHEFFIELD WED.	P
BLACKPOOL	P	EVERTON	P
CHELSEA	0	PRESTON N. E.	2
		Thompson, Finney	
		Att. 42,704	
LEEDS UNITED	P	ARSENAL	P
LEICESTER CITY	6	ASTON VILLA	1
Walker, Lynn (og),		Southren	
Riley 2, Hogg 2.		Att. 25,535	
LUTON TOWN	7	SUNDERLAND	1
Groves, Brown 2,		Fogarty.	
Turner 4.		Att. 15,932	
MANCHESTER U.	P	WOLVES	P
NEWCASTLE UTD.	P	BURNLEY	P
PORTSMOUTH	2	BOLTON W.	2
Harris, Dickinson		Hennin, Parry	
		Att. 21,950	
TOTTENHAM H.	5	MANCHESTER C.	1
Brooks, Smith 3,		Hayes.	
Robb		Att. 37,539	
WEST BROM. ALB.	3	NOTTINGHAM F.	2
Kevan 2, Robson.		Quigley, Simcoe	
		Att. 32,735	

The morning papers stated that some teams had offered United help by being prepared to loan them players subject to Football League agreement. Sheffield Wednesday said that wing-half, Don Gibson, could move to United if required. Gibson is the son-in-law of Matt Busby.

Snow and frost caused the postponement of four Division 1 games with a fifth at Old Trafford already cancelled.

Footballers throughout the country stood in silence in remembrance of those who lost their lives and those seriously injured in hospital.

Pictured above was the scene at White Hart Lane where the Manchester City players showed their respect to their fellow professionals across the City.

On the field of play Spurs found themselves a goal down at half time against City. The second half was played on a quagmire of a pitch following torrential downpours. The home side adapted better to the conditions and within five minutes of the restart should have equalised but Harmer missed from the penalty spot. Spurs continued to pile forward and Brooks scored from close range before Smith helped himself to a hat trick. Robb netted the fifth as Manchester City were completely demoralised.

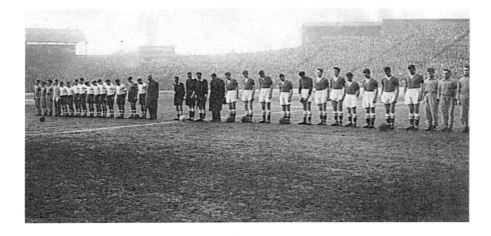

Pictured on the previous page was the scene at Stamford Bridge before the game. Chelsea fielded the youngest forward line ever to appear in League football with an average age of 18 years and 11 months.

In contrast Preston included a number of players who have made over 100 appearances. The 'old guard' proved there is no substitute for experience as goals from Thompson and Finney gave the away side the points.

Luton Town demolished Sunderland, winning 7-1 to remain in a creditable fifth position in the table. Gordon Turner scored four to bring his season's total to 26 including three hat tricks.

World Cup

The World Cup draw was made in Stockholm today giving England a very difficult qualifying group.

Group 1	*Group 2*	*Group 3*	*Group 4*
Argentina	France	Hungary	Austria
Czechoslovakia	Paraguay	Mexico	Brazil
Northern Ireland	Scotland	Sweden	England
West Germany	Yugoslavia	Wales	Russia

The tournament will be held in Sweden during June 1958.

Sun. 9th Feb.

A proposal has been submitted involving a number of European Football governing bodies, that Manchester United should be proclaimed honorary European Champions for 1958. A meeting of the European Football Union will be held on 1st March 1958 to discuss the matter.

Mon. 10th Feb.

Reports from the Rechts der Isar Hospital in Munich stated that both Matt Busby and Sports writer Frank Taylor have been taken off the danger list following improvement in their condition.

John Berry and Captain Rayment have undergone surgery including the insertion of tubes in their windpipes to assist with breathing. Both are in a critical condition with Berry still in a coma.

Professor Maurer, when questioned, said that he considered it unlikely that Berry, Edwards and Scanlon would ever play football again.

The bodies of ten victims of the Munich air crash were flown into Ringway Airport this evening and will lie in the gymnasium at the United ground tonight. Roger Byrne, Tommy Taylor, Eddie Colman, Geoff Bent and Mark Jones together with Walter Crickmer, Bert Whalley, Tom Curry and journalists Tom Jackson and Alf Clarke.

Well over 100,000 people waited in silence for up to three hours to line the route from the airport to Old Trafford, with approximately 5,000 waiting at the ground.

Another seven coffins containing the bodies of H. D. Davies, A. Ledbrooke, H. Rose, E. Thompson, F. Swift and G. Follows, all journalists, together with W. Satinoff had left the cortèges prior to its arrival at Old Trafford.

The Viscount 800 freighter had first arrived at London Airport, where the body of Bill Whelan was transferred to an Aer Lingus Dakota bound for Dublin. David Pegg's coffin was taken to Doncaster, Bela Miklos to Woking and William Cable to Swansea.

The funeral of Henry Rose, the Daily Express Sports writer, will be held in Manchester tomorrow.

Tues. 11th Feb.

Harry Gregg, Bill Foulkes and Jimmy Murphy travelled overland and by ferry and are expected to arrive in London this morning.

The FA agreed a request from United to postpone the FA Cup tie against Sheffield Wednesday, scheduled for Saturday, until Wednesday 19th February. They also announced that, in view of the extraordinary circumstances, they would waive the requirement for a player to be signed at least 14 days before the date of the tie. Any request by United to field a player who would otherwise have been ineligible will be considered on its merit.

A spokesman for the FA stated that a memorial service for the United players and officials will be held at St. Martin-in-the-Field in London at noon on Monday 17th February. On the same day at 2.30 p.m. Manchester Cathedral will hold a service for those journalists who died in the disaster.

John Berry came out of his coma today and was able to drink a small cup of tea.

Newspapers reported that Hungarian Internationals Ferenc Puskas, Zoltan Czibor and Sandor Kocsis had offered their services to Manchester United for the remainder of the season. Although these players would be of great assistance to the club it is unlikely that United will take up their offer.

A statement issued from Old Trafford has given the news that the young wing-half, Wilf McGuinness, will need a cartilage operation and is unlikely to play again this season. This is not the news that Jimmy Murphy wanted to hear on his return to Manchester.

Wed. 12th Feb.

Following the report that the FA had given United permission to sign new players prior to next Wednesday, the rumour mill went into overdrive. It was reported that Welsh Internationals Mel Charles and Ivor Allchurch from Swansea would join United for £50,000. The link of course being United Assistant Manager, Jimmy Murphy, who is also the Welsh team Manager.

The Club made their first initial move in the transfer market by asking Blackpool to name a price for transfer-listed inside-forward Ernie Taylor. The experienced player has appeared in two FA Cup Finals and, having not played in this season's FA Cup, would automatically be eligible to play for United.

Thurs. 13th Feb.

The funeral of H. D. Davies, who wrote under the pseudonym an 'Old International', for the Manchester Guardian, was held at St. Ann's church Manchester today. A large congregation filled the church and several hundred waited outside to pay their respects as the cortège left for Manchester Crematorium.

Funerals were also held for Alf Clarke of the Manchester Evening Chronicle in Manchester, George Follows of the Daily Herald in Wolverhampton, Tommy Taylor in Barnsley, Geoffrey Bent in Pendlebury, Tom Curry in Stretford and Bert Whalley in Dukinfield.

The condition of Duncan Edwards improved today when he reportedly asked for a drink. He has had an artificial kidney linked to his blood stream in an attempt to relieve the strain on his injured kidneys.

It was confirmed that £600 will be paid through the Players Union to the dependants of each of the seven players killed.

Manchester United finally made their first signing today when 33 year old Ernie Taylor joined from Blackpool for a fee of £8,000. Although Sunderland were also interested in signing the player, Taylor said that he was proud to join United and hoped that, by doing so, he could help to pay tribute to the players he had known so well.

Fri. 14ᵗʰ Feb.

Jimmy Murphy wasted no time in making his second appointment when he brought Jack Crompton back to Old Trafford as Trainer-Coach. The former United goalkeeper had spent 16 months at Luton Town as trainer and leaves the club sitting in a healthy position in the table.

The Luton chairman said that they were disappointed to lose his services but, at the same time, very pleased to help United following the terrible tragedy.

The saga of the on-off transfer of Swansea winger Cliff Jones was finally resolved today when he joined Spurs for a fee of £30,000.

Duncan Edwards was reported to have deteriorated again with his temperature rising to 103.3 degrees, although he still remains conscious. Captain Rayment and John Berry remain seriously ill. The good news to emerge was that Bobby Charlton has started his return to England today by train.

The Manchester United Disaster Fund, organised by the Lord Mayor of Manchester, has already reached a total in excess of £8,000.

More funeral services were held today for Eddie Colman at St. Clement's Church, Ordsall, Salford, Mark Jones at Wombwell Parish Church, South Yorkshire and in St. Ann's Roman Catholic Church Stretford for Walter Crickmer.

With the United v Sheffield Wednesday game postponed there will be seven FA Cup ties tomorrow. Surprisingly only three of those will include Division 1 teams as Bolton, West Brom. and Wolves strive for a place in the last eight. If successful they will, of course, be joined by either United or Sheffield Wednesday, but the draw still has a strange look about it.

Sat. 15ᵗʰ Feb.

The FA Cup matches did not produce any shock results and all the Division 1 sides will still be in the draw for the next round, albeit with West Brom. needing to come through a replay against Sheffield United.

At Molineux Wolves were in no mood to allow their Division 3 North opponents, Darlington, any leeway to gain a foothold in the game. Darlington fought hard and Wolves had to wait until the 32ⁿᵈ minute for a breakthrough when Murray scored from close range. Clamp then missed a penalty but by half time the home side were 3-0 ahead.

In the second half Murray completed his hat trick with a perfectly placed header from a cross by Deeley and the final scoreline of 6-1 was a fair reflection of the game.

259

Bramall Lane hosted the biggest crowd seen at the ground for twenty years as over 56,000 witnessed a hard fought draw between Sheffield United and West Bromwich Albion.

Allen had given the away side the lead after 17 minutes when he swept the ball into the net from a perfect pass by Kevan and the away side looked to be on their way through to the next round. Seventeen year old, Kevin Lewis had other ideas. He moved from the wing to inside-left and scored the equaliser with just over ten minutes remaining. The match had been played in a strong blustery wind blowing down the ground from one goal to the other, making the timing and accuracy of passing very difficult.

A stalemate at Ninian Park means both sides will have to replay on Thursday. Blackburn Rovers forward, Peter Dobing, who had been released by the Army to play in the game, had the best chances of the match but was thwarted on each occasion by Jones in the Cardiff goal.

In the League the Preston home match against Newcastle United was 'called off' by referee Arthur Ellis just 45 minutes before the scheduled kick-off with the pitch water logged following a prolonged period of heavy rain. A few hundred spectators were already in the ground and had to queue for a refund.

SATURDAY 15th FEBRUARY
DIVISION 1

BURNLEY	1	**LUTON TOWN**	2
Pointer		Turner, Brown	
		Att. 16,869	
EVERTON	2	**LEICESTER CITY**	2
J. Harris, Thomas.		Walsh 2	
		Att. 23,460	
MANCHESTER C.	1	**BIRMINGHAM C.**	1
McAdams.		Orritt	
(Abandoned after 40 minutes)		Att.25,000	
NOTTINGHAM F.	1	**TOTTENHAM H.**	2
Wilson		Brooks, Robb.	
		Att. 32,334	
PRESTON N. E.	P	**NEWCASTLE U.**	P
SHEFFIELD W.	2	**CHELSEA**	3
Quixall 2 (2 pens)		Greaves 3.	
		Att. 16,876	
SUNDERLAND	1	**BLACKPOOL**	4
O'Neill.		Perry, Durie 2, Mudie.	
		Att. 28,127	

F. A. CUP 5TH ROUND

BOLTON W.	3	**STOKE CITY**	1
Lofthouse, Stevens.		Cairns (pen).	
Parry.		Att. 56,667	
BRISTOL CITY	3	**BRISTOL ROV.**	4
Watkins, Etheridge,		Sykes, Ward, Meyer,	
Burden.		Bradford.	
		Att. 39,160	

CARDIFF CITY	0	BLACKBURN R.	0
		Att. 45,580	
MANCHESTER U.	P	SHEFFIELD W.	P
(Match to be played Wednesday 19th February)			
SCUNTHORPE U.	0	LIVERPOOL	1
		Murdoch.	
		Att. 23,000	
SHEFFIELD U.	1	WEST BROM. ALB.	1
Lewis.		Allen. Att. 56,150	
WEST HAM UTD.	2	FULHAM	3
Grice, Bond (pen).		Dwight, Hill, Haynes.	
		Att. 37,500	
WOLVES	6	DARLINGTON	1
Murray 3, Broadbent 2,		Bell.	
Mason.		Att. 55,778	

Blackpool gave the performance of the day racing into a 3-1 lead by half time at Roker Park. Sunderland, who are the only First Division club never to have been relegated, eventually lost the game 4-1. They sit in great danger next to the bottom of the table.

Jimmy Greaves scored a hat trick at Sheffield Wednesday to bring his season's tally to 18 goals and in the process earned the points for Chelsea in a tough game.

Luton Town continued to confound their critics by winning 2-1 at Turf Moor despite Burnley having numerous chances to win the game. The victory has moved them into third place in the table.

Sun. 16th Feb.

Mounted police were needed at Old Trafford to help control the thousands of United supporters queueing for the 18,000 available tickets for Wednesday's FA Cup game. Some people arrived at the ground before midnight to guarantee their place to see United's first game since the Munich disaster.

Bobby Charlton arrived back in London today and was met by his mother and brother. The press were asked to give them some privacy and were more than happy to oblige.

Reports from Munich indicated that there were still major concerns regarding Duncan Edwards' kidneys and he was listed as dangerously ill. This, despite the fact that he had been given another five hours of artificial kidney treatment. John Berry had made slight improvement but Captain Rayment's condition remained unchanged.

The Football League intend to send a message of thanks to the staff at the Rechts der Isar hospital for their 'wonderful care and devotion' to those injured in the disaster.

It was also agreed that collections would be held at football grounds throughout the country, with the monies raised being given to the 'Disaster Fund'.

Mon. 17th Feb.

Manchester Cathedral was the scene of a Memorial Service held for the eight journalists killed in the crash. It was estimated that about 700 people attended the service which was conducted by The Very Reverend Jones, Dean of Manchester.

At the Parish Church of St. Martin-in-the-Fields the Memorial Service was held for the Manchester United footballers, officials and the journalists who lost their lives on February 6th.

The press reported that United officials had watched Birmingham City outside-left, Alex Govan, and Spurs out of favour left-half, Jim Iley, over the weekend.

Burnley Chairman, Bob Lord, told waiting journalists that United had made an offer for outside-left Brian Pilkington. Mr Lord was scathing in his remarks to the press saying that, "Of course clubs will help United-but not to the extent of parting with star players." He went on to say that reserve players could be offered with a view to help United complete their fixtures but certainly not first team players as these were needed by their own clubs.

Jimmy Murphy had been at Turf Moor on Saturday and the 'rumour-mill' immediately linked United with Reg Pearce, Luton Town's exciting wing-half. The player could demand a fee in the region of £20,000.

Manchester United arrived at the Norbreck Hydro Hotel in Blackpool today to spend a couple of days training prior to the FA Cup match at Old Trafford on Wednesday.

Jimmy Murphy had taken the players away from Manchester in an attempt to ease the pressure on them. Harry Gregg, Bill Foulkes and new signing Ernie Taylor were all expected to train with the squad.

The televised FA Cup draw at 6.45 p.m. threw up a number of exciting ties. Not since the 1946/47 season have two Second Division teams been guaranteed a place in the semi-finals.

FULHAM	v	**BRISTOL ROVERS**
SHEFFIELD UNITED or **WEST BROMWICH ALB**	v	**MANCHESTER UNITED** or **SHEFFIELD WEDNESDAY**
CARDIFF CITY or **BLACKBURN ROVERS**	v	**LIVERPOOL**
BOLTON WANDERERS	v	**WOLVERHAMPTON W.**

Tues. 18th Feb.

A crowd of 60,000 is expected at Old Trafford tomorrow for the Cup tie that everyone wants to see. BBC television have been criticised by the Football League for issuing advance publicity stating that the match will be given five minutes of live television followed by highlights on the Sportsview programme.

This detail could affect the attendances at the other games taking place tomorrow and is contrary to the normal procedures. However, it is still hoped that the United match will be able to be covered by the television cameras.

DIVISION 1

ARSENAL	1	BOLTON WANDERERS	2
Bloomfield		Lofthouse, Gubbins	

Att. 28,425

Wed. 19th Feb.

FA Cup 5th Round

Manchester U   3   Sheffield Wed. 0

Brennan 2, Dawson.   Att. 59,848   (Receipts £8,518)

Manchester United-*Gregg, Foulkes, Greaves, Goodwin, Cope, Crowther, Webster, Taylor E., Dawson, Pearson, Brennan.*

Sheffield Wednesday-*Ryalls, Martin, Baker, Kay, Swan, O'Donnell, Wilkinson, Quixall, Johnson, Froggatt, Cargill.*

The programme for the FA Cup match (pictured on the next page) told its own story with eleven blank spaces in the places where the names of the United players should have appeared.

United supporters had expected some of the youngsters to be given a chance and so it proved with débuts for 18 year old Mark Pearson and 20 year old Shay Brennan. Ron Cope and Ian Greaves made their first appearances of the season and were joined by new signing Ernie Taylor from Blackpool.

United sprang a major surprise by signing Aston Villa wing-half, Stan Crowther, just over an hour before kick-off for a fee of £18,000. The team therefore included six players who had never appeared in the United first team.

After one minute's silence the teams emerged to a deafening roar from the 60,000 crowd, many of whom wore black armbands.

Gregg made an early save from Cargill that breathed confidence into his defence and the United faithful on the terraces. Young Mark Pearson then won a crunching tackle that showed the opposition that he would be no pushover.

As the game progressed several thousand supporters waited outside the ground unable to get a ticket but desperate to be part of the occasion interpreting every roar or groan from the crowd.

There was little to choose between the teams in the opening skirmishes and Sheffield Wednesday were not distracted, despite the noise every time a United player touched the ball. The away side had a chance when a cross eluded Gregg, but Cope was on hand to clear the danger.

As the half progressed Ernie Taylor began to marshal 'the kids' demanding the ball at every opportunity and directing proceedings, both verbally and by his actions. He came nearest to scoring with his shot from outside the penalty area hitting the foot of the post before rebounding to safety.

After 29 minutes United won a corner on the left wing and BRENNAN went over to take it. He curled the ball right-footed towards the away goal where Ryalls and two defenders failed to clear the danger. The ball ended up in the net (see picture overleaf) and the near hysterical crowd went crazy.

United held the lead until half time but within minutes of the restart it was a more determined Sheffield Wednesday who pressed the home goal. Quixall, in particular, gave the United defence a torrid time – hitting one shot just over the crossbar.

The 'Babes' held out, defending deep, with new captain Foulkes leading by example.

Tireless, eager and confident, the players never stopped running, always trying to play football in a cultured manner.

In the 70th minute United got their reward for all their endeavours when they scored again. Foulkes had headed the ball out of defence, Crowther and Taylor moved it forward quickly to Pearson. The youngster shot, only to see the ball hit the goalkeeper's legs. BRENNAN was on hand to slot home the rebound.

Six minutes from time the game was over as United scored a third. Once again Pearson was involved, crossing the ball to DAWSON just outside the six yard box. The burly centre-forward, at first, seemed to have the ball stuck between his legs but quickly adjusted to score with his right foot.

The final whistle was greeted by a wall of noise as the supporters released their last burst of energy. In the dressing rooms after the game there were emotional tears shed.

At the Isar Hospital in Munich, four injured United players were delighted when they heard the result from Old Trafford. Ray Wood took the call with Ken Morgans, Bert Scanlon and Dennis Viollet waiting anxiously. He yelled out 'We've won, we've won 3-0' and the players reportedly celebrated with a glass of champagne.

Manager, Matt Busby, still lying critically injured in another ward, knew nothing of the game as the details had been kept from him. Duncan Edwards and John Berry were also too ill to be informed.

Following his transfer from Swansea to Spurs, outside-left Cliff Jones played for the British Army against the French Army in London before he had even had the opportunity to make his debut for his new club.

Jones could not inspire his colleagues in khaki as the French won the game 2-0 despite the home side having the following forward line – Harris (Everton), Temple (Everton), Curry (Newcastle), Hitchens (Aston V.), Jones (Spurs).

In a re-arranged League match Wolves beat Leeds United 3-2 at home in front of a crowd of 35,527. Goals from Broadbent, Mason and Deeley helped them to extend their lead at the top of the table to 5 points. Leeds provided stern opposition on the night with Peyton and Forrest on target in a hard fought game.

The FA Cup 5ᵗʰ Round replay at The Hawthorns attracted a huge crowd of 57,503 and was won as expected by the home side by 4 goals to 1, with Albion scoring all the goals. Robson, Kevan 2 and Allen scored for the winners with Dugdale scoring an own goal for Sheffield United.

The match was marred by an unfortunate injury to West Brom's outside-right Frank Griffin who broke his right shin bone just after the interval and will not play again this season.

Thurs. 20ᵗʰ Feb.

Luton Town left-half, Reg Pearce, signed for Sunderland for a fee reported to be in the region of £20,000. The player, aged 28, made 75 League appearances for Luton and, apparently, on Tuesday turned down the opportunity to move to Old Trafford as Jimmy Murphy attempted to strengthen his squad. It is understood Pearce has relatives living in the North East which may have influenced his decision.

F. A. CUP 5ᵗʰ Round replay

BLACKBURN ROVERS	2	CARDIFF CITY	1
McGrath, Douglas.		Hewitt	Att. 27,000

Fri. 21ˢᵗ Feb.

Mancunians and football supporters throughout the country awoke this morning to hear and read about the story that none of them wanted to happen. Duncan Edwards had lost his fight for life in a German hospital.

The 21 year old United and England wing-half died peacefully in his sleep at 2.15a.m.following a worsening of his kidney condition during the night.

His fiancée, Molly Leach, together with his parents, who had all been staying in Munich to be near him, were the first people to be informed. After visiting the hospital to pay their last respects they thanked the staff, before it was announced that they would fly back to London in the afternoon.

The Chief Surgeon, Professor Maurer, told reporters that he had been amazed at the young man's fight for life which was a testament to his will to live and physical strength. He went on to say that, had he lived, he would never have been able to play football again and would have been permanently disabled.

The other United players in hospital who were well enough to be told cried when they heard the news, as did some of the nurses who had cared for him for the last fifteen days. His body will be flown home on Saturday and taken to Dudley.

There was better news for Viollet and Morgans who have both been informed that they can go home tomorrow but it will have to be by air. The doctors do not feel they could withstand the physical strain of travelling by road, rail and sea. The players eventually, somewhat reluctantly, agreed to this arrangement.

At Old Trafford Jimmy Murphy informed the press that he would keep the same team for tomorrow's home game against Nottingham Forest.

United Reserves

The reserve side will include a number of youngsters with the average age of the team only 17½ for the away Central League game at Sheffield Wednesday.

Saturday 22nd February

League leaders, Wolves, demolished Midlands rivals Birmingham City in the opening 45 minutes, scoring five times without reply. Despite the muddy conditions Wolves powered forward at every opportunity and Murray completed his hat trick just on the stroke of half time. The away side did pull a goal back after the interval but the win leaves Wolves five points clear at the top of the table.

Second place Preston turned on the style at Kenilworth Road against Luton, who sat just one point below them before the game.

All the goals came in the first half. North End went ahead after eighteen minutes but the home side equalised nine minutes later. The game was effectively over in the last ten minutes of the first half when Finney scored from the penalty spot following a foul on Thompson. Then Finney laid on the pass to Thompson for him to score Preston's third.

A thrilling London derby at Highbury ended in a draw as Arsenal and Spurs shared eight goals in front of 59,000 spectators.

There were goals galore at Filbert Street with eight of them ending up in the back of the Manchester City net as Leicester won 8-4.

The away side had given Leicester a shock when Johnstone opened the scoring after only three minutes. But by the half hour mark Leicester were already 3-1 ahead.

Walsh scored twice in each half to bring his season's tally to 19 League goals in 13 games. Manchester City's 30 League games have now produced 155 goals- good entertainment for the fans.

SATURDAY 22ND FEBRUARY

ARSENAL	4	TOTTENHAM H.	4
Henry (og), Clapton		Smith 2,	
Nutt, Herd.		Harmer 2(1pen)	
		Att. 59,116	

ASTON VILLA	1	CHELSEA	3
McParland.		Tindall, Mortimore,	
		Brabrook.	
		Att. 20,358	

BLACKPOOL	2	SHEFFIELD W.	2
H, Kelly (pen),		Johnson 2,	
Charnley.		Att.13,771	

BOLTON W.	2	WEST BROM. ALB.	2
Gubbins, Stevens.		Kevan 2.	
		Att.19,132	

EVERTON	1	NEWCASTLE U.	2
Thomas.		Bottom 2.	
		Att. 22,448	

LEEDS UNITED	2	PORTSMOUTH	0
Baird 2.		Att. 26,713	

LEICESTER C.	8	MANCHESTER C.	4
Walsh 4, Riley 2 (1 pen)		Johnstone 2, McAdams	
Hines, Hogg.		Barnes (pen)	
		Att. 31,017	

LUTON TOWN	1	PRESTON N. E.	3
Adam.		Taylor, Finney (pen),	
		Thompson.	
		Att. 22,549	

MANCHESTER U.	1	NOTTINGHAM F.	1
Dawson.		Imlach.	
		Att. 66,346	

SUNDERLAND	2	BURNLEY	3
O'Neill, Hannigan.		Robson 2, Pointer.	
		Att. 30,595	

WOLVES	5	BIRMINGHAM C.	1
Deeley 2, Murray 3.		Murphy.	
		Att.36,941	

United Reserves

The inexperienced United side were well beaten 4-0 at Sheffield Wednesday. The defeat has allowed Wolves to move to the top of the table.

Manchester Utd.	**1**	**Nottingham F.**	**1**
Dawson		Imlach	

Att. 66,346

Manchester United-*Gregg, Foulkes, Greaves, Goodwin, Cope, Crowther, Webster, Taylor, Dawson, Pearson, Brennan.*

Nottingham Forest-*Thomson, Whare, Thomas, Morley, McKinlay, Burkitt, Gray, Quigley, Wilson, Joyce, Imlach.*

The eyes of the football world were again focused on Old Trafford where United named the same team for their first League game since the 'Disaster'.

A crowd of over 66,000 crammed into the ground, creating a post-war League record attendance at the stadium. The fans had gathered under the shadow of the news of the death of Duncan Edwards and before the kick-off there was a strangely subdued air on the terraces and in the stands. All the admission gates at the ground were closed fifteen minutes before kick-off.

The Dean of Manchester conducted a brief Memorial Service before the teams emerged which was attended by the Yugoslav Ambassador and representatives of the Yugoslav FA and the Red Star Club. There was also a minutes silence in respect of the players, officials and journalists who had lost their lives.

The game began with snow falling on an already saturated pitch making cultured football out of the question. It was soon obvious that some of the United youngsters looked lethargic and leg weary following their exertions on Wednesday evening.

Forest dominated possession with their experienced players using short passes to dictate the play. Wilson was put clean through but somehow sliced the ball with the goal at his mercy. Quigley had a snap shot saved by Gregg but inevitably their pressure paid when they took the lead after 31 minutes.

Quigley laid the ball to Wilson on the right flank who then placed it into the penalty area. IMLACH reacted quickest and found space before driving the ball beyond Gregg.

Taylor and Pearson were the only 'bright sparks' to emerge from the opening 45 minutes. Pearson in particular caught the eye with his long sideburns giving him the appearance of a Mexican and earning him the nickname 'Pancho'. His aggressive tackling and confidence to run at defenders defied his inexperience at first team level.

During the interval Jimmy Murphy must have had effective words with his young players as it was a different United side that opened the second half. Dawson had two opportunities. The first was saved by Thomson and the second was somehow cleared inches from the goal line. Pearson beat three defenders only to see his shot cleared by Thomas. The crowd rose to the 'New Babes' urging them forward with deafening roars at every opportunity.

Taylor was now directing play, demanding the ball, hitting pinpoint passes and shouting instructions, as Forest began to wilt under the pressure.

Thomson in the Forest goal was looking more and more uncertain and on one occasion dropped a shot from Pearson. Luckily a defender cleared the danger.

Taylor continued to drive United forward in search of an equaliser. He outmanoeuvred three defenders before laying the ball into the path of Dawson, only for the burly centre-forward to have his shot saved. At the next opportunity he decided to 'go it alone' but this time Thomson pushed the ball round the post for a corner.

In the 70th minute United finally got the breakthrough that their attacking play richly deserved. From a corner there was a scramble in the Forest penalty area and DAWSON reacted quickest to score from close range.

The crowd urged the home side on and Taylor was unlucky to see a shot go just wide of the post. The noise was ear shattering but despite their best efforts United's players could not clinch the game.

Sun. 23rd Feb.

Four Memorial services were held today for the players and officials killed and injured in the Munich air disaster. These were at the Manchester Cathedral, where a congregation of approximately 2,000 attended the service with admission by ticket only, the South Manchester Synagogue, which held a service for Henry Rose of the Daily Express, the Albert Hall, where a Free Church service was attended by around 1,750 and the King's Hall, Belle Vue, Manchester, which was attended by 6,000 who took part in the Roman Catholic High Mass.

Mon. 24th Feb.

Bobby Charlton is hoping that his Army Medical Officer will pass him fit to play in the R.A.O.C. Cup Final at Didcot on Wednesday afternoon. The player, who holds the rank of Lance Corporal whilst undertaking his National Service, wants the opportunity to prove to United that he is fit, both physically and mentally, to play in the FA Cup match at West Brom. on Saturday.

He was a member of the 17th Battalion side, which included Duncan Edwards, who won the trophy last season.

Tues. 25th Feb.

The United players once again travelled to the Norbreck Hydro Hotel in Blackpool and will train in the area until the eve of the FA Cup tie on Saturday. Birmingham City have also made the Norbreck their headquarters after arriving yesterday in preparation for their game at home to Arsenal at the weekend.

Wed. 26th Feb.

The Munich Air Disaster Fund has now reached £14,200 with the monies being held for the benefit of those involved in the disaster whether they are players, officials, journalists, European Airways staff or other passengers. A management committee has been set up to administer the Fund.

Bad weather caused the postponement of the Army R.A.O.C. Cup Final at Didcot today, therefore denying Bobby Charlton the opportunity to prove his fitness.

The funeral of Duncan Edwards took place at St. Francis's Church in Dudley today. The service was conducted by the Reverend Catterall who is a keen Everton supporter.

Many professional footballers, club representatives and dignitaries attended the service with traffic being diverted as an estimated 5,000 people lined the streets and stood outside the church.

The six pall bearers were Billy Wright, Ronnie Clayton, Ray Barlow, Don Howe and his best friends Gordon Clayton and Bobby English, both from United.

Fri. 28th Feb.

United sprang a major surprise by announcing that three amateur players from the famous Bishop Auckland side will appear in the second team for the Central League match against Burnley at Old Trafford tomorrow. Warren Bradley (24) and Derek Lewin (27), pictured above, will be joined by the former England Amateur International Captain, Bob Hardisty, now aged 37, pictured below.

The young United reserve side suffered a heavy defeat last Saturday and Jimmy Murphy has decided that more experienced players are needed to help the youngsters through the remaining fixtures.

The press were informed that Matt Busby had been told yesterday of the deaths of the eight United players in the disaster. He was obviously shocked by the news and given sedatives to help him sleep.

A bulletin from the hospital today stated that he appeared to be recovering from the acute depression that the news had caused.

Johnny Berry is still on the danger list though his level of consciousness seems to be lightening. He was given an injection after a restless night to help him relax.

Co-pilot, Kenneth Rayment, remains in a critical condition.

After once again training on the beach at Blackpool, United have decided to leave out Shay Brennan for tomorrow's Cup fixture. His place in the side will be taken by Bobby Charlton who will play at outside-left in his first appearance since the European Cup tie in Belgrade.

Harry Gregg, who injured his hand in training and was sent for an X-ray, has been given the all-clear.

Albion have included former United player, Whitehouse at outside-right in place of the injured Griffin.

Earlier in the week ten inches of snow fell in Blackburn and across Lancashire. At Bolton the ground had snow drifts in places up to two foot deep. A thaw, however, has now started to melt the snow and all the clubs hosting FA Cup ties tomorrow are hopeful that the games will go ahead. Over 200,000 spectators are expected at the four Cup ties with 'grounds full' notices already posted.

Player Profile

Stanley Crowther
Born 3ʳᵈ September, 1935, Bilston, Staffordshire

After some impressive performances for Bilston Town playing at inside-right, Stan Crowther, aged 20, joined Aston Villa for a fee of £750.

The imposing 6'2" blond-haired Crowther was soon knocking on the first team door and didn't wait long for his debut. An injury to Billy Baxter, Villa's wing-half, provided the opening and manager, Eric Houghton, decided to give Crowther the No. 4 shirt on 29ᵗʰ September 1956. Bolton Wanderers were the opposition at Villa Park and, despite the goalless draw, he had an outstanding game making the position his own for the rest of the season with 24 League appearances.

Not blessed with artistic ball skills, the tough tackling no nonsense player is a hard opponent to play against. He played in all nine of Villa's FA Cup matches during 1956/57 culminating in the victory against Manchester United at Wembley. A Cup Winner's medal in his first full season brought him to the attention of the footballing world.

Selected to play for England Under 23's on three occasions, Crowther then made 28 League and Cup appearances during 1957/58 scoring 4 goals at right-half, left-half and inside-right. He joined United for a fee of £18,000 less than two hours before the kick-off against Sheffield Wednesday in the Cup, giving a cultured performance at left-half. He had special permission to play in the game having already appeared for Villa early in the Competition.

MARCH 1958

Saturday 1st March

In the FA Cup Bolton Wanderers beat Wolves to deny them the chance of a League and Cup double. The victory was somewhat fortuitous as Wolves had numerous opportunities to win the game.

Murray hit the cross-bar and Deeley rattled the post. In another raid Mullen blasted the ball over the bar when it looked easier to score.

In the final ten minutes Wolves threw everyone forward in search of an equaliser but Hopkinson and some brave defending by Hartle earned the home side a thrilling 2-1 victory. The winning goal came from a free kick by Parry after Finlayson had carried the ball beyond the edge of the penalty area whilst making a save.

In the League high flying Luton Town were surprisingly beaten by bottom placed Sheffield Wednesday with Shiner scoring twice.

SATURDAY 1st MARCH
DIVISION 1

BIRMINGHAM C.	4	ARSENAL	1
Hooper, Murphy,		Bloomfield	
Brown 2.			Att. 26,834
BURNLEY	0	EVERTON	2
		Thomas 2.	
			Att. 19,657
MANCHESTER C.	4	BLACKPOOL	3
Barnes (pen). McAdams,		Perry 2, Durie	
Barlow, H. Kelly (og)			Att. 30,621
NEWCASTLE U.	2	ASTON VILLA	4
Bottom, R. Mitchell (pen)		Smith, Hitchens 2	
		Dugdale	Att. 40,135
NOTTINGHAM F.	3	LEICESTER CITY	1
Gray, Baily, Imlach		Walsh	
			Att. 38,341
PRESTON N. E.	3	SUNDERLAND	0
Thompson 2, Baxter.			Att. 23,974
SHEFFIELD W.	2	LUTON TOWN	1
Shiner 2.		Turner.	
			Att. 17,747

F. A. CUP QUARTER FINALS

BLACKBURN R.	2	LIVERPOOL	1
Clayton, McLeod.		Murdoch	
Receipts £7,686			Att. 51,000
BOLTON W.	2	WOLVES	1
Stevens, Parry.		Mason	
Receipts £9,277			Att. 56,306
FULHAM	3	BRISTOL ROVERS	1
Hill, Stevens 2.		Bradford.	
Receipts £4,825			Att. 42,000
WEST BROM. ALB.	2	MANCHESTER U.	2
Allen, Horobin.		E. Taylor, Dawson.	
Receipts £8,050			Att. 57,574

FA Cup Quarter Final

West Brom. Alb 2   **Manchester Utd.** 2
Allen, Horobin.   Taylor, Dawson.

Att. 57,574

West Bromwich Albion-*Sanders, Howe, Williams, Dudley, Kennedy, Barlow, Whitehouse, Robson, Allen, Kevan, Horobin.*
Manchester United-*Gregg, Foulkes, Greaves, Goodwin, Cope, Crowther, Webster, Taylor, Dawson, Pearson, Charlton.*

United kicked off this eagerly anticipated Quarter-final tie to the tumultuous roar of the 15,000 travelling supporters in the capacity crowd. It did not take long for United to find their feet and after only five minutes they took the lead. The ball was pushed down the left flank to Dawson who crossed it into the penalty area. Charlton looked as though he would take a shot at goal but somehow the ball by-passed him, arriving at the feet of TAYLOR. The diminutive inside-forward made no mistake banging the ball into the net from eight yards.

West Bromwich Albion Squad

Back row L. to R. – C. Forrester, A. Jackson, C. Jackman, F. Brown, J. Sanders,
J. Kennedy, G. Lee.
Middle row – D. Kevan, D. Howe, J. Dudley, S. Williams, B. Whitehouse,
F. Griffin.
Front row – Vic Buckingham (manager), M. Setters, R. Robson, R. Barlow
(cap.), R. Horobin, R. Allen, L. Millard.

After eleven minutes Albion won a corner which was taken by Whitehouse. Horobin touched the ball onto Allen but his shot was palmed away by Gregg. However the danger was not cleared and after Kevan had another effort blocked the ball reached ALLEN who scored from barely four yards.

Taylor began to weave his magic, dictating play and marshalling his young colleagues. On one occasion he beat Kennedy and Barlow before having the ball taken from him at the last minute by Robson. In the 43rd minute United regained the lead after Taylor had seen his long range shot hit the cross-bar. The ball rebounded to DAWSON who reacted quickly and headed it beyond Sanders. Albion were always in the game but Goodwin, Cope and Crowther made life difficult for the home forwards, tackling, blocking and denying space whenever possible.

The second half opened with United looking comfortable and yet still dangerous when moving forward. Sanders saved from Charlton, Pearson shot narrowly over the bar and Dawson headed wide as United should have increased their advantage.

As the game reached the final fifteen minutes the away side began to tire and the passes became more pedestrian. Albion, sensed their opportunity as the 'Babes' looked leg weary, and in the 86th minute deservedly equalised.

Allen crashed a left foot shot from well outside the penalty area forcing Gregg to make a diving save. The goalkeeper could only push the ball into the path of HOROBIN who had the simple task of tapping the ball towards the goal-line. Gregg made a desperate attempt to prevent the ball crossing the line but the referee correctly awarded a goal.

Neither side could force a winner and after the match one newspaper reporter stated that it was the best game of football he had ever had the privilege to watch.

United Reserves

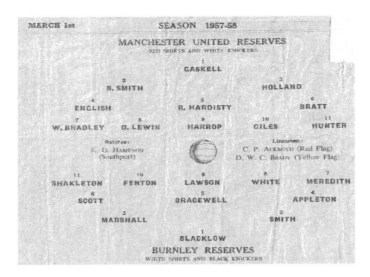

MARCH 1st   SEASON 1957-58

MANCHESTER UNITED RESERVES
RED SHIRTS AND WHITE KNICKERS.

1
GASKELL

2   3
B. SMITH   HOLLAND

4   5   6
ENGLISH   R. HARDISTY   BRATT

7   8   9   10   11
W. BRADLEY   D. LEWIN   HARROP   GILES   HUNTER

Referee: Linesmen:
K. G. HAMPSON   C. P. ACKROYD (Red Flag)
(Southport)   D. W. C. BRADY (Yellow Flag)

11   10   9   8   7
SHAKLETON   FENTON   LAWSON   WHITE   MEREDITH
6   5   4
SCOTT   BRACEWELL   APPLETON
3   2
MARSHALL   SMITH

1
BLACKLOW
BURNLEY RESERVES
WHITE SHIRTS AND BLACK KNICKERS

Veteran defender, Bob Hardisty, used his vast experience at the heart of the United Reserves defence to help the youngsters whenever possible. The two other Bishop Auckland amateurs were lively in the United attack.

Despite some early pressure from the home side it was Burnley who took the lead when Shackleton scored from a free kick. Harrop equalised for the 'Reds' with a header after 20 minutes and the game reached the interval all square.

Within a few minutes of the restart Lewin was fouled in the penalty area but Giles missed from the spot.

Neither side could force a winner as the teams shared the points in an entertaining game watched by a crowd in excess of 20,000.

	P.	W.	L.	D.	F.	A.	Pts.
Wolverhampton Wanderers	30	20	4	6	76	36	46
Preston North End ...	31	19	7	5	77	40	43
West Bromwich Albion ...	30	13	5	12	70	53	38
Luton Town ...	32	17	11	4	58	44	38
MANCHESTER UNITED...	29	15	7	7	74	48	37
Nottingham Forest ...	32	15	12	5	64	47	35
Manchester City ...	31	16	12	3	81	81	35
Chelsea ...	31	13	11	7	68	61	33
Tottenham Hotspur ...	31	13	11	7	69	67	33
Burnley ...	31	15	13	3	61	60	33
Blackpool ...	31	13	12	6	58	52	32
Bolton Wanderers ...	31	12	12	7	55	66	31
Everton ...	31	9	11	11	46	62	29
Arsenal ...	31	12	15	4	53	62	28
Birmingham City ...	30	9	13	8	54	74	26
Aston Villa ...	31	10	16	5	63	69	25
Leeds United ...	30	9	15	6	40	52	24
Leicester ...	32	10	18	4	68	84	24
Newcastle United ...	30	9	16	5	49	55	23
Portsmouth ...	30	9	16	5	52	60	23
Sheffield Wednesday ...	31	8	18	5	57	77	21
Sunderland ...	32	6	17	9	38	81	21

The organising committee for the European Cup have decided that, following a gentleman's agreement, Manchester United should be drawn against either Dortmund Borussia of Germany or Milano of Italy. This will allow them to travel to the away leg without the need to fly.

The other semi-final will be contested by Real Madrid of Spain and Vasas of Budapest.

Mon. 3rd March

The FA Cup semi-final draw made in London today has ensured that at least one team from Lancashire will be in the Final at Wembley on May 3rd.

The games to be played on March 22nd are:

Blackburn Rovers v Bolton Wanderers
at Maine Road, Manchester
West Bromwich Albion or Manchester United v Fulham
at Villa Park, Birmingham

Newspapers reported that there had been significant trouble on the football special trains transporting Liverpool supporters back from the FA Cup match at Blackburn on Saturday.

Three of the nine special trains suffered damage including 14 broken windows, 1 door ripped off and 3 electric fitting destroyed. A number of Liverpool supporters appeared in court at Blackburn charged with various offences following disturbances after the game.

One man was sent to prison for six months for assaulting a policeman and another received four months for the same offence. A third man was given a sentence of three months for breaking a shop window with a value of £45.

Another fifteen men received various fines for offences including drunk and disorderly, theft and obstructing police.

British Railways stated that they would instigate a formal enquiry to see what could be learned for future football excursions.

The United team once again travelled to Blackpool late today to be away from the Manchester area in order to concentrate on training for the Cup replay on Wednesday.

Cope and Greaves did not travel with the party as they are receiving treatment at Old Trafford for knocks they suffered on Saturday. Reserve team players, Brennan, Harrop and Jones P. will be training in Blackpool in case they are needed for the game.

Tues. 4ᵗʰ March

Manchester United were informed that they will still be allowed to sign players without having to wait the required fourteen days in respect of FA Cup games. Each case will still have to be considered on its merits.

Wed. 5ᵗʰ March

In the Inter Cities Fairs Cup Final, 1ˢᵗ Leg, London drew 2-2 against Barcelona at Stamford Bridge. Greaves and a Langley penalty late in the game earned the home side a draw.

FA Cup Quarter Final Replay

Manchester Utd.   **1**   **West Brom. Alb.**   **0**

Webster   Att. 60,523

Manchester United-Gregg, Foulkes, Greaves, Goodwin, Cope, Harrop, Webster, Taylor, Dawson, Pearson, Charlton.
West Bromwich Albion-Sanders, Howe, Williams, Dudley, Kennedy, Barlow, Whitehouse, Robson, Allen, Kevan, Horobin.

United were forced to make one change at left-half when Colin Crowther reported that he had a septic heel. Bobby Harrop (pictured below) the 21 year old England Youth International, came into the side for his debut.

Manchester Evening News

West Brom. were able to name an unchanged team. The gates were opened at 5 p.m. to allow supporters access to the ground straight from work. However one hour before kick-off, with over 60,000 in Old Trafford, the gates were locked with an estimated 30,000 still outside the ground unable to gain admittance but desperate to be part of the occasion.

A brief taped recorded message from Matt Busby was broadcast around the ground before kick-off. A thunderous roar greeted the teams as they emerged and it was Albion who made the more assured start to the game. Barlow and Dudley 'bossed' the midfield and in the opening quarter of the match Gregg was called upon to make two superb saves from Robson. In contrast the United players seemed to be struggling to put their game plan into action.

As the game progressed United's half-backs began to gain control by limiting the space available to the West Brom's forwards. This enabled Charlton and Taylor to dictate the pace of the game. Sanders saved a header from Pearson and Charlton was desperately unlucky when his powerful shot from eighteen yards hit the post and rebounded to safety.

All square at half time.

The early stages of the second half continued with the contest played at a frantic pace, but this time it was the home side who were dictating proceedings. Taylor shot over the bar and Webster wide of the post. Dawson then had a great opportunity with the goal at his mercy but lacked concentration and only partially kicked the ball. More chances came United's way – Charlton had another shot saved and Dawson rose to a cross from Pearson only to mistime his header.

West Brom., sensing that United had thrown everything at them, then began to control the game with only ten minutes remaining. Gregg was forced to bravely save at the feet of the onrushing Kevan and then made two further saves. Whitehouse hit the woodwork and Cope intervened just in time to stop Horobin scoring. With the game heading to extra time there appeared to be only one winner – Albion.

Then, with less than two minutes remaining, United broke forward. Taylor received a pass on the half way line and looking up played the ball into space down the right wing for Charlton. The outside-left easily outpaced Williams and then went beyond Kennedy who tried to obstruct him but the referee played advantage. On reaching the by-line Charlton pulled the ball across the area and WEBSTER, as cool as you like, slotted it left-footed into the net.

The crowd were hysterical and the noise deafening as Albion barely had time to restart the game before the referee blew the final whistle. United had reached the FA Cup semi-final for the second season running.

DIVISION 1

MANCHESTER CITY   1   **BIRMINGHAM CITY   1**
Barlow   Murphy

Att. 30,655

Thurs. 6th March

Manchester United players Ken Morgans and Dennis Viollet, who were released from hospital in Munich earlier in the week, arrived at Liverpool Street station in London today after travelling by boat and train. Reporters and photographers awaited their arrival but, once the players appeared, the press were jostled out of the way by police and porters.

Some of the journalists and photographers claimed that they had been manhandled in an unceremonious way by police officers in order to ensure that they were unable to interview or photograph the players.

Albert Scanlon and Ray Wood are expected to be released from hospital tomorrow. That will leave just two players, John Berry and Jackie Blanchflower, still in hospital together with Matt Busby, reporter Frank Taylor and Co-pilot Captain Rayment.

At the Princess Louise Public House in High Holborn, London a group of youngsters known as the Ballads and Blues meet every Sunday evening attracting large audiences. The folk singers have written three new ballads since the Munich Air Disaster and one of them 'The Flowers of Manchester' sung to the tune of 'High Germany' is set out below.

One cold and bitter Thursday in Munich, Germany
Seven great football stalwarts conceded victory.
Seven men will never play again who met destruction there,
The flowers of English football, the flowers of Manchester.

Matt Busby's boys were flying, returning from Belgrade.
This great United family all masters of their trade.
The pilot of the aircraft and the skipper, Captain Thain,
Three times they tried to take off and twice turned back again.

The third time down the runway disaster followed close.
There was ice upon the wings and the aircraft never rose.
It ran upon the marshy ground, it broke and overturned,
And seven of the team were killed when the battered aircraft burned.

Roger Byrne and Tommy Taylor, who were capped for England's side,
And Ireland's Billy Whelan and England's Geoff Bent died.
Mark Jones and Eddie Colman and David Pegg also,
Before the blazing wreckage went ploughing through the snow.

The trainer, coach and secretary, and a member of the crew,
Also eight sporting journalists who with United flew.
One of them was Big Swifty, we never will forget,
The greatest English 'keeper who ever graced a net.

They say that Duncan Edwards has an injury to the brain.
They say that Jackie Blanchflower will never play again.
And great Matt Busby's lying there, the father of the team,
Nine months or more will pass before he sees another game.

Oh England's finest football team, its record truly great,
Its proud successes mocked by a cruel turn of fate.
Seven men will never play again who met destruction there,
The flowers of English football, the flowers of Manchester.

Fri. 7th March

Doctors and nurses from the Rechts der Isar hospital in Munich, together with the Oberburgermeister arrived in Manchester today and will be guests at Old Trafford tomorrow. On Saturday evening they will attend a Civic Reception at Manchester Town Hall to enable the City to formally thank them.

Chief Surgeon, Professor Georg Maurer, said that he thought Matt Busby would be able to return home in about four weeks. The only survivor of the crash not doing well is Captain Rayment who is still critical.

United and Albion have both named unchanged teams for the third meeting between the sides in a week. West Brom. have stayed in Southport since Wednesday's game and desperately need two points to stay in contention with the top sides.

Ken Howley, who was the referee in charge of the two Cup games, should also have officiated the League match but has now been switched to the game at Villa Park. Mr Griffiths from Newport will now referee the game at Old Trafford as the League did not consider it would be prudent for Mr Howley to referee a game involving the same two teams for a third time in eight days.

The match is expected to attract another capacity crowd to Old Trafford.

Saturday 8th March

Championship leaders Wolves extended their lead at the top of the table to five points following an easy victory against Newcastle United. The game reached the interval goalless but soon after the restart the home side went ahead when Broadbent scored following a superb pass from Howells. They then missed a number of chances and fifteen minutes from time Newcastle equalised.

Stuart and Wright collided whilst trying to clear the ball leaving White the simple task of scoring.

This stirred Wolves back into action and two minutes later Deeley scored from a pass by Broadbent. The game had been spoiled by the frequent snow showers and slippery surface but Wolves handled the conditions better to seal the points in the final minute through Mason.

Despite a nine goal thriller at Highbury both managers expressed their dissatisfaction at the quality of the defending. Jack Crayston (Arsenal) and Ted Drake (Chelsea) told the press that both defences were wide open and the tackling non-existent.

Chelsea twice had the lead but eventually lost the game 5-4 as David Herd scored a hat trick for the home team.

A superb game at Goodison Park was spoiled when a spectator ran onto the pitch to confront Preston defender Harry Mattinson ten minutes from half time. Tommy Docherty grabbed the man and held him until the police lead him away. A few minutes later Docherty was injured after a collision with an Everton player and was carried from the field on a stretcher to a chorus of cheers from the Everton fans.

Eddie Thomas scored all four goals for Everton as they easily defeated second placed Preston by 4-2. The player has now scored seven goals in the last three games.

ARSENAL 5 Bloomfield, Herd 3, Clapton.	CHELSEA 4 Greaves 2, Block, Tindall Att. 41,620	LEICESTER C. 2 Hines, Cunningham (pen)	PORTSMOUTH 2 Harris, Gordon. Att. 30,951
ASTON VILLA 3 Lynn (pen), McParland 2.	BURNLEY 0 Att. 25,679	LUTON TOWN 1 Pacey.	MANCHESTER C. 2 Dunne (og), Sambrook Att. 16,019
BLACKPOOL 3 Perry 2, Durie.	NOTTINGHAM F. 0 Att.16,492	MANCHESTER U. 0	WEST BROM ALB. 4 Allen 2 (1pen),
BOLTON W. 1 Lofthouse.	BIRMINGHAM C. 0 Att.18,309		Greaves (og), Kevan Att. 63,479
EVERTON 4 Thomas 4.	PRESTON N.E. 2 Finney (pen), Baxter. Att. 43,291	SUNDERLAND 3 O'Neill 2, Kichenbrand.	SHEFFIELD W. 3 Aitken (og), Wilkinson, O'Donnell. Att. 22,549
LEEDS UNITED 1 Baird.	TOTTENHAM H. 2 Smith 2. Att. 23,429	WOLVES 3 Broadbent,Deeley Mason.	NEWCASTLE U. 1 White. Att.34,058

	P	W	D	L	F	A	W	D	L	F	A	Pt
Wolverhampton Wndrs	31	15	2	0	53	16	6	4	4	26	21	48
Preston North End	32	13	1	1	48	10	6	4	7	31	34	43
West Bromwich Albion	31	10	4	1	44	20	4	8	4	30	33	40
Luton Town	33	11	2	4	41	18	6	2	8	18	28	38
Manchester City	33	11	4	1	49	25	6	0	11	35	58	38
Manchester United	30	10	1	5	42	22	5	6	3	32	30	37
Nottingham Forest	33	9	2	5	38	19	6	3	8	26	31	35
Tottenham Hotspur	32	9	3	3	45	28	5	4	8	26	40	35
Blackpool	32	8	2	6	37	28	6	4	6	24	24	34
Chelsea	32	9	2	4	41	25	4	5	8	31	41	33
Burnley	32	12	1	3	41	18	3	2	11	20	45	33
Bolton Wanderers	32	8	4	5	33	28	5	3	7	23	38	33
Everton	32	4	9	4	25	23	6	2	7	25	31	31
Arsenal	32	9	2	6	46	36	4	2	9	12	30	30
Aston Villa	32	8	3	5	34	22	3	2	11	22	47	27
Birmingham City	32	5	4	6	34	32	4	5	8	21	44	27
Leicester City	33	8	4	5	46	32	2	1	13	24	54	25
Portsmouth	31	7	4	3	30	19	2	2	13	24	43	24
Leeds United	31	7	4	5	27	21	2	2	11	14	33	24
Newcastle United	31	3	3	9	21	28	6	2	8	29	30	23
Sheffield Wednesday	32	8	2	6	38	36	0	4	12	22	44	22
Sunderland	33	5	7	5	25	25	1	3	12	16	59	22

Manchester Utd.   0   West Brom. Alb.   4

Allen 2, Greaves (og) Kevan.

Att. 63,479

Manchester United-*Gregg, Foulkes, Greaves, Goodwin, Cope, Harrop, Webster, Taylor, Dawson, Pearson, Charlton.*

West Bromwich Albion-*Sanders, Howe, Williams, Dudley, Kennedy, Barlow, Whitehouse, Robson, Allen, Kevan, Horobin.*

A party of thirty doctors and nurses, who had travelled from Munich, were introduced to the crowd before the kick-off. A snow storm eased just in time to allow United Chairman, Mr Hardman, the opportunity to formally thank the medical staff for their outstanding efforts.

The cap-less spectators watched a simple but impressive ceremony as Bill Foulkes presented a bouquet in the Club's colours to Doctor Erica Maurer, wife of the Professor and Harry Gregg presented another to the youngest German nurse in the party. The trip has been arranged and sponsored by the 'Empire News' with the help of British European Airways.

The following recorded message from Matt Busby was relayed to the crowd. **"I am speaking from my bed in the Isar Hospital, Munich, where I have been since the tragic accident of just over a month ago. You will be glad, I am sure, that the remaining players here, and myself, are now considered out of danger, and this can be attributed to the wonderful treatment and attention given us by Professor Maurer and his wonderful staff, who are with you today as guests of the Club. I am obliged to the Empire News for giving me this opportunity to speak to you, for it is only in this last two or three days that I have been able to be told anything about football, and I am delighted to hear of the success and united effort made by all at Old Trafford.**

Again it is wonderful to hear that the Club have reached the semi-final of the FA Cup, and I extend my best wishes to everyone.

Finally, may I just say God bless you all".

There was then rapturous applause and cheering from the crowd.

United won the toss and decided to play against the wind on a bitterly cold day. West Brom. opened the game brightly with Barlow dominant in midfield spraying passes to both wings.

After Gregg saved an early shot from Allen it was no surprise when after only 8 minutes Albion took the lead. Kevan, who had ventured out to the right wing, whipped the ball low across the penalty area and ALLEN tapped it into the net from a few yards out. It was unfortunate that Harrop was off the field at the time receiving treatment on the touchline. United looked out of sorts and the away side continued to dictate the play. It was not until the 17th minute that United had a shot at goal.

In another attack Barlow played the ball down the wing to Horobin who then passed to Kevan. The burly forward crashed a shot at goal only to see it miss the post by inches. Dawson led a rare sortie forward but after beating Williams he was fouled by Kennedy, but nothing came of the free kick.

In the 35th minute Albion increased their lead. Allen hit a 'daisy cutter' from a tight angle and GREAVES whilst trying to prevent the ball reaching Whitehouse could only divert it into his own net.

Charlton was the outstanding forward on view and covered every blade of grass whilst trying to cajole his team-mates into action.

He shot just wide, then Pearson miss-kicked his shot in front of goal. United at last displayed some fighting spirit and Charlton almost pulled a goal back when his shot from outside the penalty area hit the post but rebounded to safety.

West Brom. could have had a penalty within a few minutes of the second half when Gregg appeared to bring down Whitehouse but the referee ruled otherwise.

The let off was short lived and in the 57th minute the visitors had a third. A centre from Whitehouse hit Cope on his body and the ball rolled gently into the path of KEVAN who made no mistake with a well place shot just inside the post. For the second time in the game the goal was scored when United were down to ten men as Taylor had left the pitch to receive treatment.

A late tackle from Pearson on Dudley earned the player a 'ticking off' from the referee as the game threatened to 'boil over' for a few minutes.

The crowd were silent for once as Albion continued to storm forward at every opportunity and on one occasion Allen headed just wide. Allen playing slightly behind Kevan was everywhere and Robson bossed the centre of the pitch as United had no answer to the onslaught.

In the 80th minute Albion scored a fourth. Kevan was tripped in the penalty area by Goodwin and ALLEN scored from the spot.

The home fans had seen enough and began to head for the turnstiles as United suffered their first defeat since 'Munich'. The injury to Ernie Taylor, which had left him as a passenger for most of the game, had destroyed any semblance of rhythm, as the youngsters had finally run out of steam.

United Reserves

Despite their lowly position in the Central League table an experienced Preston North End Reserves side were just too strong for United Reserves at Deepdale and ran out comfortable 4-0 winners.

Sun. 9th March

A train carrying Manchester City supporters back from the match with Luton Town crashed at Chinley Station in North Derbyshire last night. The special rammed into the back of a stationary train in the station but, fortunately, no one was seriously injured although one passenger was detained in Stockport Hospital overnight.

Other passengers were treated on the platform at Chinley for minor injuries. The train had run into the last carriage of the one in front resulting in glass, seats and other wreckage being spread over the platform and track.

Mon. 10th March

The party of doctors and nurses flew back home to Munich this morning. On Saturday evening they had attended a dinner at Manchester Town Hall as honoured guests of the Lord Mayor who had presented Professor Maurer with a copy of the Resolution of Thanks passed by the City Council.

Professor Maurer reiterated that he and his staff had only done their professional duty. He informed the gathering that he had received five letters offering to donate a kidney to help the late Duncan Edwards. Two Germans, a

Frenchman, a Belgian and a South African had made the offers reflecting the depth of international sympathy.

On a sadder note it was reported that Captain Rayment's left leg had been amputated.

The press were informed that United faced a fixture 'pile-up' and may be forced to play at least one mid-week game per week from now until the end of the season. The situation will be compounded if they should draw their FA Cup semi-final against Fulham.

Club physiotherapist, Ted Dalton, is treating both Ernie Taylor and Stan Crowther in a desperate race to get them both fit for Saturday's trip to Burnley. Taylor has a pulled muscle and Crowther is suffering from a septic heel.

Ken Morgans and Dennis Viollet are both expected to resume training again later this week.

Bobby Charlton returned to his Army Depot in the Midlands at the weekend and has been selected to play for the Army against the Navy at Bristol Rovers ground on Wednesday 19th March, which is only three days before the Fulham game. It is unclear at this moment in time if United will ask permission for him to miss the Forces game.

United's acting secretary, Mr Olive, stated in response to press speculation that, "although the footballers in hospital were not receiving Industrial Injuries Benefit or Sick Pay they were still getting their full wages from the Club and will continue to do so".

Albert Scanlon was discharged from hospital this morning.

Tues. 11th March

The Lord Mayor of Manchester, Alderman Lever and Mrs Lever, visited Munich today to thank the Hospital staff and Chief Burgomaster for their unstinting efforts whilst caring for the injured players and officials.

Discussions will take place to strengthen the links between the two cities.

CHELSEA   **1**   **WOLVERHAMPTON W.**   **2**
Greaves   Deeley, Showell.

Att. 46,835

Wed. 12th March

BIRMINGHAM CITY 1
Orritt.

SHEFFIELD WEDNESDAY   0

Att. 15,937

TOTTENHAM H.   4
Smith 3, Brooks.

BOLTON WANDERERS   1
Parry (pen.)

Att. 22,978

WEST BROM A.   1
Charlton (og).

LEEDS UNITED   0

Att. 16,412

The main talking point of the game at White Hart Lane was the injury suffered by Nat Lofthouse in the 55th minute. The Bolton captain was brought down by Norman in the Spurs penalty area and crashed heavily into the bone hard frosty surface. It is suspected that he may have dislocated his collar bone and will now miss the FA Cup semi-final. By a strange twist of fate his recognised deputy, Terry Allcock, who had scored five goals in ten games, was transferred to Norwich City earlier in the day.

Parry scored from the resulting penalty but Spurs easily overcame the ten men of Bolton with Bobby Smith helping himself to a hat trick.

Thurs. 13th March

Bobby Charlton has now been informed that he is required to play for his Army Unit in the re-arranged R.A.O.C. Cup Final at Didcot tomorrow afternoon. He will then have to travel back late at night in order to play in the game at Burnley.

After chasing the signature of goalkeeper, Ron Springett from Queens Park Rangers for over a week, Sheffield Wednesday finally got their man and hope that he will help in their fight against relegation. The player, who gets married soon, has agreed to the move on the condition that he is allowed to live and train in London.

Fri. 14th March

Outside-left Henderson has moved from Portsmouth to Wolves for £16,000 but looks unlikely to hold down a regular first team place. Wolves, seven points ahead of second place Preston, have Harris and Slater back in defence for the away game at Nottingham Forest.

The home side will miss the injured Imlach who has already scored fifteen goals this season.

Portsmouth immediately replaced Henderson by signing left winger Alex Govan from Birmingham City for a fee of £8,000. The player told the press that he thought he had received a raw deal at Birmingham and couldn't wait to get away quick enough. He went on to say that for the last year he has been dropped or criticised every time they had a heavy defeat or bad game.

United's influential inside-forward, Ernie Taylor, will not be risked in the game at Turf Moor tomorrow but Stan Crowther is fit to play. Bobby Harrop will switch from left-half to inside-right after two outstanding games whilst deputising for Crowther.

The switch of Harrop to inside-forward is not a complete surprise as, earlier this season; he scored twelve goals in a run of ten games for the reserve side.

Burnley have dropped centre-forward, Ray Pointer, and restored Alan Shackleton, who has not played since 14th December. Jimmy McIlroy is also fit again after missing three games.

Ken Morgans has asked if he can play in a competitive game and has now been named in the United reserve side to face Newcastle at Old Trafford.

Bobby Charlton's experience as a professional footballer proved too much for his opponents, the 4th Training Battalion, Blackdown in the final of the R.A.O.C. Cup in Didcot this afternoon.

Charlton, who played at inside-left for his Army Unit-the 17th Company, Nescliffe, scored three and made four as his side won 7-0. He received his winner's medal from Major-General Richmonds after the game before being driven by car back to Manchester in readiness for tomorrow's game.

Sat. 15th Mar.

Almost 50,000 spectators flocked to Stamford Bridge to watch a youthful Chelsea side play Blackpool. No Chelsea player was aged over twenty-three and four of them were teenagers.

Half time was reached with the game goalless despite both teams having a number of opportunities but the 'fireworks' were just about to begin.

After 51 minutes Greaves gave the home side the lead, pouncing on a poor back pass from Mudie, he smashed the ball into the net before any Blackpool defender could react.

Stanley Matthews, with his right knee bandaged, was a virtual passenger on the wing but still influenced play as Blackpool surged forward to score twice in two minutes. The first in the 64th minute was a Charnley header and the second a minute later was scored by Mudie who hit a low hard shot beyond the diving Reg Matthews.

The goals demoralised the young Chelsea side and in the 76th minute Mudie scored again with a shot from the edge of the penalty area which curled inside the top left hand corner.

Three minutes from time Perry, who had been outstanding for Blackpool, got his name on the score sheet with a header from a cross by Mudie to complete a wonderful away victory for the 'Seasiders' - their first win at Stamford Bridge for seven years.

Ron Springett kept a clean sheet in his first game for Sheffield Wednesday following his transfer from Queens Park Rangers on Friday. The goalkeeper had a good game and it was from his goal kick that Finney centred for Quixall to score the only goal of the game.

Nottingham Forest reached the interval level 1-1 with League leaders Wolves but the second half was a completely different story. Following good work by Slater, Broadbent scored a superb goal for Wolves but two minutes later Baily equalised. In the second half a hat trick by Murray, his third of the season in League and Cup games, wrapped up the points.

SATURDAY 15th MARCH

BIRMINGHAM C.	1	LUTON TOWN	1	NOTTINGHAM F.	1
Orritt.		Turner (pen)		Baily.	
		Att. 25,225			
BURNLEY	3	MANCHESTER U.	0	PORTSMOUTH	1
McIlroy, Shackleton,				Govan.	
Cheesebrough.		Att. 37,447		PRESTON N. E.	3
CHELSEA	1	BLACKPOOL	4	Finney 2, Thompson.	
Greaves.		Charnley, Mudie 2,		SHEFFIELD W.	1
		Perry. Att. 49,471		Quixall.	
MANCHESTER C.	2	ARSENAL	4	TOTTENHAM H.	0
Hayes, Barlow.		Herd (pen),			
		Bloomfield 3.		WEST BROM ALB.	4
		Att. 31,645		Robson. Kevan 2,	
NEWCASTLE U.	5	LEICESTER C.	3	Allen (pen)	
Bottom 2, White 3.		Walsh, Riley, McNeill			
		Att. 33,840			

WOLVES						4
Broadbent, Murray 3.						
					Att. 40,197	
ASTON VILLA						0
					Att.23,164	
LEEDS UNITED						0
					Att. 21,353	
BOLTON W.						0
.					Att. 24,085	
SUNDERLAND						1
Revie.					Att. 40,751	
EVERTON						0
					Att.28,771	

	P	W	D	L	F	A	P
Wolves	33	23	6	4	85	39	52
Preston N.E.	33	20	5	8	82	44	45
West Brom A.	33	16	12	5	79	53	44
Luton Town	34	17	5	12	60	47	39
Manchester City	34	17	4	13	86	87	38
Manchester U.	31	15	7	9	74	55	37
Tottenham H.	34	15	7	12	75	70	37
Blackpool	33	15	6	12	65	53	36
Notts Forest	34	15	5	14	65	54	35
Burnley	33	16	3	14	64	63	35
Chelsea	34	13	7	14	74	72	33
Bolton W.	34	13	7	14	57	71	33
Arsenal	33	14	4	15	62	68	32
Everton	33	10	11	12	50	58	31
Birmingham City	34	10	10	14	57	77	30
Aston Villa	33	11	5	17	56	70	27
Portsmouth	32	10	6	16	55	62	26
Newcastle Utd.	32	10	5	17	55	61	25
Leicester City	34	10	5	19	73	91	25
Leeds United	33	9	6	18	41	58	24
Sheffield Wed.	34	9	6	19	61	81	24
Sunderland	34	7	10	17	42	84	24

Burnley   3   Manchester Utd.   0

McIlroy, Shackleton, Cheesebrough   Att. 37,447

Burnley-*McDonald, Smith, Winton, Shannon, Adamson, Miller, Newlands, McIlroy, Shackleton, Cheesebrough, Pilkington.*

Manchester United-*Gregg, Foulkes, Greaves, Goodwin, Cope, Crowther, Webster, Harrop, Dawson, Pearson, Charlton.*

On a bright day and backed by a huge following, the white shirted United side were soon into their stride. Charlton, on the left wing, found Harrop with a well-placed pass that the player shot wide when it looked easier to score.

Brian Pilkington, (pictured below), who had been married on the morning of the game and travelled to Turf Moor straight from his wedding reception, was the next player to make an impact. He beat Foulkes then smashed a shot at goal only to see the effort miss the target.

As the game switched from end to end Burnley full-back, Smith, almost sliced the ball into his own net. Cheesebrough then drove a shot at goal, after good work by Shackleton, but Gregg blocked it. The goalkeeper was soon in action again diving bravely at the feet of Pilkington and taking a boot in the face for his troubles.

In the thirtieth minute, after a number of nasty tackles by both sides, the referee spoke to a group of players before deciding to send off Mark Pearson.

United held firm until the interval.

In the second half the vastly experienced Burnley side dictated the game and the ten men of United crumbled under the pressure. Crowther and Newlands both had their names taken in an attempt to calm the game down. Goals from McIlroy (pictured), Shackleton and Cheesebrough gave the home side a comfortable victory.

The defeat means that United have still failed to win a League game since the 'Disaster'.

United Reserves
United's 'second string' also lost their Central League game by three goals at Old Trafford. The difference being that a very strong Newcastle United side won 7-4 to virtually end any hope of the reserves winning the title.

The home side scored through Bradley, Morgans and Brennan (two) but had no answer to the constant Newcastle attacks.

Team-Gaskell, Smith, Jones, English, Hardisty, Holland, Morgans, Spratt, Brennan, Giles, Bradley.

Sun. 16ᵗʰ March

Captain Kenneth Rayment, 36 years old and Co-Pilot of the aircraft which crashed in Munich, died in hospital yesterday after never regaining consciousness. He became the 23ʳᵈ victim of the crash and leaves a widow and two children.

Mon. 17ᵗʰ March

The Football League side to face the Scottish League at Newcastle on Wednesday 26ᵗʰ March will be- **Hopkinson** *(Bolton W.),* **Howe** *(W. B. A.),* **Langley** *(Fulham),* **Clamp** *(Wolves),* **Wright** *(Wolves),* **Pearce** *(Sunderland),* **Douglas** *(Blackburn R.),* **Charlton** *(Manchester U.),* **Kevan** *(W. B. A.),* **Haynes** *(Fulham),* **Finney** *(P. N. E.).* *Reserve* **Norman** *(Tottenham H.).*

United moved into the transfer market again today announcing the signing of Tom Heron from Portadown for a reported fee of £8,000. The 21 year old left winger travelled to Manchester with his manager, Mr McKenzie, and, after signing for the 'Reds', travelled back home for a few days. The player has a groin strain at the moment and is not expected to play for the Club for at least a week.

There was good news for United when it was announced that Bobby Charlton has been given permission by the Army to join the squad for a few days prior to the Cup match. He will not now be required to play for the Army against the Navy on Wednesday.

Tues. 18th March

United, once again, travelled to Blackpool to train and stay together as a group for the next four days. Ken Morgans is with the party but Ernie Taylor remained in Manchester to receive treatment on his injured thigh, although it is hoped he will be fit for Saturday.

Newspapers reported that Albert Scanlon left Munich yesterday and was travelling by train accompanied by his wife with his right leg still in plaster.

The furore over some of the incidents in the Burnley v Manchester United game and afterwards failed to go away. Burnley Chairman, Bob Lord, denied reports that he had labelled some United players as 'Teddy Boys'. A full report of the incidents will be forwarded by Burnley to the Football Association. The match referee, Mr Oxley of Pontefract, will also be submitting a report.

LEEDS UNITED	2	**ARSENAL**	0
Meek, Peyton.			
			Att. 25,948
PORTSMOUTH	2	**WEST BROM. ALB**	2
Gordon, Dougan.		Horobin, Allen.	
			Att. 24,791
PRESTON N. E.	2	**NEWCASTLE UTD.**	1
Finney 2.		White	
			Att. 24,787

At Deepdale Tom Finney was the difference between the two teams with the centre-forward scoring both goals against struggling Newcastle United. The away side could not hold the 'Preston Plumber' who gave an exhibition of how to 'lead the line'.

Leeds, who started the day third from the bottom, moved up two places with a strong performance against Arsenal. Meek opened the scoring with a diving header *just before half time and a minute after the interval the same player had a hand in the second goal scored by Peyton.*

FA Youth Cup Fifth Round
Manchester United   6   Doncaster Rovers   2

The opening stages of the first half saw both teams checking each other out as the game moved quickly from end to end. United finally broke the deadlock ten minutes before half time when Elms scored with a header. Minutes later Giles split the away defence with a beautiful through ball to Spratt whose powerful shot beat the diving Brough. Worse was to come for the visitors as Spratt scored with a header from a centre by Lawton giving United a 3-0 interval lead.

A few minutes into the restart and United had a fourth much to the delight of the 17,000 spectators. Giles and Lawton, who seemed to be involved with everything, were once again the catalyst. As the ball was played through from Lawton to Giles, Palmer, the Doncaster full-back, sliced it into his own net in a desperate attempt to clear the danger. The Cup tie was effectively over and United began to put on a show for their supporters. Only the efforts of the Doncaster goalkeeper prevented United running up double figures. He held out under constant pressure until the 70th minute when G. Smith added a fifth.

Almost immediately Doncaster pulled a goal back through Meredith, which spurred the team on for a few minutes until Lawton netted number six. Although Doncaster scored a second goal it was United who won the game 6-2 and once again progressed to the semi-final of the FA Youth Cup.

Thurs. 20th March
Ernie Taylor did some training in Blackpool yesterday but has again returned to Old Trafford for more treatment from Ted Dalton.

All the other players reported that they are fit and raring to go and the party will move on to Droitwich tomorrow for an overnight stay before travelling to Villa Park

Fri. 21st March
Taylor passed a fitness test and the influential mid-field schemer will play tomorrow against Fulham. Webster is named at outside-right with Charlton moving to inside-left and Pearson switching to outside-left. It looks likely that Bentley will win his fitness battle and play at right-half for the 'Cottagers'.

Saturday 22nd March

FA Cup Semi-Final

FULHAM	2	MANCHESTER UTD	2

Stevens, Hill   Charlton 2.

Att. 69,745

Fulham-_Macedo, Cohen, Langley, Bentley, Stapleton, Lawler, Dwight, Hill, Stevens, Haynes, Chamberlain._

Manchester United-_Gregg, Foulkes, Greaves, Goodwin, Cope, Crowther, Webster, Taylor, Dawson, Charlton, Pearson._

Almost 30,000 fans from Manchester were among the 70,000 spectators present and gave the rebuilt United team a thunderous welcome.

Ticket touts had done a roaring trade selling 2s.6d tickets for 10s.6d. and 25s. for £3 10s.

Haynes won the toss for Fulham and almost at once Crowther was hurt in trying to parry a right wing move by the Londoners. The ex-Villa wing-half had treatment for a facial injury and soon carried on.

The ball was lively in a stiff wind and accurate control was difficult. Fulham made early use of Dwight's speed and United retaliated by giving the equally speedy Charlton the ball whenever possible.

Both Bentley and Taylor, who had been on the injured list during the week, moved quite freely. In the first ten minutes Fulham were just as good as their First Division rivals. The opening shot by Chamberlain was well wide.

CHARLTON electrified the crowd by scoring a wonderful goal in the 12th minute after being put clean through by Taylor.

United had hardly finished their celebrations when Fulham equalised. Langley, joining in attack, slipped a pass to STEVENS who scored despite Gregg rushing off his line in an attempt to block the shot (see below).

There were several causalities amongst the surging crowd and ambulance men were kept busy.

When United raised their tempo, Charlton fired a terrific shot but the goalkeeper coolly held on to the ball.

Langley suffered a painful blow to the head in a collision, but continued after treatment.

United gave their fervent supporters little to shout about for long periods as Fulham dictated the game, and seven minutes before half time HILL scored a second goal.

Langley was hurt again when Dawson accidentally kicked the back of his leg,but this time he was carried from the field with Lawler moving to left-back. Almost immediately **CHARLTON,** in injury time, equalised with another brilliant shot. The referee then blew for half time.

The second half started with Lawler still at left-back but within a few minutes a great roar heralded the re-appearance of Langley. Hobbling, he went to outside-left.

His return seemed to spur his team mates and Fulham attacked fiercely. Gregg cleared several dangerous attacks including a magnificent leaping save from a lob by Hill.

The tall Irishman fisted it over for a corner which was cleared. Stapleton had been playing well. For once, the burly Dawson, outpaced him down the wing but then slipped whilst trying to centre and the chance had gone. In the next minute Dawson was only inches wide with a fine flying header.

Langley, despite his handicap, was not a passenger making one good run down the left wing.

Dwight found himself with a gilt-edged opening ten yards out, but Gregg daringly threw himself at the right-wingers feet. It was Gregg who saved again from Chamberlain just as Dwight rushed in hoping for a rebound.

As the game entered the final fifteen minutes, it was United who began to dominate proceedings.

Macedo fisted a strong header from Taylor over the bar and pushed a shot from Charlton round the post.

Then Charlton crashed a shot against the crossbar, but United could not add to their total.

The tie will be replayed at Highbury on Wednesday afternoon.

Second Division Blackburn Rovers gave Bolton a fright at Maine Road when they took the lead after 19 minutes. A McLeod corner was headed into the net by Dobing.

Bolton centre-forward Gubbins, who was only in the side because of an injury to Lofthouse, justified his selection with an equaliser late in the half. He had run through unchallenged with the Rovers defenders claiming for offside. Worse was to follow for Blackburn as a minute later Gubbins scored again. He had skilfully trapped the ball from a long free kick by Banks and then ran through the hesitant defence before slotting home.

In the second half Blackburn threw everything at their opponents but Higgins and Hopkinson ensured a trip to Wembley in May. The quality of football on display was a great disappointment for the huge crowd as the tension of the occasion affected too many players.

In the opening minutes of the League game at Molineux Manchester City were gifted a goal when Stuart put the ball in his own net as he attempted to pass it back to his goalkeeper. Amazingly, after 36 minutes, City returned the favour when centre-half Ewing also scored an own goal. Deeley then missed a penalty for Wolves but within a few minutes the same player headed them into a 2-1 half time lead.

Within fifteen minutes of the restart Barlow had scored twice to put City 3-2 ahead and a shock result looked on the cards. Wolves attacked constantly in search of an equaliser and in the 73rd minute Mullen scored to maintain their unbeaten home record stretching back twelve months.

Excellent wins by Sunderland, Leicester City and Leeds United has thrown the relegation battle wide open. Only six points now separate the bottom eight teams although Aston Villa and Newcastle United have two games in hand on all the other sides except Portsmouth who have played one game more.

SATURDAY 22nd MARCH
DIVISION 1

ARSENAL	1	SHEFFIELD W.	0
Herd.			Att. 28,106
BLACKPOOL	4	BIRMINGHAM C.	2
Mudie, Charnley,		Hooper (pen), Astall.	
Perry 2.			Att.11,549
EVERTON	4	PORTSMOUTH	2
Williams 2,Thomas 2.		P. Harris, McClellan	
			Att. 23,179
LEEDS UNITED	1	BURNLEY	0
Meek.			Att. 24,994
LEICESTER C.	3	CHELSEA	2
Hines 2,		P. Sillett, Tindall	
Cunningham (pen).			Att. 27,849
LUTON TOWN	0	TOTTENHAM H.	0
			Att. 22,384
SUNDERLAND	2	WEST BROM. ALB.	0
O'Neill, Kichenbrand.			Att. 38,323
WOLVES	3	MANCHESTER C.	3
Ewing (og), Deeley,		Stuart (og), Barlow 2.	
Mullen.			Att.34,932

F. A. CUP SEMI-FINALS

BLACKBURN R.	1	BOLTON W.	2
Dobing.		Gubbins 2.	
At Maine Road.	Receipts £20,219		Att. 74,800
FULHAM	2	MANCHESTER U.	2
Stevens, Hill.		Charlton 2.	
At Villa Park	Receipts £19,560		Att. 69,745

	P	W	D	L	F	A	P
Wolves	34	23	7	4	88	42	53
Preston N.E.	34	21	5	8	84	45	47
West Brom A.	35	16	13	6	81	57	45
Luton Town	35	17	6	12	60	47	40
Manchester City	35	17	5	13	89	90	39
Blackpool	34	16	6	12	69	55	38
Tottenham H.	35	15	8	12	75	70	38
Manchester U.	31	15	7	9	74	55	37
Notts Forest	34	15	5	14	65	54	35
Burnley	34	16	3	15	64	64	35
Arsenal	35	15	4	16	63	70	34
Everton	34	11	11	12	54	60	33
Chelsea	35	13	7	15	76	75	33
Bolton W.	34	13	7	14	57	71	33
Birmingham City	35	10	10	15	59	81	30
Leeds United	35	11	6	18	44	58	28
Portsmouth	34	10	7	17	59	68	27
Aston Villa	33	11	5	17	56	70	27
Leicester City	35	11	5	19	76	92	27
Sunderland	35	8	10	17	44	84	26
Newcastle Utd.	33	10	5	18	56	63	25
Sheffield Wed.	35	9	6	20	62	82	24

United Reserves

Another defeat, this time 2-0 away to Liverpool, leaves the reserves five points behind Wolves albeit with a game in hand.

Leading Scorers

29 THOMPSON (PRESTON NORTH END)
29 TURNER (LUTON TOWN)
28 SMITH (TOTTENHAM HOTSPUR)
26 MURRAY (WOLVERHAMPTON WANDERERS)
24 FINNEY (PRESTON NORTH END)
23 HERD (ARSENAL)
22 GREAVES (CHELSEA)
21 DEELEY (WOLVERHAMPTON WANDERERS)
21 ROBSON (WEST BROMWICH ALBION)
20 ALLEN (WEST BROMWICH ALBION)
20 HAYES (MANCHESTER CITY)

Mon. 24th March

Following the incidents involving members of the press and United players Ken Morgans and Dennis Viollet at Liverpool Street Station on 6th March Mr Johnson, General Manager of the Eastern Region of British Railways, wrote to the secretary of the Newspaper Conference as follows – "It appears that the two Manchester United players did in fact give their consent to being interviewed by the press. They were however somewhat overcome by emotion on seeing their relatives and friends and at this stage appeared to be more concerned to get away than to see the press. When they began moving towards the cars the Railway Police assisted their passage.

It is clear that there was some misunderstanding. If any fault lay with the Railways I regret it. You may be assured that I am as anxious as the Newspaper Conference to avoid any untoward incidents at any time and to maintain our friendly relations with the press".

Tues. 25th March

BBC television have announced that they will broadcast the full ninety minutes of the FA Cup semi-final replay between Manchester United and Fulham at Highbury tomorrow afternoon.

The gates will be opened at 12 noon and a capacity crowd approaching 68,000 is expected for the first visit of United to the stadium since they beat Arsenal 5-4 before leaving for Munich.

The draw for the FA Youth Cup semi-finals has paired Manchester United with either Wolves or Bolton. The other tie will be between Chelsea and Arsenal with the games being played on or before 19th April.

Ernie Taylor has again received treatment on his bruised thigh but will, almost certainly, be fit for tomorrow. Alex Dawson is also expected to have recovered from his ankle injury. Brennan and Harrop have been added to the eleven who played on Saturday but the team will not be announced until tomorrow.

Wed. 26th March

The Football League side were forced to make four changes for the Inter-League team against the Scottish League at Newcastle because of the FA Cup replay. Banks, Allen and Robson were drafted into the side in place of Langley, Haynes and Charlton who are playing in the Cup game. In goal, McDonald replaced the injured Hopkinson.

The Football League side were far too strong for their opponents and a hat trick from Kevan and a goal from Allen secured a 4-1 victory and with it the Inter-League Championship.

Milan defeated Borussia Dortmund 4-1 in the European Cup to clinch the tie 5-2 on aggregate and they will now meet Manchester United in the semi-finals with the dates yet to be decided.

FA Cup Semi Final Replay

Manchester Utd.	5	Fulham	3

Dawson 3, Brennan, Charlton   Stevens, Chamberlain, Dwight

Att. 38,258

(At Highbury – Receipts £12,718)

Manchester United-Gregg, Foulkes, Greaves, Goodwin, Cope, Crowther, Webster, Taylor, Dawson, Charlton, Brennan.

Fulham-Macedo, Cohen, Langley, Bentley, Stapleton, Lawler, Dwight, Hill, Stevens, Haynes, Chamberlain.

The teams emerged on a mild but murky afternoon with a hint of drizzle in the air. Unexpectedly, the ground was just over half full, probably attributed to the afternoon kick-off time on a week day making it difficult for supporters of both teams to miss work to attend, and the decision to allow the game to be broadcast live on BBC TV. It had been reported that Stretford Grammar School in Manchester were allowing their pupils a half day's leave to watch the game on TV.

In a late team change Brennan was named at outside-left in place of Pearson with Charlton switching to the No. 10 shirt.

Fulham won the toss but it was United that dictated the play in the opening ten minutes determined to make no mistake at the second attempt. Macedo caught a thunderbolt shot from Goodwin on the goal-line in the opening minute but dropped the ball. He was alert to the danger and quickly regained possession.

The goalkeeper then made superb saves from Taylor and Webster to deny United again. Next it was the turn of Goodwin who stormed forward only to see his shot pushed over the crossbar by the young Fulham 'keeper.

It was no surprise when, after 15 minutes, United took the lead following a corner. Webster gained possession and crossed for DAWSON to score with a diving header. The goal stirred Fulham into action and Haynes began to control the mid-field, spraying passes all over the pitch. After 27 minutes they drew level. Haynes played a pinpoint pass into the path of STEVENS who beat Gregg with ease.

TONY MACEDO

JOHNNY HAYNES

In the 35th minute a long range shot from DAWSON was easily covered by Macedo but, somehow, he allowed the ball to slip through his hands and go over the line. The game immediately switched to the opposite end and Fulham again equalised thanks to Langley. The full-back sprinted down the left-wing before laying the ball 'on a plate' for CHAMBERLAIN to gently stroke into the net.

Still the action was not finished and right on the stroke of half time United regained the lead following another mistake by Marcedo. Taylor went on one of his mazy runs before playing the ball into the path of Brennan in the penalty area. Macedo dashed from his line to reach the ball first but fumbled his attempt to gather it cleanly allowing BRENNAN to tap it into the net.

The excited crowd waited in anticipation of the second half wondering if the outstanding quality of football on display would continue. In the opening fifteen minutes both sides cancelled each other out with defences well on top. In the 65th minute United scored a fourth. Charlton beat Cohen down the left flank before playing the ball across to DAWSON who completed his hat-trick with a well taken shot.

Fulham were still not beaten and in the 75th minute pulled a goal back following some shaky defensive play by United. Stevens crossed and DWIGHT scored despite the presence of a number of defenders who failed to mark him tightly enough. With less than eight minutes remaining Fulham had the ball in the net again but the referee ruled against them giving a handball by Haynes.

In the final minute CHARLTON finally made the game safe when he stormed forward and smashed the ball into the net. The young United side had reached the FA Cup Final for the second successive season, albeit with only two players in the side who had played in last year's Final.

Thurs. 27th March

Newspapers reported that the North-West Transport Users Consultative Committee, at a meeting in Liverpool yesterday, received a report from a British Transport official about the unseemly behaviour of Liverpool supporters returning from a match at Blackburn.

The hooligans had caused damage to the train returning to Liverpool and one of the suggestions now being considered was whether these type of football special trains should be composed of open or corridor type carriages to make it easy for Railway Police and officials to move swiftly through the train.

The report went on to state that it hoped that the hooligans would be severely dealt with by the Courts and congratulated the Railway Police on an excellent job in handling the situation.

Fri. 28th March

Match of the day tomorrow will be the all-Midlands clash between West Bromwich Albion and Wolverhampton Wanderers with a crowd of 55,000 expected at the

Hawthorns. Wolves appear clear favourites for the title but Albion should provide stiff opposition, having already earned a point at Molineux earlier in the season.

Nat Lofthouse has resumed training with a steel pin screwed into his collar bone. The Bolton Wanderers Captain is desperate to prove his fitness in time for the FA Cup Final and could yet make an appearance in three to four weeks.

United have injury problems in defence for their visit to Hillsborough with Greaves unfit. Cope will switch to left-back and Harrop will come into the side at centre-half with the forward line unchanged.

Sat. 29th March

Sheffield Wed. 1 Manchester Utd.　　0

Shiner　　　　　　　　　　　　　Att. 34,806

Sheffield Wednesday-*Springett, Staniforth, Curtis, McAnearney T., Swann, O'Donnell, Wilkinson, Quixall, Shiner, Froggatt, Finney.*

Manchester United-*Gregg, Foulkes, Cope, Goodwin, Harrop, Crowther, Webster, Taylor, Dawson, Charlton, Brennan.*

United, still seeking their first League victory since 'Munich', visited struggling Sheffield Wednesday who had a desperate need for points to move away from the foot of the table in the third meeting between the sides this season.

The game was played in a sportsmanlike manner despite its importance and both goalkeepers made some brilliant saves. The talking point of the game came in the 15th minute when a Quixall shot ended in the back of the net. On examining the net, the referee found a hole in the side netting and decided that the ball had passed through the hole and therefore awarded a goal kick.

The only goal of the game came in the 40th minute when 33 year old SHINER (pictured over) broke the deadlock with his eleventh League goal of the season.

United strove for an equaliser throughout the second half without success as Wednesday hung on to their slender lead and gained an invaluable two points.

At Deepdale the main talking point was not how easily Preston had defeated Leicester City but two missed penalties by Tom Finney. The first, after 21 minutes was awarded when Thompson was brought down by Russell, but Finney smashed his spot-kick against the upright.

The second, given in the 72nd minute for a foul on Taylor, was easily saved by Anderson. In between the two penalty incidents Finney did score with a splendid header in North End's 4-1 victory.

In a pulsating game at Fratton Park Portsmouth stormed into a 4-0 lead against Arsenal. Dougan had opened the scoring in the first minute, rounding off a great move to beat Kelsey with a low drive. Four minutes later Barnard got a second from a corner. Further goals from Gordon and Harris increased their advantage before Bloomfield pulled a goal back for the visitors just before half time.

In the second half Arsenal scored three times but a second goal from Gordon clinched the game for Portsmouth. This was the third time this season that Arsenal had been involved in a game ending with a 5-4 scoreline, only one of which they have won.

League leaders Wolves played some superb attacking football in the Midlands derby at the Hawthorns watched by the highest attendance of the day, almost 57,000.

Wolves dominated the opening exchanges and it was no surprise when they took the lead after 25 minutes through Mason. West Brom. fought back and

Finlayson was forced to make a breathtaking save from Robson and shortly afterwards Kevan had a goal disallowed for offside.

In the second half Wolves added to their tally with two goals from Murray to maintain a six point gap from Preston at the top of the table.

Wolves half-back line of Wright, Clamp and Slater were magnificent. Spurs were in top form in their game against Aston Villa and centre-forward, Bobby Smith, scored a hat trick in an eight minute spell in a whirlwind start. He scored with two headers and a shot after 13, 18 and 21 minutes. Sewell reduced the arrears but Medwin scored a fourth with a header from a cross by Smith.

In the second half Smith scored twice to bring his match total to five as Spurs won 6-2.

England team manager, Walter Winterbottom, watched the game from the stands.

SATURDAY 29th MARCH

BIRMINGHAM C.	2	EVERTON	1	
Hooper 2.		Thomas.		
				Att. 21,628
BURNLEY	2	BLACKPOOL	1	
McIlroy, Pilkington		Perry		
				Att. 20,781
CHELSEA	0	SUNDERLAND	0	
				Att. 32,929
MANCHESTER C.	1	LEEDS UNITED	0	
McAdams.				Att. 21,962
NEWCASTLE U.	3	LUTON TOWN	2	
Davies, Bottom, White.		Whitby, Turner		
				Att. 16,775
NOTTINGHAM F.	0	BOLTON W.	0	
				Att. 24,060
PORTSMOUTH	5	ARSENAL	4	
Dougan, Barnard,		Bloomfield, Clapton,		
Gordon 2, Harris.		Gunter (og), Nutt.		
				Att.25,999
PRESTON N. E.	4	LEICESTER C.	1	
Thompson 2, Finney,		Rowley.		
Mayers.				Att. 18,392
SHEFFIELD W.	1	MANCHESTER U.	0	
Shiner.				Att. 34,806
TOTTENHAM H.	6	ASTON VILLA	2	
Smith 5, Medwin		Sewell, McParland.		
				Att. 34,102
WEST BROM ALB.	0	WOLVES	3	
		Mason, Murray 2.		
				Att.56,904

	P.	W.	L.	D.	F.	A.	Pts.
Wolverhampton Wanderers	35	24	4	7	91	42	55
Preston North End ...	35	22	8	5	88	46	49
West Bromwich Albion ...	36	16	7	13	81	60	45
Manchester City	36	18	13	5	90	90	41
Luton Town ...	36	17	13	6	62	50	40
Tottenham Hotspur ...	36	16	12	8	81	72	40
Blackpool	35	16	13	6	70	57	38
MANCHESTER UNITED...	32	15	10	7	74	56	37
Burnley	35	17	15	3	66	65	37
Nottingham Forest ...	35	15	14	6	68	54	36
Chelsea	36	13	15	8	76	75	34
Arsenal	36	15	17	4	67	78	34
Bolton Wanderers ...	35	13	14	8	57	71	34
Everton	35	13	11	11	55	62	33
Birmingham City ...	36	11	15	10	61	82	32
Portsmouth ...	35	11	17	7	64	72	29
Leeds United ...	36	11	19	6	44	59	28
Newcastle United ...	36	11	18	5	59	65	27
Aston Villa	34	11	18	5	58	76	27
Leicester City ...	36	11	20	5	77	97	27
Sunderland	36	8	17	11	44	84	27
Sheffield Wednesday ...	36	10	20	6	62	82	26

United Reserves

United got back into the winning habit with a convincing 4-1 victory against Stoke City Reserves at Old Trafford. This was the second team's first victory since the air disaster, ending a run of one draw and four defeats. Pearson netted twice and Heron and Lawton added to the total.

Mon. 31ˢᵗ March

| Aston Villa | 3 | Manchester Utd | 2 |

Myerscough, Hitchens, Sewell   Webster, Dawson.

Att. 16,631

Aston Villa-*Sims, Lynn, Jones, Crowe, Dugdale, Saward, Smith, Hitchens, Sewell, Myerscough, McParland.*
Manchester United-*Gregg, Foulkes, Cope, Goodwin, Harrop, Crowther, Webster, Pearson, Dawson, Charlton Brennan.*

It was Villa who created the early opportunities and within the first few minutes Hitchens and Lynn both hit the woodwork. The misses proved costly as, after 13 minutes, United took the lead. Charlton smashed the ball goal-wards and the power of his shot surprised Sims who let the ball bounce out of his grasp. Brennan quickly seized on the chance playing the ball across the penalty area for WEBSTER to score easily.In the 35ᵗʰ minute Villa drew level after being awarded a free kick. The ball was passed to MYERSCOUGH who hit a left foot volley into the net.

With the scores level United pushed forward in the opening stages of the second half and Charlton was unlucky to see his shot hit the crossbar and rebound to safety. He was easily United's best player and at times appeared to be carrying the team on his own with little support. After sustained United pressure Villa broke away and HITCHENS scored with a clever back-heel after good work from Sewell. United were always dangerous and, eventually, their perseverance paid dividends with an equaliser. Webster received a glorious pass from Pearson, then rolled it to DAWSON for an easy goal. Two minutes later Charlton had a great opportunity to win the game. With only Sims between him and the goal he somehow failed to beat the goalkeeper and the danger was cleared.

Just when it appeared that the game would end level the home side snatched a winner with seconds remaining. United's defence appeared to have a cross from Saward well covered but SEWELL reacted quickest and was first to the ball giving Gregg no chance.

The United defenders appealed in vain to referee, Mr Williams, as it appeared that McParland was in an offside position in the build up to the goal. The official ruled that the player was not interfering with play and awarded the goal.

For United Goodwin and Crowther had both played well except, sometimes, their approach to the game was somewhat lethargic. Pearson and Charlton, as always, were a constant threat to the opposition defence.

Newspapers reported that a gold medal belonging to Stanley Matthews had been stolen from an exhibition of medals and caps at a shop in Walton, Liverpool on Saturday.

Player Profile

Donald George Revie
Born Middlesbrough 10th July 1927

Don Revie was brought up by his father after his mother died from cancer when he was only twelve years old. Like many young boys in the 1930's he was football mad and played in the streets of Middlesbrough with anything he could find as a makeshift ball.

Leaving school at fourteen he worked as an apprentice bricklayer and, whilst playing local football for Middlesbrough Swifts, was spotted by a football scout. He signed for Leicester City in August 1944 and after playing wartime football finally made his debut in the opening Second Division fixture against Manchester City on 31st August 1946. His progress in the Leicester forward line was severely hampered when he broke his right ankle in a game against Spurs. The injury was so severe that he was advised that he may not play football again. Determined to prove the medical profession wrong he fought his way back to full fitness after five months and re-established his place in the team.

The highlight of his spell at Filbert Street came in 1949 when he helped Leicester to reach the FA Cup Final. In the semi-final against Portsmouth he scored a strange goal to help his side clinch the game. With City leading 2-1 the ball was played high into the Portsmouth penalty area. Knowing that goalkeeper, Butler, had a habit of palming the ball over an opponent's head before collecting it, he anticipated the move and as the ball dropped calmly tapped it into the net.

Unfortunately he missed the Final after suffering a nasal haemorrhage which resulted in him spending time in hospital during the week leading up to the game. Without Revie, Leicester lost the match 3-1 to Wolves.

In November 1949 he moved to another Second Division club, Hull City, for £19,000 primarily to play alongside Raich Carter who was player-manager. He learned a great deal from the veteran player but could not help the club to progress to the First Division. When Carter left, Revie asked for a transfer and moved to the top tier with Manchester City in October 1951. Ernie Phillips went in the opposite direction in part-exchange with the total value of the transfer reported as between, £25,000 to £28,000.

City were struggling in the early 1950's and escaped relegation by one point in the 1952/53 season. Manager, Les McDowall, sold Ivor Broadis to Newcastle United and decided to play Revie in a deeper position just behind the forwards in the evolution of the 'Revie Plan'.

His good form earned him selection for the Football League against the Irish League at Maine Road in February 1954 and Revie made the most of his opportunity scoring a hat-trick in a 9-1 win. The following month he played for the England B team against Scotland, the game ending in a 1-1 draw. City finished the 1953/54 season sixth from the bottom of the table helped by Revie's twelve League goals.

In October 1954 he won his first Cap scoring in a 2-0 win against Northern Ireland at Windsor Park. Selected again for the National side on 2nd April 1955, he again scored in a 7-2 win over Scotland at Wembley. Although City lost in the FA Cup Final 3-1 to Newcastle United, Revie was voted Footballer of the Year as his side finished in sixth position.

He was dropped from the team for a great part of the 1955/56 season following his decision to miss two weeks of pre-season training to be with his family in Blackpool. The player had agreed with trainer, Laurie Barnett, that he would maintain his fitness levels by training whilst on holiday. Manager, McDowall, thought otherwise and fined him £27.

Despite the actions of City, Revie was selected twice by England in October 1955 and scored two goals in the International against Denmark. He was eventually reinstated into the Manchester City team and, after playing only one Cup match that season, was selected at the last minute for the Final against Birmingham City.

On the day he had, what most journalists considered, the finest game of his career, dominating the opposition with pass after pass as City won 3-1 and he was named Man of the match.

As the 1956/57 season got under way Revie was switched to right-half and it was no surprise when, in October 1956, Sunderland paid £22,000 for his services. It was in the same month that he was selected for his sixth Cap for England against Northern Ireland.

Sunderland just avoided relegation, finishing third from the bottom. The 1957/58 season has seen them struggling to stay in the top flight and retain their record of never being relegated. Revie had scored nine goals in thirty-three League appearances as at 31st March 1958.

	LEAGUE	APPS	GOALS
LEICESTER CITY	1946-1949	96	25
HULL CITY	1949-1951	76	12
MANCHESTER CITY	1951-1956	148	35
SUNDERLAND	1956-31/3/58	49	11
ENGLAND	1954-56	6	4

APRIL 1958

Tues. 1st April

Manchester United's directors met today and have decided to ask the Football Association for permission to play the two-legged European Cup Semi-Final games after the end of the English season.

United still have nine League games to play and the Cup Final and have suggested the dates of May 10th and May 17th which their opponents, F. C. Milano and the European Cup Committee, would have to agree.

The Club announced that The Munich Air Disaster Fund has now reached £32,500 and the Committee met in Manchester yesterday to approve emergency claims made by dependants of those involved in the crash.

Wed. 2nd April

The news from Old Trafford regarding a number of players who were involved in the Munich Air Crash is very encouraging.

Ken Morgans *– Back in training. Has played in reserve team.*

Dennis Viollet *– Resumed training today.*

Albert Scanlon *– Running again.*

Ray Wood *– Expected to be playing again before the end of the season.*

Also in full training is Wilf McGuinness after his cartilage operation.

Thurs. 3rd April

It was reported that Milano have indicated that they will agree to the European Cup games being played in May but have suggested two different dates. The European Cup Committee will now consider both proposals.

The Easter Football Programme starting tomorrow will, no doubt, throw up its usual array of strange results. Each team will play three games over four or five days which will include a home and away fixture against the same opposition.

Wolves are well clear at the top of the table and the bookmakers' favourites for the Championship. They meet Arsenal (twice) and Portsmouth. The most intriguing tussle is in the relegation zone where three points separate the bottom seven teams. Sunderland will meet Manchester United twice. United have decided to select from fourteen players. The three additions to the X1 who played against Aston Villa are Greaves, Taylor and McGuinness.

Good Friday, 4th April

| **Manchester Utd.** | **2** | **Sunderland** | **2** |

Charlton, Dawson. Revie, O'Neill

Att. 47,421

Manchester United-*Gregg, Foulkes, Greaves, Goodwin, Cope, Crowther, Webster, Taylor, Dawson, Charlton, Brennan.*
Sunderland-*Fraser, Hedley, Elliott, Anderson, Aitken, Pearce, Fogarty, Revie, Kichenbrand, O'neill, Grainger.*

Any neutral football fan visiting Old Trafford would have left feeling that United were somewhat fortunate to escape with a point. Don Revie, the Sunderland inside-right, dictated the pace of the game from his position just behind the forwards spraying pin-point passes to the right and left.

The opening stages of the first half saw United in dominant form and it was no surprise when they opened the scoring through a trademark CHARLTON left foot thunderbolt, which swerved and crashed into the net off a post. At this moment in the game wing-halves, Crowther and Goodwin, drove the home side forward but poor finishing denied them a second goal.

As the half time interval approached Cope made a mistake and REVIE pounced to steer the ball into the net. Sunderland resumed the second half with their 'tails up' and O'NEILL gave them the lead with a shot from the edge of the penalty area. Gregg was then called into action on more than one occasion but Sunderland failed to increase their advantage.

As is often the case after a sustained period of pressure the home side finally broke away and, with only minutes remaining, scored an equaliser. It was DAWSON, who up to this point had been very disappointing, who gained them the point. He received a pass and quickly avoided two defenders before blasting the ball beyond the diving Fraser.

Sunderland's delaying tactics during the last ten minutes had backfired and cost them dearly in their fight against relegation.

Blackpool had injury problems for their local derby against Preston. With Matthews, Harris and Peterson all unfit, eighteen year old, part-time professional and garage mechanic, John Gregson made his debut at outside-right. The youngster was not overawed by the occasion but ended up on the losing side as Preston came from a goal behind at half time to win the game 2-1 in front of Blackpool's highest attendance for six months. The win leaves North End four points behind Wolves but having played one game more.

Derek Hennin, who normally plays right-half, was called into action as an emergency centre-forward with Lofthouse injured for the game against Aston Villa. The player, who had scored two goals for Bolton this season, helped himself to a hat trick in a 4-0 victory.

At Fratton Park Derek Dougan was injured in the 13th minute and was carried from the pitch suffering from concussion.

He was examined by two doctors and allowed to return for the second half with a suspected fractured cheekbone and Portsmouth trailing 1-0.

The Irish centre-forward bravely scored twice to help his side beat Birmingham 3-2.

GOOD FRIDAY 4TH APRIL

BLACKPOOL	1	**PRESTON N.E.**	2
Mudie		Mayers, Baxter.	
		Att.29,029	
BOLTON W.	4	**ASTON VILLA**	0
Stevens, Hennin 3 (1 pen)			
		Att.19,026	
BURNLEY	2	**SHEFFIELD WED.**	0
McIlroy, Newlands.		Att.18,165	
CHELSEA	0	**NOTTINGHAM F.**	0
		Att,44,288	
EVERTON	0	**LEEDS UNITED**	1
		Baird.	
		Att.32,679	
MANCHESTER U.	2	**SUNDERLAND**	2
Charlton, Dawson.		Revie, O'Neill	
		Att.47,421	
NEWCASTLE UTD.	P	**MANCHESTER C.**	P
(Waterlogged pitch)			
PORTSMOUTH	3	**BIRMINGHAM C.**	2
Barnard, Dougan 2.		Murphy, Hooper.	
		Att.33,075	
TOTTENHAM H.	0	**WEST BROM. ALB.**	0
		Att.56,166	

Saturday 5th April

Manchester U. 0   Preston North End   0

Att. 48,413

Manchester United-*Gregg, Foulkes, Greaves, Goodwin, Cope, Crowther, Morgans, Taylor, Webster, Charlton, Heron.*
Preston North End-*Else, Cunningham, Walton, Docherty, Dunn, O'Farrell, Mayers, Thompson, Finney, Farrall, Taylor.*

United opted to drop Dawson and Scanlon and move Webster to centre-forward. In came Ken Morgans at outside-right for his first game since the Munich crash and new signing Tom Heron on debut in the No. 11 shirt.

A cold dreary windy afternoon greeted the teams as they emerged with North End led by Tom Finney who was celebrating his 36th birthday.

United kicked off with the wind behind them, playing towards the Stretford End and a quick clearance from Gregg travelled the full length of the pitch into the arms of Else in the Preston goal.

Finney beat two defenders before a timely tackle by Cope stopped his surge forward. A good chance fell to O'Farrell but his powerful first time shot was well saved. Preston were on top in the opening stages and their approach football was a joy to watch with Finney, as always, orchestrating the rhythm of their play.

A rare United raid came to nothing when Charlton shot high over the cross-bar. Heron came more into the game and gave Cunningham a few anxious moments before the danger was cleared. Midway through the half Thompson had a great opportunity to put North End ahead from a Finney pass, but the leading scorer shot wide of an open goal. The miss seemed to put some energy into the home side and Heron blasted a shot at goal which Else did well to keep out. Finney then found some space and drew Gregg from his line before crossing to Thompson only to see his colleague shoot over the bar from a few yards out and the game reached the interval scoreless.

United pressed early in the second half and Else was forced to parry a shot from Webster over the bar. As the home side pushed forward both Dunn and Cunningham were forced to head clear to break up dangerous attacks. Almost unbelievably Thompson missed a third chance to score when he outran the defence but once again shot too high with only Gregg to beat.

For once Ernie Taylor was not able to dictate the pace of the game and found Docherty and O'Farrell difficult opponents to master. Finney was next in the action but his goal-bound header was acrobatically saved by Gregg. Crowther continued to deny the Preston forwards with strong, forceful tackles breaking up their attacks.

With the game heading for a draw United mounted one last thrust, urged forward by a mighty roar, and Charlton, who had rarely been involved in the game, hit a rocket shot only to see Else somehow make a superb save.

Preston really should have won the game but the efforts of Goodwin, Cope and Crowther must not go unnoticed in a hard earned point for the home side.

	P	W	D	L	F	A	W	D	L	F	A	Pts
Wolverhampton Wndrs	36	16	3	0	57	19	9	4	4	35	23	57
Preston North End	37	16	1	1	57	12	7	5	7	33	35	52
West Bromwich Albion	38	12	4	2	49	23	4	10	6	33	39	46
Tottenham Hotspur	38	11	4	4	55	32	6	5	8	30	43	43
Manchester City	37	12	4	2	52	29	7	1	11	40	61	43
Blackpool	37	10	2	7	45	34	7	4	7	29	27	40
Luton Town	37	11	3	5	41	20	6	3	9	21	32	40
Manchester United	35	10	3	5	44	24	5	6	6	34	37	39
Burnley	37	15	1	3	48	19	3	2	13	23	51	39
Nottingham Forest	36	9	3	6	39	23	6	4	8	26	31	37
Chelsea	38	9	4	6	43	31	5	5	9	35	44	37
Bolton Wanderers	37	9	4	6	37	30	5	4	9	24	43	36
Arsenal	36	10	2	6	47	36	5	2	11	20	39	34
Birmingham City	38	7	5	6	38	34	5	5	10	31	52	34
Everton	37	5	9	6	32	30	6	2	9	26	37	33
Portsmouth	37	10	5	3	41	27	2	2	15	26	48	31
Leeds United	38	9	5	5	32	23	3	2	14	15	38	31
Aston Villa	37	10	3	5	39	25	3	2	14	24	58	31
Leicester City	37	10	4	5	54	37	2	1	15	28	63	29
Sunderland	38	6	7	6	28	31	2	5	12	19	61	28
Newcastle United	35	5	3	9	29	33	6	2	10	32	35	27
Sheffield Wednesday	38	10	2	6	40	36	0	5	15	24	50	27

EASTER SATURDAY 5TH APRIL

ARSENAL   P   NOTTINGHAM F. P
(Waterlogged pitch after snow)

ASTON VILLA 2   WEST BROM. ALB. 1
Myerscough, McParland. Allen.
Att. 31,406

BLACKPOOL 3   NEWCASTLE UTD. 2
H. Kelly (pen), Charnley, Franks, Mitchell (pen)
Mudie. Att. 18,719

BOLTON W. 0   MANCHESTER C. 2
Barlow 2.
Att. 27,733

EVERTON 3   TOTTENHAM H. 4
Hickson 2, Thomas. Clayton 2, Smith 2.
Att. 30,149

LEEDS UNITED 2   SHEFFIELD WED. 2
Baird, Meek. Shiner, Wilkinson.
Att. 26,212

LEICESTER CITY 5   BURNLEY 3
Riley 2, Rowley 2, McIlroy 2, Miller.
Walsh. Att. 26,150

LUTON TOWN 0   CHELSEA 2
Brabrook, Tindall.
Att. 15,285

MANCHESTER U. 0   PRESTON N. E. 0
Att. 48,413

SUNDERLAND 1   BIRMINGHAM C. 6
Revie. Murphy, Astall, Brown,
Hooper, Orritt 2.
Att. 34,184

WOLVES 1   PORTSMOUTH 0
Clamp (pen). Att. 31,259

An Eddie Clamp penalty gave Wolves a 1-0 win in a tough game against Portsmouth watched by a disappointingly low crowd of just over 31,000. Only Preston can now overtake them at the top of the table but with five points' advantage and a game in hand, the title looks to be heading to Molineux.

The 30,000 fans at Goodison Park were treated to a wonderful game of football. Tottenham Hotspur, orchestrated by Blanchflower, stormed into a 4-0 lead after only 51 minutes with Clayton and Smith both scoring twice.

The home supporters feared the worse but, in the 58th minute, Hickson pulled a goal back as Spurs began to relax. Eight minutes later Thomas scored from a tight angle and then with fifteen minutes remaining Hickson scored again. Spurs began to wobble and almost paid the penalty when Thomas shot inches wide as the away side hung on for a narrow 4-3 victory.

After some recent improvement Sunderland hit rock bottom in their home match against Birmingham City. The away side scored four times in the opening fifteen minutes and things got worse when Anderson was stretchered from the pitch. The final score of 6-1 leaves them one point ahead of the bottom two teams.

United Reserves

The second team were well beaten 3-0 at West Brom. and any chance of catching Wolves at the top of the Central League table now appears a forlorn hope. Their cause was not helped when full-back, Jones, scored an own goal after 13 minutes to give Albion the lead.

Easter Monday 7ᵗʰ April

Sunderland   1   Manchester Utd.   2

Fogarty,   Webster 2.   Att. 51,382

Sunderland-*Fraser, Hedley, Elliott, Anderson, Aitken, Pearce, Fogarty, Revie, Kichenbrand, O'Neill, Goodchild.*

Manchester United-*Gregg, Foulkes, Greaves, Goodwin, Harrop, McGuinness, Morgans, Taylor, Webster, Charlton, Pearson.*

United made a number of changes to the side that played against Preston on Saturday for their return Easter fixture with Sunderland at Roker Park. Tom Heron was not given permission to play by the Football League as Sunderland are still in danger of relegation and the transfer only took place after the deadline day. Pearson resumed on the left wing.

Sunderland 1957/58
*Back row – C. Hurley, J.McDonald, J. Hedley, J. Bollands,
G. Aitken, C. Grainger.
Front row – W. Bingham, S. Anderson, C. Fleming, D. Revie,
W. Elliott. Inset W. Fraser.*

Wilf McGuinness returned from injury at left half in place of Crowther who was officially 'rested'. Cope suffered a thigh injury against Preston and Harrop replaced him at centre-half.

In the Sunderland team the only change from their game at Old Trafford was Goodchild for Grainger at No.11.

On the day of the game newspapers reported that Harry Gregg had been offered bribes by letter of £250 and then £500 to lose the Cup semi-final and then the replay at Highbury.

Gregg mentioned the letters to club captain Bill Foulkes but then decided to 'laugh them off' as probably from a crank.

The game against Sunderland was a dour affair, only brightened by local boy Ernie Taylor who created both goals for Webster with some delightful play.

Sunderland had the majority of the possession and pulled a goal back through Fogarty as the teams reached the interval level at 1-1. United's defence, led by Foulkes, held out resolutely and deserved their success. Thus United won their first League game since 1st February following a run of three draws and four defeats.

Following the match it was reported that Greaves and Gregg had both been hit by objects thrown from the crowd.

EASTER MONDAY 7TH APRIL

ARSENAL	0	WOLVES	2
		Broadbent, Murray	
		Att. 51,340	
BIRMINGHAM C.	4	PORTSMOUTH	1
Hooper, Murphy,		Crawford.	
Orritt, Brown			
		Att. 23,380	
LEEDS UNITED	1	EVERTON	0
Forrest.		Att. 25,188	
LUTON TOWN	2	LEICESTER CITY	1
Gregory 2.		Hines	
		Att. 14,795	
MANCHESTER C.	2	NEWCASTLE U.	1
Hayes, Warhurst.		White. Att. 33,995	
NOTTINGHAM F.	1	CHELSEA	1
Imlach.		Gibbs. Att. 25,130	
PRESTON N.E.	2	BLACKPOOL	1
Taylor, Thompson.		Charnley.	
		Att. 32,626	
SHEFFIELD W.	1	BURNLEY	2
Shiner.		Pointer, Newlands.	
		Att. 22,417	
SUNDERLAND	1	MANCHESTER U.	2
Fogarty.		Webster 2.	
		Att. 51,382	
WEST BROM. ALB.	0	TOTTENHAM H.	2
		Medwin, Clayton.	
		Att. 26,556	

Wolves gained two more points in their quest for the First Division title but had to work extremely hard for the win. In the early stages Arsenal were the better side with Groves dictating the play, but it was Broadbent who opened the scoring

317

midway through the first half. Two Arsenal defenders had tried to clear the ball out of the mud patch in the penalty area left from the weekend snow and rain, but neither succeeded as Broadbent struck.

In the second half Herd missed a penalty for the home side before Murray sealed the win with a goal fifteen minutes from time after superb approach play by Broadbent.

Second placed Preston faced local rivals Blackpool at Deepdale in the reverse fixture from Good Friday with the same 2-1 scoreline in favour of 'The Whites'.

Finney and Matthews both missed the game through injury but the bumper Bank Holiday crowd of over 32,000 who gathered early for the 11am kick-off were treated to an enthralling encounter. Tommy Thompson scored Preston's second and his own thirty-second goal of the season to send the home fans away in good spirits to Avenham Park for the traditional Egg Rolling event.

United Reserves

The 'second string' played out a goalless draw away at Sheffield United.

Tues. 8ᵗʰ April

ASTON VILLA	**4**	**BOLTON W.**	**0**
Lynn, Hitchens, Sewell,			
Higgins (o.g.)			
			Att. 32,745
LEICESTER CITY	**4**	**LUTON TOWN**	**1**
Rowley 2, Gardiner,		Gregory.	
Hines.			
			Att. 32,480
WOLVERHAMPTON W.	**1**	**ARSENAL**	**2**
Broadbent.		Groves, Wills (pen).	
			Att. 47,501

Wolves missed a wonderful opportunity to almost clinch the title when they lost at home for the first time since March 1957. Arsenal took the lead through Groves and then Wills scored a second from the penalty spot.

The heroes of the day were the Arsenal defenders who held out for a hard earned victory despite Broadbent pulling one goal back.

Victories for Aston Villa and Leicester City eased their relegation worries.

The latest saga in the dates for the European Cup semi-final games should see United play Milan at Old Trafford on 14ᵗʰ May with the return leg one week later.

	P	W	D	L	F	A	W	D	L	F	A	Pts
Wolverhampton Wndrs	38	16	3	1	58	21	10	4	4	37	23	59
Preston North End	38	17	1	1	59	13	7	5	7	33	35	54
West Bromwich Albion	39	12	4	3	49	25	4	10	6	33	39	46
Tottenham Hotspur	39	11	4	4	55	32	7	5	8	32	43	45
Manchester City	38	13	4	2	54	30	7	1	11	40	61	45
Luton Town	39	12	3	5	43	21	6	3	10	22	36	42
Manchester United	36	10	3	5	44	24	6	6	6	36	38	41
Burnley	38	15	1	3	48	19	4	2	13	25	52	41
Blackpool	38	10	2	7	45	34	7	4	8	30	29	40
Nottingham Forest	37	9	4	6	40	24	6	4	8	26	31	38
Chelsea	39	9	4	6	43	31	5	6	9	36	45	38
Arsenal	38	10	2	7	47	38	6	2	11	22	40	36
Birmingham City	39	8	5	6	42	35	5	5	10	31	52	36
Bolton Wanderers	38	9	4	6	37	30	5	4	10	24	47	36
Everton	38	5	9	6	32	30	6	2	10	26	38	33
Aston Villa	38	11	3	5	43	25	3	2	14	24	58	33
Leeds United	39	10	5	5	33	23	3	2	14	15	38	33
Portsmouth	38	10	5	3	41	27	2	2	16	27	52	31
Leicester City	39	11	4	5	58	38	2	1	16	29	65	31
Sunderland	39	6	7	7	29	33	2	5	12	19	61	28
Newcastle United	36	5	3	9	29	33	6	2	11	33	37	27
Sheffield Wednesday	39	10	2	7	41	38	0	5	15	24	50	27

Milan still seems to be unhappy with the date of the Old Trafford fixture, stating that they think it should be played in April. If the proposed dates are implemented then Milan will have to play six matches in a seventeen day period.

Following the complaint from Mr Milward, Chief Executive of British European Airways, that the British Press intruded into the Rechts der Isar Hospital where the survivors of the Munich air disaster were receiving care, the Press Council has now fully investigated the issues raised.

In a very detailed report the Press Council issued a statement that there had been no intrusion at the hospital and that the photographers and journalists were only trying to cover the story in very difficult and trying circumstances.

Wed. 9th April

Bobby Charlton will win his first International Cap against Scotland at Hampden Park on 19th April. With only six weeks of his National Service still to complete, Charlton has been named at inside-right. Langley will also make his debut at left-back. The full England team is – **HOPKINSON** (Bolton W.), **HOWE** (W. B. A.), **LANGLEY** (Fulham), **CLAYTON** (Blackburn R.), **WRIGHT** (Wolves) captain,

SLATER (Wolves), **DOUGLAS** (Blackburn R.), **CHARLTON** (Manchester U.), **KEVAN** (W.B.A.), **HAYNES** (Fulham), **FINNEY** (P.N.E.).

Thurs. 10th April

Dennis Viollet issued a statement to say that he hopes to return to competitive action with a United side within the next two weeks. The forward, who has not played since the game against Red Star Belgrade, is desperate to prove his fitness in time for the FA Cup Final.

United 'keeper, Harry Gregg, has been released to play for Ireland against Wales in Cardiff next Wednesday and will miss United's game at Portsmouth. It is expected that his place in goal will be taken by 17 years old David Gaskell.

Fri. 11th April

United informed the press that Crowther and Cope will return to the defence for the game at White Hart Lane tomorrow in place of McGuinness and Harrop. The forward line is the same as that which played at Sunderland.

United's opponents at Wembley in three weeks' time, Bolton Wanderers, made the surprise announcement that Nat Lofthouse has recovered from his dislocated shoulder and will play for the second team against Stoke City reserves tomorrow. If everything goes to plan he will be back in the senior team later in the month.

Slater and Wright will be absent from the Wolves team for the difficult away fixture at Burnley.

Professor Georg Maurer, Head of the Rechts der Isar Hospital in Munich, has been made an Honorary C. B. E. by the Queen in recognition of his services to the victims of the Air Disaster in February.

Saturday 12th April

Ray Crawford, Portsmouth's 21 year old outside-left, was married an hour before the scheduled kick-off of the home game against Blackpool. Immediately after the fifteen minute ceremony he kissed his auburn haired bride Eileen goodbye and dashed by taxi to Fratton Park.

Unfortunately the rest of his day ended in disappointment as Portsmouth lost the match 2-1 despite Crawford having a superb game on the left wing.

At the foot of the table only Sheffield Wednesday managed to win out of the bottom six sides. The game against Everton was watched by the lowest crowd of the day in the First Division – 17,514, who had to wait until the second half for all three goals.

Table topping Wolves were made to fight all the way to earn a point at Turf Moor but Preston, in second place, failed to take advantage when they also could only achieve a draw at home to Aston Villa. The two teams clash at Molineux next Saturday and a point for Wolves will give them the title.

SATURDAY 12TH APRIL

BIRMINGHAM C.	1	LEEDS UNITED	1
Orritt.		O'Brien.

Att. 23,112

| BURNLEY | 1 | WOLVES | 1 |
| Newlands. | | Clamp (pen). |

Att. 28,539

| CHELSEA | 2 | BOLTON W. | 2 |
| P. Sillett (pen), Brabrook | | Ball (pen), Gubbins. |

Att. 27,994

| MANCHESTER C. | 3 | SUNDERLAND | 1 |
| Hart, Hayes 2. | | Kichenbrand. |

Att. 31,166

| NEWCASTLE U. | 3 | ARSENAL | 3 |
| White, Curry, Stokoe. | | Herd, Groves, Bloomfield. |

Att. 43,221

| NOTTINGHAM F. | 1 | LUTON TOWN | 0 |
| Wilson. | | |

Att. 22,085

| PORTSMOUTH | 1 | BLACKPOOL | 2 |
| Dougan. | | Perry, Durie. |

Att. 25,391

| PRESTON N. E. | 1 | ASTON VILLA | 1 |
| Mayers. | | Myerscough. |

Att. 21,053

| SHEFFIELD WED. | 2 | EVERTON | 1 |
| Quixall, Curtis. | | J. Harris. |

Att. 17,514

| TOTTENHAM H. | 1 | MANCHESTER U. | 0 |
| Harmer (pen). | | |

Att. 59,836

| WEST BROM. ALB. | 6 | LEICESTER C. | 2 |
| Robson 3, Kevan, Whitehouse 2. | | Rowley, Gardiner. |

Att. 25,241

	P	W	D	L	F	A	W	D	L	F	A	Pts
Wolverhampton Wndrs	39	16	3	1	58	21	10	5	4	38	24	60
Preston North End	39	17	2	1	60	14	7	5	7	33	35	55
West Bromwich Albion	40	13	4	3	55	27	4	10	6	33	39	48
Tottenham Hotspur	40	12	4	4	56	32	7	5	8	32	43	47
Manchester City	39	14	4	2	57	31	7	1	11	40	61	47
Blackpool	39	10	2	7	45	34	8	4	8	32	30	42
Luton Town	40	12	3	5	43	21	6	3	11	22	37	42
Burnley	39	15	2	3	49	20	4	2	13	25	52	42
Manchester United	37	10	3	5	44	24	6	6	7	36	39	41
Nottingham Forest	38	10	4	6	41	24	6	4	8	26	31	40
Chelsea	40	9	5	6	45	33	5	6	9	36	45	39
Arsenal	39	10	2	7	47	38	6	3	11	25	43	37
Birmingham City	40	8	6	6	43	36	5	5	10	31	52	37
Bolton Wanderers	39	9	4	6	37	30	5	5	10	26	49	37
Aston Villa	39	11	3	5	43	25	3	3	14	25	59	34
Leeds United	40	10	5	5	33	23	3	3	14	16	39	34
Everton	39	5	9	6	32	30	6	2	11	27	40	33
Portsmouth	39	10	5	4	42	29	2	2	16	27	52	31
Leicester City	40	11	4	5	58	38	2	1	17	31	71	31
Sheffield Wednesday	40	11	2	7	43	39	0	5	15	24	50	29
Newcastle United	37	5	4	9	32	36	6	2	11	33	37	28
Sunderland	40	6	7	7	29	33	2	5	13	20	64	28

Tottenham H   1   Manchester U.   0

Harmer (pen).   Att. 59,836

Tottenham Hotspur-Reynolds, Hills, Henry, Blanchflower, Norman, Iley, Medwin, Harmer, Smith, Clayton, Jones.

Manchester United-Gregg, Foulkes, Greaves, Goodwin, Cope, Crowther, Morgans, Taylor, Webster, Charlton, Pearson.

Spurs highest attendance of 1958, almost 60,000, gathered at White Hart Lane to see the new 'Babes' in action. In contrast to recent weeks the pitch was bone hard as the home side kicked-off facing the sun but with the wind behind them.

In the opening minutes Cliff Jones received the ball on the left wing to some ironic cheers from the home fans, who seemed to think that the winger was being starved of the ball by his jealous colleagues because of his huge transfer fee.

There was nothing to choose between the sides and it was thirteen minutes before Harmer had the first shot of the game. Spurs gradually began to dictate the play and Jim Iley in particular was prominent in driving them forward as well as having a goal-bound shot saved by Gregg.

321

Soon after Gregg gathered a shot from Blanchflower and was charged over the line by Smith only for the referee to award a free kick to United for the challenge.

Taylor and Morgans created an opening for Pearson but he failed to control the ball and lost the opportunity.

In the 43rd minute Spurs were awarded a penalty when the ball struck Crowther's arm as he tried to bring it under control. HARMER made no mistake from the spot to give Tottenham a 1-0 half time lead.

It was a determined United side that emerged for the second half and for long periods they were camped around the home side's penalty area but found it difficult to create any clear-cut openings. Pearson lobbed the ball forwards to Webster but the centre-forward didn't react quickly enough allowing Reynolds to smother the ball. A shot by Taylor was just off target and Charlton also failed to test the 'keeper with two good attempts.

At the opposite end Iley saw his shot saved by Gregg and Spurs just about deserved their victory in a spirited game played at a high tempo by both teams.

Reynolds told the press after the game that the strong wind had made his eyes water badly because of his new contact lenses but fortunately United had failed to take advantage.

United Reserves

| Manchester United | 3 | Chesterfield | 0 |

The second team were just too strong for Chesterfield at Old Trafford and reached the interval one goal ahead. It was Dawson who made the opportunity for Heron to score. In the second half further goals from Spratt and Bradley gave them a comfortable victory.

Team-*Gaskell, B. Smith, Carolan, English, Holland, McGuinness, Bradley, Brennan, Dawson, Spratt, Heron.*

Sun. 13th April

It was confirmed at the Players Union A.G.M. in Manchester that insurance payments of £500 plus a further £100 death benefit had been made to the nearest relatives of each of the eight United players killed in the Munich Air Disaster.

Mon. 14th April

SOCCER PLAYERS WAGE PROPOSALS

An extraordinary General Meeting of the Football League Management Committee will take place in London on 31st May 1958 to consider proposals to amend the weekly wage and allowances of professional footballers.

It is anticipated that this final draft will be accepted by the Clubs and implemented for the 1958/59 season.

The main proposals are as follows:

Maximum wage for a player aged 17 or over to be £20 per week throughout the year.

Minimum wage for a player aged 17 or over to be £8 per week throughout the year.

£4 win bonus, £2 for a draw and £3 for matches played outside the League and Cup structure. Up to £2 extra for playing in a televised match.

A player who agrees to be transferred may receive up to £300 in addition to his accrued share of benefits.

International appearance fee £50 per game.

It was announced that Judge Walter Stimpel, aged 41, a former Luftwaffe officer will head the inquiry into the circumstances and reasons for the crash of the B.E.A. Elizabethan Aircraft on 6th February at Munich Airport.

The Commission will meet in private on 29th and 30th April and the judge will be assisted by a Civil Airline pilot and a professor. Observers from the British Board of Civil Aviation and British European Airways will also be in attendance.

Newspapers reported that Harry Gregg, Bill Foulkes and Bobby Charlton had each received ex-gratia payments from British European Airways in part compensation. These payments have been made in advance of the establishment of liability and any final settlement figure.

Wales are still hopeful that John Charles will be released by Juventus to play in the World Cup Finals in Sweden and have named him in a provisional squad of 40 players.

United Reserves

A Warren Bradley goal earned the second team a 1-1 draw away to Aston Villa. The dropped point has ensured that Wolves will be Central League Champions as United cannot now catch them.

DIVISION 1

NEWCASTLE UNITED   **4**   **MANCHESTER CITY**   **1**
Davies, White 2, Franks.   Warhurst.

Att. 53,226

Tues. 15th April

England played a forty minute practice game against Manchester City reserves at Maine Road in preparation for Saturday's International at Hampden Park.

Despite City fielding a side with an average age of only nineteen they were still too good for England and beat their illustrious opponents 2-0 with both goals scored by Kirkman.

Wed. 16th April

The morning papers announced that Matt Busby will appear on Sportsview tonight at 9.15 p.m. on BBC television. He will be speaking from his hospital room prior to leaving for England tomorrow.

HOME INTERNATIONAL CHAMPIONSHIP

WALES	1	IRELAND	1
Hewitt.		Simpson.	
At Ninian Park, Cardiff			Att. 38,000

Portsmouth	3	Manchester U.	3
Govan, Dougan, Harris.		Taylor, Webster, Dawson.	
			Att. 39,975

Portsmouth-*Uprichard, McGhee, Wilson, Phillips, Gunter, Dickinson, Harris, Govan, Dougan, Barnard, Crawford.*

Manchester United-*Gaskell, Foulkes, Greaves, Crowther, Cope, McGuinness, Dawson, Taylor, Webster, Pearson, Morgans.*

With Gregg and Charlton on international duty this week and Cope 'rested', United made three changes to the side that lost at White Hart Lane on Saturday. Gaskell, McGuinness and Dawson came into the team.

The changes seemed to have worked as United were easily the better side in the first half and reached the interval with a 2-0 cushion following strikes from TAYLOR and WEBSTER.

GOVAN, who joined 'Pompey' recently from Birmingham City, pulled a goal back following a cross from Dickinson.

DOUGAN then equalised which stirred United into action. Following a sustained period of attack DAWSON scored to restore their advantage. However Portsmouth were not finished and in the closing minutes HARRIS equalised to the delight of the large crowd and robbed United of a point.

Ken Morgans was Man of the Match having had a hand in all three United goals.

Thurs. 17th April

After playing in last night's re-arranged game against Portsmouth, Mark Pearson heard today that he had been suspended for seven days from Monday by the Football Association. This follows his sending off in the recent game against Burnley and will result in him missing the final three League games of the season.

It must also damage his chances of being selected for United in the Cup Final.

Following the non-appearance of Matt Busby on Sportsview last night, Peter Dimmock, hosting the show, announced that Mr Busby had decided at the last minute to withdraw as he had also made a promise to hold a Press Conference in Munich organised by British European Airways.

Mr Busby left hospital today and was travelling on the Rheingold train express via the Hook of Holland. On arriving in Harwich he will travel by car to Manchester and hopes to be fit enough to lead the team out at Wembley on 3rd May.

He still has his right ankle in plaster and uses two sticks to aid his walking.

With John Berry transferred to a hospital in Manchester last Tuesday, the only survivor of the crash still in the Rechts der Isar hospital is sports writer Frank Taylor of The News Chronicle.

Fri. 18th April

Gregg and Goodwin will return to the United side for the game against Birmingham City tomorrow. The visitors will be without Smith and Brown.

Viollet will play for United reserves at Bury in his first appearance since 'Munich' desperate to prove his fitness in readiness for the Cup Final.

The European Cup Committee have asked United to play the home first-leg of their semi-final with Milano at Old Trafford on Thursday 8th May. United have agreed to the revised date providing that there is no need for a replay of the Cup Final.

Sat. 19th April
Wolves are Champions!

What a pity that this important match at Molineux should clash with the Scotland v England International and therefore rob both teams of two players. Whilst Wolves had Wright and Slater missing there is no doubt that Preston, without Docherty and Finney, were hit much harder.

Wolves were on top from the kick-off and only fifteen minutes into the first half had won six corners.

Despite the sustained pressure Else, in the North End goal, managed to deal with everything thrown at him until the 37th minute. Broadbent hit a long through pass down the middle and Preston full-back, Walton, was unfortunate that the ball struck him on his back to land at the feet of Deeley who scored with ease. Preston held out until five minutes from time when Milne inadvertently scored an own goal whilst trying to clear a difficult cross from Broadbent.

Wolves fully deserved the victory, winning the Championship trophy for the second time in their history. The Club received a number of telegrams congratulating them on their achievement including one from Matt Busby.

At the foot of the table two from Sheffield Wednesday, Sunderland, Leicester City or Newcastle United will be relegated. Sunderland were the only victors on the day, beating Nottingham Forest 3-0.

Wednesday lost at Villa Park and Leicester were comprehensively beaten 3-1 at home by Spurs. Recent record signing, Cliff Jones, finally scored his first goal for Tottenham with a header on his ninth appearance for the club.

Newcastle United gained a creditable draw away at Cup Finalists Bolton Wanderers, and ,with two games in hand on the other three teams, look the most likely to escape the drop.

It was announced that Billy Meredith, aged 81 the former Manchester City and Wales International, died today at his home in Manchester.

SATURDAY 19TH APRIL

ARSENAL	0	BURNLEY	0	
			Att. 31,440	
ASTON VILLA	2	SHEFFIELD WED.	0	
Hitchens 2.			Att. 25,995	
BLACKPOOL	2	WEST BROM. ALB.	0	
Charnley 2.			Att. 17,327	
BOLTON W.	1	NEWCASTLE U.	1	
Lofthouse.		White.		
			Att. 19,284	
EVERTON	2	MANCHESTER C.	5	
Ashworth 2.		Hayes, Hart 2,		
		Sambrook, Barnes (pen		
			Att. 31,433	
LEEDS UNITED	0	CHELSEA	0	
			Att. 20,515	
LEICESTER CITY	1	TOTTENHAM H.	3	
Gardiner.		Smith, Medwin, Jones		
			Att. 37,234	
LUTON TOWN	2	PORTSMOUTH	1	
McLeod, Turner.		Gordon.		
			Att. 12,942	
MANCHESTER U.	0	BIRMINGHAM C.	2	
		Hooper, Green.		
			Att. 39,215	
SUNDERLAND	3	NOTTINGHAM F.	0	
Revie, Elliott (pen).				
Kichenbrand.			Att. 28,753	
WOLVES	2	PRESTON N. E.	0	
Deeley, Milne (og)			Att. 46,001	

	P	W	D	L	F	A	W	D	L	F	A	Pts
Wolverhampton Wndrs	40	17	3	1	60	21	10	5	4	38	24	62
Preston North End	40	17	2	1	60	14	7	5	8	33	37	55
Tottenham Hotspur	41	12	4	4	56	32	8	5	8	35	44	49
Manchester City	41	14	4	2	57	31	8	1	12	46	67	49
West Bromwich Albion	41	13	4	3	55	27	4	10	7	33	41	48
Blackpool	40	11	2	7	47	34	8	4	8	32	30	44
Luton Town	41	13	3	5	45	22	6	3	11	22	37	44
Burnley	40	15	2	3	49	20	4	3	13	25	52	43
Manchester United	39	10	3	6	44	26	6	7	7	39	42	42
Nottingham Forest	39	10	4	6	41	24	6	4	9	26	34	40
Chelsea	41	9	5	6	45	33	5	7	9	36	45	40
Birmingham City	41	8	6	6	43	36	6	5	10	33	52	39
Arsenal	40	10	3	7	47	38	6	3	11	25	43	38
Bolton Wanderers	40	12	3	5	45	25	3	3	14	25	59	36
Aston Villa	41	10	6	5	33	23	3	3	14	16	39	35
Leeds United	40	5	9	7	34	35	6	2	11	27	40	33
Everton	41	10	6	4	45	32	2	2	17	28	54	32
Portsmouth	39	6	4	9	36	37	6	3	11	34	38	31
Newcastle United	41	11	4	6	59	41	2	1	17	31	71	31
Leicester City	41	7	7	7	32	33	2	5	13	20	64	30
Sunderland	41	11	2	7	43	39	0	5	16	24	52	29
Sheffield Wednesday												

United Reserves

Yet another defeat for the reserve side, this time 3-1 away to Bury. The good news was a goal by Viollet in his quest to prove his fitness for the Cup Final.

Manchester Utd	0	Birmingham City	2

Hooper, Green.

Att. 39,215

Manchester United-*Gregg, Foulkes, Greaves, Goodwin, Cope, Crowther, Dawson, Taylor, Webster, Pearson, Morgans.*
Birmingham City-*Schofield, Hall, Green, Larkin, Sissons, Neal, Hooper, Jones, Orritt, Murphy, Astall.*

Prior to the game the Chairman of Birmingham City Supporters Club presented a cheque for £141 to the Mayor of Manchester for the United Disaster Fund.

The away side kicked off and soon put the United defence under pressure, taking the lead after only two minutes. HOOPER (pictured) received the ball from a free kick near the half way line and raced forward beating four home players before shooting into the corner of the net with Gregg wrong-footed.

It was all Birmingham in the early stages with United having difficulty gaining any foothold in the match. Both teams struggled to control the lively ball with numerous passes going astray.

It was no surprise when Birmingham increased their lead after twenty-six minutes. Left-back, GREEN, who had ventured forward to support the attack, received the ball from Murphy just inside the penalty area and blasted it into the top corner.

As Mr Sparling from Grimsby blew the half time whistle United had just begun to look more menacing. Early in the second half Dawson had a header saved from a free kick taken by Webster. United's defence still looked shaky as Murphy dashed through the middle only to be blocked by a daring save by the 'keeper.

United responded again and Taylor forced Schofield to save on his knees. As tempers frayed Orritt had his name taken after committing a foul.

The home side just couldn't find a way through the 'Blues' strong defence and Dawson was forced to shoot from distance without success. Murphy was dangerous for the away side and once again Gregg came to the rescue by bravely diving at the forward's feet. In the final minutes United pushed everyone forward but efforts from Taylor and Pearson were easily saved by Schofield.

Once again the 'Red Devils' had failed to win a League game at home and have still not gained two points at Old Trafford since 18th January 1958.

Scotland   0   England   4

Scotland-*Younger* (Liverpool), *Parker* (Falkirk), *Haddock* (Clyde), *McColl* (Rangers), *Evans* (Celtic), *Docherty* (Preston North End) (Captain), *Herd* (Clyde), *Murray* (Hearts), *Mudie* (Blackpool), *Forrest* (Motherwell), *Ewing* (Partick Thistle).

England-*Hopkinson* (Bolton Wanderers), *Howe* (W.B.A.), *Langley* (Fulham), *Clayton* (Blackburn Rovers), *Wright* (Wolves) (Captain), *Slater* (Wolves), *Douglas* (Blackburn Rovers), *Charlton* (Manchester United), *Kevan* (W. B. A.), *Haynes* (Fulham), *Finney* (Preston North End).

A crowd of 127,857 at Hampden Park witnessed one of the poorest displays by a Scotland team for many years. Although England were never at their most fluent they still had little difficulty reaching the half time interval with a two goal advantage. The score could have been greater had it not been for two brilliant saves by Tommy Younger.

DOUGLAS gave England the lead in the 22nd minute with a well-placed header from a Charlton free kick. Then ten minutes before half time KEVAN slotted a right-foot shot into the corner of the net from a Douglas pass.

In the 65th minute Finney beat the full-back down the left flank before pulling the ball back to the edge of the penalty area where CHARLTON volleyed it beyond Younger for his first goal on his International debut. Four minutes later, after a move involving Slater and Haynes, England scored a fourth through KEVAN to clinch the Home International Championship.

Many journalists and football experts reported that, despite England's victory, the standard of football on show would be below that needed for the forthcoming World Cup Finals in Sweden.

Mon. 21st April

ARSENAL   1   **NOTTINGHAM FOREST**   1
Bloomfield.   Gray.

Att. 23,217

BOLTON WANDERERS   0   **PRESTON NORTH END**   4
Finney (pen), Hatsell 2, Thompson

Att. 24,067

MANCHESTER UNITED   0   **WOLVERHAMPTON W.**   4
Flowers, Clamp, Deeley,
Broadbent (pen).

Att. 35,467

Bolton Wanderers suffered the same fate as their Cup Final opponents when they also lost 4-0 at home, this time to Preston.

Finney was pushed in the back in the penalty area and scored from the spot (his 26th goal of the season) to give North End a narrow one goal advantage at half time.

After the interval Preston dominated proceedings, scoring three times to win easily. The fourth goal scored by Tommy Thompson was his 33rd League goal.

       Manchester Utd.   0   **Wolves.**   4
Flowers, Clamp, Deeley,
Broadbent (pen).

Att. 35,467

Manchester United-*Gaskell, Foulkes, Greaves, Goodwin, Cope, McGuinness, Dawson, Brennan, Webster, Viollet, Morgans.*
Wolverhampton Wanderers-*Dwyer, Stuart, Jones, Clamp, Wright, Flowers, Deeley, Broadbent, Murray, Booth, Mullen.*

United decided to 'rest' Crowther, Taylor and Charlton for the rearranged game against new Champions Wolves. Their places were taken by McGuinness, Brennan and Viollet, who returned for his first senior game since the Munich air crash.

Harry Gregg was in bed with a severe chill and young David Gaskell again deputised. United players formed a guard of honour to clap their opponents onto the field.

Both sides gave lacklustre performances in the opening forty-five minutes. The game only sparked into life when FLOWERS, deputising for Slater, slammed a powerful shot into the net in the 34th minute. This followed a neat inter-passing move between Booth and Murray leaving Flowers to shoot home from the edge of the penalty area.

The goal settled Wolves down and they dictated play throughout the second half. In the 60th minute they scored a second when Deeley set up CLAMP. A few minutes later DEELEY also got on the score sheet with his 23rd goal of the season.

Then in the 67th minute, Cope handled the ball in the penalty area and BROADBENT scored from the spot. The only positives to emerge from United's performance were the constant efforts of Viollet and the non-stop running of Webster. Viollet looked determined to show that he is fit and ready for the FA Cup Final in twelve days' time.

Wolverhampton Wanderers Team Group
Back row – Harris, Clamp, Stuart, Finlayson, Dwyer, Flowers, Mullen, Slater.
Middle row – Gardiner (Trainer), Deeley, Broadbent, Wright, Mason, Booth,
Cullis (Manager).
Front row – Murray, Showell.

Tues. 22nd April

The England selectors announced their provisional squad of forty players for the World Cup Finals in Sweden.

Only three players – Finney, Lofthouse and Wright – who played in the 1954 World Cup Finals are included in the group. One notable omission is Chelsea's young forward Jimmy Greaves who many experts considered would be an automatic selection.

GOALKEEPERS-Hodgkinson, (Sheffield U.), **Hopkinson** (Bolton W.), **McDonald** (Burnley), **Matthews** (Chelsea).

FULL-BACKS-Banks (Bolton W.), **Hall** (Birmingham C.), **Harris** (Wolves), Howe (W.B.A.), **Langley** (Fulham), **Sillett P.** (Chelsea).

HALF-BACKS-Barlow (W.B.A.), **Clamp** (Wolves), **Clayton R.** (Blackburn R.), **Flowers** (Wolves), **Norman** (Tottenham H.), **Setters** (W.B.A.), **Slater** (Wolves), **Smith T.** (Birmingham C.), **Wheeler** (Liverpool), **Wright** (Wolves).

FORWARDS-A'Court (Liverpool), **Allen** (W.B.A.), **Brabrook** (Chelsea), **Broadbent** (Wolves), **Charlton** (Manchester U.), **Clough** (Middlesbrough), **Deeley** (Wolves), **Douglas** (Blackburn R.), **Finney** (P.N.E.), **Hayes** (Manchester C.), **Haynes** (Fulham), **Hooper** (Birmingham C.), **Kevan** (W.B.A.), **Lofthouse** (Bolton W.), **Parry** (Bolton W.), **Pilkington** (Burnley), **Robson** (W.B.A.), **Smith** (Tottenham H.), **Thompson** (P.N.E.), **Viollet** (Manchester U.).

FA YOUTH CUP SEMI-FINAL

At Old Trafford a goal from Spratt earned United a hard fought 1-1 draw in the First Leg of the semi-final against a strong Wolves team.

Wed. 23rd April

BLACKPOOL	0	EVERTON	1
		Ashworth	
			Att. 12,981
MANCHESTER UNITED	1	NEWCASTLE UNITED	1
Dawson.		White.	
			Att. 28,573

UNDER 23 INTERNATIONAL at WREXHAM

WALES	2	ENGLAND	1
Leek, Orritt.		Clough	
			Att. 13,000

Manchester U. 1   Newcastle U.   1

Dawson.   White.   Att. 28,573

Manchester United-*Gregg, Foulkes, Greaves, Crowther, Cope, McGuinness, Dawson, Taylor, Webster, Charlton, Morgans.*

Newcastle United-*Simpson, Keith, McMichael, Scoular, Stokoe, Franks, Hughes, Davies, White, Eastham, Mitchell.*

Dennis Viollet had a groin injury and missed the game although Jimmy Murphy is still hopeful that he will be fit to play at Chelsea on Saturday. The same injury cost Viollet a place in the United team that lost to Aston Villa at Wembley last year.

There was good news for United supporters when it was announced that Gregg, Charlton and Taylor were all back in the team. Goodwin was rested and McGuinness continued at left-half.

As the teams emerged Matt Busby appeared in the Directors box receiving a tremendous ovation from the disappointingly small crowd of less than 29,000 (the lowest for any League or Cup game at the ground this season).

Despite this game being United's third League match in five days they were easily the better side in the opening exchanges and it took only eleven minutes for them to go into the lead. Taylor had been first to the ball from a corner, laying it onto DAWSON who hooked it into the net from twelve yards out. As the game progressed both sides pushed forward at every opportunity in search of a goal. Morgans saw a header kicked off the line by Keith and then both he and Dawson had goal-bound shots well saved by Simpson.

At the opposite end Gregg was also in action pushing a Mitchell 'thunderbolt' round the post and then preventing a left foot drive from Hughes from crossing the line. Cope played superbly at the heart of United's defence and Scoular was the pick of the Newcastle side, always in the right place to break down attacks and with time to push his own side forward.

Five minutes from time the away side had a strong penalty appeal turned down by the referee after Davies appeared to be fouled by Greaves. Then in the 87th minute Newcastle scored the goal that their non-stop efforts had deserved.

McGuinness conceded a corner. Eastham won a header despite a strong challenge and Mitchell pounced, only to slam the ball against the post. The ball rebounded into the path of WHITE who forced it into the net from five yards for his 22nd League goal of the season. In an amazing run he has now found the net in eight of the last ten games scoring twelve goals in all.

The game ended with the Manchester United players looking dejected in contrast to the Newcastle players who hugged and celebrated in gaining a vital point which, because of their far superior goal average, will ensure their survival in the First Division.

United were left with a difficult problem regarding the form of Ken Morgans who, during recent matches, has struggled to impose himself on the game from his left-wing position.

The dates for the semi-finals of the European Cup have finally been agreed. United will host Milan on Thursday 8ᵗʰ May with the return leg in Italy on Wednesday 14ᵗʰ May. The dates will have to be changed if the FA Cup Final results in a draw.

Thurs. 24ᵗʰ April

Manchester United revealed the badge that the players will wear at Wembley a week on Saturday. It depicts a golden eagle on a mural crown although many journalists have stated that it looks like a phoenix rising from the ashes. The badge is contained in part of Manchester City Council's new Coat of Arms.

Despite everything else happening in his life Bobby Charlton has been ordered to report to Donnington in Shropshire next Sunday with other members of the Western Command Army XI in readiness for a floodlit friendly match against Stockport County at Edgeley Park on Monday evening.

FA Youth Cup

United lost the semi-final second leg 3-1 away to Wolves and the tie 4-2 on aggregate. This was United's first defeat in the FA Youth Cup Competition since it was introduced in the 1952/53 season. Spratt once again scored their only goal.

Fri. 25th April

The First Division relegation battle will be completed tomorrow with three teams – Sheffield Wednesday, Leicester City and Sunderland – fighting to avoid the bottom two places.

Sheffield Wednesday face Champions, Wolves, at Hillsborough and even a victory is unlikely to prevent their relegation to the Second Division because of their poor goal average. A win for Wolves would take their points total to 66 which would equal Arsenal's record set in 1931.

Both Leicester and Sunderland face difficult away games in a vital fight for points, but one of them will go down.

United sprang a number of surprises when announcing their team to face Chelsea at Stamford Bridge. The forward line has been completely revamped with Charlton switching to centre-forward and Webster named at outside-left. Dawson will play on the right-wing and Viollet is fit to return at inside-left.

The normal defence of Gregg, Foulkes, Greaves, Goodwin, Cope and Crowther are selected with McGuinness on standby as twelfth man. Chelsea will have an unusual absentee as Tindall has pulled a muscle in a cricket practice match for Surrey.

The Club announced that the European Cup semi-final against Milan at Old Trafford on Thursday 8th May will be all ticket. The attendance could be affected by the BBC winning the exclusive rights to screen the game live.

Sat. 26th April

Amazingly all three teams at the foot of the table won their games which resulted in Sunderland and Sheffield Wednesday finishing in the bottom two positions. Wednesday fought tooth and nail to beat Champions, Wolves, and will provide stiff opposition to all the sides in the 2nd Division next season.

Sunderland, who were relegated because of their poor goal average, have lost their record of being the only side never to have been relegated from the top division in the history of English football.

Whilst defeating Arsenal 3-0 at Deepdale, Mayers (pictured) scored Preston's record-equalling 100th goal of the season. The side finished runners-up to Wolves and, despite putting the Arsenal defence under constant pressure for the last thirty three minutes, they could not score a fourth which would have broken their League record goals total created thirty years ago in the 2nd Division.

What a pity that the game was watched by less than 22,000, the smallest ever attendance for a League game at Deepdale against Arsenal. Their final points total of 59 was the highest they have ever achieved.

SATURDAY 26TH APRIL

BIRMINGHAM C.　0　LEICESTER C.　1
McNeill
Att. 27,607

BURNLEY　3　BOLTON W.　1
McIlroy 2, Seith.　Lofthouse.
Att. 17,419

CHELSEA　2　MANCHESTER U.　1
Cliss, Allen.　Taylor
Att. 45,011

MANCHESTER C.　1　ASTON VILLA　2
Hayes.　Smith, Sewell.
Att. 28,275

NEWCASTLE U.　1　LEEDS UTD.　2
Mitchell.　O'Brien, Baird
Att. 32,594

NOTTINGHAM F.　0　EVERTON　3
J. Harris, B. Harris 2.
Att. 16,879

PORTSMOUTH　0　SUNDERLAND　2
Kichenbrand 2.
Att. 22,545

PRESTON N. E.　3　ARSENAL　0
Thompson, Mayers 2.
Att. 21,538

SHEFFIELD WED.　2　WOLVES　1
Wilkinson, Shiner.　Flowers.
Att. 23,523

TOTTENHAM H.　2　BLACKPOOL　1
Medwin, Smith.　Charnley
Att. 37,632

WEST BROM. ALB.　4　LUTON TOWN　2
Howe, Lee 2, Allen (pen).　Turner 2 (1 pen).
Att. 20,158

		Home				Goals	Away			Goals		
	P	W	D	L	F	A	W	D	L	F	A	Pts
Wolves	42	17	3	1	60	21	11	5	5	43	26	64
Preston N.E. ..	42	18	2	1	63	14	8	5	8	37	37	59
Tottenham ..	42	13	4	4	58	33	8	5	8	35	44	51
West Brom. A.	42	14	4	3	59	29	4	10	7	33	41	50
Man. City	42	14	4	3	58	33	8	1	12	46	67	49
Burnley	41	16	2	3	52	21	4	3	13	25	52	45
Blackpool	42	11	2	8	47	35	8	4	9	33	32	44
Luton Town ..	42	13	3	5	45	22	6	3	12	24	41	44
Man. United ..	42	10	4	7	45	31	6	7	8	40	44	43
CHELSEA	42	10	5	6	47	34	5	7	9	36	45	42
Nottm. Forest .	41	10	4	7	41	27	6	5	9	27	35	41
Arsenal	42	10	4	7	48	39	6	3	12	25	46	39
Birmingham ..	42	8	6	7	43	37	6	5	10	33	52	39
Aston Villa ..	41	12	3	5	45	25	4	3	14	27	60	38
Bolton	42	9	5	7	38	35	5	5	11	27	52	38
Everton	42	5	9	7	34	35	8	2	11	31	40	37
Leeds United ..	42	10	6	5	33	23	4	3	14	18	40	37
Leicester	42	11	4	6	59	41	3	1	17	32	71	33
Newcastle	41	6	4	10	37	39	6	4	11	35	39	32
Portsmouth ..	42	10	6	5	45	34	2	2	17	28	54	32
Sunderland	42	7	7	7	32	33	3	5	13	22	64	32
Sheffield Wed. .	42	12	2	7	45	40	0	5	16	24	52	31

At Turf Moor Cup finalists Bolton Wanderers were well beaten 3-1 by Burnley. McIlroy scored the goal of the game after seven minutes when he beat two defenders before lobbing the ball over the head of the advancing Hopkinson. Bolton were always second best and the only positive they took from the game was a goal from Lofthouse, his second in three games after his return from injury.

Manchester City surprisingly lost at home to Aston Villa therefore losing the chance for talent money after relinquishing fourth position. In an astonishing season Villa's second goal in their 2-1 victory, scored by Sewell, meant that City had conceded 100 goals but had scored 104 goals, an average of almost FIVE GOALS per game.

City will be in New York on 25th May for a friendly game against Scottish Champions, Hearts. Then they move on to Canada for a further three games against the same opposition.

After losing 2-1 at White Hart Lane Blackpool immediately left for their tour of America and Australia. They will play a night game in Los Angeles on Tuesday against a Californian XI then travel on to Australia for an 11 match series.

United Reserves

In yet another disappointing performance the youthful United second team lost 2-1 at home to Huddersfield Town. Their consolation goal was scored by Giles.

Chelsea   2   Manchester U.   1

Cliss, Allen.   Taylor.

Att. 45,011

Chelsea-*Matthews, Sillett P., Sillett J., Mortimore, Scott, Casey, Brabrook, Cliss, Allen, Greaves, Harrison.*

Manchester United-*Gregg, Foulkes, Greaves, Goodwin, Cope, Crowther, Dawson, Taylor, Charlton, Viollet, Webster.*

After some morning rain it was a fine afternoon that greeted the teams as they emerged to the applause of the 45,000 fans. Webster won an early corner which was safely held by Matthews and it was United who created the first real opportunity, but Viollet slammed the ball over the cross-bar. Matthews was in action again after ten minutes when he was forced to fist away a powerful cross shot from Charlton. Against the run of play, four minutes later, 18 years old CLISS (pictured) gave Chelsea the lead with his first goal for the club. The diminutive inside-right was sent clear from a beautiful pass by Greaves and shot straight through the hands of Gregg. United were down to ten men at the time whilst Dawson was receiving attention on the touchline. Within two minutes United drew level after brilliant approach play by Charlton who, upon reaching the penalty area, laid the ball into the path of TAYLOR for an easy goal. In the 24th minute Chelsea scored a second after Brabrook and Harrison down the flanks had caused the United defence problems. ALLEN was in the right place to take advantage.

Greaves then shot against the bar as the home side reached the interval with a 2-1 lead. The second half was dominated by United for long periods but they were unable to translate their mid-field superiority into goals.

Webster had an outstanding match on the left wing and, together with the returning Viollet, looks odds-on favourites to be named in the side for Wembley.

Sun. 27th April

It was announced that the Northern Ireland and Spurs wing-half, Danny Blanchflower, had been chosen as Footballer of the Year by the Football Writers' Association.

Mon. 28th April

Newspapers reported that Manchester United had received a number of letters from supporters stating that it would be unfair if Dennis Viollet played for the team at Wembley in preference to many of the younger players who had 'stepped up to the mark' since the Munich tragedy.

The Club stated that Jimmy Murphy will select the team on merit and no preferential treatment will be given to Viollet who, unfortunately, missed last season's Cup Final through injury.

The United squad left today for Blackpool for a four day training break in a deliberate attempt once again to keep them away from the fever pitched Manchester public.

Leicester City outside-left, Derek Hogg, signed for West Bromwich Albion for a reported fee of £16,000. The player, who scored five goals during the season, will travel with his new team-mates to Spain for an end of season tour.

NEWCASTLE UNITED	1	BURNLEY	3
Bottom.		Seith, Newlands, Pointer.	

Att. 21,610

United Reserves

The Central League Fixtures were completed as United suffered a 1-0 home defeat against Derby County.

Top of Central League Table

	P	W	D	L	F	A	Pts
WOLVES	42	27	8	7	112	64	62
EVERTON	42	22	9	11	89	56	53
MANCHESTER U.	42	22	7	13	117	80	51
HUDDERSFIELD T.	42	21	9	12	87	60	51
LIVERPOOL	42	23	5	14	96	67	51

United Reserves Goal Scorers

22	Dawson,
13	Harrop, Scanlon,
10	Charlton,
8	Pegg,
6	Webster
5	Doherty, Morgans, Whelan.
4	Cope, Pearson.
3	Bradley, Spratt, Own Goals.
2	Berry, Brennan, Heron, Whitefoot.
1	Blanchflower, Giles, Goodwin, Lawton, Viollet.

Total goals 117

Tues. 29th April

United announced that their players will wear new, special lightweight boots in the FA Cup Final. The boots are especially supple and the manufacturers claim that you can play a competitive game using them after less than one hour's wear.

Jimmy Murphy today announced that the side that played at Chelsea on Saturday would represent United in the Cup Final. With a settled defence Murphy has decided to play Dawson and Webster on the wings with Viollet at inside-left.

Bolton Wanderers have also named their side which does not include any surprises, giving Lofthouse and Holden the opportunity to appear in a second Final after being on the losing side to Blackpool in 1953.

Foulkes, Charlton and Crowther all appeared in last year's Final and Ernie Taylor will play in his third, after previously being on the winning side for Newcastle United in 1951 and Blackpool in 1953.

FA Youth Cup

In the first leg of the Youth Cup Final at Stamford Bridge Chelsea, featuring a number of current first team players, overwhelmed Wolves winning 5-1 in front of 19,621 spectators.

The goals were shared between Harrison 2, Greaves, Block and Bridges. In earlier rounds Bridges (pictured) scored 7, 6, and 5 goals in easy victories.

Wed. 30ᵗʰ April

ASTON VILLA	1	NOTTINGHAM F.	1
Hitchens		Saward (og)	

Att. 21,043

Player Profile

Thomas Thompson
Born Fencehouses, Houghton-le-Spring. 10ᵗʰ Nov. 1928

Tommy Thompson signed for Newcastle United aged 17 years and made his debut in February 1948, going on to make four appearances whilst scoring two goals as Newcastle won promotion to the First Division.

Although faced with strong competition for a place in the starting X1 from Shackleton, Milburn and Robledo, 'Topper' Thompson never let the side down when called upon. He scored four goals in sixteen appearances over the next two seasons before Aston Villa decided to pay £12,500 for his signature.

Manager, George Martin, had faith in his ability and Thompson was soon rewarded with regular first team football, scoring eleven League and Cup goals in thirty-three appearances.

Although only 5ft 5ins, his strength surprised defenders and together with a blistering pace over short distances, he soon became a favourite at Villa Park.

In October 1951 Thompson scored four goals for the Football League against the League of Ireland at Goodison Park in a 9-1 victory. This performance earned him his first England cap just over a week later when he played in the No. 8 shirt at Ninian Park in a 1-1 draw against Wales with Finney at outside-right.

After averaging one goal every two games at Villa over a five year period Thompson was surprisingly allowed to move to Deepdale for a fee of £27,000 at the start of the 1955/56 season. He no doubt relished the opportunity of playing alongside Tom Finney and it took him just two minutes to score his first goal for North End, as Everton were beaten 4-0 on their home ground on the opening day of the season. He then scored in four of the next five games to firmly establish himself in the side. He ended the season with 23 League goals in 42 games and the following season improved his total to 26 in 38 League games.

This prolific form earned him his second cap as England beat Scotland 2-1 at Hampden Park. At the conclusion of the 1957/58 season he had scored 34 goals as North End finished in second place. In harness with Finney they had scored 60 goals out of 100 in League football and their dynamic partnership was the envy of many clubs.

MAY 1958

Thurs. 1st May

In an astonishing turnaround in the FA Youth Cup Final Second Leg, Wolves scored four goals in the first half against Chelsea to level the tie at 5-5. It was Farmer who scored them all. As the news filtered through, it is estimated that as many as 2000 extra fans arrived to watch the second half. They were not disappointed as, despite a goal from Greaves, Wolves scored twice through South African born Durandt to win the game 6-1 and 7-6 on aggregate.

On Tuesday 29th April the inquiry into the Munich Air Crash opened at Munich's Riem Airport, Chaired by Herr Stimpel.

The facts of the case were heard in closed session and Captain Thain, the Commander of the Elizabethan Airliner gave his evidence to the Commission.

The following day Judge Stimpel announced that, "The evidence of expert witnesses has raised many questions which can only be answered after they have made further exact calculations."

The inquiry was therefore formerly adjourned today for 4-6 weeks.

Fri. 2nd May

Matt Busby accompanied the team on their train journey to London today and will meet the Duke of Edinburgh in the players' tunnel before the kick-off. He will not lead the team out at Wembley, but instead allow his right hand man, Jimmy Murphy to have the honour.

It is expected that Professor Maurer from the Rechts der Isar Hospital and his wife will also be introduced to the Duke.

Sports journalists around the country have been voicing their opinions about who will win the FA Cup. The general consensus of opinion is that United will be too strong for Bolton and will win the trophy on a tide of emotion.

There is no doubt that this will be a close affair with Bolton having beaten United 4-0 at home in the League before losing the reverse fixture at Old Trafford 7-2, both games coming before 'Munich'.

It must be remembered that, outside of the FA Cup competition, United have only won one League game out of fourteen played and, that in itself, will give great encouragement to the Bolton players.

In what many regarded as a final trial match at Stamford Bridge this evening, an England World Cup XI defeated a Past and Present England under 23 XI by 4-2.

Despite the scoreline the England performance was not very convincing. Six players got their names on the score sheet – Finney, Haynes, Douglas and Kevan for England and A'Court and Clough for the Under 23 XI.

1957/58 Statistics

Leading Scorers

36 SMITH Tottenham H.

34 THOMPSON Preston N. E.

33 TURNER Luton Town

29 MURRAY Wolverhampton W.

26 FINNEY Preston N. E.

25 HAYES Manchester C.

24 HERD Arsenal, ROBSON W. B. A.

23 DEELEY Wolverhampton W.

22 ALLEN W. B. A., GREAVES Chelsea, WHITE Newcastle U.

		HOME			Goals		AWAY			Goals		
	P	W	D	L	F	A	W	D	L	F	A	Pts.
Wolverhampton	42	17	3	1	60	21	11	5	5	43	26	64
Preston North End	42	18	2	1	63	14	8	5	8	37	37	59
Tottenham Hotspur	42	13	4	4	58	33	8	5	8	35	44	51
West Bromwich	42	14	4	3	59	29	4	10	7	33	41	50
Manchester City	42	14	4	3	58	33	8	1	12	46	67	49
Burnley	42	16	2	3	52	21	5	3	13	28	53	47
Blackpool	42	11	2	8	47	35	8	4	9	33	32	44
Luton Town	42	13	3	5	45	22	6	3	12	24	41	44
Manchester United	42	10	4	7	45	31	6	7	8	40	44	43
Nottingham Forest	42	10	4	7	41	27	6	6	9	28	36	42
Chelsea	42	10	5	6	47	34	5	7	9	36	45	42
Arsenal	42	10	4	7	48	39	6	3	12	25	46	39
Birmingham City	42	8	6	7	43	37	6	5	10	33	52	39
Aston Villa	42	12	4	5	46	26	4	3	14	27	60	39
Bolton Wanderers	42	9	5	7	38	35	5	5	11	27	52	38
Everton	42	5	9	7	34	35	8	2	11	31	40	37
Leeds United	42	10	6	5	33	23	4	3	14	18	40	37
Leicester City	42	11	4	6	59	41	3	1	17	32	71	33
Newcastle United	42	6	4	11	38	42	6	4	11	35	39	32
Portsmouth	42	10	6	5	45	34	2	2	17	28	54	32
Sunderland	42	7	7	7	32	33	3	5	13	22	64	32
Sheffield Wednesday	42	12	2	7	45	40	0	5	16	24	52	31

Average Home League Attendances

MANCHESTER U.	43,100
TOTTENHAM H.	42,951
ARSENAL	40,137
EVERTON	39,157
CHELSEA	37,553
WOLVES.	37,317
SUNDERLAND	36,142
NEWCASTLE U.	35,696
MANCHESTER C.	32,516
W. B. A.	32,357
NOTTINGHAM F.	31,496
LEICESTER C.	31,264
BIRMINGHAM C.	29,607
ASTON VILLA	28,842
PORTSMOUTH	28,499
PRESTON N. E.	24,908
LEEDS UNITED	24,900
SHEFFIELD WED.	23,256
BURNLEY	22,251
BOLTON W.	22,080
BLACKPOOL	21,402
LUTON TOWN	18,418

Saturday 3rd May
FA Cup Final

Bolton Wanderers v Manchester Utd.

Bolton Wanderers-*Hopkinson, Hartle, Banks, Hennin, Higgins, Edwards, Birch, Stevens, Lofthouse, Parry, Holden.*
Manchester United-*Gregg, Foulkes, Greaves, Goodwin, Cope, Crowther, Dawson, Taylor, Charlton, Viollet, Webster.*

After the teams had been presented to the Duke of Edinburgh, Manchester United kicked off. It was their opponents who were earliest into their stride, spraying the ball wide whenever possible. After only three minutes LOFTHOUSE gave Bolton the lead following a corner. The ball was only partially cleared by the United defence and the burly centre-forward made no mistake with a right foot shot from six yards.

Charlton was at the hub of everything United created, switching the play from left to right in order to create space for his team-mates. Gregg was not his usual commanding figure and on two occasions dropped the ball but, fortunately, on each occasion the danger was cleared.

In the fifteenth minute Charlton lost the ball near the half way line and Wanderers stormed forward but Gregg did well to save a shot from Lofthouse.

WEST STANDING ENCLOSURE

ENTER AT TURNSTILES (See plan & conditions on back)

ENTRANCE **H** **56**

EMPIRE STADIUM, WEMBLEY
The Football Association
Cup Competition

Final Tie

SATURDAY, MAY 3rd, 1958
KICK-OFF 3 p.m.

Price 3/6

Chairman,
Wembley Stadium Limited

THIS PORTION TO BE RETAINED
This Ticket is issued on the condition that
it is not re-sold for more than its face value

Soon afterwards Banks moved forward at pace and played the ball to Birch who cut inside his marker and drilled a shot goal-wards only to see Gregg palm the ball away.

Dawson and Webster swapped wings in an attempt to re-invigorate the front line but the change did not have the desired effect. Charlton then found Viollet with a pin point pass and the inside-forward evaded one tackle before laying the ball into the path of Taylor in the penalty area. His right foot shot was pushed round the post by Hopkinson. Mid-way through the half Charlton hit a trademark right foot pile-driver from 22 yards but Hopkinson made a good save.

Neither side seemed able to put their foot on the ball to create an effective move. After three or four passes the final ball was either lost or given away.

Crowther was involved in two or three feisty challenges, both by him and against him, as Bolton refused to be intimidated. Seven minutes from the interval a long clearance found Charlton, who quickly moved forward hitting a left foot shot which the 'keeper saved. Bolton continued to attack down the wings but their final ball was often a disappointment.

Just before the whistle for half time Crowther and Stevens both received a lecture from the referee following a clash near the half-way line. In the final action Dawson won a right-wing corner and took the kick himself. For once, little Ernie Taylor escaped his marker to make good contact with a header which went just over the bar.

Half Time Bolton Wanderers 1   Manchester United 0

In the opening minute Stevens found room down the right-wing and hit a tantalising cross into the penalty area. Gregg was first to the ball, catching it cleanly above his head. Bolton pressed once more with Lofthouse creating room for himself to shoot after a move involving four Bolton players but his effort sailed over the crossbar.

At the opposite end once again it was Charlton in the thick of the action but his attempt at goal hit the post and bounced back into Hopkinson's hands.

In the 55th minute referee, Jack Sherlock, awarded Bolton a controversial second goal. Holden had played the ball to Stevens who let it go past him for Edwards. The left-half played the ball into the penalty area for Stevens to run onto and shoot at goal. Gregg palmed the ball up into the air and before he could catch it facing his own goal-line, LOFTHOUSE (pictured below) barged him into the net and the ball bobbled over the line. Gregg was left prostrate in the goal and required attention to his back from the trainer.

Although most people in the ground thought that Gregg had been unfairly charged in the back, the referee ruled otherwise. United's Assistant Manager, Jimmy Murphy, was the last person to leave the pitch after checking that his goalkeeper was ok to continue.

United stormed forward from the restart and Viollet's shot was deflected for a corner but nothing came from the kick.

Stevens then gained his revenge on Crowther with a crunching tackle after the defender had already played the ball but the referee did not even award a free kick.

Despite many of the United players' below-par performances Bobby Charlton was not one of them. He played the game at a different pace than anyone else, always moving forward at speed.

The Bolton defenders just did not give their opponents any time to settle on the ball and Banks, in particular, was outstanding. Mid-way through the second half

Webster, for once, escaped his marker and shot for goal but, as always, Hopkinson was in the right position to block the effort.

Dawson cut a lonely figure on the right-wing and the game just seemed to by-pass him. Following a series of short passes on the edge of the Bolton penalty area the ball reached Viollet but he blasted high and wide.

Crowther began to push forward more and more in an attempt to support the attack. This was necessary because Viollet, having missed many weeks of the season following the Munich crash, seemed to have lost his sharpness.

With a few minutes remaining Stevens was left prone near the wing with the Bolton players accusing Webster of an 'off the ball' incident but the referee took no action. Then, for once, Taylor found some space just inside the penalty area but his volley was too high.

In the 90th minute Lofthouse laid a pass into the path of Birch eight yards from goal. The forward and Gregg both missed the ball and Greaves raced across to clear off the goal-line.

The referee played just under four minutes of injury time with neither side able to create any opportunities.

Result Bolton Wanderers   2 Manchester United   0

After the game Matt Busby sportingly visited the Bolton dressing room to congratulate the players on their victory.

Not a classic final, but Bolton deserved their win on a day when United could not reproduce their performances from earlier rounds.

Sun. 4th May

The United team group arrived at London Road station this evening and received a tremendous welcome from a vast crowd as they travelled by bus to the Town Hall. Albert Square was a sea of red and white scarves and some of the players and staff were overcome with the emotion of the occasion.

A large crowd gathered to welcome the Bolton team home with the FA Cup. One notable absentee from the event was outside-right Brian Birch who was required to report back to his RAF Unit at Dishforth. Also missing were Eddie Hopkinson who remained in London to join the England squad for Wednesday's game against Portugal and also Tommy Banks. It is understood that Banks alighted the train at Rugby and returned to London to join up with England at the late request of the Football Association.

Wed. 7th May

It is expected that Harry Gregg will be fit to play against Milano tomorrow in the European Cup semi-final First Leg after an X-ray of his back did not reveal any damage. The goalkeeper has reportedly burned the Cap that he has worn throughout his career in disgust at his performance in the sunshine at Wembley. He will no doubt be seen wearing a new one next season.

Cope has been receiving treatment for a foot injury but should be fit to play.

Jimmy Murphy, speaking from the team's Blackpool base, said that he would not name the side until he has discussed the final selection with Matt Busby. Mr Busby had the plaster taken from his leg yesterday but it is uncertain if he will travel to Italy for the Second Leg next week.

Scotland drew 1-1 with Hungary at Hampden Park in a warm up game for the forthcoming World Cup in Sweden. The home side took the lead after 13 minutes when Leggat beat the full-back and crossed the ball into the penalty area for Mudie to head into the net. Hungary were always dangerous, moving the ball forward quickly, and after 51 minutes deservedly equalised through Fenyvesl.

England named the same team that had beaten Scotland last month for their 'friendly' game against Portugal at Wembley. Young Bobby Charlton scored the opening goal mid-way through the first half with a right foot shot from the edge of the penalty area.

In the 52nd minute Portugal equalised with a goal from Duarte. With Wembley only three quarters full, the home fans let their feelings be heard by jeering at some of the slow build-up by the England team.

Their gloom was relieved when, with just under half an hour to play, Charlton scored a second goal with a trade-mark left foot drive from 25 yards. In the 70th minute Finney was fouled in the penalty area but Langley's spot kick hit the post and was cleared to end a disappointing performance.

It was announced that Les Olive will take over as Secretary of United, succeeding Walter Crickmer who lost his life at Munich. Olive, now aged 30, has been with the Club since leaving school 16 years ago.

Thurs 8th May

Upon returning from Blackpool Jimmy Murphy and Matt Busby named the team for the match against AC Milano. They decided to rest Alex Dawson and reintroduce Ken Morgans on the right wing. With Bobby Charlton unavailable as he is with the England squad, Colin Webster will switch from outside-left to centre-forward with Mark Pearson taking his place on the wing. Gregg and Cope both passed fitness tests this morning.

Milano made two changes from the team that played against Verona on Sunday. They will be without Gastone who is now serving in the Italian Army.

European Cup Semi Final-First Leg

Manchester Utd.	**2**	**A. C. Milano**	**1**
Viollet, Taylor (pen).		Schiaffiano	

Att. 44,880

Manchester United-*Gregg, Foulkes, Greaves, Goodwin, Cope, Crowther, Morgans, Taylor, Webster, Viollet, Pearson.*

AC Milano-*Buffon, Fontana, Beraldo, Bergamaschi, Maldini, Radice, Mariani, Liedholm, Bredesen, Schiaffiano, Cucchiaroni.*

In the opening stages of the game both sides had difficulty mastering the very heavy and slippery pitch. The first real chance fell to Milano when Bredesen hit the post from a cross by Cucchiaroni. The fast moving forward line gave the United defence a torrid time and only Gregg stood in their way. He saved a shot from a free kick then bravely dived at a forward's feet.

It was no surprise when Milano took the lead after 25 minutes following a mistake by Crowther. Bredesen played the ball through the middle to SCHIAFFIANO who, despite the attention of two defenders, was still able to pass the ball beyond Gregg as he advanced from his line.

United would not let Milano settle on their advantage and six minutes before half time, following good work by Morgans, Webster and Pearson, a defender miss-kicked the ball and VIOLLET took the advantage to score.

A few minutes later Buffon dived to save from Viollet and then Morgans played the ball to Taylor who hit the crossbar as United reached the interval looking the better side.

The second half started as the first had ended with United playing some delightful attacking football roared on by the home fans. Goodwin pushed forward with more purpose and forced Buffon to make a good save.

Milano were always in the game and Foulkes did well to rob Cucchiaroni with a last ditch tackle.

Morgans began to influence the game with his probing runs at pace causing the defence problems. Taylor did his best to cover for the missing Charlton and was at the centre of everything United created.

It was disappointing that a crowd of less than 45,000 watched the game with the poor attendance blamed on the TV coverage of the match.

A C Milano squad

Back row (l to r) – Buffon, Maldini, Baraldo, Bergamaschi, Leidholm, Zannier, Zagatti, Radice, Soldan.

Front row – Fontana, Grillo, Mariani, Schiaffiano, Bean, Renie, Galli, Cucchiaroni.

In the 80th minute Maldini obstructed Viollet in the penalty area as he was charging for goal and the referee, Mr Helge from Denmark, pointed to the spot. With Maldini rolling around in agony pandemonium broke out with the Italian players hotly disputing the decision. When things had finally calmed down the experienced TAYLOR scored from the spot with the ball crashing against the underside of the bar as it entered the net.

There were no more clear-cut opportunities. The majority of the journalists and experts at the game were of the opinion that the slender one goal lead may not be sufficient to see United through the second leg.

Fri. 9th May

Newspapers reported the details of the estates of two of the United players who lost their lives in the Munich Air Crash.

David Pegg of Coppice Road, Highfields, Doncaster left £2,250 gross, £1,761 net.

Mark Jones of Kings Road, Firswood, Manchester left £800 gross, £790 net.

Both players died intestate.

Sat. 10th May

Peter Berry, the 24 year old brother of United's John Berry, was today transferred from Crystal Palace to Ipswich Town. The player had made 151 League appearances for Palace scoring 25 goals.

Manchester United left today, travelling by train and boat, to reach Milan on Monday. As expected Matt Busby was advised by his doctors not to travel and Jimmy Murphy led the party.

Fifteen players are in the group with the eleven who played in the First Leg being joined by Gaskell, McGuinness, Harrop and Dawson.

Sun. 11th May

England decided to name the same team that had beaten Scotland and Portugal in recent weeks, for the World Cup 'warm up' match in Belgrave against Yugoslavia.

Despite the 4.30 p.m. kick-off the temperature remained in the 90's for the full game as England wilted, suffering their heaviest defeat since 1954. The 5-0 scoreline could have been far worse as the home team tore England apart, hitting the crossbar twice and having three goals disallowed for off-side before half time. Hopkinson was kept fully stretched from the first to the last minute.

After an hour England were only two goals down but conceded three more in the last fifteen minutes having no answer to the constant stream of attacks. The England players appeared tired and lethargic and will need to show a vast improvement if they are to progress in the World Cup Competition.

As for Yugoslavia, they are in the same group as Scotland who must now be aware of the enormity of the task facing them.

On 14th April last, the soccer players' wage proposals were outlined, and these will be considered at the Football League Management Committee extraordinary general meeting to be held in London on 31st May.

Both Sheffield Clubs have now informed the press that they have submitted an amendment to be considered at the meeting. Their joint proposal is to limit the £20 per week payment to the football season, with players only receiving £14 in the summer. They also propose that the full payments should only be made to 15 nominated players.

It is considered highly unlikely that these proposed amendments will be accepted by the majority of the Clubs.

United's opponents on Wednesday, AC Milano, lost 4-3 to Fiorentina in an Italian League match today. Maldini did not play in the game and is rated very doubtful for the European Cup semi-final. A number of other players will need fitness tests after suffering knocks.

Mon. 12th May

Manchester United finally arrived in Milan this morning to be greeted by beautiful weather after an 18 hour train journey across France, Switzerland and Italy.

The party appeared in good spirits and Jimmy Murphy informed the press that they would train at 9.30 p.m. -the same time as the scheduled kick-off. In the meantime the players were allowed to spend the rest of the day sightseeing.

Tues. 13th May

The Press learned that last night's training session initially started with the players running and exercising. Apparently Jack Crompton, the United trainer, had decided not to bring any practice balls to Milan so that the players would have a thirst for the ball.

Eventually the trainer relented in response to some moaning from the players and the local team provided balls for the session.

United will again train this evening in a final preparation for, what will be, their 59th competitive match this season (including the Charity Shield game against Aston Villa). It is expected that United will announce an unchanged team.

Wed. 14th May

European Cup Semi-Final Second Leg

A. C. Milano 4 Manchester U. 0

Schiaffino 2, Liedholm (pen),
Danova. Att. 80,000

AC Milano-*Buffon, Fontana, Beraldo, Bergamavchi, Zannier, Radice, Donova, Bredesen, Schiaffino, Liedholm, Cucciaroni.*

Manchester United-*Gregg, Foulkes, Greaves, Goodwin, Cope, Crowther, Morgans, Taylor, Webster, Viollet, Pearson.*

United were given a hostile reception by the 80,000 fans at the San Siro Stadium as they emerged for this important game. Before the spectators had time to settle the home side took the lead to level the aggregate score. With only two minutes played SCHIAFFINO found space in the penalty area and beat Gregg from about ten yards.

The Red Devils gradually gained a small foothold in the game with Webster running at the Milano defence before shooting wide and then Viollet having a shot off target. Just before the half hour mark Ernie Taylor blasted the ball over the crossbar when he really should have done better.

Then, on thirty minutes, the referee stopped play as both teams stood for one minutes silence in respect of those who had lost their lives in the Munich Air

Crash. It seemed somewhat bizarre to carry out this stoppage part-way through the game.

The home team should have added to their tally but Danova shot too high from the edge of the penalty area. Minutes later Cucciaroni failed to test Gregg, shooting wide after good work by Schiaffino.

On the stroke of half time United won their first corner but a header from Taylor was easily saved.

After six minutes of the second half, Cope handled the ball on the line and Swedish International, LIEDHOLM, stepped forward to score from the spot. From the restart Milano nearly scored again but Greaves was on hand to clear off the line.

The referee, Mr Deusch from Germany, did not help the flow of the game with his constant whistling for trivial offences when play could have continued.

Whilst Ernie Taylor tried to insert his influence, it was obvious that the forward line missed the darting thrusts of Bobby Charlton, absent with the England squad. As the game wore on United became more stretched and the Italian side showed a wonderful fluency to their play.

The half-back line tried to 'stem the tide' and Foulkes, on one occasion, was also forced to clear off the line. On a bright note young Mark Pearson was not fazed for one moment by the red-hot environment and never let the side down.

In the 68th minute, 20 year old outside-right DANOVA netted the third goal from a lovely move, once again involving Schiaffino. With four minutes remaining SCHIAFFINO scored again for Milano to cap a superb performance by the home side.

AC Milano will now play Real Madrid in the Final in Brussels on May 28th.

* * *

The European Cup semi-final defeat in Milan seemed a perfect place to end my account of Manchester United's fascinating but sad journey through the 1957/58 season. England's exploits in the World Cup Finals and Real Madrid's victory in the European Cup will have to be told some other time.

How would the football world have changed if Munich had never happened and the original 'Busby Babes' had been able to continue their meteoric progress? We shall never know but it is interesting to consider the possible scenarios.

What if?

United, after a somewhat inconsistent start to the 1957/58 season, finally found their form around the Christmas period and by the time they beat Arsenal 5-4 on 1st

February 1958 they were six points behind Wolves in third place with fourteen games to play.

To reach a conclusion on who would have won the Championship I have first considered Wolves record over those final fourteen games (ignoring their match against United). Out of a possible 26 points they gained 20. If United had won every game including the home match against Wolves, they would have won the title by 2 points. Despite their improved form and with their involvement in the FA Cup and European Cup, this target would appear highly unlikely giving Wolves the title.

What about the FA Cup? With their vastly superior team squad strength, United should still have reached the Cup Final and the experience of the players from the previous year's Final would surely have helped them to defeat Bolton in the Wembley showpiece.

What of Europe? A stronger United side would have been expected to beat AC Milano by a better margin than 2-1, providing the normal style of drawing out the lots would have paired them together. They would have been stronger for the away leg and therefore have probably reached the Final. Winning the European Cup would have been a real possibility.

What of England in the World Cup? The three United players, Byrne, Edwards and Taylor, would almost certainly have been in the England team in Sweden. Their added ability and experience could have helped England progress further in the competition – perhaps even to the Final.

The 1966 tournament in England with Duncan Edwards aged 29 playing at left-half and captaining his country would have changed history. Alf Ramsey would no doubt have opted for the tenacity of Nobby Stiles and Bobby Moore could have found himself as a member of the non-playing squad.

What of the following ten years? The United First Team group, with the addition of the youngsters from the reserves and the junior squads, would have dominated English football over the next ten years. Each season they would have been hard to beat in both the Football League and FA Cup. Chances of progressing to the Finals in Europe would have also been increased and a win before 1968 certainly on the cards.

Whilst all these points can only be conjecture, the debate amongst football enthusiasts could go on forever and I leave you, the reader, to draw your own conclusions.

Results 1957-58

1957

AUG	24	Leicester City	a	3-0	40,214	Whelan 3
	28	EVERTON	h	3-0	59,343	Viollet, Jones (og), Taylor T.
	31	MANCHESTER C.	h	4-1	63,347	Edwards, Berry, Viollet, Taylor T.
SEP	4	Everton	a	3-3	71,868	Berry, Viollet, Whelan.
	7	LEEDS UNITED	h	5-0	50,842	Berry 2, Viollet, Taylor T. 2
	9	Blackpool	a	4-1	34,181	Whelan 2, Viollet 2
	14	Bolton Wanderers	a	0-4	48,003	
	18	BLACKPOOL	h	1-2	41,003	Edwards
	21	ARSENAL	h	4-2	47,389	Taylor T., Whelan 2, Pegg
	28	Wolves.	a	1-3	48,825	Doherty.
OCT	5	ASTON VILLA	h	4-1	43,332	Taylor T. 2, Dugdale (og), Pegg
	12	Nottingham F.	a	2-1	47,804	Whelan, Viollet
	19	PORTSMOUTH	h	0-3	39,423	
	26	W.B.A.	a	3-4	52,664	Taylor T. 2, Whelan
NOV	2	BURNLEY	h	1-0	49,689	Taylor T.
	9	Preston N. E.	a	1-1	39,066	Whelan
	16	SHEFFIELD WED.	h	2-1	41,066	Webster 2
	23	Newcastle United	a	2-1	53,950	Edwards, Taylor T.
	30	TOTTENHAM H.	h	3-4	43,307	Pegg 2, Whelan
DEC	7	Birmingham City	a	3-3	35,191	Viollet 2, Taylor T.
	14	CHELSEA	h	0-1	37,073	
	21	LEICESTER CITY	h	4-0	41,860	Scanlon, Charlton, Viollet 2
	25	LUTON TOWN	h	3-0	39,594	Edwards, Charlton, Taylor T.
	26	Luton Town	a	2-2	26,478	Scanlon, Taylor T.
	28	Manchester City	a	2-2	70,483	Viollet, Charlton

1958

JAN	11	Leeds United	a	1-1	39,401	Viollet
	18	BOLTON W	h	7-2	41,360	Charlton 3, Viollet 2, Scanlon, Edwards
FEB	1	Arsenal	a	5-4	63,578	Edwards, Charlton, Taylor T. 2, Viollet
	22	NOTTINGHAM F.	h	1-1	66,346	Dawson
MAR	8	W. B. A.	h	0-4	63,479	
	15	Burnley	a	0-3	37,447	
	29	Sheffield Wed.	a	0-1	34,806	
	31	Aston Villa	a	2-3	16,631	Webster, Dawson
APR	4	SUNDERLAND	h	2-2	47,421	Charlton, Dawson
	5	PRESTON N.E.	h	0-0	48,413	
	7	Sunderland	a	2-1	51,382	Webster 2
	12	Tottenham H.	a	0-1	59,836	
	16	Portsmouth	a	3-3	39,975	Taylor E., Webster, Dawson
	19	BIRMINGHAM C.	h	0-2	39,215	
	21	WOLVES	h	0-4	35,467	
	23	NEWCASTLE U.	h	1-1	28,573	Dawson
	26	Chelsea	a	1-2	45,011	Taylor E.

F. A. CUP

EUROPEAN CUP

APPEARANCES AND GOAL SCORERS

	LEAGUE		F.A.CUP		EUROPE	
	App.	Goals	App.	Goals	App.	Goals
BERRY J.J.	20	4			3	1
BLANCHFLOWER J.	18				2	
BRENNAN S.	5		2	3		
BYRNE R.W.	26		2		6	
CHARLTON R.	21	8	7	5	2	3
COLMAN E.	24		2		5	1
COPE R.	13		6		2	
CROWTHER S.	11		5		2	
DAWSON A.	12	5	6	5		
DOHERTY J.	1	1				
EDWARDS D.	26	6	2		5	
FOULKES W.A.	42		8		8	
GASKELL D.	3					
GOODWIN F.	16		6		3	
GREAVES I.D.	12		6		2	
GREGG H.	19		8		4	
HARROP R.	5		1			
HERON T.	1					
JONES E.P.	1					
JONES M.	10		2		4	
McGUINNESS W.	7				1	
MORGANS K.G.	13		2		4	
PEARSON M.	8		4		2	
PEGG D.	21	4			4	3
SCANLON A.	9	3	2		3	
TAYLOR E.	11	2	6	1	2	1
TAYLOR T.	25	16	2		6	3
VIOLLET D.	22	16	3	3	6	4
WEBSTER C.	20	6	6	1	5	1
WHELAN W.A.	20	12			3	2
WOOD R.E.	20				4	